SUSTAINABILITY MANAGEMENT STRATEGIES AND IMPACT IN DEVELOPING COUNTRIES

COMMUNITY, ENVIRONMENT AND DISASTER RISK MANAGEMENT VOLUME 26

SUSTAINABILITY MANAGEMENT STRATEGIES AND IMPACT IN DEVELOPING COUNTRIES

EDITED BY

MOHD FADHIL MD DIN
Universiti Teknologi Malaysia, Malaysia

NOR ELIZA ALIAS
Universiti Teknologi Malaysia, Malaysia

NORELYZA HUSSEIN
Universiti Teknologi Malaysia, Malaysia

and

NUR SYAMIMI ZAIDI
Universiti Teknologi Malaysia, Malaysia

emerald PUBLISHING

United Kingdom – North America – Japan
India – Malaysia – China

Emerald Publishing Limited
Howard House, Wagon Lane, Bingley BD16 1WA, UK

First edition 2022

British Library Cataloguing in Publication Data
A catalogue record for this book is available from the British Library

ISBN: 978-1-80262-450-2 (Print)
ISBN: 978-1-80262-449-6 (Online)
ISBN: 978-1-80262-451-9 (Epub)

ISSN: 2040-7262 (Series)

Printed and bound by CPI Group (UK) Ltd, Croydon, CR0 4YY

ISOQAR certified Management System, awarded to Emerald for adherence to Environmental standard ISO 14001:2004.

ISOQAR REGISTERED
Certificate Number 1985
ISO 14001

INVESTOR IN PEOPLE

CONTENTS

LIST OF TABLES AND FIGURES

TABLES

FIGURES

ABOUT THE AUTHORS

Nur Izieadiana Binti Abidin obtained a Bachelor's degree in Quantity Surveying and a Master's degree in Construction Management at Universiti Teknologi Malaysia (UTM). In 2019, she graduated with a Doctor of Philosophy and started her career as a Senior Lecturer at the School of Civil Engineering, Faculty of Engineering, UTM Johor Bahru campus. She has published research papers in various international journals and conference proceedings. Her research interest encompasses building retrofitting, energy efficiency, construction safety, and construction management. She was also a Member of the Scientific Committee and Technical committee in various conferences.

Nadira Binti Ahzahar, Department of Built Environment Studies & Technology, Faculty of Architecture Planning and Surveying, Universiti Teknologi MARA, Perak Branch. She is a Senior Lecturer at Universiti Teknologi MARA Perak Branch under the Department of Built Environment Studies & Technology. She has 15 years of lecturing experience in various courses in Built Environment. Her research interests are in green building and sustainable construction management. She has also published technical papers on similar topics in local and abroad.

Nor Eliza Binti Alias, PhD, Centre for Environmental Sustainability and Water Security (IPASA), School of Civil Engineering, Faculty of Engineering, UTM. She is a Senior Lecturer and a Research Fellow of the Centre for Environmental Sustainability and Water Security (IPASA), UTM. She has been involved in national and international research and consultancy projects related to water security, flood risk management, and climate change. She is an international scientist related to water security under the Japan International Cooperation Agency (JICA) and Japan Society for the Promotion of Science (JSPS) ASIAN Core Programme, Japan, as well as the Global Challenges Research Fund (GCRF), United Kingdom. She has also published high-impact technical papers on similar topics such as in the *Flood Risk Management Journal*.

Shariffah Rafidah Wan Alwi is a Professor in the School of Chemical and Energy Engineering, UTM. She previously helmed as the Director of Process Systems Engineering Centre for 10 years (2011–2021). She is an Expert Pinch Consultant for multiple industries and is among the leading researchers in Pinch Analysis technique development. She is also the Co-founder and Director of Optimal Systems Engineering Sdn Bhd, a UTM Spin-off company. She is an active consultant as well as trainers for the industries. She has won various international and national awards such as Green Talents 2009 (Germany), IChemE Highly

Commended Sir Frederick Warner Prize 2011 (UK), ASEAN Young Scientist and Technologist Award 2014, National Young Scientist Award 2015, ASEAN-US Science Prize for Women 2016 in Energy Sustainability, Malaysia Research Star Award 2016, 2018, 2019, and Top Research Scientists Malaysia 2018. She was listed as 'Asian Scientist 100' in 2017 and 'Asia's Rising Scientists' in 2020, and '8 Women Scientists from Asia You Should Know' in 2021 by AsianScientist.com.

Eeydzah Aminudin is a Senior Lecturer in the Department of Structure and Materials, UTM. Currently, she is the Co-ordinator for Master Programme in Construction Management, UTM. She completed a Bachelor and Doctor of Philosophy in Civil Engineering from UTM, which is among the ASEAN top 10 universities based on QS university ranking released in 2017. She was attached in her 4th year of teaching in UTM which previously she started her career in Universiti Tun Hussein Onn (UTHM), Batu Pahat, for almost a year. Her enthusiasm in research and education has brought her up to date more than 20 publications published while involving herself in multidisciplinary research projects, which part of it is the government initiatives projects with different fields since 2010. She has developed several award-winning research products and services that have been patented trademarked in the Malaysian construction industry.

Ferian Anggara is a Senior Lecturer at Universitas Gadjah Mada, Indonesia. His research is mainly focussed on coal, geology, and rare earth element.

Hamizah Liyana Binti Tajul Ariffin is currently an Academic Programme Co-ordinator for Masters of Science in Construction Contract Management and also a Senior Lecturer at the Department of Quantity Surveying, Faculty of Built Environment and Surveying. She obtained her Doctorate degree from the University of Salford, United Kingdom, and also part of Building Information Modelling Research Group in UTM and a Certified Trainer for Designer's Competency Training under Occupational Safety and Health for Construction Industry Management (OSHCIM). Her main research interests include, but not limited to, construction contract management, building information modelling (BIM), safety in construction, and dispute resolution in the construction industry.

Zwe Man Aung graduated from the Faculty of Civil Engineering, Yangon Technological University, Myanmar, and currently is a Master student in the Department of Construction Engineering and Management, Faculty of Civil Engineering, Ho Chi Minh City University of Technology, Vietnam National University, Ho Chi Minh City, Vietnam. His areas of research are construction risk management and claim management. He is also awarded with a scholarship for the master study in collaborative education programme (CEP) at Ho Chi Minh City University of Technology financed by Japan International Cooperation Agency (JICA) Project for ASEAN University Network/Southeast Asia Engineering Education Development Network (JICA Project for AUN/SEED-Net).

Norazura Mizal Azzmi, Department of Built Environment Studies & Technology, Faculty of Architecture, Planning And Surveying, Universiti Teknologi Mara Perak. She obtained her Master of Science in Building Technology from the School of Housing, Building and Planning, Universiti Sains Malaysia. She received her first degree in Bachelor of Science in Housing, Building and Planning majoring in Building Technology also from the same university. She joined the Centre of Studies for Building Surveying, Faculty of Architecture, Planning and Surveying, Universiti Teknologi Mara Perak, as a Permanent Lecturer in 2007 and Senior Lecturer since 2017. She is currently pursuing her PhD degree in Environmental Technology and Materials from UTM and has published papers in Journal and Indexed Proceedings locally and internationally. She has served as an Academician and also Residence Staff in Indera Mulia College, UiTM, to contribute to students' development.

Nur Fatin Syazwani Abu Bakar Postgraduate Candidate, Razak Faculty of Technology and Informatics, Universiti Teknologi Malaysia. She graduated from International Islamic University Malaysia and UTM. Possessing strong operations skill in value engineering, contract management, cost management, and project estimation via AutoCAD, SAP Ariba, Revit, CubiCost, and Icore payment system. She is a recipient of two Gold Medals, one Special Award, and one Silver Medal from innovation competitions in Korea, Taiwan, and Canada, where her research products have been copyrighted by the Intellectual Property Corporation Malaysia (MyIPO). With 11 years of working experience in mega construction projects, she was invited as an Industrial Speaker by UTM. She is a Registered Provisional Quantity Surveyor with the Board of Quantity Surveyors Malaysia and a Professional Technologist (Ts) with the Malaysia Board of Technologists (MBOT).

Denver Banlasan is currently pursuing his Master's degree in Construction Management at Ho Chi Minh City University of Technology, Vietnam National University, Ho Chi Minh City. His research interests include application of machine learning, data mining, and natural language processing techniques in construction and infrastructure management.

Leng Pau Chung (P.C.) received his PhD degree in Architecture from the UTM, Skudai Johor Malaysia. He is currently a Senior Lecturer for the Architecture Programme at The Faculty of Built Environment and Surveying, UTM. His research interests lie in the sustainable architecture in passive cooling design, sustainable housing design, industrialised building system (IBS) design, education in building information system (BIM), as well as sustainable planning and design. His interests are in sustainable built environment development and its impact on the natural environment. Also, he is currently the Principle Investigator for Research University Grant (Tier II) entitled 'Optimization of Natural Ventilation with Solar Chimney For Single Storey Terraced House in Tropical Climate and National Real Estate' and Research Coordinator Grant (NAPREC) entitled

'Challenges in Adopting Open Industrialized Building System (IBS) in the Malaysian Affordable Housing Construction Industry'.

Mohd Fadhil Md Din, Centre for Environmental Sustainability and Water Security (IPASA), School of Civil Engineering, Faculty of Engineering, UTM. Prof Ir Dr Mohd Fadhil is currently working as an Academic Administration serving as Sustainable Action Plan on the campus and is passionate about creating research and diplomatic communities in the sustainability framework. He is also one of the professional engineers in practice from the Institute of Engineer Malaysia (IEM) and the Board of Engineer Malaysia (BEM) related to water and environmental engineering. He has been involved in national and international researches related to biotechnology, water, and wastewater technology and environmental science and application. He received a great honour from the Academy Science of Malaysia (ASM) as the Associate Fellow since 2018. He also actively participates in the networking of Malaysia Sustainability University Network (MySUN) to motivate himself in the direction of sustainability in the future.

Ainarull Assikin Abdul Hadi, is one of the directors in the G7 contractor company in Malaysia. She graduated with a Master's in Business Administration (Strategic Management) from Azman Hashim International Business School, Universiti Teknologi Malaysia. She pursues her Phd at Razak Faculty of Technology and Informatics, Universiti Teknologi Malaysia, Kuala Lumpur in the area of project management, specifically on the affordable high-rise public housing projects. With more than 10 years working experience in project management, value engineering, and contract management , she has been invited as an industry speaker for postgraduate programmes by Universiti Teknologi Malaysia. She is registered with Board of Engineer Malaysia (BEM) and The Institution of Engineers, Malaysia (IEM) and also a Professional Technologist (Ts) with Malaysia Board of Technologist (MBOT).

Mohammed Hail Hakimi is a Senior Lecturer of Geology Department, Faculty of Applied Science, Taiz University, 6803 Taiz, Yemen. His research interests are unconventional energy resources, shales, geochemistry, and petrography organic.

Razali Adul Hamid is currently an Acting Dean, Faculty of Built Environment and Surveying, UTM. Research Expertise: Construction Project Management, Innovative Construction, and Project Sustainability Management. He is a Member of the Royal Institution of Chartered Surveyors UK, a Member of the Royal Institution of Surveyors Malaysia, and a Member of the Board of Quantity Surveyors Malaysia.

Siti Zubaidah Binti Hashim, Centre of Studies for Building Surveying, Department of Built Environment Studies & Technology, Faculty of Architecture Planning and Surveying, Universiti Teknologi Mara, Perak Malaysia. She is a Senior Lecturer in Universiti Teknologi MARA, Perak Branch. She was a Project Leader for Research Acculturation Grant Scheme (RAGS) under

Malaysia Greater Research Network System (MyGRANTS), Ministry of Higher Education. The grant was awarded to run research on green building incentives. She is also appointed as a green building evaluator by Melaka Green Technology for green building assessment inspection. Most of the research papers that she has published were on similar topics.

Izni Syahrizal Bin Ibrahim is an Associate Professor at the School of Civil Engineering, UTM. He received his PhD degree from the University of Nottingham, United Kingdom, in 2008. He is currently a Director at Forensic Engineering Centre (FEC), Institute for Smart Infrastructure and Innovative Construction (ISIIC) since April 2018. At the same time, he is also the Quality Manager at Civil Engineering Testing Unit (CETU) under the School of Civil Engineering, Faculty of Engineering. CETU is an accredited laboratory for MS ISO/IEC 17025: 2017 SAMM No. 804. His research area/interest is related to precast concrete construction, composite action behaviour in precast structure, steel fibre reinforced concrete, and forensic engineering investigation. He has published more than 100 technical papers in international journals and conference proceedings mainly in Structures and Materials.

Hamzat Isah, Hassan Usman Katsina Polytechnic, Katsina State Nigeria, A Registered Builder with the Council of Registered Builders of Nigeria and MSc Graduate (Building) from the Univerisiti Sains Malaysia, He is currently a Lecturer with Hassan Usman Katsina Polytechnic . His research interest is in the area of health and occupational safety.

Herda Balqis Binti Ismail is a Senior Lecturer at the School of Civil Engineering, College of Engineering, Universiti Teknologi MARA, Cawangan Johor, Kampus Pasir Gudang. Her main research interests include construction waste management, construction management, and occupational, safety, and health in construction. Currently, her research is focussed on design for safety in the construction industry.

Syuhaida Ismail, Razak Faculty of Technology and Informatics, Universiti Teknologi Malaysia, Kuala Lumpur. She is an Associate Professor of Project Management at Razak Faculty of Technology and Informatics, Universiti Teknologi Malaysia, Kuala Lumpur. She has published more than 300 technical papers, articles and books on Project Management, and recently on the COVID-19 crisis in built environment. She has received more than 50 research and professional awards, where her research products are commercialised into more than 100 Intellectual Property Rights.

Istimaroh, Faculty of Business and Management, Universitas Muhammadiyah Kalimantan Timur, Faculty of Business and Management, Universiti Tun Hussein Onn Malaysia. She graduated from the Faculty of Business and Management, Universitas Airlangga, Surabaya, Indonesia, and currently is a PhD by research student. Her study focusses on supply chain management, which includes the usage of operation management. This paper is the first that regarding supply chain management with the titled 'The Key Practices of Lean Supply Chain Management: A Review' will be published in the RCCE International Conference on sustainable 2020, UTM.

Nazhatulzalkis Jamaludin, Faculty of Architecture, Planning and Surveying, Universiti Teknologi MARA, Perak Branch. She is a Lecturer in Universiti Teknologi MARA Perak Branch under Department of Built Environment Studies & Technology. She has 15 years working experience as a Lecturer and 5 years in the construction industry. Her research interests are in Environmental Studies and Building Technology. She has also published technical papers on similar topics both local and abroad.

Noor Azreena Kamaluddin, PhD, School of Civil Engineering, College of Engineering, Universiti Teknologi MARA. She is a Senior Lecturer and Researcher at Universiti Teknologi MARA, Malaysia. She is actively involved in teaching, researching, and consultation activities. Teaching activities include lecturing, tutoring, and supervising students' theses. The main areas of research are road safety, traffic, and highway engineering. Her current research focusses on traffic safety particularly involving vulnerable road users and has led several research grants along her career. Her research concerns all aspects of safety for vulnerable road users as well as innovative methods and tools for data collection and behaviour analysis as well as safety assessments techniques. She is part of the team in developing the safety module for the p-hailing riders in Malaysia

Adetunji Kamoli is a PhD Research student in the Department of Quantity Surveying, Faculty of Built Environment and Surveying, UTM. Currently, he is researching on occupational health and safety management system in the construction industry. He had presented papers in the field of occupational health and safety at international conferences and also published papers in international journals. He is a Member of the Nigerian Institute of Quantity Surveyors (NIQS) and a registered Quantity Surveyor with the Quantity Surveyors Registration Board of Nigeria.

Santhana Krishnan, PhD, Centre for Environmental Sustainability and Water Security (IPASA), School of Civil Engineering, Faculty of Engineering, UTM. He is a Post-Doctoral Researcher (Biochemical Engineering) at the Centre for Environmental Sustainability and Water Security (IPASA), UTM. His main areas of research are Bioenergy, Fermentation, Water treatment, Bioelectrochemical systems, Nanomaterial synthesis for energy and water applications and Bioreactors development. He has been involved in national and international research and industrial projects. He has published more than 50 papers in prominent journals in Elsevier's, Springer, Wiley, and has authored 5 book chapters. His works have been cited 610 times with an h index of 14 and an i10 index of 15 to date. He has been a reviewer for various journals published by Elsevier, Wiley, RSC, and Springer.

Christine Nerisha Anak Stephen Liat, School of Civil Engineering, Faculty of Engineering, UTM. Miss Christine Nerisha Anak Stephen Liat graduated from the Faculty of Civil Engineering, UTM, Johor, Malaysia, and currently, is a Master's research student. Her study focusses on carbon tax impact in the construction industry, which includes the impact modelling and creation of green technology.

Eric Lou is a Reader in the Manchester Metropolitan University. His research investigates sustainability-led design for buildings with a specific interest in refurbishment, retrofit, and restoration of existing buildings. His expertise is in the areas of embodied energy and carbon management of materials. His interest lies in the interoperability of data for the built environment. He explores technological advancements of big data, advanced imaging, and BIM – all to create computing intelligence for the built environment.

Syamsul Hendra Bin Mahmud is a Senior Lecturer in the Department of Quantity Surveying, Faculty of Built Environment and Surveying, UTM. Research Expertise: Construction Safety Management, Construction Technology & Innovation, Cost Engineering & Quantity Surveying.

Zainuddin Abd Manan is a Professor of Chemical Engineering, the Founding Director of UTM Process Systems Engineering Centre (PROSPECT), Founding Dean of UTM Faculty of Chemical and Energy Engineering, the Founder of the UTM spin-off, Optimal Systems Engineering. He began his career as an Engineer in PETRONAS and Hume Industries and has been an academic leader, professor, researcher, consultant, and professional coach for over 25 years. As a researcher and professional practitioner, he has completed over 100 R&D and consultancy projects, has numerous patents and more than 500 publications that include 30 books/chapters, 220 refereed journals and 270 conference papers on sustainable engineering of resources (energy, power, water, emissions, and materials). He is a professional engineer, a chartered engineer, a certified energy manager, a registered electrical energy manager and the certified lead trainer for Malaysia energy managers. He has delivered over 400 invited talks in professional courses, conferences, and seminars across the world, including the 2014 Imperial College Distinguished Chemical Engineering Lecture. He has coached professionals from more than 500 national and multi-national companies.

Taslim Maulana received a Bachelor's degree (2016) in Geology from Universitas Gadjah Mada, Indonesia. His research is mainly focused on coal, geology, and petrophysics of coal.

Dianah Mazlan, School of Civil Engineering, Faculty of Engineering, UTM. She received her BEng, MEng and PhD in Civil Engineering at UTM. She actively involved in national and international research and consultancies project-related sustainable concrete/cement materials, fibre-reinforced concrete, wood/cellulose materials in cement composites, construction waste management, waste to wealth, green energy & zero energy building and sustainable development goals. Currently, she is a Research Officer in UTM Campus Sustainability, who in charge in an international project sponsored by European Commission under ERASMUS+ grant. The project is regarding Malaysia Sustainable University Network.

Masria Mustafa, School of Civil Engineering, College of Engineering, Universiti Teknologi MARA. Dr –Ing Masria Mustafa, is presently an Associate Professor at Universiti Teknologi MARA. She earned a Bachelor's degree in Civil Engineering from Universiti Sains Malaysia, Malaysia, a Master's degree from Chulalongkorn University, Thailand, and a Doctorate from Technical University of Munich, Germany. Her main areas of interests are traffic simulation and modelling, traffic operation and control, road safety, intelligent transport system (ITS) and advancement of women in transportation. To date, she has published various documents of international journals and proceedings, conferences, and chapter in book

Siti Nur Syamimi Binti Mohd Na'im, Department of Environmental Engineering, School of Civil Engineering, Faculty of Engineering, UTM. Mrs Siti Nur Syamimi graduated from the Faculty of Environmental Studies, Universiti Putra Malaysia, Selangor, Malaysia and currently, is a Master by research student in the School of Civil Engineering, Faculty of Engineering, UTM, Johor, Malaysia. Her study focusses on solid waste management; emphasis on recycling management which includes the application of waste and recycling policies towards a sustainable environment.

Najib is a Senior Lecturer at the Geological Engineering Department, Engineering Faculty, Universitas Diponegoro, Indonesia. His current interests are slope engineering, geotechnical applications, rock mechanics and tunnel engineering.

Nurul Nazleatul Najiha Binti Mohd Nazif, School of Civil Engineering, Faculty of Engineering, UTM. She graduated BASc in Sustainable Science at Universiti Malaysia Kelantan (UMK) and MEg in Civil Engineering (Environmental Management) at UTM. She is currently studying for her PHD (Environmental Engineering) in UTM. Her study focusses on the Fluorocarbon gas management in Malaysia. During her study, she has been actively involved in national and international research and consultancies projects related environmental management, waste to wealth, climate change, module development, and awareness programme. Recent year, she is working on Fluorocarbon gas management that awarded from the Ministries of Environment Japan (MOEJ) and United Nations Environment Programme (UNEP).

Norehan Norlida Mohd Noor graduated from Universiti Sains Malaysia, Penang, in Bachelor of Science (Hons) In Housing, Building and Planning majoring in Quantity Surveying, and furthered her study in Master of Science in Project Management at the same university. She received a Doctor of Philosophy in Built Environment 'Building Maintenance Budget Determination' at Universiti

Teknologi Mara, Shah Alam, Selangor. Currently, she is a Senior Lecturer who serves at Centre of Studies for Building Surveying, Department of Built Environment Studies & Technology, Faculty of Architecture, Planning and Surveying, Universiti Teknologi MARA, Perak Branch. She teaches the undergraduate programme, in building economics, and construction costs for 18 years since 2003. At the same time, she also contributes and shares her experience as the supervisor to master students. She was in the construction industry for 12 years and is experienced in leading various construction projects around Peninsular Malaysia. She is an avid researcher and writer. She received the Excellent Employee Award twice, in 2012 and 2019.

Norasmiha Binti Mhd Nor, PhD, Department for Faculty of Business and Management, Universiti Tun Hussein Onn Malaysia. She is a Lecturer and a researcher of the Centre for Operations Management, Universiti Tun Hussein Onn Malaysia. She has been involved in national and international research related to operations management.

Steven Kuba Nuhu, is a Lecturer with the Department of Minerals and Petroleum Resources Engineering, School of Engineering, Plateau State Polytechnic, Barkin-Ladi, Jos, Nigeria. He was graduated from the Federal University of Technology, Minna, Nigeria with a Master's degree in Chemical Engineering. Currently, he is a PhD student with the school of Chemical and Energy Engineering, Faculty of Engineering, UTM, Johor Bahru, Malaysia. His study focusses on Process Integration and Renewable Energy, which includes the design of hybrid multi-criteria decision-making (MCDM) methods that can be integrated with the geographic information system (GIS) for the modelling of both greenfield and brownfield eco-industrial park (EIP) site selection. The first paper was the 'Roles of Geospatial Technology in Eco-Industrial Park Site Selection: A State-of-the-art Review' published in the *Journal of Cleaner Production*. He has also co-authored a chapter "Development and Design of Eco-Industrial Park Toward Circular Economy" in the book *Process Design and Optimisation Towards Circular Economy* which is in press.

Afikah Binti Rahim is a Senior Lecturer at the Department of Geotechnics and Transportation, School of Civil Engineering, UTM. Her current interests are geology, rock mechanics, coal, enhanced coalbed methane, sorption CO_2, reservoir modelling.

Mohd Fairuz Bin Ab Rahman graduated from the University of Sheffield, UK, in BEng Mechanical Engineering, UiTM in MSc Integrated Construction Project Management and the RMIT University, Australia, in PhD Mechanical Engineering. He is registered with the Board of Engineers Malaysia as a Professional Engineer with Practising Certificate and Malaysia Board of Technologists as a Professional Technologist. He has worked with the Department of Occupational Safety and Health (DOSH/JKKP) since 2003. He has published more than 20 articles in the field of accident analysis and construction safety and health.

Nur Anis Bt Abdul Rahman is a degree holder in Building Surveying from Universiti Teknologi MARA. She is currently working as a Building Surveyor in the private sector in Kuala Lumpur. Her working experience is mainly in Facilities Management and Project Management.

Zanariah Abd. Rahman, School of Civil Engineering, College of Engineering, Universiti Teknologi MARA. She is a Senior Lecturer, a Professional Technologist and a Researcher at Universiti Teknologi MARA (UiTM), Malaysia. She is also a member of Transportation Systems, Infrastructure and Intelligent Transport (TRANSIIT) Research Interest Group at UiTM. Her works includes teaching, researches and consultation with her main research interest are in highway design and maintenance, urban transport system, pedestrian behaviour and sustainable mobility. She has led several research grants and accomplished several innovation awards with her works throughout her career in UiTM.

Muhammad Wafiy Adli Bin Ramli, School of Civil Engineering, Faculty of Engineering, UTM. He graduated with a Bachelor of Geoinformatics degree and a Master's degree in Environmental Management from UTM. Currently, he is pursuing his PhD degree which focusses on the development of an integrated disaster risk assessment in Malaysia. He has published several publications in disaster management and GIS such as Disaster Risk Index: A Review of Local Scale Concept and Methodologies.

Nur Izzati Ab Rani, School of Civil Engineering, College of Engineering, Universiti Teknologi MARA. She is a Senior Lecturer at Faculty of Civil Engineering, Universiti Teknologi Malaysia, Kuala Lumpur. She has been teaching Construction Business and Project Management related subjects. Her research area is in international construction business, project management and sustainable development, where she has published several research paper in local and international conferences and seminars. She has experience in undertaking various project management research as the member, namely related to the Coronavirus Disease 2019 (COVID-19) pandemic, constructions projects and also maritime industry.

Mohd Nadzri Md Reba is currently the Director of Geoscience and Digital Earth Centre (INSTeG) and a Senior Lecturer at Faculty of Built Environment and Surveying in UTM. As a Member of IEEE, SPIE, ISPRS, and AARS, his interest in signal processing of laser radar, remote sensing and atmospheric science has led him to publish number of ISI-cited journals and international proceedings. He has involved in national and international research and consultation in satellite oceanography, weather radar, satellite glacier mapping, multispectral UAV, high-resolution aerosol mapping, microwave lidar and tropical cyclone.

Mior Alhadi Mior Ahmad Ridzuan, Faculty of Architecture, Planning and Surveying, Universiti Teknologi MARA, Perak Branch. He was an undergraduate student of building surveying programme, Universiti Teknologi MARA Perak Branch. Now he works in Technical Department in Sitiawan Properties.

Fatin Nabihah Syahira Ridzuan, Faculty of Built Environment and Surveying, UTM. Mrs Fatin Nabihah Syahira Binti Ridzuan graduated from the Faculty of Geoinformation and Real Estate, UTM, Johor, Malaysia and currently is a Master by research student. Her study focusses on estimation of Chl-a and nutrients concentration including the development of standard ocean colour algorithms and machine learning models. The first paper regarding Chl-a estimation is titled 'Spatial variability assessment on the high-resolution Chlorophyll-a extraction from Landsat 8 imageries in Johor waters' has been published in a *Journal of Engineering Technology and Applied Physics*.

Nurfarhain Binti Mohammed Rusli obtained her BEng and MEng (Civil Engineering – Environmental Management). At present, she is a Research Officer in Centre of Lipids Engineering and Applied Research (CLEAR), UTM and is on-going her PhD (Environmental Engineering) in UTM. She has been involved in national and international research and consultancies projects related to water security, environmental management, and climate change. She joined international project related to energy efficiency and climate change includes under the JICA Programme, Japan, and industries from Japan, and the Erasmus Project from European Commission related to sustainability. Currently, she is working on climate change project under UNEP and she has published high-impact technical papers on similar topics such as in the *Cleaner Production Journal*.

Fadzlin Binti Md Sairan, PhD, Ibnu Sina Institute for Scientific and Industrial Research, UTM, Malaysia. She is a Senior Research Officer at Ibnu Sina Institute for Scientific and Industrial Research, UTM. She has been involved in several research and consultancy projects, funded by various agencies, including a grant from European Commission on water sustainability. She has almost eight years of experience in developing software for wastewater treatment plant design, air pollution, chemical risk assessment; landfill design; applied various environmental engineering simulation software, e.g., ASIM (Activated Sludge SIMulation Programme) and has written more than 30 articles in refereed journals and international conference proceedings.

Noor Nabilah Binti Sarbini is a Senior Lecturer at the School of Civil Engineering, UTM. She received her PhD (Civil Engineering) in 2014 from UTM. She is also a Registered Professional Engineer who has a wide experience in structural assessment and failure investigation. Her major interests include building assessment, forensic engineering, bridge engineering and occupational, safety and health in the construction industry.

Noor Aslinda Binti Abu Seman, PhD, Centre for Faculty of Business and Management, Universiti Tun Hussein Onn Malaysia. She is a Lecturer and a Research Fellow of the Centre for Supply Chain Management, Universiti Tun Hussein Onn Malaysia. She has been involved in national and international research related to Green supply chain management.

Bambang Setiaji, Department for Faculty of Business and Management, Universitas Muhammadiyah Kalimantan Timur. Prof Dr Bambang Setiaji is a Leader and Lecturer of the Department of Business and Management, Universitas Muhammadiyah Kalimantan Timur. He has been involved in national and international research related to development of economic and management. He has been also hoined a Short Course (Labor Economics and Development Economic) in Monash University Australia.

Siti Mazzuana Shamsuddin was born in Kuala Lumpur, Malaysia in 1980. She received Bachelor in Quantity Surveying in 2002, Masters in Science in Construction Management in 2005 and Doctor of Philosophy in Civil Engineering from UTM, Skudai, Johor, Malaysia, in 2020. She has six years of working experience before joining Universiti Teknologi MARA as a Lecturer and Senior Lecturer since 2013 in Centre of Studies in Quantity Surveying, Faculty of Achitecture Planning and Surveying, Universiti Teknologi MARA, Shah Alam, Selangor, Malaysia. She has published 18 publications and her research interests are life cycle costing, construction innovation, and sustainable development.

Takeru Shibayama, PhD, Institute of Transportation, TU Wien. He is currently a Senior Scientist at the Research Center of Transport Planning and Traffic Engineering at TU Wien, Austria. His research focusses on travel behaviour, public transport, and shared mobility, he has led a number of research projects related to organisation and policy of public transport as well as shared mobility, publishing a number of scientific papers. He led the worldwide questionnaire-based survey on COVID-19 and mobility in March–June 2020 at TU Wien. Currently, he is a Co-chair of WCTR Special Interest Group G2 National and Regional Transport Policy and Planning.

Do Tien Sy currently works at the Department of Construction Engineering and Management a Lecturer at Faculty of Civil Engineering, Ho Chi Minh City University of Technology, Vietnam National University, Ho Chi Minh City, Vietnam. He has been involved in national and international research and consultancies projects related to contract management, risk management, claim management, dispute resolution, and building information modelling (BIM). He has been participated in teaching and research in many programmes of the AUN/Seed-net organisation.

Shazwin Binti Mat Taib, PhD, Department of Environmental Engineering, School of Civil Engineering, Faculty of Engineering, UTM. She is a Senior Lecturer and a Research Fellow of the Centre for Environmental Sustainability and Water Security (IPASA), UTM. She has been involved in national and international research and consultancies projects related to climate change and water, solid waste management as well as sustainability management. International scientist related to climate change includes under the JICA and the UNEP, France. She has published 49 papers in prominent journals in Web of Science, Scopus, and has authored 6 book chapters. She is actively involved in international networking including concluding MoUs with Viet Nam National University Ho Chi Minh and National Institute of Technology, Kagoshima College as well as MoAs with Mitsubishi UFJ Morgan Stanley and E & E Solutions Inc. Japan.

Putri Basenda Tarigan, Graduate Student, Faculty of Civil Engineering, Ho Chi Minh City University of Technology – Vietnam National University. Ms Putri Basenda Tarigan graduated from Civil Engineering department in Andalas University in Indonesia. Her basic is in Structure Engineering. She was awarded CEP Scholarship to continue Master's degree with a full scholarship from AUN/SEED-Net, under the JICA programme. Currently, she is a Graduate student of Construction Management Department in Ho Chi Minh City University of Technology. She did her research that focus on optimisation of construction project. Along with her study, she has published her research in a well-known international journal.

Gabriel Ling Hoh Teck is a Senior Lecturer in the Faculty of Built Environment and Surveying of UTM. His research mainly focusses on inland and urban planning laws and public policies (governance) study, resource governance and management, new institutional economics (ecological economics), land and urban economics, climate changes and cities, common and public goods studies, property management and development process, social-ecological system framework, behavioural study, behavioural economics in real-estate valuation and management, game theory, research methodology, institutional analysis development (IAD), low-carbon society study, housing studies, social dilemmas, self-organising, and collective action theories.

Duc-Hoc Tran, PhD, Faculty of Civil Engineering, Ho Chi Minh City University of Technology – Vietnam National University. He graduated from the Department of Civil and Construction Engineering in National Taiwan University of Science and Technology in 2015. His field is focussed on automation and optimisation of construction project. He has published a lot of research in this field in many popular international journals. He just recently nominated and appointed as an Associate Professor in Ho Chi Minh University of Technology. His current profession is as a Lecturer in Construction Management Department in Ho Chi Minh City University of Technology.

Norhidayah Md Ulang holds degrees, BSc and MSc in Building Technology, School of Housing, Building and Planning, University Sains Malaysia, Malaysia, as well as PhD (Built Environment) from Civil and Building Engineering Department, Loughborough University, United Kingdom. She joined UiTM for a short period as a Lecturer in Building Surveying Department before pursuing her PhD. She joined Universiti Sains Malaysia in 2012 and currently attach to Building Engineering Technology Department in School of Housing, Building, and Planning. Her research interest is in the field of construction development process, building maintenance, construction health and safety, and energy efficiency.

Nguyen Thanh Viet received his PhD in Construction Engineering and Management from Pukyong National University (PKNU), Busan, South Korea, 2016. Currently, he is a Lecturer at the Faculty of Civil Engineering, Industrial University of Ho Chi Minh City, Ho Chi Minh City, Vietnam. His research interest includes Value Engineering in Construction, Construction Supply Chain Management, and Risk Management in Construction.

Omar Sedeeq Yousif, School of Civil Engineering, Faculty of Engineering, UTM. He graduated from the Department of Civil Engineering, University of Mosul, and obtained his Master of Engineering in Construction Management from UTM, Johor, Malaysia, and currently is a PhD candidate at the same Faculty in UTM. His research focusses on construction management, construction informatics, and sustainable initiatives. He has also published high-impact technical papers on similar topics such as in the green highway initiatives and management journals.

Zulkifli Bin Yusop, Centre for Environmental Sustainability and Water Security (IPASA), School of Civil Engineering, Faculty of Engineering, UTM. Prof Dr Zulkifli Yusop is a Senior Professor and a Senior Fellow of the Centre for Environmental Sustainability and Water Security (IPASA), UTM. His research interests include water management, climate change impact on water resources, non-point source pollution, and integrated river basin management. He has authored and co-authored about 400 articles, of which 105 are indexed in ISI, 50 in Scopus, 30 book chapters, 8 books, and the rest are proceedings. He is currently working on a RM 7.8 million research grant from the UK Research Institute (UKRI) on water security together with other collaborators from UK, India, Ethiopia, and Columbia.

Hareyani Zabidi is a Senior Lecturer at School of Material and Mineral Resources, Engineering Campus, Universiti Sains Malaysia. Her current interests are karst, rock mechanics, tunnel modelling, and mineral resources.

Intan Bayani Bin Zakaria, Centre of studies for Building Surveying, Department of Built Environment Studies & Technology, Faculty of Architecture Planning and Surveying, Universiti Teknologi Mara, Perak Malaysia. She is a Senior Lecturer in University Teknologi MARA Perak Branch and currently doing her PhD at Universiti Malaya, Malaysia. Her research is on the indoor air pollution for non-landed kindergarten building. She has 11 years working experience as a lecturer. In addition, she was also involved in higher education programmes such as syllabus review, accreditation process, student internship, and student's final project supervision. She has also published papers on similar topics local and abroad journal.

Rozana Zakaria currently serves as an Associate Professor and Head of Research Group, GreenPROMPT at School of Civil Engineering, Faculty of Engineering, UTM. Her expertise is highly concentrated on construction and project management with specialization in sustainable construction, sustainable building, and infrastructure, which respond highly to sustainable urban development.

Rosli Bin Mohamad Zin currently served as an Associates Chair of Quality and Strategy for School of Civil Engineering, Faculty of Engineering, UTM. His research areas are construction management, constructability, and green construction.

PREFACE

This book intends to share research works in the field of current niche area in sustainability management, beyond modern strategies and showcasing impact in developing countries. The work is a collection of various impactful research works presented during the Regional Conference of Civil Engineering and Sustainable Development Goals 2020 (RCCE & SDGs 2020), which held from 7 to 9 November 2021, co-organised together with UTM, MySUN, and AUN/SEED-Net, Japan. Contributing authors are from Malaysia, Vietnam, and Nigeria, whose research covers a range of sustainable management fields, from construction management, covid-19 impact to socio-economics, green initiatives, engineering, to framework and policies.

The importance of sustainability strategies and identification of impacts in developing countries is a vital element in physical and/or social development. The content of this book is concurrent to the SDGs awareness to provide information to the public, researchers, planners, and stakeholders dealing implicit and explicitly to sustainable development. A huge gratitude to all contributors involved in the production of this book.

PART A

MANAGEMENT AND STRATEGIES

CHAPTER 1

A REVIEW ON CARBON TAX FOR MALAYSIA CONSTRUCTION INDUSTRY

Christine Nerisha Anak Stephen Liat, Eeydzah Aminudin, Eric Lou, Gabriel Ling Hoh Teck, Leng Pau Chung, Rosli Mohamad Zin and Rozana Zakaria

ABSTRACT

Oversupplied emission basically will create a global economic downturn, which will lead to the implications for the climate action more broadly. Though the pandemic has test the resilience of carbon initiatives, there is urgency in identifying the carbon tax to strengthen as jurisdiction around the world ambitious in adopting and mitigating the targets as an introductory of the associated policy tools. Based on different situations and disciplines, the carbon tax model is simulated in different ways. The purpose of this study is to compare the available approaches that have been utilised by researchers and to determine the methods that suitable the most. The carbon tax and its influence on the construction sector are being benchmark and discussed as the whole of this document. A bibliometric approach is the method in this study in between the keyword of a carbon tax and the construction industry based on the data available in database of Scopus and Web of Science to foresee the interconnection between the knowledge of understanding and definition. The definition of carbon tax is the Pigovian tax that is designed to reduce the greenhouse gases (GHGs) emitted with aim to act as a green tax and been paid by the

Sustainability Management Strategies and Impact in Developing Countries
Community, Environment and Disaster Risk Management, Volume 26, 3–13

ISSN: 2040-7262/doi:10.1108/S2040-726220220000026001

industries that emitted GHGs as for the carbon emission reduction agenda. The implementation is parallel to the other government policies and in sync to the sustainable development goals.

Keywords: Carbon tax; sustainable development goals; green tax; carbon emissions reduction; construction sector; greenhouse gases

1. INTRODUCTION

In the last decade, the world surface temperature increased 0.74 ± 0.18°C (1.33 ± 0.32°F) as reported by the Intergovernmental Panel on Climate Change (IPCC) in 2007 as the impacts of climate change or global warming. There is a general scientific consensus on global warming that is mainly due to the development of human CO_2 from fossil fuels, so it draws widespread attention to long-term regulation of CO_2 emissions. Failure to resolve climate change could cause an economic loss of about 5% of the world's gross domestic product (GDP) according to Stern's Climate Change Economics Assessment (Stern, 2006). Losses may amount to as much as 20 per cent of world economic production in more extreme scenarios. In comparison, to prevent the worst impacts of climate change, the expense of cutting greenhouse gas (GHG) emissions may be limited to as little as 1 per cent of global GDP annually.

Since a decade ago, countries have been seriously considering what can be done to cope with global warming and reduce carbon emissions. In 1997, the Kyoto Protocol first defined legally binding goals linked to the United Nations Framework Convention on Climate Change for 37 developed countries and the European Community for the reduction of GHG emissions. The latest effort took place in Madrid, Spain, in December 2019, where the worldwide countries and leaders have agreed to make commitments to reduce the emission level from the respective country and European Union agreed on The European Green Deal in which the emission level should reach zero in 2050. It stresses the urgent need to tackle climate change in compliance with the concept of shared yet distinct obligations and capacities, agrees that global temperature rises should be below 2°C, and undertakes to take steps compatible with science and based on equity and finance plans to achieve this objective.

1.1. Construction Industry Carbon Emission

In the environmental protection of both the in-build development phase and the in-service performance condition, the construction sector plays an important role. In 2008, the United Nations Environment Programme (UNEP) estimated that construction of buildings especially is responsible for more than one-third of the total energy usage and carbon emissions (Cheng, Pouffary, Svenningsen, & Callaway, 2008). Construction industries hold the third highest GHG emissions among the United States industrial sectors. One hundred and thirty-one MMTCO2e are emitted by the construction site in 2002 as reported by the United States Environmental

Protection Agency (US EPA, 2008). This value represents 1.7% of total US emissions, or equivalent to 6% of US industrial carbon emissions. The segregation within the total carbon emissions by the construction industry, 76% emissions result from fossil fuel combustion for on- and off-road construction equipment, and 24% come from purchased electricity (Lu, Zhu, & Cui, 2012). Unfortunately, the total emissions from the construction industries should be much higher as EPA estimated excluded the emissions from materials extraction, transportation, productions, consumptions, and disposal. The number of materials used in the construction industries is huge; hence, the magnitude of the carbon emissions of this sector is higher due to the embodied carbon. The four major sources of carbon emissions in construction are embodied building materials (81.6–86.7%), transporting building materials (6.1–8.4%), equipment energy consumption (6.4–8.6%), and disposal of construction debris (Yan, Shen, Fan, Wang, & Zhang, 2010)

Thus, carbon emission from the construction industry is considered critical especially in the operation stage of the life cycle due to the usage of energy to power up the buildings. Policy-makers and the Government shall pay attention to the emission contribution from the construction as the emission can be out of control if not managed properly.

1.2. Malaysia Initiatives to Lower the Country Total Carbon Emission

By 2020, Malaysia's carbon emissions will be expected to reduce by 40 per cent (compared to 2005 levels), and by 2030, the emissions will be reduced by 45 per cent (compared to 2005 levels). Malaysia faces the same dilemma as other emerging nations in decarbonising its energy-centric economy while contending with population growth pressures and high levels of poverty. In 2006, three years before Prime Minister Razak's public declaration, Malaysia began cutting carbon emissions. Many policies and strategic plans have been implemented since then to reorient the country towards a future with fewer carbon-intensive activities. On the list of measures is the addition of palm biodiesel to diesel fuel (The National Biofuel Policy, 2006), the creation of the Sustainable Energy Development Authority to promote the use of renewable energy in power generation (KeTTHA, 2017b), and promotion of public transportation while limiting private vehicle ownership (National Land Public Transport Master Plan).

The government plan contains multisectoral initiatives to reduce GHG emission intensity by 45 per cent by 2030 and to boost economic growth via the use of green technologies. The plan was released in December 2017. Malaysia plans to double its current modal share of 20 per cent in the transportation industry to 40 per cent by 2030 (KeTTHA, 2017a, 2017b). Additionally, 100 per cent of newly registered vehicles must be hybrid or electric, according to the Master Plan (KeTTHA, 2017a). Also on the agenda are proposals to increase the use of compressed natural gas (CNG) and to raise the fuel standards for automobiles, develop green building certification systems, and improve waste management (KeTTHA, 2017a).

For land use and forestry emissions, Malaysia measures carbon intensity both per capita and per unit of GDP. GHG emissions in 2011 were 9.97 tonnes

CO_2 equivalent per capita and 0.41 tonnes CO_2 equivalent per thousand ringgits, respectively (a 9.8 per cent and a 23 per cent drop in intensity from 2005 levels). 2011 GHG emissions were 0.94 tonnes CO_2 equivalent per capita and 0.04 tonnes CO_2 equivalent per thousand Ringgit (respectively, 20.7 and 32.5 per cent decreases from 2005 levels) when LULUCF removals are included (Ministry of Natural Resources and Environment, 2015).

1.3. Carbon Tax in General

Pigovian tax, named after the economist Pigou, is the genesis of carbon taxes as a charge on market activity that creates a 'disservice'. In principle, a Pigovian tax corrects for market failure by adding a charge to the market price, at a rate that represents the societal harm of the activity, to correct for undesired or inefficient market outcomes. Coase (1960) referred to these expenses as 'externalities', or societal costs that are not reflected in private market prices. In economic theory, a carbon tax is generally considered the 'first-best' or 'optimal' option for addressing the externality of human carbon dioxide emissions (Bertram et al., 2015). Critics do, however, point out that carbon prices are not without flaws. 'Climate capitalism' (Newell & Patterson, 2010) as well as restricted technocentric and economic worldviews arising from restrictive monodisciplinary perspectives have been implicated in the prioritising of carbon taxes in political economics (Kirby & O'Mahony, 2018).

2. METHODOLOGY

The research questions are 'What is the impact of the carbon tax in the construction industry?', 'Will carbon tax will impact the legislation of the construction management?', 'Do carbon emissions from the construction will reduce if a carbon tax is implemented?', and 'Why a carbon tax is preferable to move the conventional method to a greener technology?'. The databases selected in this review are the Scopus and Web of Science due to the reliability of the data and quality plus the available resources in the databases. Next, after used the keywords such as 'Carbon Tax AND Construction Industry', 'Carbon Tax AND Green Building Strategy', and 'Impacts of Carbon Tax', the screening will be conducted to select the best references. Due to the lack of availability of carbon tax in construction industry research, other impacts from different sectors were analysed and assimilated to the situation of the construction industry. VOSviewer software is used to illustrate the carbon tax relationship with the construction industry. VOSviewer is a program to build and visualise bibliometric networks. For example, these networks can involve journals, scholars, or individual publications, and they can be established based on citation, bibliographic coupling, co-citation, or relationships with co-authorship. Text-mining functionality is also available in VOSviewer, which can be used to build and visualise co-occurrence networks of important words extracted from a body of scientific literature.

3. CARBON TAX AS CARBON EMISSION REDUCTION STRATEGY

Carbon taxes value carbon dioxide that is released to the atmosphere, thus the impact of the carbon dioxide emission must be cost to carter the bad impacts (Sumner, Bird, & Dobos, 2011). While this role is necessarily given by all carbon taxes, policy objectives can differ. Carbon taxes are mainly used to minimise GHG emissions by putting emissions costs on the table, but carbon tax may also boost revenues to support carbon reduction measures or to build demand. Some countries are not yet ready to implement carbon tax especially the developing country due to the fear of tax will add more burden to the country.

A carbon tax can act as a carbon emission reduction strategy for the construction sector to support the current legislation. Green buildings strategy is legislated for sustainable energy development and the construction activities that used low-carbon technology as well as use available natural resources (Conefrey, Gerald, Valeri, & Tol, 2013). The purpose of green buildings is to reduce and minimise the carbon emissions from the construction materials, manufacturing machines, and labour that can ensure an indoor environment quality for building occupants (Chen, & Jim, 2011; Roe & Mell, 2013). A carbon tax can complement the green building strategy to fully operate as the carbon emission reduction strategy. The carbon footprint of green buildings is the calculated carbon dioxide emissions for the whole life cycle of the buildings, which can help to identify the critical area for energy consumption management and identify the pollutions. It is vital to determine the sources of the carbon emissions that come from a direct activity and indirect carbon emissions from the construction process (Tsai, Yang, Huang, & Wu, 2016). Construction firms are responsible for measuring and reporting the green building carbon footprint for occupants and achieving the goal of reducing CO_2 emissions. It is not one-sided responsibility; hence, construction industry practitioners must overcome this problem and counter back with solutions such as using recycled material for construction, deploy higher productivity machinery to the site, and use greener technology that emits less carbon dioxide as less energy usage.

3.1. Relationship between the Carbon Tax and Construction Industry

A carbon tax's primary goal is to reduce emissions of GHGs; most existing carbon policies lack defined processes or standards for determining the success of policies in lowering emissions, although some have sought to measure their benefits. Cumulative carbon tax effects are difficult to assess since numerous things influence overall carbon dioxide emissions, including economic development and other environmental regulations. Considerations for design are based on capital expenses and viability from the developer's point of view. Prospective renters must pay a carbon fee for the whole life of the home. As a result, the developers would only be affected by a small fraction of the additional cost if the building is not commissioned for its use. Because they are not accountable for building energy conservation and do not have a long-term interest in buildings

(British Standards Institution (BSI), 2004), architects, consultants, and contractors have no duty or legitimate rationale for changing their activities. Cost savings are created when customers switch from more expensive high-efficiency equipment to less-expensive high-efficiency equipment within the same technology class. Customers will also gravitate towards better-performing models within the same technology class as a result of the carbon tax.

Using content analysis via analysing the distribution of the keywords of the publication, VOSviewer software is chosen as the medium to interpret the data. The keyword co-occurrence network of the carbon tax and construction industry (see Fig. 1.1) was constructed by the VOSviewer software. The size of the nodes and words illustrated the weights of the nodes. The bigger the size of the node and word, the heavy the weight of the occurrence. The distance between two different nodes shows the strength of the relation between the two nodes. Shorter distances give the meaning of a strong relationship between the two nodes. The line between two nodes or keywords revealed that the keywords have appeared together. A thicker line means more co-occurrence between the two keywords. The nodes of a similar colour are called a cluster.

VOSviewer had helped to divide the related publications into five clusters. Referring to Table 1.1, the keyword of 'emission control' has the highest occurrences of 70. Other keywords are 'pollution tax' (42), 'carbon taxes' (51), 'carbon dioxide' (50), and 'carbon' (47).

Through the content analysis, the relationship between the carbon tax and the construction industry can be revealed. Carbon tax acts as the emission control legislation to reduce the amount of carbon dioxide emissions from the construction sector. The carbon tax is a pollution tax, where the tax is based on

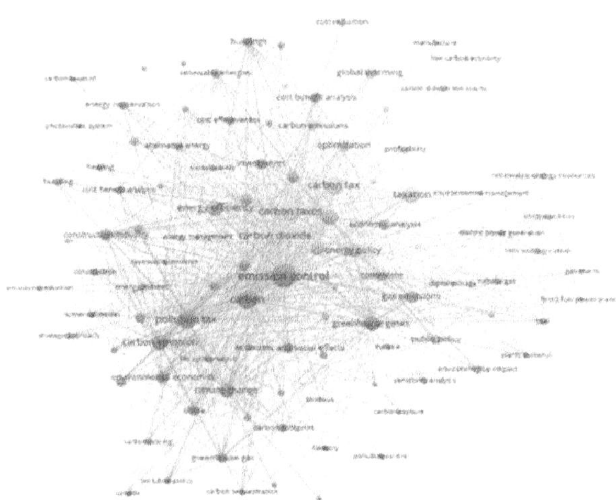

Fig. 1.1. Keyword's Co-occurrence Network of the Carbon Tax and Construction Industry-related Publications. Adapted from the Software VOSviewer Using the Data Extracted from Scopus Database.

Table 1.1. The Top 10 Keywords of the 'Carbon Tax' and 'Construction Industry'-related Publications.

No.	Keyword	Occurrences	Total Link Strength
1	Emission control	70	627
2	Pollution tax	42	417
3	Carbon taxes	51	410
4	Carbon dioxide	50	409
5	Carbon	47	398
6	Taxation	38	357
7	Carbon tax	48	329
8	Costs	36	322
9	Carbon emission	33	306
10	Greenhouse gases	29	275

Adapted from the Software VOSviewer.

the amount of pollution of carbon dioxide. It is believed that carbon tax can push the construction industry to become a digitalised sector by moving forward the conventional technology to efficient and greener technology.

3.2. Framework to Analyse the Impacts of Carbon Tax

Among climate protection strategies, carbon pricing is usually recognised as the most effective way of decreasing pollution. It has been implemented in many forms in many nations. Scholars have studied the carbon tax and its consequences in great detail. This study simulates the carbon emission reductions from different carbon tax levels by utilising the Dynamic Integrated Climate-Economy (DICE) model (Nordhaus, 1993).

Climate change may be mitigated by equitable carbon tax policies, according to a study of Greece's energy production business (Floros, & Vlachou, 2005). There will be some economic benefits from a reasonable carbon tax (Pearce, 1991). As well as allowing businesses the opportunity to alter their production and service processes in order to reduce emissions, the revenues may also be used to finance other environmentally beneficial projects. A study of 55 nations over the previous 20 years revealed that carbon taxes would reduce CO_2 emissions and enhance local environmental quality (He et al., 2019). This report examines China's need for and practicality of a carbon tax as well as its core aims and principles, as well as its basic material and implementation mechanisms (Zhu, Qian, Jiang, & Mbroh, 2020).

The available models used to analyze the impacts of carbon tax are MARKAL (Market Allocation of Technologies), LEAP (Long-Range Energy Alternatives Planning), CGE (Computable General Equilibrium), Input-Output (Wu & Han), System Dynamics (Morshedi, & Kashani, 2020), and Logistic Regression (Asar, & Wu, 2020). Table 1.2 lists the specifics of each of the methods.

The real economic system is primarily stimulated by the energy-economic model, and the focus of the model is on the different suppliers and consumers who aim to maximise utility. It's a common tool for studying energy, environmental, and economic policies. The energy technology model is a broad dynamic

Table 1.2. The Methodology Used by Other Authors to Analyse the Impacts of the Carbon Tax.

Method	References	Details
MARKAL	Jaskólski (2016)	Implications of emissions trading for Poland's long-term technological transition
LEAP	Rivera-González, Bolonio, Mazadiego, and Valencia-Chapi (2019)	Long-term electricity supply and demand forecasting (2018–2040): an application of the LEAP model to a sustainable power-generating system in Ecuador
CGE	Machado, Cunha, Walter, Faaij, and Guilhoto (2020)	A CGE-based life cycle study of an economy's ability to cut Brazilian GHG emissions by 2030
Input–output	Wu and Han (2020)	The shifting patterns of China's green GDP in light of climate change: an analysis using the economic input–output life cycle assessment model
Dynamic Model	Morshedi and Kashani (2020)	A system dynamics model is being developed to assess the housing market's reaction to vulnerability reduction promotion measures
Logistic Regression Model	Asar and Wu (2020)	In the logistic regression model, an improved and efficient biased estimation approach was developed

energy optimisation model developed by international research institutions that are widely used in national, regional, and industry-level research on energy system optimisation and emission reduction (Yang et al., 2020). In contrast to the energy technology model, the energy economy model concentrates on the relationships between energy and other sectors while ignoring the technological elements of the internal energy system. The energy technology model is excellent for low-carbon research in the power sector because it allows thorough analysis, estimate, and optimisation from the viewpoints of energy supply, conversion, and demand.

4. CONCLUSION

This study is mainly focus on the carbon tax for the construction industry. The important conclusion is that the construction industry's largest source of carbon dioxide emissions is the transportation sector. Due to the facts that carbon price encourages the use of greener materials and technologies, the decreasing amount of the energy consumption in the building sector is one of the success factors of the implementation. Although the primary goal of a carbon tax is to reduce GHG emissions, most existing carbon policies lack defined procedures or criteria for determining the success of policies in decreasing emissions, though some have sought to analyse their benefits. It can be difficult to assess the cumulative effects of a carbon tax since numerous factors, such as economic development and other environmental regulations, can influence overall carbon dioxide emissions. Despite the difficulty in estimating the impact of a carbon tax, when emissions are evaluated, assessment, monitoring, and programme evaluation are required to evaluate the policy's impact.

To study the impacts of a carbon tax in the construction industry, a thorough study must be conducted using the methodology or modelling the impacts using models or frameworks such as the CGE model, Input–Output model, and MARKAL model. The result of carbon reduction can be directly illustrated compared to the 'safe' approach such as using renewable energy and green technology adoption because it only impacted a small portion of the sector and not the whole sector. Carbon emissions will be reduced more effectively if an entire industry works together to reduce emissions by adopting green technologies in order to avoid a massive carbon tax. A carbon tax must be implemented on the general amount of carbon dioxide emissions in every sector. With the current situation of Malaysia that used the implementation of renewable energy to reduce the carbon emission, this method is to be seen not relevant in a few decades due to the high demand of fuel and energy usage. This method might be worked for a few years before it falls due to the industry that grows fast with a lot of mega-production or mega factories in the country. Hence, a carbon tax can be proposed solely on the construction industry exclusively in Malaysia.

Japanese researchers Wakiyama and Zusman (2016) found that governments must adjust rates and revenue recycling provisions for each sector's specific characteristics to encourage emissions reductions among the iron & steel, chemical, and equipment industries in Japan. To create a tax that is more generally applicable, it is necessary to consider more than just the rate or the pace of growth. This decision has important ramifications for how revenues are viewed by the public, as well as for equitable issues and cost factors. That is also the case for the construction sector as every sector has significant features that contributed to carbon emissions. Carbon taxes are a good complement to other policies and measures necessary to reduce emissions, according to decades of empirical research and policy experience. To accomplish substantial emissions reductions, a variety of policies and actions must be implemented, and carbon prices can provide further assistance and avoid recovery. Social acceptability, political feasibility, and cost-effective emissions reductions of lower intensity routes are all consistent with achieving deep emissions reductions over the long term.

ACKNOWLEDGEMENTS

Authors would also like to acknowledge UTM Collaborative Research Grant (CRG) No. Q.J130000.2451.07G95 and R.J130000.7351.4B693 for supporting throughout the whole study.

REFERENCES

Asar, Y., & Wu, J. (2020). An improved and efficient biased estimation technique in logistic regression model. *Communications in Statistics – Theory and Methods*, *49*(9), 2237–2252.

Bertram, C, Luderer G, Pietzcker R. C., et al. (2015). Complementing carbon prices with technology policies to keep climate targets within reach. *Nat Clim Change*, *5*, 235–239. doi: 10.1038/nclimate2514

British Standards Institution (BSI). (2004). *Environmental management systems – Requirements with guidelines for use*. London: ISO140001.

Chen, W. Y., & Jim, C. Y. (2011). Resident valuation and expectation of the urban greening project in Zhuhai, China. *Journal of Environmental Planning and Management*, *54*(7), 851–869.

Cheng, C., Pouffary, S., Svenningsen, N., & Callaway, M. (2008). *The Kyoto protocol, the clean development mechanism, and the building and construction sector – A report for UNEP sustainable buildings & construction initiative*. Paris: United Nations Environment Programme.

Coase, R. H. (1960). The Problem of Social Cost. *The Journal of Law & Economics, 3*, 1–44. Retrieved from http://www.jstor.org/stable/724810

Conefrey, T., Gerald, J. D. F., Valeri, L. M., & Tol, R. S. J. (2013). The impact of a carbon tax on economic growth and carbon dioxide emissions in Ireland. *Journal of Environmental Planning and Management*, *56*(7), 934–952.

Floros, N., & Vlachou, A. (2005). Energy demand and energy-related CO_2 emissions in Greek manufacturing: Assessing the impact of a carbon tax. *Energy Economics*, *27*(3), 387–413.

He, P., Chen, L., Zou, X., Li, S., Shen, H., & Jian, J. (2019). Energy taxes, carbon dioxide emissions, energy consumption, and economic consequences: A comparative study of Nordic and G7 countries. *Sustainability*, *11*(21), 6100.

IEA. (2011). *Key world energy STATISTICS* (p. 43). Paris Cedex: International Energy Agency (IEA).

IPCC. (2007a). Summary for policymakers. In S. Solomon et al. (Eds.), Climate change 2007: The physical science basis. Contribution of Working Group I to the Fourth Assessment Report of the Intergovernmental Panel on Climate Change. Cambridge University Press, Cambridge.

IPCC. (2007b). *The physical science basis*. Cambridge: Cambridge University Press.

Jaskólski, M. (2016). Modelling long-term technological transition of Polish power system using MARKAL: Emission trade impact, *Energy Policy*, *97*, 365–377.

KeTTHA. (2017a). *Green technology master plan Malaysia 2017–2030*. Putrajaya: Ministry of Energy, Green Technology and Water.

KeTTHA. (2017b). National green technology master plan. Retrieved from https://lcs-rnet.org/pdf/locarnet_meetings/2015/4th_annual%20meeting/day1/KS1-2.pdf. Accessed on July 31, 2021.

Kirby. P., & O'Mahony, T. (2018). The Political Economy of the Low-Carbon Transition: Pathways Beyond Techno-optimism, International Political Economy Series, Cham, UK: Palgrave Macmillan.

Lu, Y., Zhu, X., & Cui, Q. (2012). Effectiveness and equity implications of carbon policies in the United States construction industry. Building and Environment, 49, 259–269. https://doi.org/10.1016/j.buildenv.2011.10.002

Machado, P. G., Cunha, M., Walter, A., Faaij, A., & Guilhoto, J. J. M. (2020). The potential of an economy to reduce Brazilian GHG emissions towards 2030: A CGE-based life cycle analysis. *Biofuels, Bioproducts, and Biorefining*, *14*(2), 265–285.

Ministry of Natural Resources and Environment. (2015). Malaysia Biennial Update Report To The UNFCCC.

Ministry of Plantation Industries and Commodities Malaysia. (2006). The National Biofuel Policy. Government of Malaysia.

Morshedi, M. A., & Kashani, H. (2020). A system dynamics model to evaluate the housing market response to vulnerability reduction promotion policies. *International Journal of Disaster Risk Reduction*, *44*, Article ID 101438.

Newell, P., & Paterson, M. (2010). Climate Capitalism: Global Warming and the Transformation of the Global Economy, Cambridge: Cambridge University Press. doi: 10.1017/CBO9780511761850

Nordhaus, W. (1993). Optimal greenhouse-gas reductions and tax policy in the "DICE" model. *The American Economic Review*, *83*, 313–317.

Pearce, D. (1991). The role of carbon taxes in adjusting to global warming. *The Economic Journal*, *101*(407), 938–948.

Rivera-González, L., Bolonio, D., Mazadiego, L. F., & Valencia-Chapi, R. (2019). Long-term electricity supply and demand forecast (2018–2040): A LEAP model application towards a sustainable power generation system in Ecuador. *Sustainability*, *11*(19), 5316.

Roe, M., & Mell, I. (2013). Negotiating value and priorities: Evaluating the demands of green infrastructure development. *Journal of Environmental Planning and Management*, *56*(5), 650–673.

Stern, N. (2006). *Stern review on the economics of climate change*. Cambridge: The Office of Climate Change.

Sumner, J., Bird, L., & Dobos, H. (2011). Carbon taxes: A review of experience and policy design considerations. *Climate Policy*, *11*(2), 922–943.

Tsai, W.-H., Yang, C.-H., Huang, C.-T., & Wu, Y.-Y. (2016). The impact of the carbon tax policy on green building strategy. *Journal of Environmental Planning and Management*, *60*, 1–27.

U.S. EPA. (2008). *Quantifying greenhouse gas emissions from key industrial sectors in the United States*. Washington, DC: U.S. Environmental Protection Agency.

Wakiyama, T., & Zusman, E. (2016). What would be the effects of a carbon tax in Japan: An historic analysis of subsidies and fuel pricing on the iron & steel, chemical, and machinery industries. *AIMS Energy*, *4*(4), 606–632. https://doi.org/10.3934/energy.2016.4.606

Wu, S., & Han, H. (2020). Sectoral changing patterns of China's green GDP considering climate change: An investigation based on the economic input-output life cycle assessment model. *Journal of Cleaner Production*, *251*, Article ID 119764.

Yan, H., Shen, Q. P., Fan, L. C. H., Wang, Y. W., & Zhang, L. (2010). Greenhouse gas emissions in building construction: A case study of One Peking in Hong Kong. *Building and Environment*, *45*(4), 949–955.

Yang, J., Li, Q., Li, M., Zhu, W., Yang, Z., Qu, W., … Li, H. (2020). In situ decoration of selenide on copper foam for the efficient immobilization of gaseous elemental mercury. *Environmental Science & Technology*, *54*(3), 2022–2030.

Zhu, N., Qian, L., Jiang, D., & Mbroh, N. (2020). A simulation study of China's imposing carbon tax against American carbon tariffs. *Journal of Cleaner Production*, *243*, Article ID 118467.

CHAPTER 2

DISASTER RISK MANAGEMENT: AN OVERVIEW OF DISASTER RISK ASSESSMENT IN ASEAN COUNTRIES

Muhammad Wafiy Adli Ramli, Nor Eliza Binti Alias, Zulkifli bin Yusop and Shazwin Mat Taib

ABSTRACT

This chapter reviews and compares Southeast Asia country practices on global, regional, and local practices for disaster risk assessment (DRA). DRA research and practices include and create a disaster risk management (DRM) solution. There are 11 countries in Southeast Asia, but only 10 countries are members of the Association of Southeast Asian Nations (ASEAN), except Timor-Leste. The key objective of ASEAN's formation is cooperation in economic growth, social, regional peace and cultural development, disaster management cooperation, and humanitarian assistance at the regional level. The DRM system practiced in ASEAN member countries is discussed in this chapter. Furthermore, the system and findings of DRAs are also addressed. Globally, two DRA structures are discussed and compared, namely Index of Risk Management (INFORM) and World Risk Index (WRI). In addition, regional vulnerability assessment guidelines for regional and national levels are discussed. However, several selected studies and practices such as the Indonesian Risk Index (InaRISK) are being discussed at the local level. Overall, there is space for improvement of coordination in terms of data and

Sustainability Management Strategies and Impact in Developing Countries
Community, Environment and Disaster Risk Management, Volume 26, 15–27

Published under exclusive licence by Emerald Publishing Limited
ISSN: 2040-7262/doi:10.1108/S2040-726220220000026002

technology sharing for DRM, especially for assessment. The finding of this review highlighted the complexity of DRA at the global and regional levels and encouraging community DRA among the ASEAN members.

Keywords: Association of Southeast Asian Nations; disaster risk assessment; Index for Risk Management (INFORM); World Risk Index (WRI); regional vulnerability assessment; Indonesian Risk Index (InaRISK)

1. INTRODUCTION

Disaster is often defined as a result of the combination of danger, exposure, current vulnerability condition, and the inadequate capacity or step to mitigate and cope with the possible negative consequences (UNISDR, 2009). The disaster terms are also consistently associated with the natural hazard. There are several natural hazards, such as floods, earthquakes, landslides, tsunami, and others. According to the World Risk Report, 4,120 disasters were registered worldwide from 2002 until 2012, with more than a million people affected and at least US$1.5 billion economic damages reported (IFRC, 2018). A total of 574 recorded disasters, triggered by earthquakes, floods, landslides, and heatwaves, killed nearly 32,550 people during 2015, affected more than 108 million people, and caused damage of US$70.3 billion (IFRC, 2016). Based on this, disaster risk management (DRM) plays a vital role in ensuring society's safety and security, including protecting the country's governance. DRM is a systematic method of implementing the techniques, policies, and enhanced coping capacities to administrative orders, organisations, and organisational skills and capacities to mitigate the adverse effects of hazards and disaster risk (González et al., 2018). The current DRM activity is more focussed on prevention and preparedness than in the past, with the majority of countries or organisations focussing more on post-emergency response. Overall, DRM's main objective is to minimise, avoid, and shift the adverse effect of hazards by detection and mitigation programmes (Lin, 2018). Overall, the primary goal of DRM is to mitigate, eliminate, and shifting the adverse hazard impact by mitigation, prevention, and preparedness programmes. Every country, government, or organisation needs an orderly and robust disaster risk reduction (DRR) plan to succeed in all DRM programmes to ensure DRM activities run smoothly.

DRR is the policy or practice of disaster risk mitigation through a concerted effort to analyse and control disasters' causative factors, including decreased risk exposure, decreased vulnerability of individuals and property, wise land, environmental management, and enhanced preparedness for adverse effects (UNISDR, 2009). In 2005, Japan presented the Hyogo Framework, the international strategy for disaster reduction at The World Conference on Disaster Reduction at Hyogo. This framework serves as a national guideline for DRR. The Sendai Framework for Disaster Reduction 2015–2030 was adopted in 2015 as a continuation of the Hyogo Framework. Both frameworks advocate for greater DRM at the national and local levels, as well as at the global and regional levels. In Sendai Framework, four priorities need to be focussed on by the government at local, national, regional, and global levels (UNISDR, 2015). The four priorities are:

(i) Understanding disaster risk.
(ii) Strengthening disaster risk governance to manage disaster risk.
(iii) Investing in DRR for resilience.
(iv) Enhancing disaster preparedness for effective response and 'Build Back Better' in recovery, rehabilitation, and reconstruction.

Each of the priorities has its objectives or action to be achieved at the local, national, regional, and global levels. The action includes strengthening the disaster risk assessment (DRA). The strengthening of DRA involves the development of regional DRA and maps and encourages the strengthening of baselines and periodically evaluating, in line with national circumstances, disaster risk, vulnerability, capability, exposure, hazard characteristics, and potential sequential effects (UNISDR, 2015). DRA is a method (quantitative or qualitative) to evaluate the existence and degree of disaster risk by analysing potential hazards and assessing current exposure and vulnerability conditions that could affect the people, property, facilities, livelihoods, and environment on which they depend (UNISDR, 2017). Regional DRA is a key to defining high-risk regions and ultimately enhancing the disaster prevention and mitigation capability of vulnerable regions.

1.1. Association of Southeast Asian Nations (ASEAN) Countries

ASEAN or Association of Southeast Asian Nations is an international organisation founded in 1967 to foster peace and stability in the Southeast Asia for the advancement of social, economic, and cultural. The ASEAN organisation consists of only five member states (Malaysia, Indonesia, Thailand, Philippines, and Singapore) at the beginning of its formation. The association now has five additional members (Vietnam, Myanmar, Laos, Brunei, and Cambodia). In comparison to other world regions, the ASEAN region has experienced rapid economic growth over the last decade. It is considered as the most competitive regional organisation in the developing world (Do et al., 2020). With 5.1% of gross domestic product (GDP), ASEAN's economic growth remained robust in 2018, while the slowdown in trade growth was driven by strong domestic demand and investment (ASEAN, 2019). ASEAN is the fifth largest economy globally, with a 650 million population (ASEAN, 2020).

The population of ASEAN is commonly regarded as a mixture of intrusion-line civilisations. Each member state has its uniqueness and culture, such as Malaysia and Indonesia, with the majority is Muslim, Christian (Philippines), Buddhist (Thailand), and Confucian (Vietnam) (Carney & Gedajlovic, 2002). ASEAN adopts a holistic approach to securing a peaceful, healthy, and prosperous region, strengthening its ability to address current and emerging problems, overcome disagreements, and strengthen maritime security and cooperation.

Following the Indian Ocean Tsunamis (2004), Cyclone Nargis (2008), and Typhoon Haiyan (2013), the need for organised regional cooperation between ASEAN member states has gained momentum. In 2006, the ASEAN member state bounded with an Agreement on Disaster Management and Emergency Response. The purpose of this agreement is to provide an efficient framework to achieve a significant reduction of disaster losses in the lives and social, economic, and environmental properties of the contracting parties and to respond jointly to disaster emergencies through national conceit and enhanced regional and international cooperation efforts (ASEAN, 2010). This agreement also establishes the ASEAN Coordinating Centre for Humanitarian Assistance to facilitate and coordinate disaster among the member states bound to the agreement. This agreement also strengthens the disaster reduction cooperation in terms of policies, operational mechanism, plans, and communication system among the member states in the Southeast Asian region.

Southeast Asia is considered as a disaster risk hotspot, including Oceania, Central America, and West and Central Africa (Heintze et al., 2018). In this chapter, the review focuses on ASEAN countries' actions and practices in DRA at global, regional, national, and local levels. This article reviews current DRM and DRA research and practice in the ASEAN region and countries, comparatively at the local, national, regional, and global levels. This review will benefit the decision-makers, technical analysis, and researcher, especially among the ASEAN members.

2. DRM IN ASEAN COUNTRIES

DRM includes risk 'dimensioning' and risk measurement in order to ensure that not only the potential physical harm, victims, and economic damages, but also social, organisational, and operational variables are considered (Cardona, 2007). In the ASEAN region, the cooperation on DRM started in 1970 by establishing an expert working group as a consequence from the Declaration on ASEAN Concord 1 in 1976 and Declaration on Mutual Assistance on Natural Disasters. Although the cooperation of DRM in ASEAN started in 1970, the momentum gained in early 2000 after the increasing numbers of natural disaster events in this region (Petz, 2014). The ASEAN Agreement on Disaster Management and Emergency Response (AADMER) was signed by all 10 member states in 2005 and entered into force in 2009. The agreement envisions disaster-resilient nations and safer communities in the ASEAN region. One of the two objectives in AADMER is to respond to disaster emergencies jointly (CEDMHA, 2019).

At the national level, each country has its organisational structure for disaster management. All this ASEAN country disaster management involving inter-sectoral cooperation is led by the National Disaster Management Agency (NADMA). For example, in Malaysia, the lead agencies are the NADMA, Vietnam, the Ministry of Agriculture and Rural Development (MARD). Simultaneously, Brunei is the National Disaster Management Centre (NDMC). The main responsible for these leading national agencies is national disaster management coordination to provide effective preparedness, response, prevention and mitigation, and rehabilitation and recovery. The coordination operation also could be different in terms of scale level, like Malaysia and Thailand. If the disaster occurs on a small scale, the district chief, mayor, or executive will head the operation. However, if a vast scale disaster occurs, the prime minister will lead the national emergency operation (CEDMHA, 2018b).

3. DRA IN ASEAN COUNTRIES

DRA is a method (qualitative or quantitative) to assess the existence or magnitude of disaster risk by evaluating the conditions of exposure and vulnerability that could affect people, property, facilities, livelihoods, and the environment (UNISDR, 2017). The DRA consists of two main components: hazard and vulnerability, although studies expanded the concept with additional components such as capacity and exposure. Hazard assessment usually focusses on the extent and magnitude of the hazard. The assessment includes the probability that it could occur in the future. In contrast, a vulnerability assessment is to evaluate the susceptibility towards the exposed element. The vulnerability aspect varies, including physical, social, cultural, economic, and environmental factors (UNISDR, 2009). In this study, the DRA discussion and review focussed on the practice and research at local, regional, and global levels among the ASEAN member states.

3.1. Local Level

Each member has its own DRA practices or works to conduct disaster assessments at the local level, focussing on particular areas or the whole country. Gibson et al. (2000) described scale as 'the spatial, temporal, quantitative, or analytical dimensions used to measure and study any phenomenon'. The spatial scale of DRA may vary depending on the objectives of the DRA being conducted. It could be at the state, province, district, sub-district, or community level – the majority of countries conduct DRAs based on administrative boundaries or specific disaster events. Table 2.1 shows the six ASEAN countries' DRA practices targeting different component risk (hazard and vulnerability) and scale. Each of these countries has its purpose and objectives to achieve.

Table 2.1 shows the DRA approach from several ASEAN countries. Overall, all of the countries listed in Table 2.1 employ the basic concept of risk component, which consists of two main components, hazards, and vulnerabilities. The difference is in terms of hazard type and vulnerability component of the study. Other countries' DRA practices, for example, include multiple hazard types, with the exception of Malaysia, which focuses on flood hazards (DID, 2003). The other countries listed are conducting assessments based on different hazard types such as landslides, storms, typhoons, earthquakes, forest fires, droughts, and cold snaps. There are various types of hazards that occur in the ASEAN countries. In comparison to other countries, Malaysia is frequently hit with floods, especially during

Table 2.1. The Practices of Disaster Risk Assessment (DRA) from Several ASEAN Members.

Countries	Hazard(s)	Vulnerability	Scale	Agency	References
Cambodia	Flood, Fire, Drought	Socioeconomic	Administrative Boundary (Province and District)	ADPC, National Committee for Disaster Management (NCDM), Cambodia Humanitarian Forum (CHF), Bill and Melinda Gates Foundation	(ADPC, 2018)
Indonesia	Earthquake, Tsunami, volcano, landslide, flood, land, and forest fire	1. Social 2. Physical 3. Economic 4. Environment	Administrative boundary (province and district)	National Disaster Management Authority (NDMA)	(NDMA, 2017)
Laos	Biological, climatological, hydro-meteorological, and man-made	Health, education, transportation, hydropower, and housing	Administrative boundary (province and district)	ADPC, National Disaster Management Office (NDMO)	(ADPC, 2010a, 2010b)
Malaysia	Flood	Damage assessment	Catchment scale	Department of Irrigation and Drainage (DID)	(DID, 2003)
Philippines	Typhoon, flood, and earthquake	Damage assessment	Administrative boundary (provincial, city, municipal)	National Disaster Risk Reduction and Management Council (NDRRMC)	(Swiss NGO DRR Platform, 2014)
Vietnam	Typhoon, flood, drought, coldsnap	1. Physical 2. Social 3. Awareness	Community-based (village)	Disaster Management Authority (DMA), Join Advocacy Networking Initiatives in Vietnam	(DMC, 2015; JANI, 2008)

the monsoon season (CEDMHA, 2016). Other countries, such as Indonesia and the Philippines, are continuously exposed to multiple types of hazards including floods, landslides, volcano eruptions, and typhoons (CEDMHA, 2018a).

In terms of the vulnerability component, the ASEAN countries practise various dimensions of vulnerability. Indonesia focuses on four main dimensions: economic, social, physical, and environmental. Meanwhile, Cambodia concentrates on socioeconomic, and Vietnam on physical, social, and awareness. Each dimension consists of indicators such as several lost lives, economic losses, and property damages. These indicators serve as criteria to classify which areas are more or less vulnerable to disasters. However, the risk description for Malaysia and the Philippines is based on damaged assessment. Suppose that an area experiences severe damage to the plantation, road, and building, increasing the area's risk. In Laos, vulnerability factors include health, education, transportation, hydropower, and housing (ADPC, 2010b).

Given the prevalence of DRA approach, the spatial scale is an essential factor that needs to be considered. A scale is an essential tool, especially for improving vulnerability assessment. Table 2.1 shows that some countries practise multiple spatial scales while others use a single scale for vulnerability assessment. There are pros and cons in using a small or more significant spatial scale. However, the smaller scale will give better details and capture complexity (Fekete, Damm, & Birkmann, 2010). The community-level DRA in Vietnam allows analysis on people's perception such as awareness towards risk (DMC, 2015). The other countries (Cambodia, Laos, and Indonesia) apply the approach on subnational administrative boundaries (province and district levels) with a larger spatial scale and better data availability.

All these DRA practices need cooperation, partnership, and support from the government and other agencies. For low-income countries such as Cambodia, the Cambodian government is supported by other organisations such as the Asian Disaster Preparedness Center (ADPC) and the international foundation. As for Indonesia, the government's effort in providing the website of Indonesian Risk Index (InaRISK) to show the risk zones in their countries should be applauded. This can provide information to the people and create awareness among the people in the risk zones. People can also easily access disaster risk information through the website.

3.2. Regional and National Levels

Regional DRA is an essential practice in assessing natural risks in order to identify high-risk regions and ultimately improve vulnerable disaster regions' prevention and mitigation capacity (Chen, Chen, Ma, & Chen, 2019). In addition, DRA aims to identify threats and risks from a national perspective at the national level, similar to what it does at the regional level (Lin, 2018). The ASEAN Regional Risk and Vulnerability Assessment (RVA) guidelines were developed at the regional level by the ASEAN member states, the ASEAN Secretariat, the ASEAN Partnership Group, and the ASEAN Humanitarian Assistance (AHA) Centre. This document provides guidelines for conducting RVA at the national level to the ASEAN member state.

The main goals of these guidelines are for the two-level regional and national levels. The primary goals are to cross-boundary assessment to identify high-risk areas among the member states at the regional level. For the national level, this document guides the member to start the national risk assessment at the subnational or local level (Bell, Bausch, Morath, & Livengood, 2017).

The approach used for risk analysis and evaluation using a composite index. Regional RVA consists of three main components: hazard (multi-hazard exposure), vulnerability, and DRM capacity. There are eight hazard types listed in these guidelines, namely flood, landslides, cyclones, earthquake, tsunami, drought, volcanoes, and forest fire. In terms of vulnerability, nine factors, which influence the affected area's vulnerability, include population, gender, health, water and sanitation, education, communications, transportation, and environmental pressures. The last component in this approach is DRM capacity. This component's primary purpose is to analyse the DRM capacity based on Hyogo and Sendai's framework. The component is used as regional monitoring for the implementation of Hyogo and Sendai framework priorities.

In terms of implementation among the ASEAN members, these guidelines were not well published except for the DRM capacity component. DRM capacity is used to monitor each member state's progress to adopt the Hyogo Framework action to reduce hazards and vulnerability. The progress report for DRM capacity has documented in the disaster management handbook produced by the Centre for Excellence in Disaster Management and Humanitarian Assistance (CEDMHA, 2018a, 2019, 2020). This RVA framework serves as a reference among the ASEAN both at the subnational and at the local levels.

3.3. Global Level

There are two common approaches from DRA globally: World Risk Index (WRI) and the Index for Risk Management (INFORM). Both approaches are used for comparisons and analysis between countries to determine the risk ranking. For WRI, the works to develop and publish a global risk index started in 2011 (Birkmann et al., 2011), while INFORM started in 2013 (De Groeve, 2014). WRI development is a collaborative effort between the United Nations (UN) and the United Nations University-Institute for Environment and Human Security (UNU-EHS). The theoretical concept for WRI derives disaster risk as people are exposed to hazards and vulnerability (de Almeida et al., 2016). The approaches allow risk comparisons among the 173 countries. INFORM approach is an effort between the UN agencies, donors, non-government organisation (NGO), and research institutions. The main objective is to make DRA a holistic and flexible approach that is generally accepted, accessible and regularly updated, transparent, and provides assessments on multi-hazard humanitarian risk indexes at global coverage and regional levels, including climatic variables (De Groeve, 2014).

INFORM approach consists of three main components: hazard and exposure, vulnerability, and lack of coping capacity. Hazard and exposure component is divided into two categories: natural and human. Natural hazard consists of five types: earthquakes, floods, drought, tsunami, and typhoon. In contrast, human hazard category consists of three hazard types: conflict intensity, regime stability, and extrajudicial and unlawful killings. There are two categories for the vulnerability component. Each category consists of socioeconomic (development and deprivation, inequality, and aid dependency) and vulnerable groups (uprooted people and other vulnerable groups). The lack of coping capacities, which include institutional and infrastructure categories, is the final component of this approach.

WRI concept is based on a traditional concept to define risk as exposure (hazard) and vulnerability. The exposure component is the countries exposed to earthquakes, storms, floods, droughts, and sea-level rise. The vulnerability component for these categories is divided into three categories that are susceptibility, coping capacity, and adaptive capacity. Susceptibility defines the risk of harm and injury in the event of a natural disaster. The sub-category of susceptibility consists of housing conditions, public infrastructure, nutrition, poverty and dependencies, and economic capacity and income distribution. Coping and adaptive capacities are the next two categories in the vulnerability component. Coping capacity is the ability to reduce the impact of hazard damage and adaptive capacity is the capacity of communities' strategies and planning to transform after the negative impact of hazard exposure. The sub-categories for coping capacities include government and authorities, disaster preparedness and early warning, medical services, social networks, and material coverage. Education and research, gender equity, environmental status and ecosystem protection, adaptation strategies, and investments are all sub-categories of adaptive capacities.

So, there are differences in terms of structural concepts between these two approaches. The INFORM concept focuses on two types of hazards (natural and human), while WRI focuses on natural hazards. The way these two concepts derive vulnerability also contrasts with WRI's focus on three vulnerability dimensions. However, the INFORM vulnerability concept is based on intrinsic and extrinsic vulnerability, which refers to external factors that influence risk. The vulnerability concept from INFORM was adapted from previous research (Cardona, 2002).

There are several previous studies implementing the WRI concept at the national and local scales. In previous study by Almeida et al. (2016), the WRI concept was implemented at the municipal level to develop the Disaster Risk Index in Brazil (DRIB). However, modification is needed from these studies to improve this approach's validity in order to implement this concept. The modifications are in terms of data, structure calculation, and removal of some indicators. The same approach was adapted by Zhou et al. (2015) to develop the Disaster Risk Index in China (DRIC). The study used the WRI concept to develop risk index at the province level but data modifications and removal of some indicators are required. Although the concept could be used as a starting point to develop the DRA at a smaller scale (national, subnational, or local levels), it must be modified. The detailed information and complexity of risk are captured at the local level, which is different at the global and local levels.

Fig. 2.1 shows the graph risk index of 11 ASEAN countries for WRI (Himmelsbach et al., 2019) and INFORM (INFORM, 2019). Based on the graph, there are differences between the highest risk countries for both risk indexes. Brunei has the highest WRI risk index among ASEAN countries, while Myanmar has the

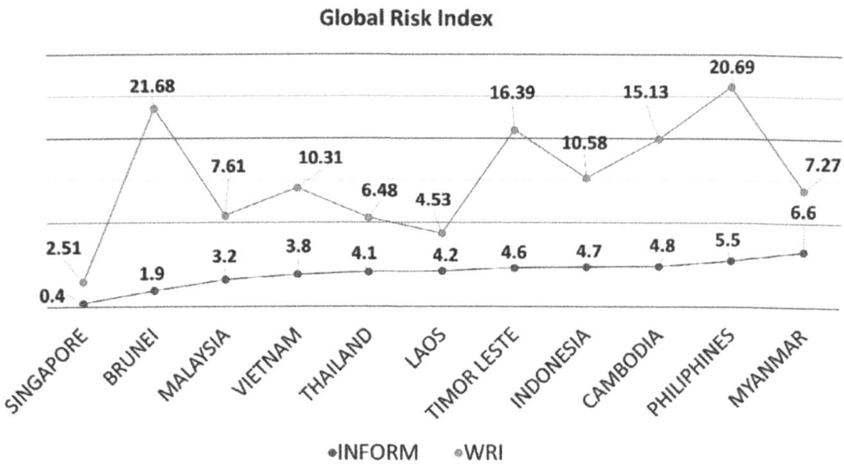

Fig. 2.1. The Risk Index Graph for WRI and INFORM for ASEAN Countries in 2019.

highest INFORM risk index. Brunei has the highest WRI because of the high risk of sea-level rise, which is mainly affected by the strong influence of sea-level rise (Welle, & Birkmann, 2015). The INFORM risk index does not consider the sea-level rise in the risk index development. However, the INFORM risk index is higher in Myanmar because the approach is regarded as a human hazard, thus increasing the risk index. The main reason is Myanmar's humanitarian crisis. The Rohingya, one of Myanmar's ethnic groups, is facing extreme human rights violation by the ruling government (Ibrahim, & Mohd Akahsah, 2020). As a result of the humanitarian crisis, Myanmar is ranked as the country with the highest risk on the INFORM index.

The Philippines is the second-highest risk for both approaches, while Singapore has the lowest risk among the ASEAN countries. The Philippines is a country that is exposed to a variety of hazards. Typhoons are the most frequent hazard in the Philippines. The super typhoon Haiyan, which annihilates the Central Philippines, is the strongest typhoon of 2013 (Seriño et al., 2021). The National Disaster Risk Reduction Management Council (NDRRMC) reported that 3,424,593 families, or 16,078,181 persons, were affected, with a total of 689 injuries and 28 deaths (NDRRMC, 2015). In contrast, Singapore is the less prone area to disaster among the 11 ASEAN countries. Both indexes indicate that Singapore is the safest country from natural and human hazards. Although Singapore is located outside the Pacific Rim of Fire, Singapore has a vital role in this region in disaster management and humanitarian assistance efforts (CEDMHA, 2017).

4. CONCLUSION

This chapter presents a review on the DRA practised among ASEAN countries at the global, regional, and local levels. The main purpose is to review the concept and approach being used by ASEAN countries on the local level, as well as at regional and global levels. Overall at the local level, there are various approaches among the ASEAN countries reviewed in this study. Countries like Indonesia, Cambodia, and the Philippines focus the DRA in multi-hazard type, whereas Malaysia focuses solely on single-hazard type. However, other ASEAN countries should follow the Indonesian approach, as the DRA results if the county is published on the website (InaRISK). The website allows citizens to access the risk assessment information in the country easily.

ASEAN organisations are also working into developing regional RVA that can be used by all members. An ASEAN member state can use the regional RVA as a reference to develop a DRA at the local level. The regional approaches, in particular, allow the member states to monitor the progress of the Hyogo frameworks in order to reduce hazard and vulnerability. There are two common approaches for DRA, namely the WRI and INFORM index. Both have different concepts to determine risks in terms of hazard, vulnerability, and capacity. So, the different concepts produce different outcomes for both concepts. The INFORM index approach combines natural and human hazards into the risk assessment, whereas the WRI only uses natural hazard risk assessment. Despite that the DRA applicable at the global or regional scales, previous studies have shown that it can be used at the local level with some modifications. Thus, it is concluded that the DRA, at any level, plays a vital role in providing information to decision-makers towards reducing the disaster risk and understanding risk in the specific area.

ACKNOWLEDGEMENTS

VThe authors would like to express their gratitude to the Malaysian Ministry of Education for funding through the Fundamental Research Grant Scheme (FRGS) (FRGS/1/2018/WAB05/UTM/02/6) [R.J130000.7851.5F032], UTM Fundamental Research Grant [Q.J130000.2551.20H75], Malaysia Research University Network Grant [R.J130000.7851.4L897], the special Malaysia-Japan International Institute of Technology (MJIIT) grant [R.J130000.7722.4J282], UTM ZAMALAH for sponsorship, and the Malaysian Ministry of Education for GUP 2018 grant [QJ130000.2522.19H68].

REFERENCES

ADPC. (2010a). *Developing a national risk profile of Lao PDR (Part 1)*. Bangkok: Asian Disaster Preparedness Center.

ADPC. (2010b). *Developing a national risk profile of Lao PDR (Part2)*. Bangkok: Asian Disaster Preparedness Center.

ADPC. (2018). Cambodia baseline assessment country report (Issue September 2018). Retrieved from https://app.adpc.net/publications/cambodia-baseline-assessment-report

ASEAN. (2010). *ASEAN Agreement on Disaster Management and Emergency Response*.

ASEAN. (2019). ASEAN Economic Integration Brief (2019). In 1–8.

ASEAN. (2020). The Fourth Industrial Revolution, Pandemics and the Future of Work - RevUnit. *The Asian Magazine*, 04. http://blog.revunit.com/fourth-industrial-revolution-future-work/

Bell, H., Bausch, D., Morath, D., & Livengood, J. (2017). *ASEAN regional RVA: Guidelines for implementation*. Bangkok: ASEAN Committee.

Birkmann, J., Krause, D., Setiadi, N. J., Suarez, D.-C., Welle, T., & Wolfertz, J. (2011). World risk report: Focus governance and civil society. *Unu-Ehs*. Retrieved from http://www.preventionweb.net/files/21709_worldriskreport2011.pdf

Cardona, O. D. (2002). Estimación holística del riesgo sísmico utilizando sistemas dinámicos complejos [Universitat Politècnica de Catalunya]. *Universitat Politècnica de Catalunya*. Retrieved from http://www.tdx.cat/handle/10803/6219

Cardona, O. D. (2007). Indicators for Disaster Risk Management: Disaster Risk Communication Tools from a Holistic Perspective. *Valtellina 2007, 20 Anni Di Sviluppo E Protezione Del Territotio, February*, 1–15. http://understandrisk.org/sites/default/files/01CardonaSystemofIndicators_0.pdf

Carney, M., & Gedajlovic, E. (2002). The Co-evolution of Institutional Environments and Organizational Strategies: The Rise of Family Business Groups in the ASEAN Region. *Organization Studies*, *23*(1), 1–29. https://doi.org/10.1177/0170840602231001

CEDMHA. (2016). *Malaysia: Disaster Management Reference Handbook 2016* (Issue 7 January 2016). Centre for Excellence in Disaster Managment and Humanitarian Assistance. http://reliefweb.int/report/malaysia/malaysia-disaster-management-reference-handbook-2016

CEDMHA. (2017). *Singapore Disaster Mangement Reference Handbook* (Issue 2017).

CEDMHA. (2018a). Philippines Disaster Management Reference Handbook. Retrieved from http://reliefweb.int/map/chile/chilelocation-map-2013

CEDMHA. (2018b). *Thailand Disaster Management Reference Handbook*. http://reliefweb.int/map/chile/chilelocation-map-2013

CEDMHA. (2019). *ASEAN disaster management reference handbook*. Center for Excellence in Disaster & Humanitarian Assistance (Issue March). Retrieved from http://reliefweb.int/map/chile/chilelocation-map-2013

CEDMHA. (2020). *Myanmar disaster management reference handbook* (Issue March). https://reliefweb.int/report/myanmar/myanmar-disaster-management-reference-handbook-march-2020

Chen, N., Chen, L., Ma, Y., & Chen, A. (2019). Regional disaster risk assessment of China based on self-organizing map : Clustering, visualization and ranking. *International Journal of Disaster Risk Reduction*, *33*(June 2018), 196–206. https://doi.org/10.1016/j.ijdrr.2018.10.005

de Almeida, L. Q., Welle, T., Birkmann, J., Queiroz, L., Almeida, D., Welle, T., … Birkmann, J. (2016). Disaster risk indicators in Brazil: A proposal based on the world risk index. *International Journal of Disaster Risk Reduction*, *17*(April), 251–272. https://doi.org/10.1016/j.ijdrr.2016.04.007

De Groeve, T. (2014). Scientific policy report – Index for risk management – INFORM. *European Commission*, *53*(9), 194. https://doi.org/10.2788/78658

Department of Irrigation and Drainage Malaysia (DID). (2003). *National register of river basins updating of condition of flooding in Malaysia*. Volume 2.5: State Report for Johor. Department of Irrigation and Drainage, Malaysia, 2(October), 1–45. Retrieved from http://www.water.gov.my/images/stories/BTB/Vol2.5JohorStateReport.pdf

DID. (2003). *Flood Damage Assessment of 26 April 2001 Flooding Affecting The Klang Valley and The Generalised Procedure and Guidelines for Assessment of Flood Damages* (Vol. 2, Issue October 2003).

DMC. (2015). Community-based disaster risk assessment guide. http://dmc.gov.vn/Uploads/Thu vien tai lieu/Tai lieu tham khao/SCDM II project report/CBDRA EN Clean_MARD UNDP Jun 2015.pdf?lang=vi-VN

Do, H., Patel, C., Budhwar, P., Katou, A. A., Arora, B., & Dao, M. (2020). Institutionalism and its effect on HRM in the ASEAN context: Challenges and opportunities for future research. *Human Resource Management Review*, *30*(4), 100729. https://doi.org/10.1016/j.hrmr.2019.100729

Fekete, A., Damm, M., & Birkmann, J. (2010). Scales as a challenge for vulnerability assessment. *Natural Hazards*, *55*(3), 729–747. https://doi.org/10.1007/s11069-009-9445-5

Gibson, C. C., Ostrom, E., & Ahn, T. K. (2000). The concept of scale and the human dimensions of global change: A survey. *Ecological Economics*, *32*(2), 217–239. https://doi.org/10.1016/S0921-8009(99)00092-0

González, D. P., Monsalve, M., Moris, R., & Herrera, C. (2018). Risk and Resilience Monitor: Development of multiscale and multilevel indicators for disaster risk management for the communes and urban areas of Chile. *Applied Geography*, *94*(November 2017), 262–271. https://doi.org/10.1016/j.apgeog.2018.03.004

Heintze, H. J., Kirch, L., Kuppers, B., Mann, H., Mischo, F., Mucke, P., Pazdriernt, T., Prutz, R., Radtke, K., Strube, F., & Weller, D. (2018). *World Risk Report 2018 Focus: Child Protection and Children's Rights*.

Himmelsbach, J., Forster, T., Radtke, K., Day, J., Forster, T., Himmelsbach, J., Korte, L., Mucke, P., Thielbörger, P., & Weller, D. (2019). *World Risk Report 2019 Focus: Water Supply*.

Ibrahim, H., & Mohd Akahsah, N. (2020). The Rohingya crisis: Demand for international pressure for a change in Myanmar. *Environment-Behaviour Proceedings Journal*, *5*(SI1), 85–90. https://doi.org/10.21834/ebpj.v5isi1.2302

IFRC. (2016). *Resilience : saving lives today*.

IFRC. (2018). *World Disaster Report 2018: Leaving No One Behind*.

INFORM. (2019). INFORM report 2019. Retrieved from https://reliefweb.int/sites/reliefweb.int/files/resources/Inform 2019 WEB spreads.pdf%0Ahttp://files/140/Inform 2019 WEB spreads.pdf

JANI. (2008). Community based disaster risk management in Vietnam. https://www.preventionweb.net/publication/framework-community-based-disaster-risk-management-vietnam

Lin, L. (2018). Integrating a national risk assessment into a disaster risk management system: Process and practice. *International Journal of Disaster Risk Reduction*, *27*(April 2017), 625–631. https://doi.org/10.1016/j.ijdrr.2017.08.004

National Disaster Management Authority (NDMA). (n.d.). inaRISK. Retrieved March 1, 2021, from http://inarisk.bnpb.go.id/

NDRRMC. (n.d.). Disaster reports. 2015. Retrieved from https://ndrrmc.gov.ph/index.php/disaster-reports.html. Accessed February 1, 2021

Petz, D. (2014). Strengthening Regional and National Capacity for Disaster Risk Management: The Case of ASEAN. *Brookings Institution, Brookings-LSE Project on Internal Displacement*, 45. https://www.brookings.edu/wp-content/uploads/2016/06/Strengthening-Regional-and-National-Capacity-for-DRM-Case-of-ASEAN-November-5-2014.pdf

Seriño, M. N. V., Cavero, J. A., Cuizon, J., Ratilla, T. C., Ramoneda, B. M., Bellezas, M. H. I., & Ceniza, M. J. C. (2021). Impact of the 2013 super typhoon Haiyan on the livelihood of small-scale coconut farmers in Leyte island, Philippines. *International Journal of Disaster Risk Reduction*, *52*(October 2020). https://doi.org/10.1016/j.ijdrr.2020.101939

Swiss NGO DRR Platform. (2014). Disaster risk reduction and management in the Philippines (Issue July). https://www.shareweb.ch/site/DRR/Documents/About Us/Risk_Assessment_Philippines_2014.pdf

UNISDR. (2009). 2009 UNISDR Terminology on Disaster Risk Reduction. In *United Nation*. https://doi.org/10.1021/cen-v064n005.p003

UNISDR. (2015). Sendai Framework for Disaster Risk Reduction 2015 - 2030. In *Sendai Framework for Disaster Risk Reduction 2015 - 2030* (Issue March). https://doi.org/A/CONF.224/CRP.1

UNISDR. (2017). *National Disaster Risk Assessment: Governance System, Methodologies, and Use of Results* (S. Safaie (ed.); Consultati). United Nation Office for Disaster Risk Reduction (UNISDR).

Welle, T., & Birkmann, J. (2015). The world risk index – An approach to assess risk and vulnerability on a global scale. *Journal of Extreme Events*, *2*(01), 1550003. https://doi.org/10.1142/S2345737615500037

Zhou, Y., Liu, Y., Wu, W., & Li, N. (2015). Integrated risk assessment of multi-hazards in China. *Natural Hazards*, *78*(1), 257–280. https://doi.org/10.1007/s11069-015-1713-y

CHAPTER 3

DECISION CRITERIA FOR RETROFITTING EXISTING CAMPUS WITH GREEN ROOF

Nur Izieadiana Abidin, Rozana Zakaria and Siti Mazzuana Shamsuddin

ABSTRACT

The Greenery system on buildings is an interesting approach to address the urban, and environmental issues yet provide economic and social benefits. The educational campus in Higher Learning Institution (HLI) has been regarded as a small city that can implement the greenery system area. Green roofs have rapidly become a key in sustainable building development and design features for urban cities and have started being applied in a campus building. However, the built environment in the campus is mostly covered with the existing buildings. Several studies also conducted green roof aspects but with a vast focus on the new building design. Thus, there is an urgent need to identify retrofitting criteria on green roof implementation for existing buildings to achieve optimal solutions. This chapter aims to identify the influential criteria for implementing green roof initiatives in the educational building of HLI. A list of 12 green roof criteria has been identified based on design and economics. A questionnaire has been designed and distributed to architects as important stakeholders in green roof development. The results obtained were analysed with factor analysis based on principal component analysis with Varimax Rotation and Factor Score to categorise and rank according to the importance of criteria. The outcomes of this study showed that design criteria should concern waterproofing, drainage, and access; economic criteria are construction costs, return

Sustainability Management Strategies and Impact in Developing Countries
Community, Environment and Disaster Risk Management, Volume 26, 29–35

Published under exclusive licence by Emerald Publishing Limited
ISSN: 2040-7262/doi:10.1108/S2040-726220220000026003

on investment, and maintenance cost. This study enables decision-makers to consider the criteria established during the decision of retrofitting an existing building with a green roof.

Keywords: Criteria; decision-making; retrofitting; green roof; campus; existing building

1. INTRODUCTION

The development of buildings has made the planet become saturated with structures, and over the twentieth century, the world's population has rapidly lived with the urbanised environment. Urbanisation can bring both positive and negative impacts; however, one of the major impacts is the environment due to the decreases of land covered with vegetation (Charles, Vidyaratne, & Melagoda, 2019). Thus, climate change has been recognised as one of the significant risks in the future because buildings are primarily responsible for greenhouse gases emission (Cascone, Catania, Gagliano, & Sciuto, 2018). Buildings also are responsible for 40% of the total world annual energy consumption, which has attracted serious attention by many, including researchers, architects, engineers, facilities managers, authorities, and property developers, to have green construction to achieve sustainable development. Thus, the green roof has been one of the viable solutions and effective strategies to mitigate the issue by converting the existing building surfaces to become multifunctional land cover with vegetation (Charles et al., 2019). In the context of retrofitting, the green roof has been proved to contribute to significant benefits where all types of a green roof are feasible to be implemented. However, there are several important considerations, whether tangible or intangible, for green roof retrofit. This has been concerned by most owners, such as structural capability, initial costs, maintenance costs, and other requirements. However, there is still a lack of study conducted related to the decision-making for green roof retrofitting. This chapter is to identify and assess the most influential criteria for green roof retrofitting to provide an insight for the decision-makers for effective implementation.

2. RETROFITTING WITH GREEN ROOF

Green roofs are also known as vegetated roofs installed on the top of a building considered a best management practice to manage storm water run-off, heat reduction, green spaces, and habitat de-fragmentation. There are two categories of green roofs, which are intensive and extensive, in which intensive comes with a soil thickness of >15 cm that needs strong structural support to allow for mixtures of trees, bushes, and grass. On the other hand, an intensive green roof usually applies to a large commercial building that consists of pedestrian access. While the extensive green roof comes with a soil thickness of around 5–15 cm, which only requires short vegetation to covers the roof (Barnhart et al., 2021).

In comparing to new building development, most existing buildings were developed before establishing a law that regulates the building energy consumption standards. However, nowadays, there have been limited areas available to build for new buildings, making the existing building more important to apply for sustainable initiatives through retrofitting approach. Thus, the installation of the green roof has significantly increased to new buildings due to the growing interest of the public, private institutions, and the international scientific community to the sustainability issue. However, only a few studies and implementation concern green roofs installation for existing buildings (Cascone et al., 2018). As a case study conducted by Silva, Gomes, and Silva (2016) in Lisbon, the author revealed that 79% of Lisbon is suitable for a green roof, with 52% suitable for retrofits. Furthermore, Castleton, Stovin, Beck, and Davison (2010) have conducted a review for green roof installation on existing buildings where the author identified costs and structural implications to retrofits existing buildings. Besides, Berardi (2017) analysed the benefits of green roof retrofits in terms of energy and microclimate based on case studies conducted on the campus of Toronto University, where the results have proved that green roof retrofits reduced the building energy consumption.

Meanwhile, this research focuses on the assessment of green roof implementation based on the methodology of multicriteria to consider multidimensional criteria of design, economic, and occupant's comfort. According to Kontokosta (2016), the concern towards the decision-making process is beneficial in helping the owners and asset managers for investment in retrofitting. Mcintyre and Snodgrass (2010) supported that building retrofitting was conducted for several reasons, such as reducing energy usage, improving indoor quality, and improving user's level of satisfaction. When the reasons have been clarified, this influences the decision-making process in terms of economic, technical, and technological involved. Therefore, the decision-making in retrofitting should be implemented from the early stage to select the best among numerous available options to suits the building condition.

3. METHODOLOGY

3.1. Data Collection

A questionnaire survey has been directly distributed to the Architects as respondents registered under the Institute of Architect Malaysia and has professional certification of green building. A sampling method used in this chapter is random sampling techniques that allow to obtain maximum data. It is accounted that the registered architects under the Institute of Architect Malaysia in Kuala Lumpur are 210, in Selangor are 158, and in Johor Bahru are 21. The reason for selecting these States is to ease the researcher in meeting the respondents in helping to answer the questionnaire. According to Sekaran (2000), the reliable number to distribute the questionnaire is 191 based on the total sampling of 389. However, due to limitation to find an Architect with green building certified professional, only 85 respondents successfully respond to the survey, which indicated a response rate of 33.46%. The survey specifically required the respondent to state the degree of importance for each criterion according to the 5-point scale given. The establishment of criteria is based on the reviewing process from secondary data published journals, books, and online articles, thus, for the reason to obtain data about criteria affecting the decision of green roof retrofitting.

3.2. Data Analysis

Subsequently, Factor Analysis has been adopted as a data reduction method to prioritise and rank the item based on the factor loading (FL) scores. To perform the Factor Analysis, there are several protocols involved. First is to assess the Kaiser–Meyer–Olkin (KMO) with the minimum acceptable value is 0.50. Second is Barlett's Test of Sphericity (P) with the minimum value $P < 0.50$. Third is the selection with the Factor of extraction to produce the smallest number of factors. After that is to select the factor rotation for an interpretation with the number of criteria under the Factor. The last protocol is to determine the FL with the minimum suggested value is 0.50 (Pallant, 2014). The Factor Analysis performed in this chapter is based on the adoption of principal component analysis with Varimax Rotation as a factor extraction and factor rotation method with the FL 0.50.

Once many criteria have been reduced based on the FL 0.50 and above, the findings were further analysed with Factor Score (FS). FS allows for further verification and justification of the ranked of variables developed based on the numerical value assign. FS is calculated by multiplying the FL with the average mean value, Y. Thus, the multiplying result will be the FS, for each of the sub-criteria, Factor score of sub-criteria (Fssc) (Dien & Frishkoff, 2005).

4. ANALYSIS AND RESULTS

4.1. KMO and Barlett's Test of Sphericity

Prior to conducting the principal component analysis, the first essential step is to determine the sampling adequacy and statistically significance which can be obtained based on the KMO and Barlett's test of Sphericity. Table 3.1 shows the result of sampling adequacy with the KMO 0.913, which exceeds the recommended value of 0.50 and the Barlett's Test of Sphericity also indicated as statistically significant with Sig 0.000; $P < 0.05$.

Table 3.1. Barlett's Test of Sphericity and KMO Analysis.

KMO and Bartlett's Test		
KMO measure of sampling adequacy		0.913
Bartlett's test of Sphericity	Approx. Chi-square	3,046.501
	df	666
	Sig.	0.000

4.2. FS – Criteria Affecting the Decision for Green Roof Retrofitting

Meanwhile, based on the surveys obtained, all the criteria are ranked in descending order according to the level of importance with the minimum value of 0.50, by using principal component analysis with Varimax Rotation and the Weightage Factor. The results of the list of most influential criteria for green roof retrofitting are presented in Table 3.2.

Economic criteria consist of five sub-criteria with the FL value of 0.50 and above, which fall as significant criteria for green roof retrofitting. The priority has been given to the construction costs, followed by return on investment, maintenance costs, estimation for energy and cost reduction, and the payback period. The construction cost can vary based on site location, accessibility, storage of materials on or off-site, transportation distance, project period, roof height, and the desired growing plants (Culnane et al., 2014; Mclntyre & Snodgrass, 2010). Return on investment measures the efficiency or profitability from the investment made, making comparisons based on the different alternatives, while the payback period is the years needed to obtain back the money from the investment (Miller et al., 2011). Besides, maintenance costs are the required costs to maintain the green roof condition periodically (Pack & Kuhn, 2003). Estimation of energy and cost savings has always been an important consideration when implementing a sustainable or green building, especially reducing electricity cost (Berardi, 2017; Mclntyre et al., 2010).

For design criteria, seven sub-criteria are achieved for a FL of 0.50 and above that consists of waterproofing, drainage, accessibility, irrigation system, structural capacity, regulations and local laws, and types of green roof. Waterproofing has been the main influential criteria to protect the building from water leaking, since some roofs require special treatment before the adaption of the green roof. The second influential criteria are the drainage system to accommodate rainfall and discharge the storm water due to severe weather (Culnane et al., 2014). Then, the criteria of accessibility is beneficial for maintenance work purposes, and it's

Table 3.2. FL and FS for Green Roof.

Criteria	*Sub-criteria*	*FL*	*Mean (Y)*	*FS, FSsc*
Economic criteria	Construction costs	0.761	3.920	2.950
	Return on investment	0.729	3.880	2.826
	Maintenance costs	0.705	3.930	2.733
	Estimation for energy and cost reduction	0.675	3.930	2.616
	Payback period	0.578	3.720	2.240
			3.876	13.364
Design criteria	Waterproofing	0.711	3.920	2.762
	Drainage	0.699	3.930	2.716
	Accessibility	0.691	3.850	2.685
	Irrigation system	0.658	3.810	2.556
	Structural capacity	0.649	3.850	2.521
	Regulations and local laws	0.562	3.930	2.183
	Type of green roofs	0.515	3.910	2.000
			3.885	17.423

taken to another level if the green roof is intended to be designed for the public used to view the surrounding (Peck & Kuhn, 2003). The irrigation system has become another important criterion by ensuring for adequate water supply to ensure the survival and aesthetical of the trees. Green roof consists of several layers; thus, structural capacity has become the next influential criteria. Other than layers, the plant weight also needs to be part of the structural capacity as it tends to be heavier when it reaches the maturity level (Culnane et al., 2014). The structural capacity criteria are undeniable to have a relation with the type of green roof required whether to go for extensive and intensive type where the difference is based on the substrate layer (Berardi, 2017). Above all, the design criteria shall comply with the regulations and local law, such as the planning permit for replacement or built-up new structures, structural load capacity compliance, and safety regulations (Culnane et al., 2014).

5. CONCLUSIONS

The existing built environment has contributed to many global greenhouse gas emissions where the adoption of currently has become vital solution. Among several retrofitting initiatives, the green roof is known as the viable approach to offer environmental benefits that reduce the operational carbon emissions, reduce the heat urban island effect, increase biodiversity, storm water run-off, and improve the building temperature. However, before implementing retrofitting, it is understandable that many criteria should be considered. Thus, the design and economic criteria presented in this chapter represent the most significant criteria found for the implementation of retrofitting in an existing building with a green roof. The design criteria were strongly influenced by the technical attributes of the building, such as waterproofing, drainage system, accessibility, structural condition, types of green roof, and to follow the regulations and local laws. For economic, the concern criteria are construction costs, return on investment, maintenance costs, the achievement of energy and cost savings, and the payback period. Future study is planning to cover other criteria where these include the site assessment, occupants' comfort, and others. The development of the decision criteria in this chapter is able to promote green roof implementation, especially for existing buildings through retrofitting approach and to serve for interested stakeholders with the required information during their decision-making process. This can be used as initial data for the building project to be considered for green roof retrofitting.

ACKNOWLEDGEMENTS

This work was financially supported by Universiti Teknologi Malaysia, Research University Grant (Vot no: 18J10).

REFERENCES

Barnhart, B., Pettus, P., Halama, J., McKane, R., Mayer, P., & Djang, K. (2021). Modeling the hydrologic effects of watershed-scale green roof implementation in the Pacific Northwest United States. *Journal Environmental Management*, *277*, 111418. doi:10.1016/j.jenvman.2020.111418.

Berardi, U. (2017). A cross-country comparison of the building energy consumptions and their trends. *Resource Conservation and Recycling*, *123*, 230–241. doi:10.1016/j.resconrec.2016.03.014.

Cascone, S., Catania, F., Gagliano, A., & Sciuto, G. A. (2018). A comprehensive study on green roof performance for retrofitting existing buildings. *Building and Environment*, *136*(2), 227–239. doi:10.1016/j.buildenv.2018.03.052.

Castleton, H. F., Stovin, V., Beck, S. B. M., & Davison, J. B. (2010). Green roofs; building energy savings and the potential for retrofit. *Energy and Buildings*, *42*(10), 1582–1591. doi:10.1016/j.enbuild.2010.05.004.

Charles, S., Vidyaratne, H., & Melagoda, D. G. (2019). Prospects and restraints of green roofs for high-rise buildings in Sri Lanka. *Built Environment Project and Asset Management*, *10*(2), 246–260. doi:10.1108/BEPAM-11-2018-0150.

Culnane, N., Edwards, P., Gammon, J., Hitchcock, K., Innes, S., Katigbak, R., … Webster, R. (2014). *Victoria's guide to green roofs, walls and facades*. Canberra: National Library of Australia.

Dien, J., & Frishkoff, G. (2005). *Introduction to principal components analysis of event- related potentials*. Cambridge: MIT Press.

Kontokosta, C. E. (2016). Modeling the energy retrofit decision in commercial office buildings. *Energy and Buildings*, *131*, 1–20. doi:10.1016/j.enbuild.2016.08.062.

Mclytyre, L., & Snodgrass, E. C. (2010). *The green roof manual: a professional guide to design, installation, and maintenance*. Portland: Timber Press.

Miller, C., Berg, S., Berghage, R., Bass, B., Leal, T. M., Hussain, S., … Gaffin, S. (2011). *The benefits and challenges of green roofs on public and commercial buildings. A report of the United States General Services Administration*. Washington, DC: General Service Administration.

Pallant, J. (2014). *SPSS survival manual. A step by step guide to data analysis using SPSS for Windows version 12*. Sydney: Allen & Unwin.

Peck, S. W., & Kuhn, M. (2003). *Design guidelines for green roofs*. Toronto: Ontario Association of Architects.

Sekaran, U. (2000). *Research method for business: A skill building approach*. Hoboken, NJ: John Wiley & Sons.

Silva, C. M., Gomes, M. G., & Silva, M. (2016). Green roofs energy performance in Mediterranean climate. *Energy and Buildings*, *116*, 318–325. doi:10.1016/j.enbuild.2016.01.012

CHAPTER 4

INTRODUCING NEW PARAMETER IN GREEN BUILDING INCENTIVES TO ENHANCE SUSTAINABLE DEVELOPMENT PARADIGM IN MALAYSIA

Siti Zubaidah Binti Hashim, Nadira Ahzahar, Intan Bayani Bin Zakaria and Norehan Norlida Mohd Noor

ABSTRACT

Green building is an outcome of a design that focuses on increasing the efficiency of resources use energy and national environment. A variety of assessment programmes were developed, such as green building incentive (GBI) had been implemented in Malaysia as a strong indication for the key player in the construction industry to use the opportunity for their companies by embracing the idea of green building focussing on renewable energies, energy conservation, green building, waste management, and support service. However, the current situation reveals that the incentives were not effective enough to encourage the key players to apply the green building concept in their development. The purpose of this research is to produce a new parameter of GBIs for construction key players in Malaysia. The participants of this research were among the implementer and policy maker in helping to produce new parameter on green building incentives in Malaysia. The significant of this new parameter is to provide some guidance to the government in

Sustainability Management Strategies and Impact in Developing Countries
Community, Environment and Disaster Risk Management, Volume 26, 37–44

Published under exclusive licence by Emerald Publishing Limited
ISSN: 2040-7262/doi:10.1108/S2040-726220220000026004

improving and strengthen the prior incentive, hence increase the participation of key building players in green building development in Malaysia. Apart from that, the green incentives are considered to be valuable tools in generating interest, in creating a motive for the adoption of green building practices over conventional practices and in eliminating knowledge gaps.

Keywords: Green building; incentive; sustainability; environment; green development; construction

1. INTRODUCTION

Green building as an indicator to increase the efficiency of using a resource in a building while it can reduce the impact of construction project has on humans, health, and the environment (Ab. Azis, Sipan, & Sapri, 2013). There are many building lifecycles that can be managed with green building concept in mind such as design, construction, operation, maintenance, and waste disposal. Green buildings generally have a smaller carbon footprint and offer a level of cost effectiveness that is superior to conventional buildings. Green buildings give a benefit to the financial and social aspect directly to their stakeholders and indirectly to the public (Hashim, Zakaria, Ahzahar, Mat Yasin, & Aziz, 2016).

Green incentive is an analysis of the current state of green building incentives (GBIs) at the state and local levels. The key players included developers, investors, owners, and so on (Samari, Godrati, Esmaelifir, Olfat, & Mohd Shafie, 2013). The purpose of GBIs is to be use in the private and public sectors and to encourage the key players in construction industry to use a green building concept in their new building development by establishing them as the smartest choice in new development (Richardson & Lynes, 2007).

The Government of Malaysia has offered the GBIs to all the key players in construction industry. The purpose of the GBI is to encourage all the key players to involve in sustainable development to save the environment. Besides that, it's an efficient utilisation of resources.

2. LITERATURE REVIEW

2.1. Green Building Definition

Green building is always relating to environment and health. The purpose of green building is to remove a negative impact towards the environment and building occupants. Hence, it is also designed for economic and environmental performances, where it takes consideration on the climate and cultural needs of the local while providing on the productivity of occupants who does not take their safety and health for granted (Howe & Gerrard, 2010). Green building also can be defined as guidance to be followed in building structures. It also goes through an environmentally friendly process without any harmful resources to be considered throughout the building life cycle. All of this will fulfil what the conventional method is missing and increase in terms of economy, durability, utility, and comfort (Howe & Gerrard, 2010).

2.2. Green Building Incentives

In Malaysia, there are three types of incentives that have been introduced by the government to support the development of green building in Malaysia. The three categories of GBIs according to Van Pottelsberghe (2003) are as follows:

(i) Financial incentives are a monetary provided by the government as a financial support for developers who propose or are willing to be involved in green development. There are various financial incentives provided, such as grants, loans, fund, vouchers, rebates, etc. Financial support is more targeted and has better budget control (Van Pottelsberghe, 2003). The advantages of financial incentives are direct benefit to customer and ease of administration. However, developing countries compared to developed countries, which are more matured in green market, need higher level of incentives, and it is considered as high-cost programmes that could become a disadvantage for financial incentives (Ghodrati, Samari, Wira, & Shafiei, 2012).

(ii) Fiscal incentive is less much common as financial incentives. Many journals and researchers have combined the fiscal instrument into financial incentives. However, it is not a direct monetary given by the government to encourage developers like financial incentives. Fiscal incentives are more likely a privilege given by the government, in terms of exclusion from paying any tax but only given to qualified projects (Manasan & Parel, 2012). Fiscal can be classified as profit based, capital investment based, labour based, sales based, import and export based, and other particular expenses based. Fiscal is more neutral, more predictable for companies, wider reach, very low on administrative cost, and more accessible (Van Pottelsberghe, 2003).

(iii) Structural incentive is related to the expenditure in an indirect way. It is because the administrative incentives do not require the expenditure of funds outside of staff time and do not directly reduce city or country income. The most common new building incentives offered by local governments are incentive to claim the green building certificate, incentive claimed once certificate issued for new building, and upgrade of existing buildings.

2.3. GBIs Implementing in Malaysia

Government has provided several incentives in order to support the development of green building construction in Malaysia. The incentives that have been offered are tax breaks and loans. The incentive that has been introduced by the government is to help the small construction companies to develop green building in Malaysia. The policy-maker made a several changes to GBIs starting from 1986 to 2019. Most of the changes are focusing on the fiscal aspects, such as tax allowance on capital expenditure, tax exemption on using an energy efficiency elements or products, and structural incentives for stamp duty exemption. The changes made do not involve much on the financial aspects as fiscal aspects involve indirectly on the financial for the government or policy-maker.

3. METHODOLOGY

The objective of this research is to identify the new parameter of GBI that can be implementing in Malaysia to encourage all construction key players to involve in green development, such as developer, consultant, investor, local authority, and contractor. The quantitative method has been chosen for this research by distributing questionnaires for three key locations, which are Pulau Pinang, Putrajaya, and Melaka. All those states have implemented a green building concept in their development. Primary data and secondary data were collected for analysing the present study. A total of 41 questionnaires were distributed and 33 questionnaires were returned. The method of distribution was by hand and email. The collected data were analysed with suitable statistical tools. An extensive literature review on GBIs has been carried out through desk study by peer-reviewed journals papers, reports, and published and unpublished manuscripts. Current implementation of GBIs in Malaysia are evaluated by comparing data based on the category of incentives (Ghodrati et al., 2012).

In order to introduce an appropriate incentive for green building fund in Malaysia, this research has listed the best options that have been recognised by literature review. There are three types of GBI that have been identified namely, Type 1 – Financial Incentive, Type 2 – Fiscal Incentives, and Type 3 – Structural or Administrative Incentives.

3.1. Financial Incentives

(i) *Grants and Scheme*: Feed-in tariff in electrical consume is eligible renewable energy producer will be paid a set from their power generate and will purchased by power companies within period 15–20 years.

(ii) *Fund*: Used a Green Technology and renewable energy fund under 'Feed-in tariff' offers of 60% guarantee of the financing amount and a rebate of 2% on the interest or profit rate changed by the financial institutions.

(iii) *Fund*: Consumer purchased a green product more than minimum point must contribute 1.6% of their bill towards the fund. The fund is then used to sponsor other approval holders for the next coming years.

3.2. Fiscal Incentives

(i) Using renewable energy resources such as biomass, solar, etc., will consider in an income tax exemption of 100% of the statutory income for 10 years. Import duty and sales exemption on equipment are used to generate energy.

(ii) Sales and tax exemption on equipment purchased from local manufactures.

(iii) Building obtaining Green Building Index certificate.

(iv) 100% tax exemption of the amount of qualifying expenditure.

(v) Generate renewable energy for own consumption.

(vi) 100% investment tax allowance on the qualifying capital expenditure incurred within five years.
(vii) Provide energy conservation services.
(viii) 100% investment tax allowance on the qualifying capital expenditure incurred within five years.

3.3. Structural/Administrative Incentives

(i) Incentives to claim certificate by developers of green building.
(ii) Incentive claimed once certificate issued for new building and upgrade of existing buildings.
(iii) Exemption based on additional cost to obtain GBI certificate.
(iv) Exemption for transferring ownership of GBI-certified green building.

4. ANALYSIS AND FINDINGS

4.1. The Sample Size and Respondent

The questionnaires were sent to 10 private companies whom were involved directly in the green building system and five government agencies including local authority that act as policy regulators and decision-makers. The overall total population in this research involved 41 respondents categorised into five different groups, namely (i) private developer; (ii) investor; (iii) local authority; (iv) consultant; and (v) main contractor. Out of the 41, a total of 33 respondents gave their feedback at a response rate of 80.5%.

Table 4.1 shows frequency agreement among the respondents on the questionnaire given. It clarifies that the investor group dominated the category with the highest percentage of 100% of total sample or amounted three respondents, followed by the local authority and government agency with 11 respondents or 91.7%. The third and fourth highest responses are from developer group and consultant group, respectively, amounted to eight respondents or 80.0%, and the smallest number of responses totalled three out of six respondents or 50% is a main contractor group. The entire sample size for this research amounts to 33 individuals or within 80.5%, which is sufficient and complies with the sampling frame to produce a meaningful analysis.

In the five categories that took part in the survey, only one group represented the Government as a policy-maker and GBI provider, while the other four groups were placed under the same category as the implementer. This research is to determine the most appropriate incentives to be implemented in Malaysia. GBIs along this research was, generated from the literature and previous study, are classified as three variants: (i) financial; (ii) fiscal; and (iii) structural or administrative.

The results that emerge from the frequency of acceptance or agree towards the incentives list as suggested are moderate. There are nine types of incentives scored ranging from 80% to 90%, while five other types of incentives were scored between 65% and 79%, only proving that the incentive options were not favoured.

Table 4.1. Frequency Calculation for All Respondent Groups: 'Agreed on Types of Green Building Incentives in Malaysia'.

Suggestion of GBIs in Malaysia		Agree (%)	Strongly Agree (%)	Total (%)
Financial incentives				
1.0	Loan of Green Homes Program			
1a	Up to RM15,000 per residential	48.5	27.3	75.8
1b	Up to RM30,000 to retrofit	45.5	33.3	78.8
2.0	Rebates			
2a	Commercial Bathroom Retrofit Program	42.4	24.2	66.7
2b	Solar Rebates – Clean Energy Centre	45.5	30.3	75.8
2c	Solar Rebates – New Homes with ENERGY STAR Program	54.5	30.3	84.8
2d	HEAT Energy Audit	48.5	27.3	75.8
2e	On-Site Renewable Distributed Generation Program	54.5	30.3	84.8
3.0	Grants and Scheme			
3a	Solar Energy Grant Program	60.6	27.3	87.9
3b	Scheme for Existing Buildings and Premises	66.7	21.2	87.9
4.0	Fund			
4a	Design for Efficiency Scheme	60.6	24.2	84.8
Fiscal incentives				
5	Tax exemption			
5.1	Solar – Property Tax	60.6	24.2	84.8
6	Energy-efficient Commercial Buildings Tax Reduction	57.6	27.3	84.8
7	Solar – Income Tax	45.5	42.4	87.9
Structural/Administrative Incentives				
8	Technical Assistance Industrial Uses	33.3	51.5	84.8

Table 4.2 shows the ranking of the variables (in three variants) in the context of concurrence among the respondents, as the green building expert, to propose the best option of incentives in Malaysia setting.

5. CONCLUSION

From the analysis that has been done shows have a several incentives could be implement and added value in current GBI based on Table 4.2, to come out with appropriate planning for Malaysia's green development. Most of the respondents are requested to increase an incentive in financial aspect compared to fiscal and structural. It shows that it can help on the initial cost of green building construction for of this research development. From this research, the policy-maker needs to form a group that consists of expert person in green building development to revise and improve a current GBI. The researchers believe that this research could be a benchmark for Malaysian government in improving the incentives. Further research is needed to focus on the procedure and regulation. Apart from that, awareness among construction key players in Malaysia should be focussed to ensure that they have enough information and knowledge about GBIs for their green development.

Table 4.2. New Parameter of GBIs.

	Financial Incentives		
1	Loans	Green Jobs/Green Homes Programme	Up to RM15,000 per residential customer to retrofit a home Up to RM30,000 to retrofit each qualifying commercial building.
		Solar – Rebates	Clean Energy Centre provides rebates for very small solar projects of 5 kW or less per building. New Homes with ENERGY STAR Programme provide rebates for PV system between 3.6 and 10 kW servicing residential projects
		On-Site Renewable Distributed Generation Program	Rebate for the installation of a qualified PV system at a non-residential facility; a maximum incentive for any PV project is RM1 mil
3	Grants and Scheme	Solar Energy Grant Program	Provides grants up to RM4,000 to install solar water heating systems and up to RM30,000 to install PV system
		Scheme for Existing Buildings and Premises	Energy improvement work involve installation of equipment; it provided cash incentive up to 50% of qualifying cost
4	Fund	Design for Efficiency Scheme	Encourage new facilities or expansion project for EE improvement in early stage. Funding up to 50% of qualifying cost or capped at RM600k
	Fiscal incentives		
1	Tax Exemption	Solar – Property Tax	Up to 100% of the value added by solar energy systems is exempted from local property taxes for a 30 years period
2	Solar – Income Tax		Income tax credit equal to 25% (up to RM5,000) of the cost of equipment and installation of an eligible PV or solar thermal system in a residential or multi-family residential building.
	Structural incentives		
1	Technical assistance industrial uses		Provide services on compliance assistant and on-site technical support for manufacturing companies to reduce toxic use, improve energy efficiency and conserve water and other resources

REFERENCES

Ab. Azis, S. S., Sipan, I., & Sapri, M. (2013). The potential of implementing property tax incentives on green building in Malaysia. *American Journal of Economics*, *3*(2), 63–67. doi:10.59231/j.economics.20130302.01.

Ghodrati, N., Samari, M., Wira, M., & Shafiei, M. (2012). Investigation on government financial incentives to simulate green homes purchase. *World Applied Sciences Journal*, *20*(6), 832–841.

Hashim, S. Z., Zakaria, I. B., Ahzahar, N., Mat Yasin, M. F. & Aziz, A. H. (2016). Implementation of green building incentives for construction key players in Malaysia. *International Journal of Engineering and Technology*, *8*(2), 1039–1044.

Howe, J. C., & Gerrard, M. B. (2010). *The law of green buildings*. Chicago, IL: American Bar Association.

Manasan, R. G., & Parel, D. (2012). The need (or not) for fiscal incentives. Retrieved from http://pidswebs.pids.gov.ph.

Richardson, G. R. A., & Lynes, J. K. (2007). Institutional motivation and barriers to the construction of green building on campus – A case study of the University of Waterloo, *Ontario. International Journal of Sustainability in Higher Education*, *8*(3), 339–354.

Samari, M., Godrati, N., Esmaielifar R., Olfad, P., & Mohd Shafie, M. W. (2013). The investigation of the barriers in developing green building in Malaysia. *Modern Applied Science*, *27*(2).

Van Pottelsberghe, P. B. (2003). *Evaluation of current fiscal incentives for business R&D in Belgium*. Solvay Business School Working Papers, University libre De Bruxelles, pp. 8–12.

CHAPTER 5

RECOMMENDATIONS FOR MINIMISING CONSTRUCTION CLAIMS: ACHIEVING SUSTAINABLE RELATIONSHIPS AMONG STAKEHOLDERS

Do Tien Sy, Zwe Man Aung and Nguyen Thanh Viet

ABSTRACT

Claims and disputes are often unavoidable in the construction industry due to its unique and complex characteristics involving the massive investment of capital, lengthy project duration, and multiple project stakeholders. This chapter intends to identify the critical construction claims attributes, compare the perceptions of major stakeholders on different claim attributes, and investigate the contrast of the top five claim attributes between this study and previous ones. The literature review resulted in 48 claim attributes responsible for the construction project schedule delays. These attributes were then presented to Vietnam construction industry (VCI) practitioners in the form of a questionnaire survey. Data analysis was done based on the collected 113 qualified samples. Relative importance index (RII) was applied to determine the ranking of claim attributes. The results were that the top five causes of claims, that is, payment delays, mistakes by contractor during construction stage, delays in work progress by the contractor, financial failure of the contractor, and frequently changing requirements by the owner, lead to the schedule delays in VCI. These findings can assist the local industry practitioners and foreign companies seeking a share in the VCI market in understanding the causes of construction

Sustainability Management Strategies and Impact in Developing Countries
Community, Environment and Disaster Risk Management, Volume 26, 45–60

Published under exclusive licence by Emerald Publishing Limited
ISSN: 2040-7262/doi:10.1108/S2040-726220220000026005

claims comprehensively and formulating the countermeasures to minimise their impacts and hence reduce the unnecessary losses and raise the likelihood of success as well as maintain sustainable relationships among stakeholders.

Keywords: Construction projects; construction claims; sustainable relationships; schedule delays; relative importance index (RII); Vietnam

1. INTRODUCTION

Construction industry has always been a measure for success in the development of both national and global economic situations. However, construction projects nowadays are dynamic, risky, complex, and large-scale with the involvement of dissimilar, prospectively multicultural stakeholders. It is often infeasible to finish the project without any deviations from the primary plan, and hence, changes and claims occur (Hai, 2019; Vo, Nguyen, & Le Hoang Thuy To Nguyen, 2020). Construction claims can be defined as the demand for the compensation of additional money and extension of project duration for the work extra to the primary contract. It has a significant impact on the time and cost performance of the construction projects (Hai, 2019; Kumaraswamy, 1997; Wilson, 1982).

In Vietnam, the construction industry is one of the pivotal pillars supporting economic growth. The growth rate of the Vietnam construction industry (VCI) has been increasing 15% annually for the previous 10 years. In 2002, VCI contributed to 39% of the Vietnam GDP growth rate. In 2011, the number escalated up to 41.1%. With the support from the Vietnam government's endorsement of industrialisation and injection of foreign investment capital through the Official Development Assistance (ODA) programme, the growth rate of VCI has been in a stable and thriving state over the years (Khanh, & Kim, 2014; Le, 2017; Nguyen & Ogunlana, 2004).

Despite the vigorous development and growth of the VCI, the claims and disputes arising in the VCI are also increasing each year. The leading arbitration centre in Vietnam, the Vietnam International Arbitration Centre (VIAC), reported that the number of disputes settled at VIAC in 2019 is 274, which is a 52.2% increase from its previous year with total dispute values of around 6.7 thousand billion VND (290 million dollars), of which construction industry accounted for 12% of it (Vietnam International Arbitration Centre, 2018). Construction claims also have a significant impact on the time performance of projects in VCI. Most construction projects in VCI fail to finish the project on time and have been experiencing schedule delays regularly (Le-Hoai, Lee, & Lee, 2008). Besides, construction claims can affect sustainable relationships among stakeholders, which significantly impact the project performance (S. Y. Kim, & Nguyen, 2018).

In order to improve the project performance, especially the time performance, and maintain sustainable relationships among stakeholders, the primary project stakeholders, including project owners, contractors, and consultants, therefore, need to catch onto the causes of claims and prevent them from occurring. This chapter intends to identify the claim attributes affecting the time performance of construction projects in VCI as well as to give recommendations for minimising construction claims.

2. LITERATURE REVIEW

The study on construction claims has invariably received a significant amount of attention from researchers all over the world. Enshassi, Choudhry, and El-ghandour (2009) investigated the causes of claims in Palestinian construction projects from the aspect of the contractor by distributing a questionnaire survey and interviewing Palestinian contractors in the Gaza strip. The analysis was done applying the relative importance index (RII). The findings are that awarding bids to the lower bidder, border closures, residents' inference during project implementation, road blockage, and difficulties in passing between cities and governorate are the leading causes of claims. 'Choi and Kim (2016), aimed to identify the causes of claims and disputes in Korean construction projects from the construction companies' perspective based on FIDIC red books through Failure Mode and Effects Analysis (FMEA), and Delphi method. The results of their study indicate that delay in work progress by the contractor is one of the top 10 dispute risk factors. On the other hand, Zaneldin (2006) studied the types, causes, and severity of claims in UAE construction projects through the analysis of RII. The results show that changes and extra work types of claims are the most frequent, while contract ambiguity is ranked last. For the causes of claims, change/variation orders is the most frequent, while delay caused by owner and oral change orders by owner rank second and third, respectively. The same author, Zaneldin (2020), conducted another study for construction claims in UAE in 2020. The results are similar to the previous one, except for types of claims; changes and delay are the most frequent ones, and for the causes of claims, the first two rankings are the same, excluding changes in material and labour cost, which ranks third.

Similar studies about construction claims have also been conducted in ASEAN countries. Hardjomuljadi (2014) emphasised the casual factors of construction claims in the hydroelectric projects in Indonesia from each party's viewpoint involved in project execution. The results indicate that the most important main causal factor is inefficiency and disruption, which can be considered a common discussion for all claims and disputes because it involves both time and money. Recently, Kongchasing and Sua-lam (2021), examined the factors leading to construction delays from both Thailand contractors' and consultants' perspectives through the Delphi technique. The results are that shortage of qualified labour, change orders made by owners, and insufficient financial liquidity on the part of the contractor were three critical factors affecting the construction schedule to both the contractors and the consultants.

In Vietnam, Hai (2019) intended to survey the claim practices in the VCI by collecting data from both contractors and consultants. The analysis is done by RII, and the results show that time extensions claim, change order claim, and design-related claims are three crucial types of claims that frequently occurred in VCI. Recently, Vo et al. (2020), conducted a questionnaire survey among the industry practitioners of Ho Chi Minh City, Vietnam, with 117 observations to understand the causes of disputes in VCI. Through the technique of RII and exploratory factor analysis, it is determined that diversity of working style among the parties, reluctance to work, and poor teamwork ate top three dispute casual attributes, and six groups of dispute factor, that is, cooperation, technology, economics, productivity, information, and behaviour are achieved.

From the literature review, it resulted in 48 claim attributes, engendering the project schedule delays in VCI, presented in Appendices 1 and 2. Moreover, a review of the aforementioned studies indicates that the study of construction claims based on their impact on the time performance of the construction projects VCI has yet to be performed.

3. METHODOLOGY

The aim of this research is to investigate the critical claim attributes and their categories in VCI. The research methodology adopted for this research is shown in Fig. 5.1, which can be broken down into three main steps:

Step 1 – Identify claim attributes causing schedule delay and collect data. The claim attributes affecting the schedule delay in construction projects are first collected through literature review. A set of preliminary questionnaires is developed based on those claim attributes. Five-point Likert scale is applied for this questionnaire survey. Respondents are requested to choose one out of five options (from 1 = 'no effect' to 5 = 'very strong effect') to determine the impact of claim attributes engendering the construction delays from the contractor's perspective. A pilot survey is conducted to confirm the reliability of the preliminary questionnaire design by measuring the internal consistency. Internal consistency reliability by using Cronbach's alpha coefficient measures the degree to which all single sets of items

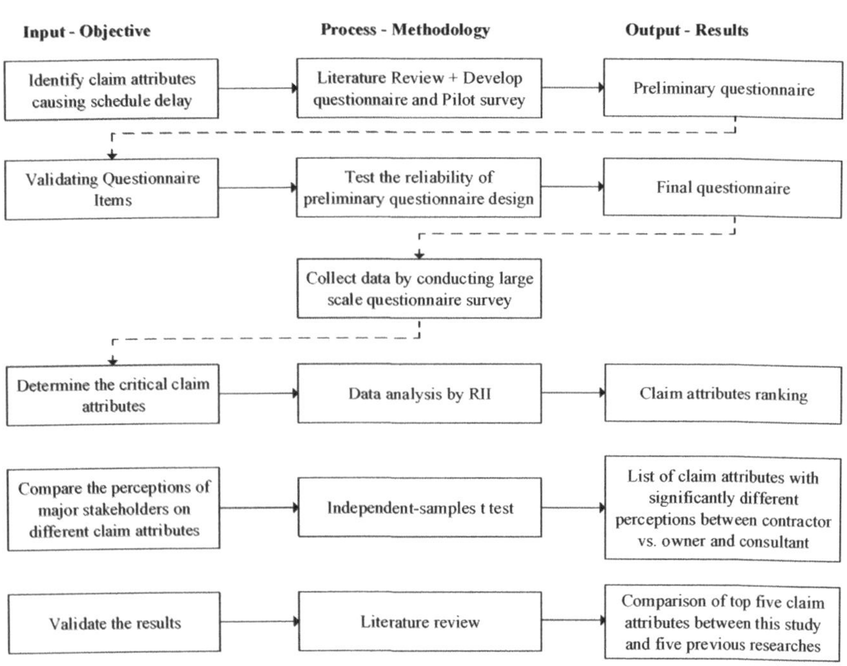

Fig. 5.1. Research Flowchart.

represent the similar construct. The Cronbach's alpha coefficient is calculated by dividing the true score variance to the observed score variance. A test is considered reliable if there are minimum amount of errors, that means higher coefficient value (Ursachi, Horodnic, & Zait, 2015). Cronbach's alpha coefficient value ranges from 0 to 1. After finalising the questionnaire form, a large-scale questionnaire survey is conducted among the industrial practitioners in VCI. The questionnaires are handed out using both physical copies and soft copies via email. They were then completed by gathering feedback from the participants, and all these responses were stored in the Google Form. The majority of respondents were from contractors, the rest being owners, consultants, subcontractors, and suppliers.

Step 2 – Determine the critical claim attributes. RII is applied to determine the ranking of claim attributes triggering the construction projects' schedule delays. The detailed discussion of top five claim attributes in VCI based on RII ranking is mentioned in the next section. RII formula for the five-point Likert type scale is shown in equation 1.

$$\text{RII} = \frac{\sum_{i=1}^{5} a_i x_i}{5N} \tag{1}$$

where, a_i is a constant expressing the weight of the *i*th response, x_i is the frequency of the *i*th response of the total responses for each clause, i is the response category index, where $i = 1, 2, 3, 4$, and 5, respectively, N is the total number of respondents. RII value is ranged from 0 to 1 (Enshassi et al., 2009).

Step 3 – Compare the perceptions of major stakeholders on different claim attributes. Statistical Package for Social Sciences software (SPSS 26.0) is utilised for independent samples *t*-test to compare the difference in perspectives between two respondent groups: owner + consultant and contractor, on construction claim attributes in VCI.

Step 4 – Validate the results. To validate the findings from this study, a literature review is conducted to compare the top five claim attributes between this study and previous ones.

4. DATA ANALYSES, RESULTS, AND DISCUSSION

4.1. Critical Claim Attributes

Through literature review, 48 claim attributes were obtained, and a preliminary questionnaire was designed based on these attributes. A pilot survey was conducted among 15 experts in VCI. In this study, Cronbach's alpha coefficient was used to determine the reliability of the preliminary questionnaire design by measuring internal consistency among factors. The result of the test was 0.953, which is greater than 0.5, thus affirming the reliability of the questionnaire item at the 5% significance level (Wang, & Yuan, 2011).

The finalised questionnaire form was distributed among the VCI practitioners. The feedback from the respondents was stored in Google Form. One hundred and twenty-six observations were collected. Out of which, 13 were rejected due to incomplete and inconsistent answers. There were 113 qualified observations in total for the data analysis. Information required of the respondents included type of organisation, work experience, knowledge about construction claims, and experience in handling with construction claims.

There were 60 (53.1%) contractors, 25 (22.1%) consultants, 24 (21.2%) owners, and 4 (3.5%) subcontractors and suppliers for types of organisation the respondents work for. With regard to working experience, 47 (41.6%) of the respondents had less than five years of working experience, 44 (38.9%) had 5–10 years of experience, 13 (11.5) had 11–15 years of experience, and 9 (8%) had over 15 years of experience. Additionally, 108 (95.5%) of the respondents had knowledge about construction claims, 71 (62.8%) had experience in working for construction claims, and 42 (37.2%) had no experience in handling construction claims. The five respondents with no knowledge about construction claims were explained clearly about the definition and process of construction claims and requested to answer the questionnaire survey again. Hence, based on the above-mentioned statistics, respondents could provide sound judgement about the effect of construction claims on schedule delays as majority of them had knowledge about construction claims.

The RII ranking of 48 claim attributes affecting construction schedule delays is presented in Appendices 1 and 2. The top five claim attributes were: payment delays (RII = 0.819; $R = 1$), mistakes by contractor during construction stage (RII = 0.804; $R = 2$), delays in work progress by the contractor (RII = 0.798; $R = 3$), financial failure of the contractor (RII = 0.791, $R = 4$), and frequently changing requirements by the owner (RII = 0.781, $R = 5$).

'Payment delays' is defined as the failure of the owner to make payments to the contractor on time, resulting in the delay of the work progress by the contractor and finally affecting the time performance of the construction projects (Enshassi et al., 2009; Mohamed, Ibrahim, & Soliman, 2014; Vo et al., 2020; Zaneldin, 2020). This attribute was ranked first and, it is the most crucial claim attribute engendering the schedule delays of the construction in VCI. This might be due to the fact that Vietnamese construction companies have suffered dismal business failure due to terrible financial problems and risks coupled with prior competition (Hai, 2019). When delays in the payment occurred, contractors, especially from the small and medium construction enterprises, might not have enough financial capacity to continue the project, therefore, resulted in construction schedule delays. Moreover, when the owner delayed the payment to main contractors, payment to subcontractors by main contractors might be hindered. As a result, the confidence of main contractors/subcontractors' confidence on owner/main contractors might have plummeted for the payment issue, which can hamper the sustainable relationships among them in the current project or future projects.

'Mistakes by contractor during construction stage' means that the workers and engineers under the contractors committed some human errors such as misreading of design by site engineers, misunderstanding of engineers' instructions by workers; therefore, extra work and rework have to be performed and additional time and money will be consumed from the contractor (Zaneldin, 2006, 2020). This factor was ranked second because, in developing countries, similar to Vietnam, there is always a shortage of skilled labours and engineers. Due to the technical inadequacy of the workers, human errors occurred during the execution of construction, which brings on rework and extra work, and finally, delaying the schedule (Kongchasing & Sua-Iam, 2021). Moreover, mistakes and errors in construction by contractors can lead to poor quality of construction projects, which are not satisfied by owners and consultants. This reduces the opportunity for collaboration between the contractors and the owners in the next projects. In other words, their sustainable relationships could be broken.

'Delays in work progress by the contractor' implies that the contractor failed to perform the work in accordance with the planned schedule (Vo et al., 2020; Zaneldin, 2006, 2020). This was ranked third. Most construction projects in Vietnam are behind schedule due to poor infrastructure and underdeveloped management mechanisms (S. Kim, Van Tuan, & Ogunlana, 2009). Owner might claim against the contractor if there is a significant delay in work progress, which results in the consummation of more time and budget of the project. Furthermore, in severe cases, the owner can put the contractor on their blacklist if they do not want to build a sustainable relationship with the contractor in the future anymore.

'Financial failure of the contractor' indicates that the contractor did not have enough financial capability and failed to continue the project before the payment was done by the owner (Kongchasing & Sua-Iam, 2021; Zaneldin, 2006, 2020). This factor ranked fourth. A major issue affecting the contractor's lack of financial liquidity is the contractor's work performance (Nasirzadeh, Mazandaranizadeh, & Rouhparvar, 2016). When the contractor performed the poor quality of work, the consultant considered the work unqualified, and the owner might not pay the contractor. This has a serious impact on the contractor's finance, and the contractor might fail to meet the financial obligations entailed to run the project, and in serious cases, there might be stopping of work, which resulted in construction claims between owner and contractor. Additionally, if the project was halted due to the contractor's failure in financial issues, the owner might have to select a new contractor, thus bringing to an end to the sustainable relationship with the current contractor.

'Frequently Changing Requirements by the Owner' is defined as that owner makes variation orders (i.e., work changes) frequently, which is terrible for the contractor, especially if that scope of work is already in progress (Enshassi et al., 2009; Kongchasing & Sua-Iam, 2021; Zaneldin, 2006, 2020) This factor ranked fifth. From the contractors' perspective, change orders mean additional costs and extra scope of work, which means that the project will take longer than the planned schedule (Kongchasing & Sua-Iam, 2021). Owner should extend the project deadline in the contract while issuing the change order. Otherwise, the contractor might claim against the owner if the owner issues unrealistic scope changes repeatedly, triggering more time delays and over-budget of the project, thus hindering the sustainable relationship among project stakeholders.

4.2. Different Perceptions of Major Stakeholders on Claim Attributes

To clarify the different perceptions of two respondent groups, owner + consultant and contractor, on claim attributes in VCI, their perceptions were compared through independent sample t-test method (at $\alpha = 5\%$) with the aid of SPSS software (SPSS 26.0). The reason as to why the perceptions of these two respondent

Table 5.1. Claim Attributes with Significantly Different Perceptions of Owner + Consultant and Contractor Groups under an Independent Sample *t*-Test.

Claim Attributes		Levene's Test for Equality of Variances						*T*-test for Equality of Means	
		Assumption	*F*	Sig.	*t*	df	Sig. (2-tailed)	Mean Diff.	Std. Error Diff.
Owner + Consultant Versus Contractor									
C34	Unfair risk allocation	Equal variances not assumed	4.489	0.036	2.467	104.569	0.015*	0.410	0.166
C24	Uncertainty of project scope	Equal variances assumed	0.168	0.683	2.283	107	0.024*	0.440	0.193
C38	Time extensions/ EOT	Equal variances not assumed	6.211	0.014	2.102	85.324	0.039*	0.361	0.172

Notes: * Significant, *p*-value (<0.05).

groups were compared is that usually, in a construction project, the consultants represent the interests of the owner and hence, their approach to claims issues are quite similar, whereas owner stands for his own benefits, resulting in two separate groups for the perceptions in claim attributes. The number of owner + consultant group was 49 (43.3%) out of the whole respondents, and contractor group count was 60 (53.1%). The null hypothesis is that there is no significant difference between the owner + consultant and contractor sectors' perceptions. The claim attributes with significant differences between owner + consultant and contractor groups under an independent sample *t*-test are displayed in Table 5.1.

The survey data revealed three claim attributes (3 out of 48) with significantly different perceptions (p-value < 0.05) between owner + consultant and the contractor groups, as shown in Table 5.1. The claim attributes with the significant different perceptions between owner + consultant and contractor groups are unfair risk allocation, uncertainty of project scope, and time extensions/ extension of time (EOT). These differences in the perceptions of owner + consultant and contractor group are due to the fact that each stakeholder in the project has their own interests to protect, thus, resulting in different priorities and viewpoints (Bal, Bryde, Fearon, & Ochieng, 2013).

Unfair risk allocation implies the unreasonable distribution of risks by the project stakeholders and results in excessive risk exposure to the contractor. Risk is one of the underlying reasons for claims, and the probability of claim occurrence is higher in the projects that transfer more risks to the contractor (Council, 2007). Owner and consultant transfer the risks to the contractor to minimise the impact on them, whereas the contractor does not want to shoulder the responsibilities of risks as much as possible. This causes a significant difference in the perspectives of owner + consultant and contractor for the case of risk allocation.

Uncertainty of project scope is defined as ambiguities in project stakeholders' decisions while setting the project scope, resulting in changes of project scope in the later stages of the project. When a contractor's work is delayed or interrupted due to changes in the scope of the project, he will usually seek compensation to cover the unanticipated costs (Al-Qershi & Kishore, 2017). Owner and consultant team will try to keep down the compensation time and cost for their benefits, hence, triggering the split in the viewpoints of owner + consultant and contractor groups to protect each side's profits. On that account, there was a significant difference between the perceptions of owner + consultant and contractor factions for the uncertainty of project scope claim attribute in VCI.

Time extensions/EOT means the construction of a project or a part of the project is not completed within the time period initially intended and as specified in the contract. This can occur due to failure to obtain necessary permits for the work, poor workmanship, and site conditions, which differ from the expectations (Al-Qershi & Kishore, 2017). EOT is one of the fundamental causes of claims, and there have always been controversies and arguments on settling it objectively between owner + consultant and contractor groups. Owner and consultants want to finish the project as early as possible and do not want to extend the project to generate more profit unless the responsibilities for the delays lie in their own fault. On the other hand, when the project is delayed, the contractor wants to submit the notice for EOT to the consultant for delays caused by both owner and contractor to shrink the amount of compensation necessary to hand over to the owner. Therefore, this results in significantly different perceptions between owner + consultant and contractor factions on time extensions/EOT.

4.3. Validation of the Results

To validate the list of critical claim attributes in this study, the top five critical claim attributes affecting the time performance of construction projects in VCI, which are identified in the previous section, are further examined by comparing with the results from previous five researches in other countries, as presented in Table 5.2. Even though these studies have different research objectives and methodology, their findings can be analogised to perceive the trait of crucial claim attributes in other countries.

Table 5.2. Comparison of Top Five Claim Attributes between This Study and Previous Studies.

Top five claim factors from the survey	Rank					This study
	Zaneldin (2006)	Zaneldin (2020)	Kongchasing and Sua-Iam (2021)	Mohamed et al. (2014)	Al-Qershi and Kishore (2017)	Vietnam
	UAE	UAE	Thailand	Egypt	India	
Payment delays	1	4	5	–	1	8
Mistakes by contractor during construction stage	2	18	17	–	–	39
Delays in work progress by the contractor	3	10	18	–	–	7
Financial failure of the contractor	4	10	19	3	–	18
Frequently changing requirements by the owner	5	1	1	2	6	3

Based on the findings from Table 5.2, 'payment delays' is the most critical claim attribute affecting the time performance of construction projects in VCI. This claim attribute is also the most important one in the Egyptian construction industry (first rank) and quite dominant in other construction industries, too; UAE (2006 – fourth rank), UAE (2020 – fifth rank), and India (eighth rank). Therefore, it can be presumed that 'payment delays' is one of the significant claim attributes encountered in most countries' construction industries.

'Mistakes by contractor during construction stage' is considered one of the crucial claim attributes in Vietnam (second rank in this study). However, it is not critical in UAE (2006 – 18th rank), UAE (2020 – 17th rank), and India (39th rank). In contrast to these countries, Vietnam is a developing country, experiencing the shortage in skilled labours and engineers, the insufficient technical capability of contractors, and hence, human errors and mistakes occur frequently during construction. 'Delays in work progress by contractor' is one of the major claim attributes in VCI (rank third). Nonetheless, it is not dominant in UAE (2006 – 10th rank), UAE (2020 – 18th rank), and India (7th rank). This is because most Vietnam construction projects are suffering schedule delays due to inadequate claim management mechanisms. Therefore, these two claim attributes, 'mistakes by contractor during construction stage' and 'delays in work progress by contractor' are two unique types of claim attributes for VCI.

Interestingly, 'financial failure of the contractor' is one the major claim attributes in Vietnam (fourth rank in this study) and Thailand (third rank). Thailand and Vietnam are both developing countries with similar geographical locations in South East Asia, and hence, there might be some resemblances in the viewpoint of industrial practitioners of these two countries. On the other hand, it is not crucial in UAE (2006 – 10th rank), UAE (2020 – 19th rank), and India (18th rank).

Similar to 'payment delays', 'frequently changing requirements by the owner' is one of the dominant claim attributes in Vietnam (fifth rank in this study), UAE (2006 – first rank), UAE (2020 – first rank), Thailand (second rank), Egypt (sixth rank), and India (third rank). This attribute is one of the principal causes of construction claims in most construction industries, and hence, it corresponds to the fact that it is one of the critical claim attributes in most countries.

5. CONCLUSION

Claims in constructions have received significant attention from researchers. This study explored the critical construction claims attributes affecting the time performance of the projects in the VCI. RII was applied to rank the critical claim attributes. The results showed that payment delays, mistakes by contractor during construction stage, delays in work progress by the contractor, financial failure of the contractor, and frequently changing requirements by the owner were the top five factors triggering the schedule delays in VCI construction projects. The three claim attributes with significantly different perceptions between major stakeholders in VCI construction projects are unfair risk allocation, uncertainty of project scope, and time extensions/EOT. Detailed understanding about construction claims and their causes can reduce unnecessary losses, improve the business performance of project stakeholders, and preserve sustainable relationships among the project stakeholders in VCI. Although this study was performed in Vietnam, these results could also be applied in other construction industries too, especially in the case of developing countries; this can provide as a valuable reference.

6. RECOMMENDATIONS

Based on this study, with the developing countries in mind, the following points can be recommended to minimise the construction claims:

Owner should pay special attention to the following factors:

- Handover the progress payment to the contractor on time; otherwise, it will hinder the contractor's work progress, and in severe cases, the contractor will halt the project, claim against the owner.
- Minimise change orders, especially during construction, to avoid schedule delays and the occurrence of claims.

Contractor should consider the following factors:

- Prepare required skilled labours and engineers to reduce human mistakes and errors during the time of construction.
- Establish a strategy on how to deal with tighter schedule requirements.
- Accumulate adequate financial resources and manage the project cash flow effectively.

Finally, it is necessary to enhance the cooperative relationship between project stakeholders to increase their expected benefits and improve the overall project benefits, hence, achieving sustainable relationships among project stakeholders.

ACKNOWLEDGEMENTS

This research is funded by Japan International Cooperation Agency Project for ASEAN University Network/Southeast Asia Engineering Education Development Network (JICA Project for AUN/SEED-Net) in the framework of Collaborative Education Program (CEP) under Program Contract No. HCMUT CEP 2101.

REFERENCES

Al-Qershi, M. T., & Kishore, R. (2017). Claim causes and types in Indian construction industry – Contractor's perspective. *American Journal of Civil Engineering and Architecture*, *5*(5), 196–203.

Aryal, S., & Dahal, K. R. (2018). A review of causes and effects of dispute in the construction projects of Nepal. *Journal of Steel Structures & Construction*, *4*(2), 144.

Bal, M., Bryde, D., Fearon, D., & Ochieng, E. (2013). Stakeholder engagement: Achieving sustainability in the construction sector. *Sustainability (Switzerland)*, *5*(2), 695–710.

Chaphalkar, N. B., Iyer, K. C., & Patil, S. K. (2015). Prediction of outcome of construction dispute claims using multilayer perceptron neural network model. *International Journal of Project Management*, *33*(8), 1827–1835.

Choi, S. H., & Kim, Y. S. (2016). Priority analysis of dispute factors in overseas construction based on FIDIC contract conditions. *KSCE Journal of Civil Engineering*, *20*(6), 2124–2133.

Council, N. R. (2007). *Reducing construction costs: Uses of best dispute resolution practices by project owners – Proceedings report. Federal Facilities Council Technical Report* No. 149. National Academies Press, Washington, DC.

Enshassi, A., Choudhry, R. M., & El-ghandour, S. (2009). Contractors' perception towards causes of claims in construction projects. *International Journal of Construction Management*, *9*(1), 79–92.

Hai, D. T. (2019). Assessment of contractors' claims on construction projects in Vietnam. *The Open Civil Engineering Journal*, *13*(1), 218–228.

Hardjomuljadi, S. (2014). Factor analysis on causal of construction claims and disputes in Indonesia (with reference to the construction of hydroelectric power project in Indonesia). *International Journal of Applied Engineering Research*, *9*(22), 12421–12445.

Illankoon, I. M. C. S., Tam, V. W. Y., Le, K. N., & Ranadewa, K. A. T. O. (2019). Causes of disputes, factors affecting dispute resolution and effective alternative dispute resolution for Sri Lankan construction industry. *International Journal of Construction Management*, *0*, 1–11.

Khanh, H. D., & Kim, S. Y. (2014). Evaluating impact of waste factors on project performance cost in Vietnam. *KSCE Journal of Civil Engineering*, *18*(7), 1923–1933.

Kim, S., Van Tuan, N., & Ogunlana, S. O. (2009). Quantifying schedule risk in construction projects using Bayesian belief networks. *International Journal of Project Management*, *27*(1), 39–50.

Kim, S. Y., & Nguyen, V. T. (2018). A Structural model for the impact of supply chain relationship traits on project performance in construction. *Production Planning and Control*, *29*(2), 170–183.

Kongchasing, N., & Sua-Iam, G. (2021). The major causes of construction delays identified using the Delphi technique: Perspectives of contractors and consultants in Thailand. *International Journal of Civil Engineering*, *19*(3), 319–338.

Kumaraswamy, M. M. (1997). Conflicts, claims and disputes in construction. *Engineering, Construction and Architectural Management*, *4*(2), 95–111.

Le, N. (2017). Vietnam construction industry performance issues and potential solutions. *Journal for the Advancement of Performance Information and Value*, *9*(2), 7–20.

Le-Hoai, L., Dang, C. N., Lee, S. B., & Lee, Y. D. (2019). Benchmarking claim causes against contractors in emerging markets: empirical case study. *International Journal of Construction Management*, *19*(4), 307–316.

Le-Hoai, L., Lee, Y. D., & Lee, J. Y. (2008). Delay and cost overruns in Vietnam large construction projects: A comparison with other selected countries. *KSCE Journal of Civil Engineering*, *12*(6), 367–377.

Love, P., Davis, P., Ellis, J., & Cheung, S. O. (2010). Dispute causation: Identification of pathogenic influences in construction. *Engineering, Construction and Architectural Management*, *17*(4), 404–423.

Mohamed, H. H., Ibrahim, A. H., & Soliman, A. (2014). Reducing construction disputes through effective claims management. *American Journal of Civil Engineering and Architecture*, *2*(6), 186–196.

Nasirzadeh, F., Mazandaranizadeh, H., & Rouhparvar, M. (2016). Quantitative risk allocation in construction projects using cooperative-bargaining game theory. *International Journal of Civil Engineering*, *14*(3), 161–170.

Nguyen, L. D., & Ogunlana, S. O. (2004). A study on project success factors in large construction projects in Vietnam, *Engineering, Construction and Architectural Management*, *11*(6), 404–413.

Parchami Jalal, M., Noorzai, E., & Yavari Roushan, T. (2019). Root cause analysis of the most frequent claims in the building industry through the SCoP 3 E Ishikawa Diagram. *Journal of Legal Affairs and Dispute Resolution in Engineering and Construction*, *11*(2), 04519004.

Parikh, D., Joshi, G. J., & Patel, D. A. (2019). Development of prediction models for claim cause analyses in highway projects. *Journal of Legal Affairs and Dispute Resolution in Engineering and Construction*, *11*(4), 04519018.

Sibanyama, G., Muya, M., & Kaliba, C. (2012). An overview of construction claims: A case study of the Zambian construction industry. *International Journal of Construction Management*, *12*(1), 65–81.

Stamatiou, D. R. I., Kirytopoulos, K. A., Ponis, S. T., Gayialis, S., & Tatsiopoulos, I. (2019). A process reference model for claims management in construction supply chains: The contractors' perspective. *International Journal of Construction Management*, *19*(5), 382–400.

Ursachi, G., Horodnic, I. A., & Zait, A. (2015). How reliable are measurement scales? External factors with indirect influence on reliability estimators. *Procedia Economics and Finance*, *20*(15), 679–686.

Vietnam International Arbitration Centre. (2018). *Annual report*. VIAC.

Vo, K. D., Nguyen, P. T., & Le Hoang Thuy To Nguyen, Q. (2020). Disputes in managing projects: A case study of construction industry in Vietnam. *Journal of Asian Finance, Economics and Business*, *7*(8), 635–644.

Wang, J., & Yuan, H. (2011). Factors affecting contractors' risk attitudes in construction projects: Case study from China. *International Journal of Project Management*, *29*(2), 209–219.

Wilson, R. L. (1982). Prevention and resolution of construction claims. *Journal of the Construction Division*, *108*(3), 390–405.

Zaneldin, E. K. (2006). Construction claims in United Arab Emirates: Types, causes, and frequency. *International Journal of Project Management*, *24*(5), 453–459.

Zaneldin, E. K. (2020). Investigating the types, causes and severity of claims in construction projects in the UAE. *International Journal of Construction Management*, *20*(5), 385–401.

APPENDIX

Appendix 1: List of 48 Claim Attributes from Literature Review

Code	Claims Affecting the Delays of Construction Schedule	[1]	[2]	[3]	[4]	[5]	[6]	[7]	[8]	[9]	[10]	[11]	[12]	[13]	Occurrence
C1	Payment delays	✓	✓	✓		✓	✓	✓	✓	✓		✓	✓	✓	11
C2	Variation initiated by the owner		✓	✓	✓			✓	✓	✓		✓	✓	✓	9
C3	Late giving of possession to the site by the owner	✓	✓	✓			✓	✓	✓	✓					7
C4	Inclement weather condition	✓		✓		✓			✓	✓	✓			✓	7
C5	Changes in government regulations	✓				✓		✓	✓	✓	✓		✓		7
C6	Unforeseen site conditions	✓	✓	✓		✓	✓		✓	✓					7
C7	Bad quality of contractor's works		✓	✓			✓	✓		✓			✓		6
C8	Delays in executing the changes of the works				✓	✓	✓		✓	✓			✓		6
C9	Price fluctuation of construction materials	✓				✓	✓	✓			✓		✓		6
C10	Different Description of item in BOQ than what was mentioned in specifications	✓		✓			✓	✓	✓	✓					6
C11	Pricing of extra items not included in the contract of BOQ	✓		✓			✓		✓	✓			✓		6
C12	Force majeure				✓	✓	✓	✓		✓					5
C13	Ambiguities in contract documents	✓					✓	✓	✓					✓	5
C14	Poor planning and resourcing by contractor/consultants		✓					✓		✓	✓		✓		5
C15	Inadequate/incomplete specifications and drawings	✓				✓			✓		✓		✓		5
C16	Different interpretations of the contract provisions	✓	✓						✓		✓				4
C17	Price of scope changes		✓		✓			✓		✓					4
C18	Poor contract management & supervision	✓				✓		✓			✓				4
C19	Financial failure of the contractor		✓			✓				✓			✓		4
C20	Low contract price due to high competition		✓	✓						✓			✓		4
C21	Delays in work progress by the contractor						✓			✓			✓	✓	4
C22	Inadequate investigation before bidding by the contractor			✓		✓		✓		✓					4
C23	Incomplete/erroneous contract documentation		✓		✓	✓					✓				4
C24	Uncertainty of project scope	✓	✓											✓	3
C25	Delay in obtaining approvals by the owner	✓					✓		✓						3
C26	Bad communication between parties									✓	✓			✓	3

C27	Price escalation									✓			✓	✓	3
C28	Owner interference	✓				✓								✓	3
C29	Lack of understanding & agreement in contract document		✓			✓					✓				3
C30	Slow decision-making of the owner	✓								✓				✓	3
C31	Unrealistic expectations by the owner		✓			✓								✓	3
C32	Nominated subcontractors/suppliers/subcontracting problems		✓						✓				✓		3
C33	Variations due to design errors					✓			✓	✓					3
C34	Unfair risk allocation		✓	✓							✓				3
C35	Technical inadequacy of the contractor					✓				✓	✓				3
C36	Difficulty in justifying the ambiguity of drawings	✓								✓		✓			3
C37	Overestimating/Underestimating construction schedule								✓	✓			✓		3
C38	Time extensions/EOT						✓		✓			✓			3
C39	Shortage in material					✓				✓					2
C40	Poor quality of design			✓										✓	2
C41	Acceleration and stop-and-go operation by the owner						✓	✓							2
C42	Frequently changing requirements by the owner	✓				✓									2
C43	Poor controlling and monitoring of the owner to his supervision team	✓							✓						2
C44	Mistakes by contractor during construction stage					✓							✓		2
C45	Waiting time for approval of tests and inspection					✓			✓						2
C46	Complex construction methods					✓									1
C47	Delays in choosing the type of contract	✓													1
C48	Complex drawing preparation and approval process					✓									1

Notes: [1]: Enshassi et al. (2009); [2]: Love, Davis, Ellis, and Cheung (2010); [3]: Sibanyama, Muya, and Kaliba (2012); [4]: Chaphalkar, Iyer, and Patil (2015); [5]: Aryal and Dahal (2018); [6]: Stamatiou, Kirytopoulos, Ponis, Gayialis, and Tatsiopoulos (2019); [7]: Parikh, Joshi, and Patel (2019); [8]: Parchami Jalal, Noorzai, and Yavari Roushan (2019); [9]: Le-Hoai, Dang, Lee, and Lee (2019); [10]: Illankoon, Tam, Le, and Ranadewa (2019); [11]: Hai (2019); [12]: Zaneldin (2020); [13]: Vo et al. (2020)

Appendix 2: Ranking of Claim Attributes Engendering Construction Schedule Delays

Code	Claim Attributes	RII	Rank
C1	Payment delays	0.819	1
C44	Mistakes by contractor during construction stage	0.804	2
C21	Delays in work progress by the contractor	0.798	3
C19	Financial failure of the contractor	0.791	4
C42	Frequently changing requirements by the owner	0.781	5
C2	Variations initiated by the owner	0.779	6
C3	Late giving of possession to the site by the owner	0.770	7
C30	Slow decision-making of the owner	0.766	8
C7	Bad quality of contractor's works	0.763	9
C35	Technical inadequacy of the contractor	0.750	10
C41	Acceleration and stop-and-go operation by the owner	0.736	11
C46	Complex construction method	0.735	12
C22	Inadequate investigation before bidding by the contractor	0.731	13
C25	Delay in obtaining approvals by the owner	0.729	14
C14	Poor planning and resourcing by contractor/consultants	0.729	15
C37	Overestimating/underestimating construction schedule	0.729	16
C33	Variations due to design errors	0.719	17
C15	Inadequate/incomplete specifications and drawings	0.710	18
C40	Poor quality of design	0.704	19
C45	Waiting time for approval of tests and inspection	0.704	20
C17	Price of scope changes	0.701	21
C38	Time extensions/EOT	0.701	22
C26	Bad communication between parties	0.701	23
C13	Ambiguities in contract documents	0.690	24
C39	Shortage in material	0.685	25
C32	Nominated subcontractors/suppliers/subcontracting problems	0.683	26
C20	Low contract price due to high competition	0.680	27
C48	Complex drawing preparation and approval process	0.676	28
C28	Owner interference	0.674	29
C31	Unrealistic expectations by the owner	0.674	30
C5	Changes in government regulations	0.671	31
C6	Unforeseen site conditions	0.671	32
C16	Different interpretations of the contract provisions	0.669	33
C8	Delays in executing the changes of works	0.667	34
C12	Force majeure	0.655	35
C34	Unfair risk allocation	0.655	36
C24	Uncertainty of project scope	0.653	37
C23	Incomplete/erroneous contract documentation	0.651	38
C18	Poor contract management and supervision	0.650	39
C27	Price escalation	0.648	40
C10	Different description of item in BOQ than what was mentioned in the specifications	0.646	41
C29	Lack of understanding and agreement in contract document	0.644	42
C43	Poor controlling and monitoring of the owner to his/her supervision team	0.644	43
C4	Inclement weather condition	0.630	44
C11	Pricing of extra items not included in the contract or BOQ	0.616	45
C9	Price fluctuation of construction materials	0.611	46
C36	Difficulty in justifying the ambiguity of drawings	0.588	47
C47	Delays in choosing the type of contract	0.588	48

CHAPTER 6

THE KEY PRACTICES OF LEAN SUPPLY CHAIN MANAGEMENT TOWARDS SUSTAINABLE PERFORMANCE: A REVIEW

Istimaroh, Noor Aslinda Binti Abu Seman, Bambang Setiaji and Norasmiha Binti Mhd Nor

ABSTRACT

A crucial aspect of supply chain management (SCM) is the formulation of lean supply chain management (LSCM). In this sense, the key practices are extended towards the LSCM settings as alternative strategies and several frameworks were developed to help companies to make choices based on production disruption. Studies in this field have focussed mainly on SCM. Although manufacturing businesses recognise the necessity of effective SCM, but little study has been done on manufacturing LSCM. The behaviour and the potential for significant impacts on sustainable performance (SP) in manufacturing companies can vary with time and variations for approaches of the LSCM key practices. This chapter, therefore, focusses on main practices for LSCM on the basis of evaluations of experts in the Malaysian manufacturing sector in order to achieve SP in manufacturing companies. The aim of this chapter is to identify the key practices in LSCM on SP. Hence, this chapter reviewed 172 articles published from 2015 to 2019, used the methodology for SLR with three main steps: literature review planning, reviewing, and reporting. As a result, there are evidence that the key practices for LSCM used in

Sustainability Management Strategies and Impact in Developing Countries
Community, Environment and Disaster Risk Management, Volume 26, 61–74

Published under exclusive licence by Emerald Publishing Limited
ISSN: 2040-7262/doi:10.1108/S2040-726220220000026006

previous studies are (1) customer relationship management, (2) supplier relationship management, (3) just in time manufacturing, (4) waste reduction, (5) cost reduction, and (6) minimise inventory level. In manufacturing industries, LSCM is more complex. Insights on the causing issues and SP are provided. Finally, this chapter contributes to SCM and literature on sustainability and has managerial implications for companies to improve SP more effectively.

Keywords: Lean supply chain management; customer relationship management; supplier relationship management; waste reduction; just in time manufacturing; sustainable performance

1. INTRODUCTION

Malaysian manufacturing firms face significant challenges in terms of production and supply instability as well as costs in responding to local and foreign competitors. Hence, in Malaysia, lean supply chain management (LSCM) is the best strategy for most manufacturing companies for improving market efficiency and supply chain management (SCM) and boosting their corporate performance. The behaviour and the potential for significant impacts on sustainable performance (SP) in manufacturing companies can vary with time and variations for approaches of the LSCM key practices. In addition, many companies that have adopted LSCM to improve their performance also want to be seen to be managing their businesses responsibly and to be aware of the impact that their activities are having on society. Therefore, the firms also should raise their SP. On the other hand, this analysis of practices LSCM should be addressed from both a company's point of view and a supply chain's point of view (Nimeh et al., 2018). Thus, the perspective of inter-organisational operations was identified to propose in new challenges opportunities for future research.

The LSCM is referred with implementing lean principles throughout the whole supply chain (Tortorella et al., 2018). According to Vitasek (2005), the LSCM is defined as a group of organisations directly connected by upstream and downstream flows of goods, resources, information, and funds that cooperate in reducing costs and waste by efficient pulling in of what is required to meet the needs of the individual customer. Hence, many companies are adopting LSCM approaches to cost reduction, waste removal, and efficiency by increasing global competition among enterprises (Sagnak & Kazancoglu, 2016). LSCM is adopted as a new business model, where enhanced returns are generated through cooperation and not through negotiation or the imposition of power over supply chain partners (Purvis et al., 2014; Chiromo et al., 2015; Khorasani et al., 2019). In line with this integrated LSCM view, the total flow from raw products to the final customer has considered as an integrated entire in lean supply chains in that companies interface in the economic arrangements of assets governed by various contextual factors, such as tier level, raw material geographical location, and company size (Boonstonsatit & Jungthawan, 2015).

In addition, a number of studies examined several LSCM practices and bundles in isolation, offering an intimate look at their use and advantages. Gold et al. (2013) investigated how the usage of just-in-time (JIT) in purchasing, production, selling, and information reduced the logistical costs of suppliers and consumers, and suggested that adopting these practices benefits both of them. Further evidence is found in Jean et al. (2014), who studied the influence of knowledge and learning on product innovation and services development from the customer–supplier relationships along the supply chain. These studies generally raise arguments to support a positive impact on the performance of certain LSCM practices, although they are usually examined from a very limited standpoint.

Many studies are focusing on how companies may integrate their processes with customers and suppliers, as well as how LSCM practices should be aligned with the mission of the organization (Qrunfleh & Tarafdar, 2014; Nimeh et al., 2018; Iranmanesh et al., 2019). The companies can achieve a more successful implementation by eliminating unnecessary or even contradicting efforts in the implementation of LSCM practices as a result of this identification. This perspective aids in anticipating problems and establishing convergent development initiatives, as well as creating appropriate expectations during the implementation process (Huo et al., 2019). The supplier relationship is expected to reduce costs and increase the trust of organisation cooperation (Marodin et al., 2017). The difference between success and failure in reaching the sustainable performance of SCM implementation may be explained by LSCM practices. Particularly, Manufacturing companies in the developing countries must enhance their competitiveness by using LSCM in competitive and dynamic markets (Marodin et al., 2017; Nimeh et al., 2018). In other word, the organizations have used LSCM practices within value added to the products include waste reduction and minimize inventory (Mallak et al., 2018; Qrunfleh & Tarafdar, 2013; Wen Chiet et al., 2019). Lastly, if companies can reduce inventory levels to a minimum, the company will have more inventory space, which will sell faster. Minimise inventory also means fewer funds for the excess inventory handling of workers. This enables you to focus on efforts elsewhere and in a properly sized warehouse. This paper assists in identifying LSCM practices in the context of a specific developing countries. Thus, it offers appropriate advice and verified practices for Malaysian manufacturing firms to evaluate and implement LSCM practices. The study also adds to the body of knowledge on SCM in developing countries, which is currently lacking.

2. LITERATURE REVIEW

2.1. Supply Chain Management

According to Wang et al. (2016), SCM is defined as the design and seamless management, the process of value added through the organisation's boundaries to satisfy the end customer by providing the needed goods or services. Different from (Yazdani et al., 2017) defined SCM is the philosophy of management directed for integrating the network upstream linkages to downstream that has performing process and activities specifically to optimise value for satisfying the customer with the output of products and services. Usually, the SCM covers managing and relationship turnover of the goods, services, and information within producers, manufacturers, and customers (Frazzon et al., 2017; Tortorella et al., 2018). This also includes coordination, and network partners, who could be manufacturers, intermediaries, third-party operation; providers, and customers. More simply, SCM *essentially* combines the management of supply and demand within and through businesses (Gilal et al., 2017).

Furthermore, Madhavan et al. (2015) suggested that the implementation of SCM needs coordination with another organisation to integrate the process and function of the supply chain. In addition, developed countries have implemented SCM considerably than by developing countries. Even though, utilising SCM was more efficient and effective for the companies (Ahmed & Huma, 2018), LSCM has focussed on general independent and the initiatives integrative (Das, 2018; Huo et al., 2019; Vamsi & Jasti, 2017), which helped the integration process to lean manufacturing and SCM practices (Cudney & Elrod, 2010). In addition, Li et al. (2015) suggested for manufacturing companies looking to maintain and improve their competitiveness, enhancing the efficiency and effectiveness of supply chains (SCs) is the most essential concern. Lean management may be integrated into SCM to save costs, shorten delivery times, and increase the efficiency of supply chains. Lean is becoming more popular as a method of managing the supply chain, and it has the potential to become a sustainable concept for directing businesses toward world-class overall performance (Halldórsson et al., 2015; Tseng & Liao, 2015). Implementing LSCM practices has become a trend in the global marketplace and is one of the most common strategies used by manufacturing companies (Mani et al., 2018; Nag et al., 2014). Thus, Gold et al. (2013) concluded that SP and LSCM efficiency should be researched systematically through a paradigm of support for the company's strategic in the global business environment (Çankaya & Sezen, 2019), which also maximised the profit of companies since SCM covers planning and manufacturing operations management to carry the product or services to the market place. Therefore, the flow of raw material to the delivery of the completed products or services is becoming presently considerable to organisations as part of the SCM. As a result, organisations tend to achieve better performance in the sustainability of their businesses.

2.2. Lean Supply Chain Management

According to Chiet et al. (2019), the lean supply chain is the organisation's maximising operational process and minimising overall manufacturing cost. LSCM also includes taking measures to reduce all kinds of waste throughout the supply chain, with the purpose of minimizing lead time and costs of production (Chiromo et al., 2015). In different researches, lean supply chain can be defined as a set of organisations that is linked by upstream and downstream directly to reduce cost and waste (any resource consuming activity with no added value) that also meet with the needs of customers (Jasti, & Kodali, 2015; Totorella et al., 2017).

Wu et al. (2015) suggested that lean supply chain should enable customer-free supplier flow of goods, services, and technology. This approach takes the form of a long-term engagement to supply chain partners with a collaborative, systemic waste elimination throughout the chain, away from the current 'trading mentality' in which short-term and market-driven profit targets are very dependent and the ability to strongly negotiate with their supplier or customer (Agarwal et al., 2006; Yusuf et al., 2013). However, due to lack of awareness and an improper implementation approach, many organisations have been struggling to implement LSCM practices (Jasti, & Kodali, 2015; Nimeh et al., 2018; Tortorella et al., 2018). Furthermore, several studies focussed only on single aspects of the LSCM, with very few researchers working both upstream and downstream (Carvalho et al., 2017; Jasti & Kurra, 2017). Moreover, despite the fact that the LSCM theory and concepts have been not yet fully developed (Jasti & Kodali, 2015), instead of a generalisation of the LSCM framework (Perez et al., 2010), most studies have been restricted to a given sector. Therefore, the LSCM is developed based on attributes of supply chain focus, type of product, market demand, and market leader (Arif-Uz-Zaman & Ahsan, 2014). Moreover, Huo et al. (2019) argued that the scope in the lean supply chain focusses on the objectives and goal of the supply chain corporate. Hence, LSCM seems to be able to solve many problems for manufacturing companies. However, relatively few LSCM studies were done in manufacturing, and few literature reviews were conducted in order to synthesise knowledge throughout the studies.

2.3. Practices of LSCM

The changing business environment has to necessary include changes in its supply chain style, but there is no answer about how to change in the current literature (Eltawy & Gallear, 2017). Therefore, this has made it interesting to investigate the gap that evidences the relationship of LSCM practices on companies from emerging countries to become global and SP (Jurado & Fuentes, 2014; Shee et al., 2018) whereby the decisions on supply chain design become important for the firm to achieve a competitive advantage (Huo et al., 2019). Moreover, the evidence on the relationship of the lean supply chain has additional challenges that rely on the firm from emerging markets that are struggling to become a lean supply chain and integrate the global market at the same time (Blos et al., 2015). On the other hand, organisations become competitive and thrive to focus on all internal aspects of the supply chain. LSCM is one such entity that enhances competitiveness and flexibility (Boonsthonsatit & Jungthawan, 2015). In addition, LSCM also has a positive effect on supply chain performance (Nimeh et al., 2018).

However, not all can follow the same set of practices as it is dependent on a collection of contextual variables to implement any particular management practices. Understanding the relationship between lean supply chain practices and contextual variables helps to predict challenges and sets the right goal for implementation (Morita et al., 2018). Considering that an effective LSCM handles fluctuations in demand, interruptions in the process flow, product movement, and cost in tackling the complexities (Cooper & Slagmulder, 2017). In order to gain competitive advantage globally, businesses are required to build relationships with multiple providers and customers (Gunasekaran et al., 2015).

Furthermore, Ratnayake and Chaudry, (2017) conducted a study on the lean supply chain principles and practices impact on sustainability performance, the improvement of performance to be achieved the whole chain (Huo et al., 2019; Iranmanesh et al., 2019). Moreover, reducing business risk through reduced inventories, elimination of waste, and reduced cost (Manzouri et al., 2013; Tortorella et al., 2017; Susila et al., 2020) were used as the selected dimensions of the studies. Therefore, all the dimensions were found to have a positive impact in the internal implementation on customers and suppliers relationship. Additionally, Azevedo and Carvalho (2016) and Nimeh (2018) have considered lean supply chains through the adoption of management techniques and practices such as just in time, suppliers, and customers relationship. The results have empirically validated lean supply chain practices, namely elimination of waste, supplier relationship management, customer relationship management, and just in time (Nimeh et al., 2018; Qrunfleh & Tarafdar, 2013; G. Tortorella et al., 2018b) to be considered as the dimensions of lean supply chain. On the other hand, researchers such as Marodin et al. (2017) have determined the following LSCM practices: elimination of waste, continuous improvement, top management commitment, customers–suppliers relationship management, and continuous improvement as the lean supply chain dimensions in their research. Based on the literature reviewed in this chapter, six practices of the lean supply chain were used most widely and commonly: customer relationship, supplier relationship, just-in-time manufacturing, waste reduction, minimise inventory, and cost reduction. These six lean supply chain practices are described in Table 6.1.

3. METHODOLOGY

This chapter focusses on the direction of the lean supply chain studies, which have been arranged using the systematic literature review. Systematic literature review is used to map the area uncertainty in the study and recommended for future research (Jurado & Fuentes, 2014). This study has reviewed a total of 172 articles from different studies that have been categorised in potential guidelines.

Defining the search terms, the ‘Supply Chain’, ‘Lean Supply Chain’, ‘Sustainable’, and ‘Performance’ keywords are used for data collection. The following keywords were used in four variations: Lean AND Supply Chain, Sustainable AND Performance; and Lean Supply Chain AND Firm Performance. Two operating and design perspectives can describe the lean supply chain primarily. We also ensured that the selected keywords cover both aspects fully. Lean Supply Chain, for example, includes lean supply chain manufacturing/production, operations, purchasing, procurement, performance measurement, and product design. The primary importance of this chapter is to conduct a systematic literature review to identify key practices for LSCM in manufacturing industry. In the literature of LSCM on sustainable manufacturing, only a few other studies have been published. Besides that, other potential keywords relating to SP were also used in our quest attempts instead of ‘economic’, ‘social’, and ‘environmental’.

Table 6.1. Critical factors of Lean Supply Chain into Sustainable Performance.

Critical Factors	Description/Definition	Authors/Years
Customer relationships	The success of the firms is not only the effective and efficiency in internal operations but also the linked internal processes with the external operations such as customer relationship	Abdallah et al. (2014), Jasti and Kodali (2015), Halldórsson et al. (2015), Saha et al. (2015), Salojärvi et al. (2015), Carvalho et al. (2017), Marodin et al. (2017), Vamsi and Jasti (2017), Kang et al. (2018), Shee et al. (2018), and Nimeh et al. (2018)
Supplier relationships	Supplier relationship is an important element to enhance competitiveness through organisational boundaries	Abdallah et al. (2014), Liu et al. (2013), Azevedo and Carvalho (2016), Tortorella et al. (2017), Carvalho et al. (2017), Nimeh et al. (2018), Yang et al. (2018), Khorasani et al. (2019), Fadaki et al. (2019), and Iranmanesh et al. (2019)
Just-in-time manufacturing	Just in time ensures the deliveries from suppliers such as delivering amount the needed, high frequency, at the right time to the right place, and also the small size	Liu et al. (2013), Jurado et al. (2014), Saha et al. (2015), Salojärvi et al. (2015), Halldórsson et al. (2015), Jasti and Kodali (2015), and Nordin and Adebambo (2016)
Waste reduction	The lean supply chain can decrease lower cost, inventory level, and shorten the lead time	Qrunfleh and Tarafdar (2013), Ahsan et al.,(2014), Tortorella et al. (2017), and Nimeh et al. (2018)
Minimise inventory level	The cellular processes could create a continuous flow that is able to an alternative to eliminate inventories in the production steps.	Qrunfleh and Tarafdar (2013), Boonsthonsatit and Jungthawan (2015), Tortorella et al. (2016), Marodin et al. (2017), and Fadaki et al. (2019)
Cost reduction	The lean supply chain is one of the key factors for many companies that will influence the activities and performances such as low inventory, cost reduction, and improve lead time.	Abdallah et al. (2014), Hsiao and Chen (2014), Kinyua (2015), Jasti and Kodali (2015), Nimeh et al. (2018), Fadaki et al. (2019), and Susila et al. (2020)

Source: Computed data analysis by authors.

As a result, there were 935 collected and stored journal articles (conference papers, books, and book chapters excluded) for the specified search terms using the title, abstracts, and keywords search from the Scopus Database at the beginning of the quest. The cycle starts with the collection of contingent (sustainable) variables. A few Scopus databases belonging to the referenced, high-ranking journals from various disciplines were chosen to classify the similarities of the studies. Furthermore, the method proposed by Khorasani et al. (2019) has been used to conduct a systematic review of literature. Thus selected, profiled, and reviewed 935 journal articles were published between 2015 and 2019. A total of 41 papers were also selected for a qualitative analysis based on their high relevance to research objective.

4. DESCRIPTIVE STATISTICS

4.1. Overview of Studies

The concept of the lean supply chain has interested many researchers and the number of studies has continued to increase every year. Even though the number of researchers established in 2017 was slightly lower than in 2016, for the next years until 2019 the number has raised significantly. This signifies that the lean supply chain is important to research project needed for further research as shown in Fig. 6.1(a).

Fig. 6.1(a) represents the number of papers published between 2015 and 2019. The majority of the selected papers were reflected the growing importance of

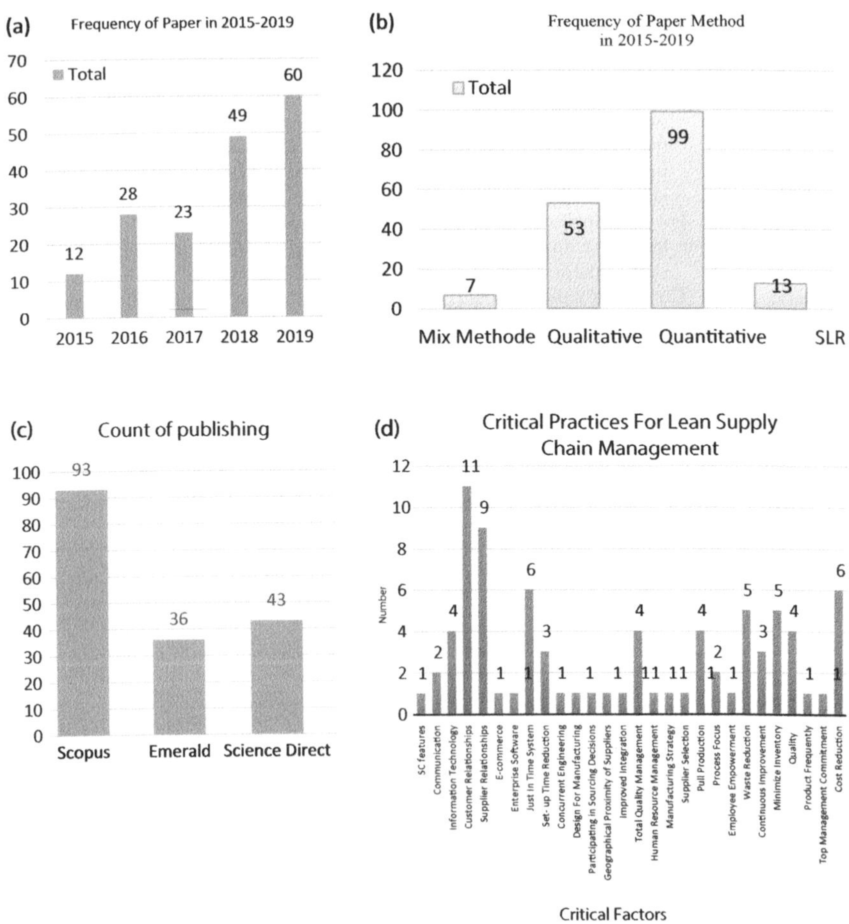

Fig. 6.1. The Overview of This Study is Described by (a) Number of Papers of Publication Year, (b) Number of Papers in Research Method of Publication Year, (c) Publisher and Count of Publishing, and (d) Critical Practices for Lean Supply Chain Management. *Source*: Computed Data Analysis by Authors.

LSCM and SP. This paper has also been classified by the methodology used; it is divided into four groups: systematic literary review (SLR), quantitative, qualitative, and mixed methode. Fig. 6.1(b), shows that the studies clearly show that 8% of articles contain literature, 58% of quantitative, 31% of qualitative, and 4% of the articles falling within the mixed method category. Therefore, it is important to note that SLR publications are scarce and only began to appear significantly in the period 2015–2019, as the number of publications witnessed increased in the same time period. The quantitative method is higher than other methods in this study because the quantitative method was applied in examining the research objective on the relationship among the variables that were measured and the result that have been provided and also the evidence of the findings in the research with statistical number and figures (Brandenburg et al., 2014).

In Fig. 6.1(b), the number of papers in research method of publication year shows the importance of the different journals start the research in the aspect of lean supply chain and SP in the manufacturing industry. More precisely, publishers related to science citation have published more papers. Specifically, attention is given by researchers for implementing LSCM practices.

In Fig. 6.1(c), three electronic databases were used for the relating search of the article, namely (1) Scopus, which offers cross-disciplinary research in various subject areas such as science and social science, electric and electronic methods, and arts; (2) Emerald is a scientific database that offers consistent and extensive articles in the scientific, technological and medical fields, and science and engineering research; (3) ScienceDirect, a widespread database of science. These databases encompass the LSCM practices and SP to identify a wide-ranging range of related approaches.

4.2. Critical Practices of LSCM

The lean supply chain is a system for satisfying the customer through optimised resources. Hence, implementing the lean supply chain could be the best approach to achieve greater profit and SP. The lean supply chain has also contributed to the minimised cost and the maximised profit of businesses. Eventually, the contributions have the result for customer loyalty.

From Fig. 6.1(d), there are six critical practices that were identified for the lean supply chain in this literature review that are using more than five researchers. These include supplier relationships, customer relationships, cost reduction, just-in-time system, and minimise inventory levels and waste reduction on SP (economic, environmental, and social) performance as shown in Fig. 6.1(d). Moreover, Fig. 6.1(d) indicates the critical practices for lean supply chain as shown and explained in Table 1, whereby the crucial factors are linked to the implementation of the lean supply chain practices from different authors and years. Hence, the results of the study showed that LSCM practices had significant and positive effects on production efficiency, namely just-in-time system and customer relationship. This verified and justified previous studies on the existence of positive effects on manufacturing performance of these practices (Li and Lin, 2006; Nordin & Adebambo, 2016; Saha et al., 2015; Salojärvi et al., 2015).

Moreover, the findings confirmed that all LSCM practices have a major positive impact on supply chain performance as referred from earlier literature.

Additionally, it was also found that the LSCM is a perfect method for enhancing supply chain performance for manufacturing companies. Reduced costs, quality improvement, speed of delivery, and increased flexibility can be anticipated (Vaart et al., 2008; Abdallah et al., 2014; Hsiao & Chen, 2014; Kinyua, 2015). Furthermore, the short-term strategy has a long-term impact upon the commitment to supply chain partners and on a partnership with the mechanism of reducing waste in the entire chain. Such results are in line with the studies from Boonsthonsatit and Jungthawan (2015) and Tortorella (2016), which stated that efficient information flow from the end customer to all tiers of the chain is essential so that each agent converts these data into valuable information to schedule production and minimise inventory levels.

As companies are positioned farther from the end customers, this information may be amplified, entailing noise effects that can cause overproduction effects (Selvarajah & Zhang, 2014; Rasyid et al., 2017). In addition, a number of studies focussed exclusively on individual aspects of LSCM (Thatte et al., 2013; Galankashi & Helmi, 2016) and very few researchers (Abdallah et al., 2014; Ayoub & Abdallah, 2019; Nimeh et al., 2018; Saha et al., 2015) tackled both upstream (supplier relationship) (Kang et al., 2018; Mallak et al., 2018) and downstream (customer relationships) (Abdallah et al., 2014; Kang et al., 2018; Shee et al., 2018) organisation operations (Jasti & Kodali, 2015; Tortorella et al., 2017; Gefen et al., 2019).

From Table 1, it can be summarised that the critical practices of LSCM into SP are identified after journal studies. Even though this chapter identified the practices that have complemented the lean supply chain, they are also valuable for initiating SP in the manufacturing industries. In addition, the practices that have been identified can be analysed with key practices relationship used by other analysis tools such as Smart-PLS.

In addition, there is still an ambitious, diverse, scalable and realistic method to track, analyse, and further enhance the genuinely SP of organisations through managers, engineers, and experts. The findings of this review paper are intended to contribute to the growth efforts of a lean supply chain and SP relationships by offering detailed guidance.

5. FUTURE RESEARCH PERSPECTIVE

This systematic literature reviewed the key practices of LSCM to SP proposed to new future research opportunities. First, future research could involve the reward in the SCM system in order to achieve SP in the supply chain, including the suppliers, customers, and manufacturers who can do evaluation to better improve in performance. Secondly, for maintaining SCM and improving SP, future research should explore techniques for maintaining all activities even though with the limited resources. And lastly, future research can develop on new methodologies, frameworks, and tools that could help with the achievement of truly SP organisations and supply chains compliant with the proposed ultimate objective concept by considering stakeholders (suppliers, customers, employees, owners, creditors, and society, respectively).

6. CONCLUSION

From the bundles of the lean supply chain practices that have been proposed by some researchers, this study have empirically identified six key of interrelated and internally consistent LSCM practices such as (1) customer relationship implicates many activities among problem-solving, creating customer relationships for long times, increasing customer satisfaction, rapid response to a customer complaint, and enhancing customer loyalty; (2) Supplier relationships are supposed to lower costs and improve credibility, raise accountability and strengthen technology and design skills of SC partners, align capabilities and develop learning routines, and eliminate wasteful time and activities. (3) just-in-time manufacturing has shown increased performance of the firm; (4) waste reduction has also provided a technique for manufacturing companies that used to increase efficiency and best performance; (5) cost reduction; and (6) minimise inventory level that has caused by poor quality or by late delivery times, unstable production schedules and fluctuations and poor customer demand forecast. In this study, the researchers have identified critical factors in the implementation of LSCM in manufacturing industries, especially in Malaysia, which supplement LSCM. In a systematic literature review, the researcher has summarised that the outcomes can helpful for practitioners and researchers in manufacturing and the supply chain. Furthermore, the author stressed practices in the LSCM model to achieve best companies' performance. Although the findings presented are still in the initial phase, an analysis of the SCM complementary and the SP can be a significant step in the implementation of LSCM practices. This study was furthered by the opinion of government and industry experts to provide an insight into the implementation of LSCM for manufacturing companies in Malaysia. Eventually, the researchers believe that this study will be valuable for future directions of lean supply chain studies and also contributing to all functions as well.

ACKNOWLEDGEMENTS

The researchers thank to Research Management Center (RMC) for financing them with the research fund: VOT E15501 from the Faculty of Technology Management and Business, Universiti Tun Hussein Onn Malaysia, and Faculty of Management and Business, Universitas Muhammadiyah Kalimantan Timur (Indonesia) that have provided all the necessary facilities for completing of this study.

REFERENCES

Abdul-Rashid, S. H. et al. (2017). The impact of sustainable manufacturing practices on sustainability performance: Empirical evidence from Malaysia. *International Journal of Operations and Production Management*, *37*(2), 182–204.

Abdallah, A. B., Obeidat, B. Y., & Aqqad, N. O. (2014). The impact of supply chain management practices on supply chain performance in Jordan: The moderating effect of competitive intensity. *International Business Research*, *7*(3), 13–27.

Agarwal, A., Shankar, R., & Tiwari, M. K. (2006). Modeling the metrics of lean, agile and leagile supply chain: An ANP-based approach. *European Journal of Operational Research, 173*(1), 211–225.

Ahmed, W., & Huma, S. (2018). Impact of lean and agile strategies on supply chain risk management. *Total Quality Management and Business Excellence, 32*(1–2), 33–56.

Arif-Uz-Zaman, K., & Ahsan, A. M. M. N. (2014). Lean supply chain performance measurement. *International Journal of Productivity and Performance Management, 63*(5), 588–612.

Ayoub, H. F., & Abdallah, A. B. (2019). The effect of supply chain agility on export performance: The mediating roles of supply chain responsiveness and innovativeness. *Journal of Manufacturing Technology Management, 30*(5), 821–839.

Azevado, S. G., Carvalho, H., & Machado, V. C. (2016). Benchmarking: An International Journal LARG index: A benchmarking tool for improving the leanness, agility, resilience and greenness of the automotive supply chain. *The Eletronic Library, 34*(1), 1–5.

Blos, M. F., Hoeflich, S. L., & Miyagi, P. E. (2015). A general supply chain continuity management framework. *Procedia Computer Science, 55*(Itqm), 1160–1164.

Boonsthonsatit, K., & Jungthawan, S. (2015). Lean supply chain management-based value stream mapping in a case of Thailand automotive industry. *4th IEEE international conference on advanced logistics and transport*, pp. 65–69.

Brandenburg, M., et al. (2014). Quantitative models for sustainable supply chain management: Developments and directions. *European Journal of Operational Research, 233*(2), 299–312.

Carvalho, H., et al. (2017) 'Modelling green and lean supply chains: An eco-efficiency perspective. *Resources, Conservation and Recycling, 120*, 75–87.

Chiromo, F., Nel, A., & Sebele, T. O. (2015). *Lean manufacturing challenges in a South African clothing company. International Association For Management of Technology*, 265–274.

Cooper, R., & Slagmulder, R. (2017). *Supply chain development for the lean enterprise: Interorganizational cost management* (pp. 1–510). Portland, OR: Productivity Inc.

Cudney, E., & Elrod, C. (2010). Incorporating lean concepts into supply chain management. *International Journal of Six Sigma and Competitive Advantage, 6*(1–2), 12–30.

Das, D. (2018). The impact of sustainable supply chain management practices on firm performance: Lessons from Indian organizations. *Journal of Cleaner Production, 203*, 179–196.

Eltawy, N., & Gallear, D. (2017). Leanness and agility: A comparative theoretical view. *Industrial Management and Data Systems, 117*(1), 149–165.

Fadaki, M., Rahman, S., & Chan, C. (2019). Quantifying the degree of supply chain leagility and assessing its impact on firm performance. *Asia Pacific Journal of Marketing and Logistics, 31*(1), 246–264.

Frazzon, E., et al. (2017). Simulation-based analysis of a supplier–manufacturer relationship in lean supply chains. *International Journal of Lean Six Sigma, 8*(3), 262–274.

Galankashi, M. R., & Helmi, S. A. (2016). Assessment of hybrid Lean-Agile (Leagile) supply chain strategies. *Journal of Manufacturing Technology Management, 27*(4), 470–482.

Gefen, D., et al. (2019). Editor's comments : An update and extension to SEM guidelines for administrative and social science research. *MIS Quarterly, 35*(2), 3–14.

Gilal, F. G., et al. (2017). Supply chain management practices and product development: A moderated mediation model of supply chain responsiveness, organization structure, and research and development. *Journal of Advanced Manufacturing Systems, 16*(1), 35–56.

Gold, S., Hahn, R., & Seuring, S. (2013). Sustainable supply chain management in "Base of the Pyramid" food projects – A path to triple bottom line approaches for multinationals?. *International Business Review, 22*(5), 784–799.

Hallavo, V. (2015). Superior performance through supply chain fit: A synthesis. *Supply Chain Management, 20*(1), 71–82.

Halldórsson, Á., Hsuan, J., & Kotzab, H. (2015). Complementary theories to supply chain management revisited – From borrowing theories to theorizing. *Supply Chain Management, 20*(6), 574–586.

Hsiao, L., & Chen, Y. J. (2014). Strategic motive for introducing internet channels in a supply chain. *Production and Operations Management, 23*(1), 36–47.

Huo, B., Gu, M., & Wang, Z. (2019). Green or lean? A supply chain approach to sustainable performance. *Journal of Cleaner Production, 216*, 152–166.

Iranmanesh, M., Zailani, S., Hyun, S. S., Ali, M. H., & Kim, K. (2019). Impact of lean manufacturing practices on firms' sustainable performance: Lean culture as a moderator. *Sustainability (Switzerland)*, *11*(4), 1093–1112.

Jasti, N. V. K., & Kodali, R. (2015). A critical review of lean supply chain management frameworks: Proposed framework. *Production Planning and Control*, *26*(13), 1051–1068.

Jasti, N. V. K., & Kurra, S. (2017). An empirical investigation on lean supply chain management frameworks in Indian manufacturing industry. *International Journal of Productivity and Performance Management*, *66*(6), 699–723.

Jean, R. J. B., Sinkovics, R. R., & Hiebaum, T. P. (2014). The effects of supplier involvement and knowledge protection on product innovation in customer–supplier relationships: A study of global automotive suppliers in China. *Journal of Product Innovation Management*, *31*(1), 98–113.

Kang, M., et al. (2018). Supply chain integration and its impact on sustainability. *Industrial Management and Data Systems*, *118*(9), 1749–1765.

Khorasani, S. T., Cross, J., & Maghazei, O. (2019). Lean supply chain management in healthcare: A systematic review and meta-study. *International Journal of Lean Six Sigma*, *11*(1), 1–34.

Kinyua, B. K. (2015). An assessment of just in time procurement system on organization. *European Journal of Business and Social Sciences*, *4*(5), 40–53.

Li, S., & Lin, B. (2006). Accessing information sharing and information quality in supply chain management. *Decision Support Systems*, *42*(3), 1641–1656.

Li, X., Wu, Q., & Holsapple, C. W. (2015). Best-value supply chains and firms' competitive performance: Empirical studies of their linkage. *International Journal of Operations and Production Management*, *35*(12), 1688–1709.

Liu, H., et al. (2013). The impact of IT capabilities on firm performance: The mediating roles of absorptive capacity and supply chain agility. *Decision Support Systems*, *54*(3), 1452–1462.

Madhavan, M., Kaliaperumal, C., & Muthuvel, S. (2015). Mediation effects of sustainable supply chain strategies on supply chain functions and firm performance. *International Journal of Business Performance and Supply Chain Modelling*, *7*(3), 292–304.

Mallak, S. K., et al. (2018). Toward sustainable solid waste minimization by manufacturing firms in Malaysia: Strengths and weaknesses. *Environmental Monitoring and Assessment*, *190*(10), 575–581.

Mani, V., Gunasekaran, A., & Delgado, C. (2018). Enhancing supply chain performance through supplier social sustainability: An emerging economy perspective. *International Journal of Production Economics*, *195*, 259–272.

Manzouri, M., et al. (2013). Lean supply chain practices in the Halal food. *International Journal of Lean Six Sigma*, *4*(4), 389–408.

Marodin, G. A., et al. (2017) 'The moderating effect of Lean supply chain management on the impact of Lean shop floor practices on quality and inventory', *Supply Chain Management*, *22*(6), 473–485.

Martínez-Jurado, P. J., & Moyano-Fuentes, J. (2014). Lean management, supply chain management and sustainability: A literature review. *Journal of Cleaner Production*, *85*, 134–150.

Morita, M., Machuca, J. A. D., & Pérez Díez de los Ríos, J. L. (2018). Integration of product development capability and supply chain capability: The driver for high performance adaptation. *International Journal of Production Economics*, *200*(March), 68–82.

Nag, B., Han, C., & Yao, D. Q. (2014). Mapping supply chain strategy: An industry analysis. *Journal of Manufacturing Technology Management*, *25*(3), 351–370.

Nimeh, H. A., Abdallah, A. B., & Sweis, R. (2018). Lean supply chain management practices and performance: Empirical evidence from manufacturing companies, *International Journal of Supply Chain Management*, *7*(1), 1–15.

Nordin, N., & Adebambo, H. O. (2016). Descriptive analysis of sustainable manufacturing indicators in Malaysian manufacturing firms. *Journal of Mechanical Engineering and Sciences*, *10*(2), 2126–2133.

Perez, C., et al. (2010). Development of lean supply chains: A case study of the Catalan pork sector. *Supply Chain Management*, *15*(1), 55–68.

Purvis, L., Gosling, J., & Naim, M. M. (2014). The development of a lean, agile and leagile supply network taxonomy based on differing types of flexibility. *International Journal of Production Economics*, *151*, 100–111.

Qrunfleh, S., & Tarafdar, M. (2013). Lean and agile supply chain strategies and supply chain: The role of strategic supplier partnership and postponement. *Supply Chain Management: An International Journal*, *18*(6), 571–582.

Qrunfleh, S., & Tarafdar, M. (2014). Supply chain information systems strategy: Impacts on supply chain performance and firm performance. *International Journal of Production Economics*, *147*, 340–350.

Ratnayake, R. M. C., & Chaudry, O. (2017). Maintaining sustainable performance in operating petroleum assets via a lean-six-sigma approach: A case study from engineering support services. *International Journal of Lean Six Sigma*, *8*(1), 33–52.

Sagnak, M., & Kazancoglu, Y. (2016). Integration of green lean approach with six sigma: An application for flue gas emissions. *Journal of Cleaner Production*, *127*, 112–118.

Saha, S., et al. (2015). Mail-in-rebate coupled with revenue sharing and downward direct discount for supply chain coordination. *International Journal of Operational Research*, *23*(4), 451–476.

Salojärvi, H., et al. (2015). Synergistic effect of technology and customer relationship orientations: Consequences for market performance. *Journal of Business and Industrial Marketing*, *30*(5), 511–520.

Selvarajah, E., & Zhang, R. (2014). Supply chain scheduling at the manufacturer to minimize inventory holding and delivery costs. *International Journal of Production Economics*, *147*(Part A), 117–124.

Shee, H., Miah, S. J., & Fairfield, L. (2018). *The impact of cloud-enabled process integration on supply chain performance and fi rm sustainability: The moderating role of top management*, *6*(July), 500–517.

Susila, I., et al. (2020). Supply chain strategy in stabilization of products price: Case study beef price in Indonesia. *International Journal of Supply Chain Management*, *9*(4), 1055–1062.

Thatte, A. A., Rao, S. S., & Nathan, T. S. R. (2013). Impact of SCM practices of a firm on supply chain responsiveness and competitive and advantage of a firm. *The Journal of Applied Business Research*, *29*(2), 499–530.

Tortorella, G., et al. (2018). Lean supply chain practices: An exploratory study on their relationship. *International Journal of Logistics Management*, *29*(3), 1049–1076.

Tortorella, G. L., Miorando, R., & Marodin, G. (2017). Lean supply chain management: Empirical research on practices, contexts and performance. *International Journal of Production Economics*, *193*(July), 98–112.

Tortorella, G. L., Miorando, R., & Tlapa, D. (2017). Implementation of lean supply chain: An empirical research on the effect of context. *TQM Journal*, *29*(4), 610–623.

Tseng, P. H., & Liao, C. H. (2015). Supply chain integration, information technology, market orientation and firm performance in container shipping firms. *International Journal of Logistics Management*, *26*(1), 82–106.

Vamsi, N., & Jasti, K. (2017). An empirical investigation on lean supply chain management frameworks in Indian manufacturing industry.

van der Vaart, T., & van Donk, D. P. (2008). A critical review of survey-based research in supply chain integration. *International Journal of Production Economics*, *111*(1), 42–55.

Wang, G., et al. (2016). Big data analytics in logistics and supply chain management: Certain investigations for research and applications. *International Journal of Production Economics*, *176*, 98–110.

Wen Chiet, C., et al. (2019). The integration of lean and green manufacturing for Malaysian manufacturers: A literature review to explore the synergies between lean and green model. *IOP Conference Series: Earth and Environmental Science*, *268*(1), 34–39.

Yazdani, M., et al. (2017). A group decision making support system in logistics and supply chain management. *Expert Systems with Applications*, *88*, 376–392.

Yildiz Çankaya, S., & Sezen, B. (2019). Effects of green supply chain management practices on sustainability performance. *Journal of Manufacturing Technology Management*, *30*(1), 98–121.

Yusuf, Y. Y., et al. (2013). The UK oil and gas supply chains : An empirical analysis of adoption of sustainable measures and performance outcomes. *International Journal of Production Economics*, *146*(2), 501–514.

CHAPTER 7

TIME COST QUALITY TRADE-OFF IN REPETITIVE CONSTRUCTION PROJECT FOR SUSTAINABLE CONSTRUCTION PROJECT

Duc-Hoc Tran and Putri Basenda Tarigan

ABSTRACT

The concept of sustainability is about the relationships among people, the planet, and profit. Nowadays, it has been spread to many areas, including construction projects. Sustainability in construction projects has been so important in the present time. It is commonly pointed to the environment and construction materials. Nevertheless, it is also important in construction management which addresses sustainable project scheduling. Sustainable project scheduling will help to deliver the project under the deadlines, within the available budget, and also ensuring about the quality of the works. This study presents the trade-off among time, cost, and quality in the construction project to provide the decision-maker some alternative solutions in the planning phase to conduct a sustainable construction project. Multi-objective optimisation using Symbiotic Organism Search (SOS) algorithm is done to find the best solutions to the problem under investigation. Then, fuzzy logic approach is utilised to model the diverse environment and uncertainty in the construction project. A case study in repetitive construction project is analysed to see the capability of the model to work in time cost quality trade-off to reach into a sustainable construction project.

Keywords: Time cost quality trade-off; optimisation in construction project; sustainable construction project; multi-objective optimisation; repetitive project; uncertainty in construction project

Sustainability Management Strategies and Impact in Developing Countries
Community, Environment and Disaster Risk Management, Volume 26, 75–85

Published under exclusive licence by Emerald Publishing Limited
ISSN: 2040-7262/doi:10.1108/S2040-726220220000026007

1. INTRODUCTION

Sustainable development is how the human makes the development sustainable, by ensuring that the development meets the needs of present time without arbitrating the futures (Robert, Parris, & Leiserowitz, 2005). In construction especially, the concept of sustainable development has been widely applied in many areas, such as the planning, design, maintenance, and even the rehabilitation of the project (Zavadskas, Šaparauskas, & Antucheviciene, 2018). Then, intensely it becomes one of the key factors to define the successfulness to complete a construction project (Schultmann & Sunke, 2007). A sustainable construction project will be an effort to achieve a project completion by doing economic development, increasing social health, and reducing the negative impact on the environment (Wu, 2017). It integrates these three factors to utilise the present resources and offer the same for the next generation. In other words, it tries to satisfy current needs but also protecting the environment and resources for future use (Chawla, Chanda, Angra, & Chawla, 2018).

Many researches have been done for the sustainability field. Most of those are focussed on the materials; it is about using environmentally friendly materials, natural resources like sunlight, reuse-suitable materials, and the idea to avoid the hazard (Schultmann & Sunke, 2007). Alongside with this, sustainability must also focus on business operations, which has an impact on the planning, scheduling, and execution of the construction project (Chawla et al., 2018). It aims to deliver the project under the deadlines, within the available budget, and also ensuring the quality of the works. To reach a long-life profitable project, especially for a construction project, which is often implemented in an uncertain environment, there is a project management tool that can be used to deal with this problem, called multi-objective optimisation (Cinelli, Coles, & Kirwan, 2014). This tool can be used to optimise many objectives that the users want. There has been existed optimisation among time, cost, quality, and sometimes researchers pair it to risk, environment, and even resources (Ahari & Niaki, 2013; Altuwaim & El-Rayes, 2018; Banihashemi, Khalilzadeh, Shahraki, Malkhalifeh, & Ahmadizadeh, 2020; El Bassuony, 2018; El-Rayes & Kandil, 2005; El-Rayes & Moselhi, 2001; Eshtehardian, Afshar, & Abbasnia, 2008, 2009; Huang, Zou, & Zhang, 2016; Kalhor, Khanzadi, Eshtehardian, & Afshar, 2011; Luong, Tran, & Nguyen, 2018; Mohammadipour & Sadjadi, 2016; Tran, Cheng, & Prayogo, 2016; Tran, Luong-Duc, Duong, Le, & Pham, 2018; Zhang, Du, & Zhang, 2014; Zhang & Xing, 2010). Some of these researches were considering the uncertain environment of a construction project, but some others were not. Due to the uniqueness of construction project, which describes many and various uncertain events that are likely to occur, the analysis considering uncertainty is better to present the real condition of a construction project (El Bassuony, 2018).

In this study, the trade-off among time, cost, and quality in the construction project is analysed by considering the uncertainty subjected to the uncertain environment of the construction project to reach out to a sustainable project. Specifically, the model was designed to solve repetitive construction projects, which are dominant and very common nowadays (El-Rayes & Moselhi, 2001).

High-rise buildings, highways, bridges, multiple housing, and pipeline projects are instances of repetitive projects. It consists of similar activities that are repeated in some units (Photios & Yang, 2016). Utilising fuzzy logic approach and Symbiotic Organism Search (SOS) algorithm, the objective of this study will be searching for the most effective and optimum execution option that can be done to implement a construction project by carrying the sustainable value in the construction project. Besides, the tardiness cost and reward due to the late and early completion are also considered to make a better depiction of the construction project.

2. PROPOSED TIME COST QUALITY TRADE-OFF FOR SUSTAINABLE PROJECT SCHEDULING

Sustainable project scheduling intends to deliver the project within the target time, by spending the available budget, and also ensure the quality, which addresses the sustainable result for the present and long term (Dasović, Galić, & Klanšek, 2020). The optimisation among time, cost, and quality explores the alternative solutions to conduct the construction project to result in the shortest project duration with the minimum total cost and maximum quality. To reach out to the objective, the model in this study is developed according to following subsections.

2.1. Fuzzy Logic Approach to Model Uncertainty

Construction projects consist of complex tasks and are often implemented in a dynamic environment. Some uncertain conditions may appear in the construction site, such as the weather, site and equipment condition, the availability of the resources, and even the efficiency of the labourers (Bakry, Moselhi, & Zayed, 2016). These will impact the project output and performance. The time, cost, and quality of the project will be impacted by uncertain conditions (Eshtehardian et al., 2009). In this study, fuzzy logic approach is adopted to model the uncertain condition for the analysis. It will be used to model the uncertain time and cost of each task in the construction project.

Fuzzy logic was first introduced by Lotfi A. Zadeh (1965). This approach can process vagueness and inaccurate information into a definite conclusion (Al Zarrad & Fonseca, 2018). Many kinds of fuzzy can be used to form the uncertainty, but in this study, triangular fuzzy number (TFN) is used. TFN can be seen in Fig. 7.1b.

The horizontal axis is the duration of the task, and the vertical axis is the level of uncertainty in the project. a, b, and c are the uncertain time, which are the optimistic, most likely, and pessimistic time, respectively. α is the membership value, which describes the uncertainty level. As the α increases, from 0 to 1, it indicates that the uncertainty level is lower, but as it decreases from 1 to 0, the level of uncertainty of the project is increased. It can be seen from the triangle that when the uncertainty becomes higher, the duration range of a task in the project becomes wider. $t-$ and $t+$ indicate the optimistic and pessimistic time for each uncertainty level. It can be calculated from the basic formula of TFN in equation (1). Then t is the crisp number that can be got from defuzzification.

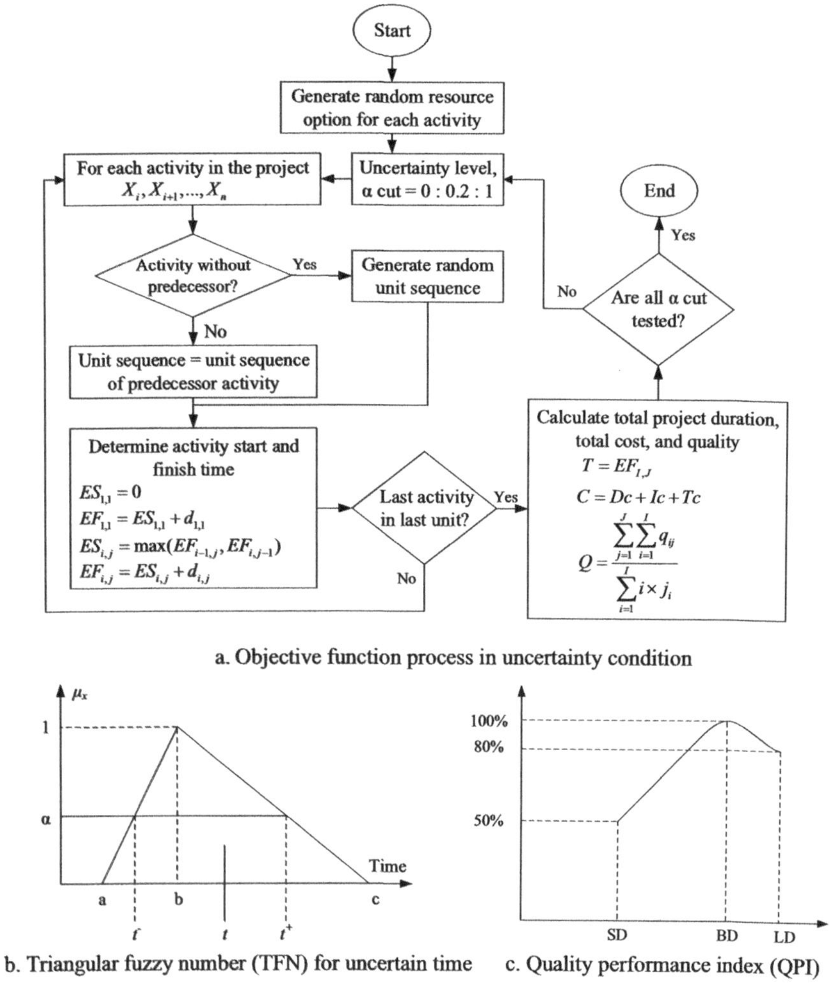

Fig. 7.1. Scheduling and Estimating Process. (a) Objective Function Process in Uncertainty Condition. (b) Triangular Fuzzy Number (TFN) for Uncertain Time. (c) Quality Performance Index (QPI).

Defuzzification is a process to convert fuzzy number into a crisp one, so it becomes a definite number. The method of defuzzification used in this study is the centroid method. It uses the centroid of the area under the membership value as the crisp value. As in Fig. 7.1b, t is the crisp number, which means that the most efficient time to do the task is within t. The defuzzification to get the deterministic number can be done by equation (2). F^* is the crisp number, and $F\mu A$ is the function of the moment in the fuzzy diagram with variable x (Eshtehardian et al., 2009).

$$\mu_x = \begin{cases} 0, x \le a \\ \dfrac{x-a}{b-a}, a \le x \le b \\ \dfrac{c-x}{c-b}, b \le x \le c \\ 0, x \ge c \end{cases} \tag{1}$$

$$F^* = \frac{\int F\mu_A x dx}{\int F\mu_A dx} \tag{2}$$

2.2. Scheduling and Estimating the Project

This is done to predict the total duration, total cost, and also overall quality of the construction project. For the schedule, this study used soft logic to schedule the project. This is very suitable, especially for the repetitive project, which has some similar activities that must be repeated in some units. Soft logic is a non-unit scheduling method. This means that the unit arrangement is flexible. It is not bound which units an activity must done first, then followed by the next unit. As long as the scheduling arrangement results in a shorter duration, it is a better way to do the activity (Huang et al., 2016). For example, if there is one activity that must be done for five units, the unit arrangement for the activity can be 3–4–2–1–5 or 2–1–3–5–4. It is not bounded that the activity must be done in 1–2–3–4–5. Later in the optimisation process, a random unit arrangement is defined by the algorithm. Then, the early start (*ES*), early finish (*EF*), and the total project duration are calculated (*T*). The formulation for these is served in Eqs. (3)–(6). *i,j* means the activity *i* in unit *j*, and $d_{i,j}$ means the duration of activity *i* in unit *j*.

$$ES_{1,1} = 0 \tag{3}$$

$$EF_{1,1} = ES_{1,1} + d_{1,1} \tag{4}$$

$$ES_{i,j} = \max(EF_{i-1,j}, EF_{i,j-1}) \tag{5}$$

$$EF_{i,j} = ES_{i,j} + d_{i,j} \tag{6}$$

After scheduling the activities, the next step is to estimate the total cost of the project. The total cost being considered in this model is the direct cost (*Dc*), indirect cost (*Ic*), tardiness cost (*Tc*), and reward (*r*). The direct cost is the sum of all activity cost (c_{ij}) in the project, the indirect cost is assumed as a constant number per day (c_{in}), the tardiness and reward are then estimated based on the duration of the project completion. If it can finish earlier than the target time, a constant reward per day will be added; otherwise, the project will be punished by tardiness cost. These costs are formulated in equation (7) and (8). Tardiness and reward are formulated in equations (9) and (10).

$$Dc = \sum_{j=1}^{J} \sum_{i=1}^{I} c_{ij} \tag{7}$$

$$Ic = T \times c_{in} \tag{8}$$

$$Tc = \frac{\left(e^{\frac{T-T_t}{Tt}} - 1\right) \times (Dc + Ic)}{10} \tag{9}$$

$$r = c_1(T_t - T) \tag{10}$$

e is the exponential number and Tt is the target time that is set up before starting the project. The reward regarding the early completion of the project is assumed to be a constant number c_1 per day. These equations are on the basis of previous research (Zhang et al., 2014) but modified a little bit to maintain common numbers.

The last process is estimating the overall quality of the project. The overall quality of the project depends on the quality of each activity in the project (Tran et al., 2018). This quality somehow can describe the sustainability of the construction project. This study will rate the quality of each alternative in each activity of the project. The quality of each activity is defined by its execution time. This method is called quality performance index (QPI), which is also already used by previous researchers (Tran et al., 2018; Zhang et al., 2014). The quality is represented by %, from 0% to 100%. The concept of QPI is that there is a best duration to do the activity and got the highest quality, which is 100%. As the duration is shortened, the quality will be lower, and as it is extended, the quality will also become lower but still higher than when it is shortened. This means that when the duration is shortened, then there is no enough time to maximise the quality of the work, and when the duration is extended, it means that the resource cannot work properly to maximise the result. This is why these situations result in lower quality. The QPI can be calculated by equations (11) and (12). Fig. 7.1© describes the QPI.

$$BD_{i,j} = SD_{i,j} + 0.613(LD_{i,j} - SD_{i,j}) \tag{11}$$

$$QPI_{i,j} = a_{i,j} \times t_{i,j}^{\ 2} + b_{i,j} \times t_{i,j} + c_{i,j} \tag{12}$$

$a_{i,j}$, $b_{i,j}$, $c_{i,j}$ are the coefficients determined by the quadratic function based on the best duration of the activity (see Fig. 7.1c). $t_{i,j}$ is the duration of activity i in unit j. SD, BD, and LD are the shortest duration, best duration, and longer duration, respectively. The best duration is formulated in equation (11). The time, cost, and quality are calculated for all alternatives and each level of uncertainty (α cut). The α cut is tested from 0, 0.2, 0.4, 0.6, 0.8, and 1. This is to see the relation of time, cost, and quality in the lower and higher uncertainty level. Fig. 7.1 describes the flowchart of the scheduling and estimating process.

3. CASE STUDY

A case study of a repetitive construction project is analysed in this study to the effectiveness of the model. The case study is a concrete bridge project, which also has been used before by previous researchers (Hyari & El-Rayes, 2006; Selinger, 1980; Tran et al., 2018). This intends to compare the result of the proposed model to the literature and to see the capability of the model itself. The project consists of five main activities: excavation, foundation, columns, beams, and slabs work. These activities need to be done for four units, as the bridge has four piers and three main spans. There is more than one alternative that can be used to execute the project. These alternatives are different from each other in terms of the construction method, material quality, labour hours, duration, cost, and obviously will be different in the quality. The project data of the case study are in optimistic (O), most likely (M), and pessimistic (P) condition (see Table 7.1).

Table 7.1. Project Data of the Case Study.

Activity	Unit	Alternatives	Time (Day)			Cost ($)		
			O	M	P	O	M	P
1	1	1	10	12.5	18	40,000	50,000	75,000
1	2	1	14	15.6	19	40,000	50,000	75,000
1	3	1	8	10.8	15	40,000	50,000	75,000
1	4	1	15	16.7	20	40,000	50,000	75,000
2	1	1	10	11.5	15	76,500	80,000	92,300
2	1	2	13	14.4	17	64,200	70,000	86,900
2	1	3	18	19.2	22	55,600	60,000	70,200
2	2	1	11	12.0	15	76,500	80,000	92,300
2	2	2	14	15.0	18	64,200	70,000	86,900
2	2	3	18	20.0	25	55,600	60,000	70,200
2	3	1	8	10.5	15	76,500	80,000	92,300
2	3	2	11	13.1	16	64,200	70,000	86,900
2	3	3	16	17.5	21	55,600	60,000	70,200
2	4	1	8	10	14	76,500	80,000	92,300
2	4	2	10	12.5	17	64,200	70,000	86,900
2	4	3	13	16.7	21	55,600	60,000	70,200
3	1	1	16	18.1	24	64,000	70,000	81,000
3	1	2	14	15.1	21	73,600	80,000	93,200
3	1	3	10	12.9	16	94,500	100,000	113,200
3	2	1	13	15	22	64,000	70,000	81,000
3	2	2	10	12.5	17	73,600	80,000	93,200
3	2	3	8	10.7	17	94,500	100,000	113,200
3	3	1	20	22.5	30	64,000	70,000	81,000

(*Continued*)

Table 7.1. (*Continued*)

Activity	Unit	Alternatives	Time (Day)			Cost ($)		
			O	M	P	O	M	P
3	3	2	17	18.8	24	73,600	80,000	93,200
3	3	3	14	16.1	22	94,500	100,000	113,200
3	4	1	15	17.5	23	64,000	70,000	81,000
3	4	2	12	14.6	22	73,600	80,000	93,200
3	4	3	10	12.5	21	94,500	100,000	113,200
4	1	1	7	8.6	13	59,300	65,000	77,600
4	1	2	8	10	15	66,700	70,000	83,600
4	1	3	10	12	18	75,000	80,000	92,100
4	1	4	13	15	20	85,000	90,000	98,300
4	2	1	7	9.3	16	59,300	65,000	77,600
4	2	2	9	10.8	16	66,700	70,000	83,600
4	2	3	11	13	20	75,000	80,000	92,100
4	2	4	14	16.3	21	85,000	90,000	98,300
4	3	1	8	10.2	16	59,300	65,000	77,600
4	3	2	10	11.9	17	66,700	70,000	83,600
4	3	3	12	14.3	21	75,000	80,000	92,100
4	3	4	15	17.8	25	85,000	90,000	98,300
4	4	1	7	8	12	59,300	65,000	77,600
4	4	2	8	9.4	15	66,700	70,000	83,600
4	4	3	9	11.3	19	75,000	80,000	92,100
4	4	4	12	14.1	22	85,000	90,000	98,300
5	2	1	14	15.8	23	49,000	55,000	63,000
5	2	2	16	17.8	25	63,000	65,000	73,200
5	3	1	11	13.1	20	49,000	55,000	63,000
5	3	2	13	14.7	22	63,000	65,000	73,200
5	4	1	13	16.7	24	49,000	55,000	63,000
5	4	2	16	18.8	26	63,000	65,000	73,200

Notes: Indirect cost = $5,000/day; initial cost = $120,000.

In the optimisation process, the number of generations and ecosystem size is necessary to be defined. The number of generation represents how many iterations the model will run until it reaches the optimum solution, while the ecosystem size means the number of the solution produced by each generation/iteration. The model was run in 100 generations and 50 ecosystem sizes. The result is shown in Table 7.2.

The solutions (Table 7.2) are the selected solutions in terms of the shortest project duration, minimum total cost, and maximum quality. The first solution, which was the solution with the shortest duration, can be reached by executing the project with 1.1.3.1.1 resource option. This means that the first activity is done by resource option 1, the second activity is done by resource option 1, the third activity by resource option 3, and so on. The unit sequence gives the unit arrangement for each activity. There are uncertainty levels from 0 to 1, which means this solution is tested to six levels of uncertainty. The total duration, cost, and quality from each uncertainty level are also served in the table. The whole solution of this study is present in 3D view in Fig. 7.2. The symbol +, □, *, •, ○, and x represent the uncertainty level from 0, 0.2, 0.4, 0.6, 0.8, and 1, respectively.

Table 7.2. Optimum Solutions from the Case Study.

Sorted By	Resource Option	Unit Sequence/ Activity	Uncertainty Level	Project Performance		
				Time (Days)	Cost ($)	Quality (%)
Time	1.1.3.1.1	3.2.1.4	0	117.5	2,150,800	0.874
		3.2.1.4	0.2	116.2	2,133,900	0.865
		3.2.1.4	0.4	115.0	2,118,700	0.857
		3.2.1.4	0.6	114.0	2,105,800	0.850
		3.1.2.4	0.8	113.3	2,096,400	0.844
			1	104.4	1,983,600	0.760
Cost	1.2.2.1.1	3.2.4.1	0	123.0	2,071,200	0.929
		3.2.4.1	0.2	121.8	2,054,400	0.922
		3.2.4.1	0.4	120.6	2,039,200	0.916
		3.2.4.1	0.6	119.7	2,026,300	0.910
		3.4.1.2	0.8	119.0	2,016,900	0.905
			1	110.7	1,903,200	0.835
Quality	1.3.1.4.2	3.4.2.1	0	151.0	2,320,100	0.984
		3.4.2.1	0.2	149.4	2,300,000	0.984
		3.4.2.1	0.4	147.9	2,282,000	0.984
		3.4.2.1	0.6	146.6	2,266,800	0.984
		4.3.1.2	0.8	145.7	2,255,700	0.983
			1	135.1	2,126,100	0.961

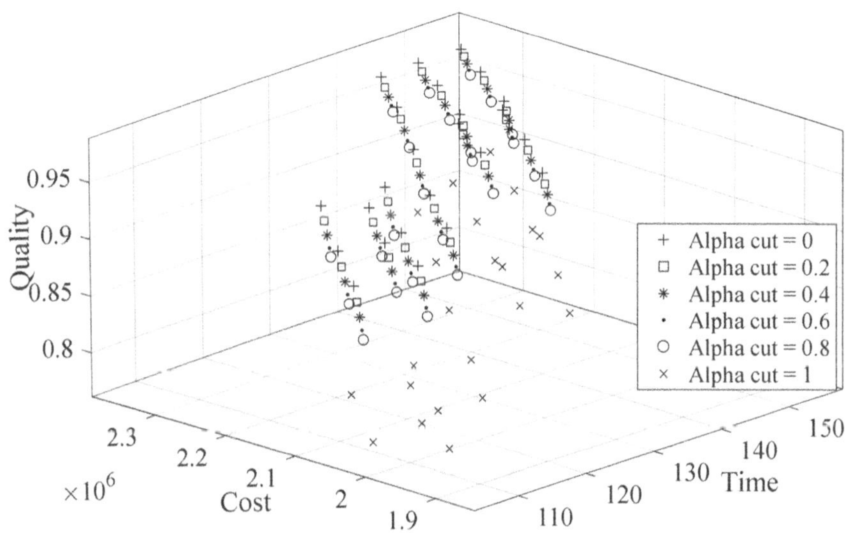

Fig. 7.2. Time–Cost–Quality Trade-off of the Optimum Solution in the Case Study.

From the result in Table 7.2, one can see that as the uncertainty increases from 1 to 0, the total duration, total cost, and also quality increase. Time and cost increase as the safety to maintain the project deliver in time and in budget. The higher uncertainty level indicates that the project faces a harder condition and that it needs more time or more resources, which will cost higher. As the quality refers to QPI, the shorter duration will make the quality fall. That is why, in the higher duration and cost, the quality is higher. This could represent the objective of the sustainability, which is to deliver the project in time, in budget, and with the highest quality/sustainability.

The result of the study can be compared very well to the result of previous research. It can get the shortest duration and the highest quality. The soft logic method of scheduling used in this study is effective to search for the shortest project duration. The model is powerful since it provides more alternative solutions in different levels of uncertainty. These solutions could provide the decision-maker many alternatives to execute the project based on the uncertainty level of their consideration. The decision-maker highly considers the uncertainty, which means they want to protect the project from uncertainties, they may choose uncertainty level 0; otherwise, they chose the higher number.

4. CONCLUSION AND RECOMMENDATION

Sustainable must be considered in planning a construction project. It helps to achieve a project completion by doing economic development, increasing social health, and reducing the negative impact on the environment. Sustainable planning for a construction project can be done by doing multi-objective optimisation. Optimisation among time, cost, and quality is one kind of optimisation that plans to achieve sustainability objectives, which are to deliver the project in time, in budget, and with the highest quality.

One case study is analysed to see the performance of the model. The result is well compared to previous research. The total duration, total cost, and quality are very good and competitive. By doing the soft logic, the result of this study can find the shortest duration comparing to previous research. The quality is also higher than previous research. The result of this study is excellent since it could give more alternative solutions in many levels of uncertainty. The algorithm used in this study is recommended to be used in the further study because it is really simple and fast. However, this study only depicts the sustainability together in 'quality' terms. Further study can be done to add sustainability's function to be optimised.

REFERENCES

Ahari, R. M., & Niaki, S. T. A. (2013). Fuzzy optimization in cost, time and quality trade-off in software projects with quality obtained by fuzzy rule base. *International Journal of Modeling and Optimization*, *3*(2), 176–179.

Al-Zarrad, M. A., & Fonseca, D. (2018). A new model to improve project time-cost trade-off in uncertain environments. *Contemporary Issues and Research in Operations Management*, *6*, 96–112.

Altuwaim, A., & El-Rayes, K. (2018). Optimizing the scheduling of repetitive construction to minimize interruption cost. *Journal of Construction Engineering and Management*, *144*(7), 04018051-1–04018051-12.

Bakry, I., Moselhi, O., & Zayed, T. (2016). Optimized scheduling and buffering of repetitive construction projects under uncertainty. *Engineering, Construction, and Architectural Management*, *23*(6), 782–800.

Banihashemi, S. A., Khalilzadeh, M., Shahraki, A., Malkhalifeh, M. R., & Ahmadizadeh, S. S. R. (2020). Optimization of environmental impacts of construction projects: A time–cost–quality trade-off approach. *International Journal of Environmental Science and Technology*, *18*(3), 631–646.

Chawla, V. K., Chanda, A. K., Angra, S., & Chawla, G. R. (2018). The sustainable project management: A review and future possibilities. *Journal of Project Management*, *3*(3), 157–170.

Cinelli, M., Coles, S. R., & Kirwan, K. (2014). Analysis of the potentials of multi-criteria decision analysis methods to conduct sustainability assessment. *Ecological Indicators*, *46*, 138–148.

Dasović, B., Galić, M., & Klanšek, U. (2020). A survey on integration of optimization and project management tools for sustainable construction scheduling. *Sustainability*, *12*(8), 1–18.

El Bassuony, M. M. (2018). *Time-cost-quality trade-off analysis for construction projects*. Thesis, The American University in Cairo.

El-Rayes, K., & Kandil, A. (2005). Time-cost-quality trade-off analysis for highway construction. *Journal of Construction Engineering and Management*, *131*, 477–486.

El-Rayes, K., & Moselhi, O. (2001). Optimizing resource utilization for repetitive construction projects. *Journal of Construction Engineering and Management*, *127*, 18–27.

Eshtehardian, E., Afshar, A., & Abbasnia, R. (2008). Time–cost optimization: Using GA and fuzzy sets theory for uncertainties in cost. *Construction Management and Economics*, *26*(7), 679–691.

Eshtehardian, E., Afshar, A., & Abbasnia, R. (2009). Fuzzy-based MOGA approach to stochastic time-cost trade-off problem. *Automation in Construction*, *18*(5), 692–701.

Huang, Y., Zou, X., & Zhang, L. (2016). Genetic algorithm-based method for the deadline problem in repetitive construction projects considering soft logic. *Journal of Management in Engineering*, *32*(4), 04016002-1–04016002-9.

Hyari, K., & El-Rayes, K. (2006). Optimal planning and scheduling for repetitive construction projects. *Journal of Management in Engineering*, *22*, 11–19.

Kalhor, E., Khanzadi, M., Eshtehardian, E., & Afshar, A. (2011). Stochastic time–cost optimization using non-dominated archiving ant colony approach. *Automation in Construction*, *20*(8), 1193–1203.

Luong, D.-L., Tran, D.-H., & Nguyen, P. T. (2018). Optimizing multi-mode time–cost–quality trade-off of construction project using opposition multiple objective difference evolution. *International Journal of Construction Management*, *21*(3), 271–283.

Mohammadipour, F., & Sadjadi, S. J. (2016). Project cost–quality–risk tradeoff analysis in a time-constrained problem. *Computers & Industrial Engineering*, *95*, 111–121.

Photios, G. I., & Yang, I. T. (2016). Repetitive scheduling method: requirements, modeling, and implementation. *Journal of Construction Engineering and Management*, *142*(5).

Robert, K. W., Parris, T. M., & Leiserowitz, A. A. (2005). What is sustainable development? Goals, indicators, values, and practice. *Environment: Science and Policy for Sustainable Development*, *47*(3), 8–21.

Schultmann, F., & Sunke, N. (2007). Sustainable management of construction projects. *CIB World Building Congress*.

Selinger, S. (1980). Construction planning for linear projects. *Journal of Construction Division, American Society of Civil Engineers*, *2*, 195–205.

Tran, D.-H., Cheng, M.-Y., & Prayogo, D. (2016). A novel multiple objective symbiotic organisms search (MOSOS) for time–cost–labor utilization tradeoff problem. *Knowledge-Based Systems*, *94*, 132–145.

Tran, D.-H., Luong-Duc, L., Duong, M.-T., Le, T.-N., & Pham, A.-D. (2018). Opposition multiple objective symbiotic organisms search (OMOSOS) for time, cost, quality and work continuity tradeoff in repetitive projects. *Journal of Computational Design and Engineering*, *5*(2), 160–172.

Wu, G. (2017). A multi-objective trade-off model in sustainable construction projects. *Sustainability*, *9*(11), 1–18.

Zavadskas, E., Šaparauskas, J., & Antucheviciene, J. (2018). Sustainability in construction engineering. *Sustainability*, *10*(7), 1–18.

Zhang, H., & Xing, F. (2010). Fuzzy-multi-objective particle swarm optimization for time–cost–quality tradeoff in construction. *Automation in Construction*, *19*(8), 1067–1075.

Zhang, L., Du, J., & Zhang, S. (2014). Solution to the time–cost–quality trade-off problem in construction projects based on immune genetic particle swarm optimization. *Journal of Management in Engineering*, *30*, 163–172.

CHAPTER 8

WASTE MINIMISATION GOVERNANCE THROUGH STANDARDISED RECYCLING RATE IN HIGHER EDUCATION INSTITUTIONS IN MALAYSIA

Siti Nur Syamimi Mohd Na'im, Mohd Fadhil Md Din, Santhana Krishnan, Shazwin Mat Taib and Fadzlin Md Sairan

ABSTRACT

Sustainable recycling activities in higher education institutions (HEIs) are crucial as it serves as a common benchmark to a community that is socially and environmentally responsible. This chapter presents a suitable case study of HEIs in Malaysia reporting on recycling rate, monitoring the recycling patterns, and matching the significant recycling policy in the HEIs. Therefore, four HEIs including Universiti Teknologi Malaysia (UTM), Universiti Malaya (UM), Universiti Kebangsaan Malaysia (UKM) and Universiti Putra Malaysia (UPM) were selected as the suitable case studies to examine the practices of recycling activities. These four HEIs are Malaysian research universities that are ranked in the top 300 in the UI Green Metric World University Rankings. Several findings and previous works were reviewed; further steps to set a recycling target were identified and served as a guidance of the standard recycling rate. Results showed the selected HEIs reflected the low percentage of recycling rate in the range of 0.03–29.26%, depending on its practices and policy.

Sustainability Management Strategies and Impact in Developing Countries
Community, Environment and Disaster Risk Management, Volume 26, 87–102

ISSN: 2040-7262/doi:10.1108/S2040-726220220000026008

Three phases of planning have been structured to target the recycling rate at HEIs in Malaysia with the First Plan (2025), Second Plan (2035) and Third Plan (2040) towards the recycling rates of 20%, 30% and 40%, respectively. The recommendations for the HEIs formulate recycling policies and recycling rates, and for waste management, academia and research centres to play a more active role in increasing the efficiency of recycling activities for a positive impact on the recycling rate in HEIs.

Keywords: Standardising recycling rate; recycling policies; recycling setting plans; recycling management; higher education institutions; National Solid Waste Management Policy

1. INTRODUCTION

Solid waste at higher education institutions (HEIs) is one of the most important issues discussed by the Ministry of Higher Education (MOHE) and other agencies related to solid waste management as it raises more complex issues rather than an impact on the campus operation per se. Rising in student enrolment every year directly contributes to the increase in the amount of solid waste produced each day – as HEIs yielded few tonnes of solid waste every day and the number increasingly associated with the location, facility and distribution of wastes. With a waste generation rate per capita of 0.5–0.8 kg/person/day, the total number of HEIs' students of almost 1.8 million will produce more than a thousand tonnes of waste per day (The Star, 2019; Kementerian Pendidikan Tinggi, 2018). The exponential growth of this amount of solid waste is one of the major issues at the HEIs and it should serve as a benchmarking agenda to the community that is socially and environmentally responsible. Thus, sustainable waste management should be considered to reduce the large amount of solid waste to be handled by HEIs management and to work towards a more sustainable society. The maturity of sustainability initiatives implementation in campus sustainability has been seen as an integrative and transformative approach that needs to acknowledge the issues of multifunction and complexity are in line with the sustainability paradigm.

Given that solid waste management costs a lot especially in terms of waste disposal, most HEIs have taken steps to minimise their daily waste generation through various initiative programmes. According to the Environmental Protection Agency (2016), 'Waste Minimisation is an effort to reduce the use of resources and recycle useful goods before opting for high-cost methods such as energy recovery, treatment and waste disposal'. Basically, waste reduction and recycling are at the top rank within the waste hierarchy compared to energy recovery, treatment or disposal. In addition to reducing the cost of solid waste management, these waste reduction and recycling initiatives can facilitate the work of solid waste management in HEIs. According to Chifari, Piano, Matsumoto, and Tasaki (2017) in the study 'does recyclable separation reduce the cost of municipal waste management in Japan' the results showed the segregation of recyclables for recycling purposes can reduce the processing costs at the treatment facilities. However, recycling has been most practised when waste reduction is not seen as practical economically. A study by Zhang, Williams, Kemp, and Smith (2011) emphasises the HEIs as small municipalities that contributed significantly in developing sustainable waste management by using the University of Southampton (UoS) as a case study.

Recycling is the process of collecting and processing materials that can still be used from disposal and turning them into new products (Environmental Protection Agency, 2020). Recycling is beneficial to reduce the solid waste generated to be sent for disposal. This practice can have a rapid positive effect in reducing waste disposal, and at the same time, HEIs' revenue can be increased through the sale of recyclables. Recycling can reduce greenhouse gasses, saving material and energy, lowering impacts on human health and discovering new jobs. Nonetheless, recycling practices are different from the two practices because as a result of the sale of recyclables, the practitioners will receive a reward in terms of money or other goods such as coupons, necessities or points that need to be collected for certain activities. This practice will be easy to implement continuously and is very difficult to break because pleasant behaviour encourages your brain to release dopamine that strengthens the habit and creates the craving to do it again (Schultz, 1998). As HEIs produce more waste, disposal sites are filling up. Recycling is the best practice that can be implemented in a short time and has a positive impact on waste management in HEIs. In the context of waste management, waste minimisation in Malaysia is given as part of the solid waste management system, regulated by the Solid Waste and Public Cleansing Management Act 2007 (Act 672). The act covers the aspects of waste generation and collection, transportation, recovery or treatment, and disposal, and includes several mechanisms to overcome crucial issues related to solid waste management in Malaysia.

The development of solid waste management policies in Malaysia is parallel with the increment in solid waste generation in this country. The momentum of recycling practices in Malaysia encourages the government to include recycling matters in the country's solid waste management policy. Solid waste management policies in the country can be summarised with a study conducted by Agamuthu and Victor (2011), which emphasises the evolution of waste policy in Malaysia. The waste-related policy in Malaysia began in 1998 with Action Plan for Beautiful and Clean Malaysia (ABC) highlighting the uniformity of the country's more environmentally friendly solid waste management system and accepted by the community by 2010. Then in 2005, the government adopted a National Strategic Plan for Solid Waste Management in Malaysia (NSP) that targeted six strategies, pointing out the guidance on recycling legislative, institutional along with infrastructural planning and management. Through the NSP plan, target setting has been set up with an aim of 22% reduction and recovery as well as 100% waste segregation of resources implemented by 2020. In 2006, the Master Plan on National Waste Minimisation (Ministry of Housing & Local Government, 2006) was launched with the objective of providing the vision, strategy and functions of stakeholders in reducing solid waste disposal in Malaysia. The plan also aims to achieve a recycling rate of 11% in 2010. The National Solid Waste Management Policy (NSWM), formed in 2006, emphasises the implementation of a sustainable plus environmental, social and economic friendly solid waste management system. This policy affirmed the 3R practices that emphasise waste management according to the hierarchy in the implementation of this policy. SWM Corporation has also formulated a strategic plan for 2009–2013 by focussing on seven areas including public awareness programmes. This strategic plan provides for 3R practices to achieve 30% public awareness related to 3R and target recycling rate at 40% by 2013. The last policy cited in this study is the Tenth Malaysian Plan (10MP) for a period of five years (2011–2015). This 10MP has allocations related to 3R practices towards sustainable waste management.

The Eleventh Malaysia Plan is the last five-year plan (2016–2020) in realising Vision 2020. This plan also underlined matters related to 3R practices with the attention on separating waste at the source to achieve a recycling rate of 22% by 2020 (The Economic Planning Unit, Malaysia Prime Minister's Department, 2015). Recently, Malaysia practised the National Solid Waste Management Policy 2016 (National Solid Waste Management Department, 2016) in implementing solid waste management based on the waste management hierarchy and prioritising 3R practices. This policy is an improved version of the amendment based on the achievements in the policies of NSP 2005, MWM 2006 and NSWM 2006 as well as taking into account initiatives related to solid waste management that can be applied from the Eleventh Malaysia Plan document. The six objectives in this policy focus on solid waste management in terms of costs, mitigation initiatives, technology involvement, environmentally friendly and public health and legal involvement. There are six thrusts in this policy of which only thrusts 1 and 6 focus on 3R practices. Thrust 1 is an effort to reduce solid waste generation and optimise resource utilisation. Among the strategies formulated to support this thrust is the improvement of 3R practices at the household, institutional, commercial and industrial levels as well as the introduction of new mechanisms to encourage recycling activities. While thrust 6 is an effort to increase capacity and human capital development. Skills in the solid waste sector are very important to meet the set standards. Planned strategies include the development of human capital capabilities, the enhancement of knowledge and skills in the solid waste sector as well as the improvement of competencies to stakeholders. Here it can be seen that every year 3R practices, especially recycling, are gaining ground in solid waste management policies in Malaysia. This is because recycling is seen to help reduce solid waste disposal and the existence of this policy can provide guidance to waste management and the community in creating a more sustainable environment.

Generally, the recycling rate is presented as a percentage of waste recycled over the total waste generated. The increment in the value of the recycling rate is shown as the progress in recycling activities. The recycling rate has gained attention among policy-makers to monitor the performance of recycling policies and the rate of natural resources savings, but there is still no standard value set to assess the level of the recycling rate in HEIs. For example, each country sets a recycling rate target that the country needs to achieve for a certain period of time. Developing countries such as Malaysia set a target of a 40% recycling rate among Malaysians by 2025 with the achievement of recycling at 28.1% by 2020 (BHOnline, 2020). Developed countries such as Germany, which is also the best country in recycling practices, have succeeded in achieving and maintaining the country's recycling rate at 50–60% and targeted a recycling percentage of 65% by 2020, which was expected to be easy for the country (Neligan, 2018). The effectiveness of the recycling system in Germany can be proven by a study conducted at the University of Bamberg, Germany, on the participation of students and staff in the segregation and recycling of waste. The results of the study found that students urge waste management on campus to be more competent in an effort to curb waste production as much as possible through waste segregation and recycling. Students also stated that they are ready to commit to waste reduction and recycling waste inevitable initiatives (Achter, 2018). Here it can be proved that Germans including university students understand the importance and benefits of recycling.

Here it is clear that the setting of the recycling rate target is very important to track the performance of recycling practices. In the case of HEIs, this recycling rate target is needed to divert the waste from disposal towards sustainable institutions. This chapter discusses the recycling rate pattern for Malaysia's HEIs case studies and sets the recycling rate target associated with the recycling policy for HEIs in Malaysia.

2. METHODOLOGY

2.1. Case Study of Recycling Rate

In this study, four HEIs have been selected for the case studies, which are Universiti Teknologi Malaysia (UTM), Universiti Malaya (UM), Universiti Kebangsaan Malaysia (UKM) and Universiti Putra Malaysia (UPM). These four HEIs are also listed in UI Green Metric World University Rankings, which aims to assess the current situation on a green campus, electricity usage, energy, water and transportation. These six indicators have several specific percentages in assessing the rating of each sector including waste indicators (18%). Waste treatment and recycling activities are among major factors to keep the environment green and sustainable campus. The HEIs' activities such as learning and teaching activities (especially meals preparation at the cafeteria and formal meetings), programmes and campaigns generated a lot of waste. Therefore, several initiatives and programmes such as recycling programmes as well as policy limit the use of plastic and paper on the campus.

These four HEIs are research universities among 15 universities in Malaysia that are ranked in the top 300 in the UI Green Metric World University Rankings. Based on the rank according to the waste indicator in 2019, UM is ranked 68th in the world making the UM the best HEIs in Malaysia in waste management. Then followed by UPM, UTM and UKM with positions at 91, 227, 277 and 288, respectively, worldwide. Although it is seen that two HEIs in Malaysia have managed to place among the top 100 in the world, waste management and recycling practices in HEIs need to be strengthened to increase the waste indicator scores of each HEIs and raise the position for a better rank. Therefore, this study is very important in determining the recycling rate target for HEIs in Malaysia as a guide to improve recycling performance in their respective HEIs.

In this study, the data for the number of recyclables and the amount of waste generated have been obtained from the solid waste management of each HEIs. The data had been collected from the HEIs in the form of secondary data (reports) for a given assessment period, preferably five years (2015–2019).

The recycling rate is a method of monitoring used to assess the performance of the recycling activities by looking at the percentage of the amount of material isolated for recycling from the total amount of waste generated. The calculation of the recycling rate is based on the following equation:

$$\text{Recycling rate} = \frac{\text{total waste collected for recycling}}{\text{total waste generated}} \times 100 \quad (1)$$

3. RESULTS AND DISCUSSION

3.1. Setting the Recycling Rate

The main objective of recycling is to reduce the amount of waste disposed of the landfills. By converting and managing certain waste, the rate of disposal can be reduced significantly and recycling optimisation can be achieved, simultaneously. Generally, solid waste management will highlight the efficacy of the recycling collection and find alternative ways for final disposal. In this case, the National Solid Waste Management Policy is important for the extension of the landfill life due to the proper solid waste management at the basic structure (Sreenivasan, Govindan, Chinnasami, & Kadiresu, 2012).

Some of the developed and developing countries in Asia are beginning to set national recycling targets as an initiative towards their national development. Table 8.1 shows the national recycling targets from several Asian countries, as well as the EU and the US practices. Also, this revision summarises the targets and policies used by the selected countries in Asia. The target setting by these countries explains that standardising recycling rates and targets helps to monitor and compare recycling performance, respectively.

3.2. Attempts at Recycling Rate Standardisation

Coordination of definition and standardising the recycling rate is very substantial to facilitate the understanding. Back in 2009, in developing countries in Asia, a forum called the Regional 3R Forum in Asia and the Pacific was launched to advocate the recycling practices and 3R-related indicators for the Asian regional level (Asia Recycling Circulation Policy Research Group, 2014). A scientific community such as International Solid Waste Association (ISWA) and international forums such as the Regional 3R Forum in Asia and the Pacific will be formed when a recycling rate standardisation is needed for international comparisons in Asia and overcoming challenges when standardising. One of the challenges in standardising the recycling rate in Asia is the lack or absence of waste-related data stored due to a lack of emphasis on systematic data storage systems. Therefore, working group members need to redouble their efforts by reviewing and collecting

Table 8.1. National Recycling Target Setting in Asian Countries, EU and the USA.

Country	Target	Policy
Malaysia	Solid waste management goals to achieve a diversion rate of 40% from landfills and a 22% recycling rate by 2020	National Solid Waste Policy 2016 Eleventh Malaysia Plan 2015–2020
Japan	Cyclical use rate: cyclical use amount/(cyclical use amount + amount of natural resource input) 18% by 2025 The recycling rate of MSW is monitored, but the target was not set	The 4th Fundamental Plan for Establishing Sound Material Cycle Society (Government of Japan, 2018)
Philippines	Diversion rate: 25 % of all solid waste, through reuse, recycling and composting, and other resource recovery activity Potential diversion rate through composting (60%) and recycling (15%) (2019)	Ecological Solid Waste Management Act 2000 (Republic Act No. 9003) (Governance of Philippine, 2001)
Singapore	Recycling rate = Total waste recycled/Total waste generated (70% in 2030) 59% in 2019	A lively and liveable Singapore: strategies for sustainable growth (The Inter-Ministerial Committee on Sustainable Development, 2009)
Vietnam	To collect and treat, within environmental standards, 100% of daily life solid waste in urban centres, 90% of which will be recycled, reused as recovered energy or used as input for organic fertiliser production	Viet Nam strategy for integrated solid waste management until 2025 and vision towards 2050 (Government of Viet Nam, 2009)
EU	Target for recycling 65% of municipal waste by 2030 Target for recycling 75% of packaging waste by 2030 Target to reduce the disposal of municipal waste to landfills by 10% by 2030	Circular Economy Package Waste: Review of Waste Policy and Legislation (European Commission, 2014)
USA	National Recycling Goal will increase to 50% by 2030	National Framework for Advancing the U.S. Recycling System. (United States Environmental Protection Agency, 2019)
	By 2018, 500,000 tonnes of virgin materials were counterbalanced by the reuse or recycling of waste products.	Fiscal Year 2014–2018 EPA Strategic Plan (United States Environmental Protection Agency, 2014)

information related to waste management description and calculation from the generation, collection and recycling stages. Hereof, Regional 3R Forum in Asia and the Pacific members have taken additional initiatives by forming Asia Pacific 3R White Paper to monitor the performance of the 3R policy implemented in the Asian region.

There is also a study reviewed on the challenges in standardising the recycling rate and target setting in the Asia context by Hotta, Visvanathan and Kojima (2016). The authors have taken into account many forms and levels in waste recovery including recycling rate, collection rate, diversion rate and cyclic use rate. Results showed that there were four major types of recycling indicators. The authors emphasised that the recycling rate definition and calculation depend on the process involved or taken into account whether the emphasis is on the input side, resource recovery, proper collection or alternative to the final disposal. In this regard, the authors also point out that the major challenge that will be faced when defining recycling and recycling rates is specifying numerators and denominators. Although this recycling rate is said to be popular and easy to understand, various definitions and calculations cause confusion and complexity to use it as an indicator. Therefore, a standard definition is needed to enable it to be a uniform elementary indicator.

Many initiatives towards recycling have been undertaken by HEIs especially in Asia in an effort towards sustainable development. In fact, there are many studies that examine the characteristics of waste generated on campus to see the opportunities that can be taken from the separation of recyclables from the waste generated. A study conducted in 2015 by Arazo (2015) at Misamis Oriental State College of Agriculture and Technology (MOSCAT), the Philippines, to look at the composition of solid waste generated on the campus. The results of the study found that almost 55 wt.% of recyclables consisting of paper, plastic, glass, iron and textiles were successfully separated in this four-week study. This means recycling initiatives are able to reduce more than half of the waste generated on campus from being disposed of at landfills. Similarly, Moqbel (2018) conducted a study at the University of Jordan to review the composition of waste for four different periods; regular semester, semester break, summer semester as well as during the fasting season (Ramadan). The study successfully segregated 64% of recyclables from the total amount of waste generated during the four periods. This waste composition information is able to show recycling opportunities as well as waste reduction strategies on campus.

There are also studies on the composition of this waste in the context of HEIs in Malaysia. The study on the potential of utilising waste generated at Universiti Malaysia Sarawak (UNIMAS) by Zawawi, Rosli, Bustami, Mispan, and Ramli (2015) focuses on four main sources in the West campus. In this study, 25% of the recyclables segregated from the total consisted of mixed paper, plastic bottles, boxes and aluminium. The rate of 25% of the recyclables is also estimated to generate an income of RM126.43 from the sale of these materials. In addition to reducing a quarter of the waste generated, this initiative is also able to increase campus revenue with the sales of recyclables. The composition of solid waste at Universiti Teknologi MARA (UiTM) Perak was also studied by Ishak, Mahayuddin and Mohamed (2015) to identify the type, amount and composition of waste in student accommodation areas. The four-week study found that almost 45% of recyclables can be segregated from being disposed of, which consists of paper, aluminium, glass and plastic. The result of a high recycling rate is also found from a study at Universiti Teknologi MARA (UiTM) Pasir Gudang, which is 66% with the highest composition of aluminium (24%) (Ismail et al., 2018). This trend is slightly different from previous studies where the recycled material with the highest percentage of composition is paper or plastic. However, with this high recycling rate, it is able to generate income for the campus of RM42.50, not including glass materials. These studies prove that researchers and solid waste management in HEIs, including in Malaysia, are aware of the benefits that can be obtained from active recycling activities. The standardisation of recycling rate targets for HEIs in Malaysia is seen as very important to monitor the performance of recycling rates as well as a motivator for campus residents to always practice recycling to achieve the set targets.

3.3. Malaysian HEIs Recycling Rate

This study intends to propose a common recycling rate, monitor the performance of recycling and carefully target the setting of recycling policy in four HEIs, UTM, UM, UKM and UPM. The findings from the study will improve the performance of recycling practice in four HEIs in an effort towards the Green Campus.

Fig. 8.1a shows UTM recycling data for the consecutive three years (2017–2019). The result shows an increment in the percentage of recycling rates. UTM successfully recycled their waste in 2017 at a rate of 0.03%, increasing to 0.09% in 2018 and further improving to 0.11% in 2019. However, the overall recycling rate is insignificant, with the percentage not even reaching 1%. Furthermore, the increase in the recycling rate is relatively significant to sustainable performance in recycling practices at UTM. The low percentage of recycling activities in UTM is likely because the recycling practice on campus has only started as early as 2011 with the launch of 'Monday is UTM Recycling Day' (Zen, Subramaniam, Sulaiman, Omar, & Salim, 2016). However, this initiative on recycling practices has been effective since 2018 with the conversion of the UTM's multi-stream recycling system to single-stream recycling. So it is not surprising that the recycling rate in UTM is very low considering the campus residents are still new to this practice at that time. But, looking at the very good increase from 2017 to 2019, it is certain that recycling practices in UTM now have a much better recycling rate. Acurio, Rossin, Teixeira, and Zepeda (1998) and de Vega, Benítez, and Barreto (2008) identify the provision of waste management and a waste profile as the basic empirical information needed to support correct decision-making, leading to a better understanding of solid waste management systems in campuses.

Recycling rates for UM from 2017 to 2019 are shown in Fig. 8.1b. UM recycling percentage was relatively high in 2017 with 9.44% but decreased in 2018 by 7.2% and 5% in 2019. The percentage value for the recycling rate in UM is higher than in UTM because recycling initiatives in UM began in early 2010 with the launch of the Zero Waste Campaign (ZWC) to become a campus with zero-waste disposed to landfills (Yusoff, 2018). The practice of waste management is also supported by their living laboratory initiatives and flagship programme on the development of Intelligent Recycle Centre (IRC) to boost behaviour and inculcate the best practice of recyclables drop-off. These efforts succeeded in diverting 620 tons of waste from been disposed to landfills thus reducing the cost of waste management operations (collection fee and landfill gate fee) by RM97, 758 over a period of five years (2012–2016) (Yusoff, 2018). Yet, the recycling rate at UM decreased due to the increase in the amount of waste generated. Based on Fig. 8.1b, the amount of recyclables increased every year, as well as the amount of waste produced also multiplied many times over. This means that initiatives and campaigns to raise awareness of recycling practices among UM campus residents need to be further enhanced to encourage them to separate recyclables

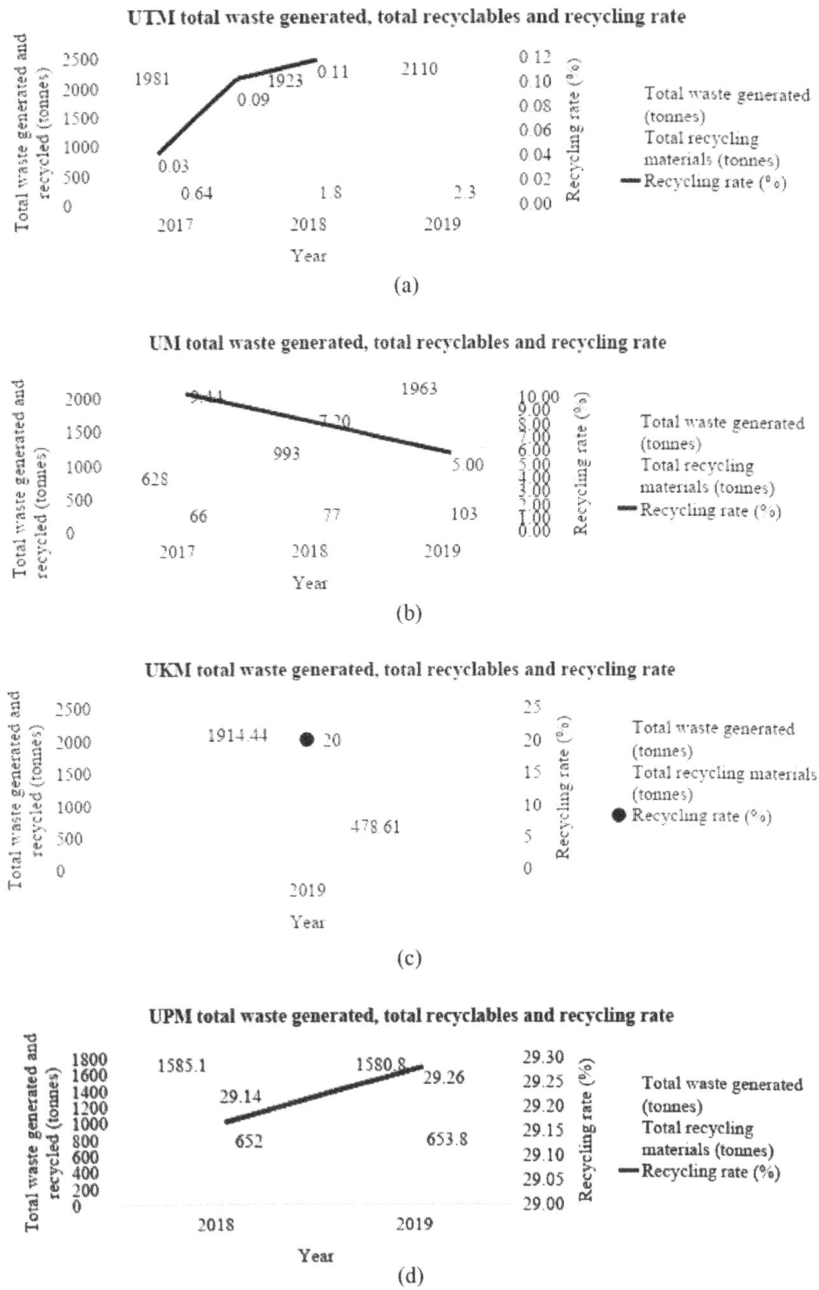

Fig. 8.1. (a) UTM Total Waste Generated, Total Recyclables and Recycling Rate in 2017–2019; (b) UM Total Waste Generated, Total Recyclables and Recycling Rate in 2017–2019; (c) UKM Total Waste Generated, Total Recyclables and Recycling Rate in 2019; and (d) UPM Total Waste Generated, Total Recyclables and Recycling Rate in 2018 and 2019.

from landfills to landfills. Directly, a high amount of recyclables will increase the percentage of recycling rates at UM. In addition, the capacity of the recyclables collection centre at UM also plays an important role in increasing the rate of recycling on campus. The limited capacity of the collection centre resulted in the entry of collected recyclables also limited. The process of segregation and collection of recyclables will be delayed due to insufficient area to carry out the process. Recyclables that do not fit to be collected at the centre are also likely to be sent to the disposal route. Therefore, a study needs to be done to review the capacity requirements at the recyclables collection centre on campus in line to the daily waste increment.

Recycling data for UKM only available in 2019 with a percentage of recycling rate of 20% (Fig. 8.1c). This is among a top rank in recycling percentage as compared to the previous two HEIs, which are UTM and UM. However, a proper trend or pattern for recycling rates in UKM could not be made as to the reported data for one year only. Nonetheless, with the initiative to establish Pusat Kitar Semula in UKM (PKS-UKM) since 2010 as a result of cooperation with Alam Flora Sdn. Bhd. is able to encourage UKM campus residents to recycle to increase the recycling rate to a high percentage value. This effort is in line with the purpose of establishing this recycling center which focuses on improving the recycling management system, improving the existence of recycling centers and facilities as well as promoting recycling awareness campaigns within the UKM campus. The existence of PKS-UKM is able to reduce waste disposal to landfills and also able to increase campus income by an estimated RM200–RM600 per month (Tiew et al., 2019). Recycling efforts at UKM were enhanced with the existence of a two bins recycling system in 2010. The two bins recycling system or a single-stream recycling system is a method of collecting recyclables in one bin without having to be separated at the source, while non-recyclables are put in another bin. The system is said to successfully promote recycling practices by segregating recyclables of almost 50% of the total waste generated (Tiew, Watanabe, Basri, Zain, & Basri, 2011). Recycling practices at UKM are further enhanced with the initiative of a recycling entrepreneurship programme that targets students and staff at UKM. The activities such as the recyclables design competition, sale of recyclables to the PKS-UKM as well as sale of used reading materials are carried out (Er, Nawi, Tee, Ibrahim, & Bachok, 2019). This effort can instil recycling practices among campus residents, increase the recycling rate on campus and be able to highlight the image of PKS-UKM as a major recycling initiative in UKM.

Fig. 8.1d shows the percentage of recycling rates for UPM for a period of two years (2018–2019). The recycling rate at UPM is high and has increased significantly, from 29.14% in 2018 to 29.26% in 2019. Despite this, recycling data at UPM may be less accurate as recycling information is only obtained from the National Solid Waste Management Department (2015) (as the technical and academic research publication). In the estimation study, it was confirmed that the recycling performance at UPM is highly top rank compared to the other previous three HEIs. It is likely that UPM has started this recycling initiative earlier and has carried out various recycling programmes on campus both increasing the recycling rate among campus residents.

3.4. Recycling Rate Targets in Malaysian's HEIs

In the previous sub-section on attempts to standardize recycling rate targets, common and practical definitions were seen as the basic things that should be set in advance to systematise the categorisation of recyclable materials taken into account in the study. The first thing to do before recycling is to plan the material to be recycled and ensure that the material is recycled correctly. In this study, the recyclables for all HEIs in Malaysia include paper products, glass products, tetra pack, hard plastic products, tin and aluminium cans, electronic waste and textiles. Compost material is not included in this study as it is categorised under the composting process or organic decomposition classification.

The National Solid Waste Management Policy was formally approved in 2006. This policy focuses on reducing the generation of solid waste through 3R and needs to be implemented consistently. As a result, the national recycling rate could significantly increase from 5% in 2005 to 28% in 2020 and is confident that the target of a 40% recycling rate by 2025 could be achieved (Appendix 1).

The data of Malaysian Recycling Rate explained that starting with 5% in 2005, it has set another 15% target for 2015. Based on the graph, the recycling rate in Malaysia shows the target rate increased at a value of 1% annually from 2005 to 2015. However, in 2020, the new recycling rate is recommended at 22%. This is an additional 2% from the previous year's target. The reason for the additional target by the Malaysian government is the expectation of the successful recycling rate target aligned with the efforts and initiatives undertaken by several agencies and local governments. The government's expectations are correct as it turns out that Malaysia managed to achieve a recycling rate of 28.1% by 2020, more than it projected. Therefore, most recently, the government has set Malaysia's recycling rate at 40% by 2025 and believes this value is achievable in the next four years.

Despite the efforts of national policy, HEIs make a further benchmark in setting comprehensive recycling rate targets. With this, the objectives of this study can be achieved. Using the recycling rate results for four HEIs (UTM, UM, UKM and UPM) in Malaysia as a guide and reference, the range of recycling rates obtained are found to be 0.03–29.26%. Three phases of planning have been structured to target the recycling rate at the HEIS in Malaysia with the First Plan (2025), Second Plan (2035) and Third Plan (2040) with recycling rates of 20%, 30% and 40%, respectively (Appendix 2).

Therefore, the consensus of 20% rate is set because although there are some HEIs such as UKM and UPM have managed to achieve it. Based on the above value, it is a starting value that can be practised by any HEIs that has not practised recycling or is still in their initial stage. The selected 20% (as the targeted recycling rate) is possible to achieve due to the various initiatives that have been done on campus as well as the way of thinking of campus residents who are already exposed to recycling practices from various sources. For HEIs that have successfully achieved a value of 20%, make this target as a bottom limit to monitor the performance of recycling practices on their respective HEIs to always have a rate of more than 20%. These HEIs can also draft plans to achieve the Second Plan recycling rate target at 30%. The study by de Vega et al. (2008) on the several important factors in the success, endurance and spread of recycling programmes in most universities in the

United States found out that the introduction of a new waste system requires different structural frameworks of change such as the introduction of economic incentives and information campaigns as persuasive strategies to stimulate behaviors as an integrated approach with solid waste management in a campus organisation.

4. CONCLUSION

Recycling is among the priority of solid waste management in reducing the disposal of solid waste in landfills. A standardised recycling rate could help waste management to monitor the performance of recycling practices in HEIs in Malaysia. The study on four HEIs, UTM, UM, UKM and UPM as case studies found that the recycling rate of HEIs in Malaysia is ranged from 0.03% to 29.26%. This means that the recycling rate in HEIs in Malaysia is still at low levels. However, even some of the HEIs recorded a very low recycling agenda at their university, the setting of the recycling rate for all HEIs should be par at the percentage of 20%, which is estimated to be achieved by 2025.

Various specific policies related to recycling in HEIs have been formulated to encourage campus residents to practice any recycling activities. Recycling programs and campaigns held by the HEIs management aim to expose and familiarize campus residents with recycling practices, as well as improve more sustainable campus recycling management. Yet the biggest constraint for HEIs is especially in the Asian context where data related to waste and recycling are less or not recorded. This complicates the process of analysis and standardisation of recycling rate targets in HEIs.

Recommendations for future studies to better collect recycling data for longer periods; 5–10 years due to the availability of more thorough and long-term data can show the trends and patterns of recycling practices in HEIs in Malaysia more accurately. Moreover, short-term data collection is also very important, namely monthly observations for a period of one year. These short-term observations can also show trends and patterns of recycling practices on campus on a seasonal basis; active semesters and semester breaks; during major events such as convocation ceremonies, university carnivals or major sports tournaments. In addition, studies related to recycling policy in HEIs are seen as important to be taken into account in future studies to see the relationship between operations and recycling governance in the HEIs involved.

ACKNOWLEDGEMENTS

The authors gratefully acknowledge the research grant and financial support provided by the MOHE and UTM under the MRUN grant number: R.J130000.7805.4L886.

REFERENCES

Achter, P. (2018). Bei umweltgerechter Mülltrennung mitmachen Universität Bamberg. Retrieved from https://www.uni-bamberg.de/news/artikel/nachhaltigkeit-muelltrennung-test/ (in German).

Acurio, G., Rossin, A., Teixeira, P. F., & Zepeda, F. (1998). *Diagnosis of municipal solid waste management in Latin America and the Caribbean.* Washington, DC: Pan American Health Organization, World Health Organization.

Agamuthu, P., & Victor, D. (2011). Policy evolution of solid waste management in Malaysia. In: Presented at the *International Solid Waste Association World Congress*, October, Daegu, Korea.

Arazo, R. O. (2015). Compositions of solid wastes generated from a school campus. *IJRET: International Journal of Research in Engineering and Technology*, *4*(10), 2319–1163.

Asia Recycling Circulation Policy Research Group. (2014). *3R policy indicator factsheets, Ver. 1.Hayama: IGES.*

BHOnline. (2020, August 2). SWCorp tingkat sasaran kadar kitar semula 40 peratus menjelang 2025. Retrieved from https://www.bharian.com.my/berita/nasional/2020/08/717133/swcorp-tingkat-sasaran-kadar-kitar-semula-40-peratus-menjelang-2025

Chifari, R., Piano, S. L., Matsumoto, S., & Tasaki, T. (2017). Does recyclable separation reduce the cost of municipal waste management in Japan? *Waste Management*, *60*, 32–41.

de Vega, C. A., Benítez, S. O., & Barreto, M. E. R. (2008). Solid waste characterization and recycling potential for a university campus. *Waste Management*, *28*, S21–S26.

Environmental Protection Agency. (2016, February). Wastes – hazardous waste – waste minimization. Retrieved from https://archive.epa.gov/epawaste/hazard/wastemin/web/html/faqs.html

Environmental Protection Agency. (2020). Recycling basics. Retrieved from https://www.epa.gov/recycle/recycling-basics

Er, A. C., Nawi, N. F. M., Tee, M. Y., Ibrahim, N. I., & Bachok, N. (2019). Entrepreneurial recycling initiatives towards campus sustainability. *International Journal of Business & Society*, *20*(1), 247–259.

European Commission. (2014). *Circular economy package waste: Review of waste policy and legislation.*Brussels: EC.

Government of Japan. (2018). The 4th fundamental plan for establishing sound material cycle society. Retrieved from https://www.env.go.jp/recycle/recycle/circul/keikaku/pam4_E.pdf

Government of Philippine. (2001). Republic Act No. 9003 Metro Manila. Retrieved from https://emb.gov.ph/wp-content/uploads/2015/09/RA-9003.pdf

Government of Viet Nam (2009). *Decision on Approving the National Strategy of Integrated Solid Waste Management up to 2025, Vision towards 2050*. Retrieved from https://www.uncrd.or.jp/content/documents/PM%20Decision%20of%20Approval%20of%20NSISWM%20(Eng).pdf

Hotta, Y., Visvanathan, C., & Kojima, M. (2016). Recycling rate and target setting: challenges for standardized measurement. *Journal of Material Cycles and Waste Management*, *18*(1), 14–21.

Ishak, N. R., Mahayuddin, S. A., & Mohamed, M. R. (2015). Generation and composition of solid waste in university campus. In R. Hashim & A. B. Abdul Majeed (Eds.),. *Proceedings of the colloquium on administrative science and technology* (Chapter 13 pp. 119–126). Singapore: Springer.

Ismail, H. B., Hassan, A. C., Jamal, M. H., Martin, J., Salleh, M. Z. M., Chik, W. S. W., & Yusof, N. A. U. (2018). Potential revenue from solid waste recycling practices in faculty of civil engineering UiTM Johor, Pasir Gudang campus. *Journal of Fundamental and Applied Sciences*, *10*, 2540–2550.

Kementerian Pendidikan Tinggi. (2018). Statistik Pendidikan Tinggi 2018. Retrieved from https://www.moe.gov.my/muat-turun/laporan-dan-statistik/pendidikan-tinggi/buku-perangkaan/2018-10/2401-statistik-pendidikan-tinggi-2018-bab-1-pdf/file

Moqbel, S. (2018). *Solid waste management in educational institutions: The case of the* University of Jordan. *Environmental Research, Engineering and Management*, *74*(2), 23–33.

National Solid Waste Management Department. (2015). *Final lab report solid waste management lab 2015*. Malaysia: Ministry of Housing and Local Government.

National Solid Waste Management Department. (2016). *National solid waste management policy 2016*. Malaysia: National Solid Waste Management Department.

Neligan, A. (2018). *2025 recycling target: Only 10 EU countries on track* (No. 28/2018). Köln: IW-Kurzbericht.

Perbadanan Pengurusan Sisa Pepejal dan Pembersihan Awam. (2018). Kadar kitar semula kebangsaan mengikut tahunan [Data file]. Retrieved from https://www.data.gov.my/data/dataset/eeae205e-7715-406a-93f5-55f5d87509ac/resource/fa11f252-9d95-4f0f-87ac-a2ce4d17f76f/download/kadar-kitar-semula-kebangsaan-mengikut-tahunan.xlsx

Schultz, W. (1998). Predictive reward signal of dopamine neurons. *Journal of Neurophysiology*, *80*(1), 1–27.

Solid Waste and Public Cleansing Management Act 2007 (Act 672), Malaysia.

Sreenivasan, J., Govindan, M., Chinnasami, M., & Kadiresu, I. (2012). Solid waste management in Malaysia – A move towards sustainability. *Waste Management: An Integrated Visions, 2005*(April 2005), 55–70.

The Economic Planning Unit, Malaysia Prime Minister's Department. (2015). *Eleventh Malaysia plan 2016–2020: Anchoring growth on people* (Chapter 5 p. 372). Putrajaya: Economic Planning Unit.

The Inter-Ministerial Committee on Sustainable Development. (2009). *A lively and liveable Singapore: strategies for sustainable growth*. Singapore: Ministry of the Environment and Water Resources and Ministry of National Development.

The Star. (2019, July 30). Generating more waste than ever. Retrieved from https://www.thestar.com.my/news/nation/2019/07/30/generating-more-waste-than-ever

Tiew, K. G., Basri, N. E. A., Watanabe, K., Zain, S. M., Er, A. C., & Deng, H. (2019). Higher educational institutions recycling management in Malaysia. *International Journal of Business and Society*, *20*(1), 277–285.

Tiew, K. G., Watanabe, K., Basri, N. A., Zain, S. M., & Basri, H. (2011). Reducing waste disposal from Universiti Kebangsaan Malaysia campus by 2-bins recycling system. *Journal of Civil Engineering, Science and Technology*, *2*(1), 31–35.

United States Environmental Protection Agency. (2014). *Fiscal year 2014–2018 EPA strategic plan*. Washington, DC: United States Environmental Protection Agency.

United States Environmental Protection Agency. (2019). *National framework for advancing the U.S. recycling system*. Washington, DC: United States Environmental Protection Agency.

Yusoff, S. (2018). Toward integrated and sustainable waste management system in University of Malaya: UM zero waste campaign. In R. Fitri Sari, H. Hadiyanto & N. Suwartha (Eds.). E3S web of conferences (Vol. 48, p. 04007.). Indonesia: EDP Sciences.

Zawawi, M. H., Rosli, N. A., Bustami, R. A., Mispan, N. H., & Ramli, M. Z. (2015). Potential of utilizing solid waste generated in UNIMAS west campus. In A. E. Ismail, et. al (Eds.). *Applied mechanics and materials* (Vol. 773, pp. 1073–1078). Trans Tech Publications Ltd.

Zen, I. S., Subramaniam, D., Sulaiman, H., Omar, W., & Salim, M. R. (2016). Institutionalize waste minimization governance towards campus sustainability: A case study of Green Office initiatives in Universiti Teknologi Malaysia. *Journal of Cleaner Production*, *135*, 1407–1422.

Zhang, N., Williams, I. D., Kemp, S., & Smith, N. F. (2011). Greening academia: Developing sustainable waste management at higher education institutions. *Waste Management*, *31*(7), 1606–1616.

Appendix 1: Malaysia National Recycling Rate (Bhonline, 2020; Perbadanan Pengurusan Sisa Pepejal Dan Pembersihan Awam, 2018).

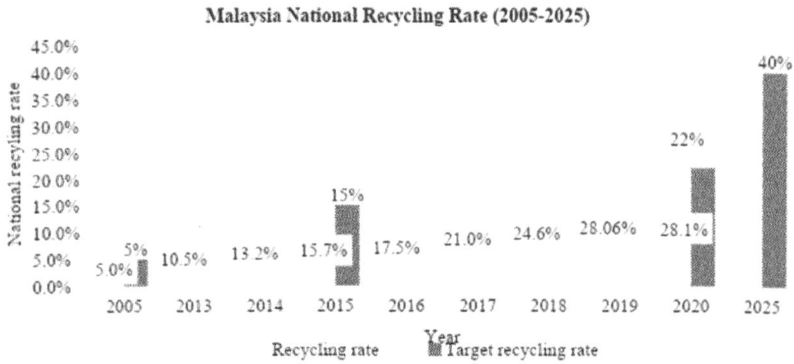

Appendix 2: Targets Recycling Rate for Malaysia's HEIs.

Year	Recycling Rate
First Plan (2025)	20%
Second Plan (2035)	30%
Third Plan (2040)	40%

CHAPTER 9

WEB-BASED BIG DATA INTEGRATION VISUALISATION SOLUTIONS

Omar Sedeeq Yousif and Rozana Zakaria

ABSTRACT

Industries' projects are associated with large amounts of data throughout the project lifecycle. As the size of the projects grows, so does the data associate with the projects. To generate useful information from Big Data, appropriate predictive analysis and data visualisation tools are required. Therefore, the use of visualisation techniques will target this expected evolution of big data. Thus, this study aims to give an overview of the migrations of an existing computer-based application, used to analyse multidata sources of enterprises, to a web-based application. Essential development aspects were concerned with the process of application development, platform development, software utilisation, and efficient display interface according to the enterprise's requirement. Two solutions such as Microsoft Power Business Intelligence (BI) and the Dynamic Web System have been presented that proven to be widespread because these solutions have met the enterprises' requirements in terms of expenses, policy, security, maintenance, and interactive interface. Also, an assessment of these solutions and challenges to adopting has been presented. Eventually, the system developed on the web overcomes computer-based systems in solving their problems such as deploying and maintaining applications and providing efficient and richer user interfaces for users. The web-based visualisation application has wide beneficial features; it provides high-performance real-time data analysis, data multimodal visualisation, and friendly to use.

Sustainability Management Strategies and Impact in Developing Countries
Community, Environment and Disaster Risk Management, Volume 26, 103–117

Published under exclusive licence by Emerald Publishing Limited
ISSN: 2040-7262/doi:10.1108/S2040-726220220000026009

Web-based applications will increase confidence in decision-making based on data visualisation, which will positively reflect on comprehensive data analysis processes for project success.

Keywords: Big data; data analysis; data management; data visualisation; information technology; technological innovation

1. INTRODUCTION

Companies with high data generation and digitalisation are developing too fast all around the world, which means more data, information, and decision need. So, there is a need for tools that allow companies to monitor their data generation as well as their performance (Storey & Song, 2017). These companies' goal is to collect, save, and analyse more data and enhance their performance by data-driven decision-making. To achieve this, many companies have a dedicated data management team to deal with data problems and analyse their big data. Moreover, others are still in the early stage of changing their structure and their willingness to use new business intelligence (BI) and big data applications (Geno Armstrong, 2019; Su, 2019).

Organisations are currently facing some hurdles to become more data-dependent. Many companies still fear big data as a buzzword and a common phrase. Moreover, some companies still operate with the principle of intuition and experience in making their daily decisions. As a result, data-driven decisions to increase the effectiveness of their performance led companies to compete to adopt this principle quickly. This competition created an opportunity to search for a new approach to start integrating big data and improving business management (Erraissi & Belangour, 2020).

It is not a big deal and difficult to imagine some data, but that will generate great sight and benefits. To obtain these benefits, information must be extracted and analysed from the vast amount of data to grow and forecast business and profits (Patgiri, 2018). This is critical in today's world. The large amount and complex data can be visualised and presented simply and effectively. The governmental, construction, services, and a wide list of sectors have started adopting web-based applications and used as an improvement to their businesses and work process. Recently, strong competition between companies to achieve speed and accuracy in applications showed the need to employ web-based methods and tools for development and to keep pace with the fast advancement in global business (Yahaya, Ibrahim, & Deraman, 2017). It has become difficult to move from raw data to extracting information with simple tools without any human intervention in the process. Web-based data analysis and visualisation tools will reduce human intervention in every step of the process, which allows all users to analyse and obtain information quickly and effectively. These applications will facilitate the process of analysing data into information after integrating and visualising it for use by all parties (Ali, Gupta, Nayak, & Lenka, 2016). For human consumption, graphical formats are the best method. The valuable data and information become easily comprehended and actionable. Common visualisation methods can be classified into diagrams, charts, and plots. The diagrams, charts, and plots consist of bars, lines, scatter, maps, and areas graphs (Kung, 2015).

Therefore, this study aims to draw insights into the specific areas of web-based big data visualisation research. The research objectives encompass: to identify and classify the data sources; to set up a plan for the web-based development process; and to map out the current solutions of big data integration visualisation research. Two types of data visualisation solutions are proposed that currently dominating the solutions of web-based applications such as the Microsoft Power BI and the Dynamic Web Systems, and assess these solutions to highlight the challenges and barriers to adopting these solutions. The integration and visualisation of big data will affect industries in general; the results from this research will constitute a motivation to create the awareness that we need to provide web-based solutions for data management. As a result, it will push companies to prepare to improve their capabilities in the use of web applications as well as stimulate talent and prepare to engage in the next blast of big data technology in the world.

2. IDENTIFICATION AND CLASSIFICATION OF DATA

Data management is needed to enhance the evaluation of efficiency. The development of the country depends on the advancement of the data of the industries (Yousif et al., 2021), the nature of the work process in the projects, which is dynamic, and depends on large data sharing between the various stakeholders to be gathered and processed (Gara, Zakaria, Aminudin, Adzar, & Yousif, 2021). At present, the data is stored in databases different from each other and that data is shaped in many structural forms, comprises structured and unstructured data stored in the clouds, computer, picture data and various project data stored in papers (Ajayi et al., 2019; Foote, 2019; Madanayake & Egbu, 2019).

During the lifecycle phases of the project, the data is generated from conception to completion. The stream of data, which is often large in size, is different in shapes and with a dynamic property. Extensive activities lead to a data stream, and multifaceted data reflects the characteristics of this stream (Aouad, Kagioglou, Cooper, Hinks, & Sexton, 1999; Bilal et al., 2016).

Further, the advancement of data processes through the popular employment of these data shall be the new limit of industry revolution and advancement. This is supported by Harenberg (2017), who mentioned real-time data utilisation as the new supporter of advancement in industries. The data that companies use for data analysis reflects the strong use of standard BI technologies in big data. Practically all types of data are on the rise. This offers further proof that companies are increasingly aware of their data's value and want to utilise it accordingly. In turn, this rapid data growth has left organisations to be overwhelmed with a large amount of data such that managers and potential users are drowning in data while thirsting for information (Bange, Grosser, & Janoschek, 2015).

3. DATA VISUALISATION PROCESS

Web-based visualisation solutions use engineering, scientific, and management essentials and methodical approaches to implement, establish, and preserve premium quality web applications successfully. Its purpose is to have a web-based application development control, minimise risks and maximise the quality, maintainability, and scalability of web applications (Yahaya et al., 2017). There are many limitations for practitioners in adopting the appropriate methodology and processes of web-based visualisation development. The web-based application development process requires many processes more than just a visual design and a user interface UI, but there are more complex steps and activities, and following systematic steps to reach the ideal integrated development such as planning, design, system selection, browser, protection, and various tests to ensure quality and security and performance evaluation. The development process requires regular maintenance and continuous updates simultaneously with the introduction of new jobs and with the continued growth of the use of web applications (Li et al., 2018).

The development process is divided into sequential steps. One step is taken; after the requirements are collected, analysed, and designed for that step a prototype is implemented and it is given to the customer for the evaluation. According to the feedback, the developer does some modifications. If that prototype is acceptable for customer, developer can pass to the second step. This is done until an acceptable system is delivered (Woldesenbet, Jeong, & Park, 2016). Since the development process is divided into sequential steps, each step starts as soon as the previous one is finished, and the full cycle leads to a prototype, this cycle provides the flexibility to redesign or improve one of the steps, if necessary (Taleb, Dssouli, & Serhani, 2015). Otherwise, it would be difficult to make some modifications and uncover important issues early before problems or faulty assumptions can lead to disaster after implementing the whole project. Besides, it is an efficient modal for the customer too. The client's knowledge of the project grows as the project grows so that they can interface effectively with management (Hussien, Sulaiman, & Shamsuddin, 2016), this whole process can be shown in Fig. 9.1.

4. DATA VISUALISATION SOLUTIONS

Interactive and smart visualisation technologies are recent technologies; one of their advantages is that they can deal with user interventions in a fast time and without a stated effort. One of the advantages of the power of these advanced technologies is that they can quickly discover important information in the data and turn them into valuable assets that will be used as a result of the decision-making processes (Carlisle, 2018; Patgiri, 2018).

Big data has many different types of sources, ranging from physical sources such as sensors, the Internet of things, and engineering equipment to social types and transactions; this unique diversity gives it the character of anarchy, inaccuracy, and disorganisation. The large size, speed, and diversity of flow are a

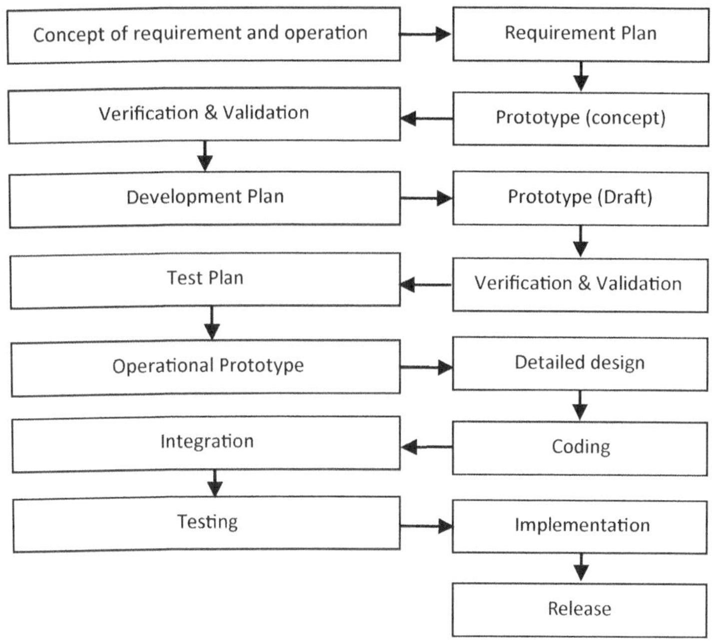

Fig. 9.1. Data Visualisation Process.

huge challenge for users. The magnitude of this data is similar to something like 'ocean to swimmer'. Procedures and regulations must be followed in the process of searching for data and the tools of integration and visualisation to prevent losing control of the process of merging data from its various sources together to reveal the information hidden inside the big and chaotic data. In this chapter, we talked about another vital model 'V', which is visualisation. The visualisation with its various tools aims to display and analyse data and provide a large and clear picture to help users formulate critical questions and then ask exploratory and discreet answers (Kung, 2015).

Due to the increasing volume and types of big data, managing and tracking of web systems are becoming increasingly essential. It led to the need to record and analyse the activities of individual and shared networks and devices. Based on Wagner et al. (2015), the analysis and visualisation of data nowadays require the use of new and innovative methods and technologies, as the data at present face an unprecedented large increase due to technological advancement and therefore it leads us to analyse the growing volume of data resulting from these technologies, and this is a time-consuming process. These innovative solutions for data visualisation and analysis will contribute to improving the analysis process concerning disclosure, comparison, and summary of data samples. To this regard, we had analysed the available, common, powerful, and effective visualisation solutions in the market and found two options that suit for most of the industries and proven their success in developing a web-based application as follows.

4.1. Microsoft Power BI

The Microsoft Power BI is one of the latest data analytics and visualisation tools; it is a user-friendly and easy tool with dashboard, reports, and variety datasets. It provides many visualisation types to deliver interactive reports and geo-map visualisation. Power BI is a software developed by Microsoft that utilised for analysing and visualising data from various and varied types of data. It's a simple application especially for data and business analysts. Therefore, it's appropriate for the data visualisation process (Ferrari & Russo, 2016).

Power BI contains a few panels that each has a specific function such as data source option, visualisation option, and fields list. Once the data had been loaded into the Power BI field list, the data analyst can choose any visualisation types such as bar and column chart, pie chart, line chart, geographical maps, or metrics to produce data visualisation based on the objective of reports (Lachev & Price, 2018). Fig. 9.2 (a) displays the Power BI visualisation application that we developed to monitor the green highway performance in Malaysia. This application monitors real-time data management for highway agencies.

Microsoft has produced this Power BI programme, which is a modern and effective application to analyse and visualise data, easy to use, and intelligible by users. The programme can be easily obtained from Microsoft's online platform. One of the advantages of this programme is that it gives freedom to explore and visualise various data analysis methods using the features available in it, and it allows the creation and sharing of reports online with other users easily (Microsoft, 2020). This programme has many features that include a waterfall, matrix, donut, and area charts. Also, it supports many formatting for their charts like setting colours, titles, and legends. It must be mentioning the sources support that include SweetIQ, Zendesk, GitHub, and Twilio. Finally, this programme can link to a wide range of databases like SQL Server, MySQL, and SQLite.

Power BI enables users to view, coordinate, and modify information and visualisations through a web browser and the software installed on a computer (Power BI Desktop). Another benefit that supports active participation and cooperation is the ability to support groups and allow the team to monitor reports and modify data easily. It must be mentioned that the programme can be linked with another programme produced by Microsoft, which is Excel, where it is possible to import and transfer data and reports to and from the two programmes easily, and reports and information can be viewed through Excel Online (Gowthami & Kumar, 2017; Negru, 2018).

4.2. Dynamic Web System

A web-based application is an application that uses a website as the visualisation interface. Users access the application from any computer or smartphone connected to the Internet using a standard browser. The browser is one of the essential applications available on the OS on mobiles and computers. To run a web-based application, the client machine needs an internet connection and a web browser, which are available for different operating systems. The browser competition has begun over having more HTML capabilities and displaying unique

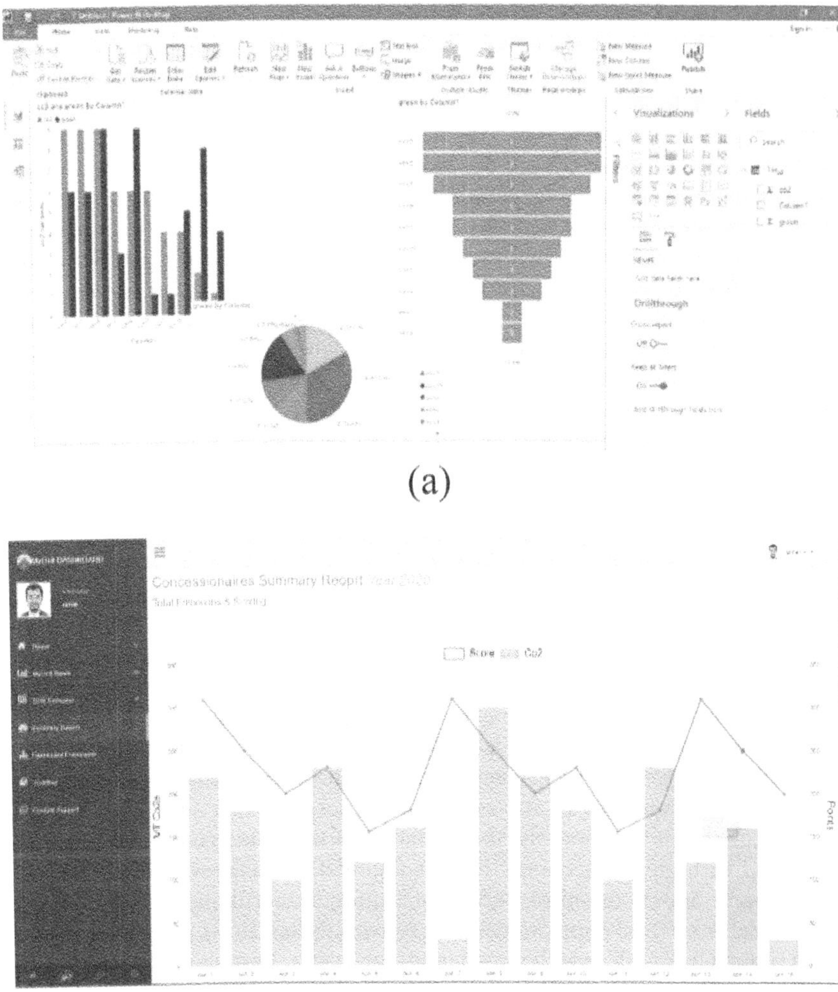

(a)

(b)

Fig. 9.2. (a) Data Visualisation using Power BI for Green Highway Performance Monitoring; (b) Web-based Application for Green Highway Performance Monitoring.

features. But after HTML5 was invented, a variety of premium browsers featured and integrated for display such as Firefox, Microsoft Edge, Google Chrome, and Opera. HTML5 is more than just a series of plane HTML elements. It also can control how it is displayed. This has made it possible to create unique and special websites that appear identically in all modern browsers (Himschoot, 2019).

One advantage of web-based application is that application's updates are performed in the server. By that, users will benefit the updates immediately and will not waste their time downloading/installing the applications. However, the user who wants to work on the Excel application must pay an additional cost to purchase Microsoft Office applications. On the other hand, using web-based applications may be less expensive and more flexible to modify as it requires the user to have only a web browser and an internet connection.

To develop a dynamic website, the designer needs to use four major components that work together (Rosen & Shklar, 2009). They are a web server, databases, server-side script, and operating systems. When the user tries to access a web page, the following steps are performed: First, a client computer calls a page from the web server via www; second, the web server sends the client the title of the relevant page; third, if the page that client wanted is a dynamic page, web server interprets dynamic page and generates HTML pages; fourth, an HTML page that generated from a dynamic page is sent to the client by a web server; fifth, client shows the HTML page on the screen that reaches it. The combination of the components previously mentioned is called a solution stack (Taivalsaari, Mikkonen, Pautasso, & Systä, 2017).

Multitechnologies used to implement different models: use HTML and Cascading Style Sheets (CSS) to build up basic static UI; use JavaScript and jQuery to archive the processing data dynamically; and use Hypertext Preprocessor PHP language to control models' logical function and MySQL database. The integration of these powerful technologies helps development more efficiently (Xu, 2017).

PHP is a reliable and efficient programming language to build web systems. It is implemented on the server and is included in the HTML language. It gained the title of the most popular language in the internet industry today because of the clarity of design, its wonderfully organised units, and its integration of various technologies. To implement, it must be included with HTML files and integrated with them. It can also execute compiler code that enables to achieve security encryption and optimise the operation of the code to make the code run faster and with greater accuracy. PHP is a global language with many unique features, and one of the most important feature is that it supports almost all types of databases and popular operating systems (Sklar, 2016). It is used to build highly interactive and appealing dynamic web pages. Distinguished users such as Harvard University and the prominent social networking site Facebook are using it, and this is a clear evidence for its popularity, credibility, and strength (Han & Golparvar-Fard, 2017). Data visualisation requires high-interactive abilities for users. PHP's advantages will make development more efficient and easier to maintain.

A PHP is an efficient alternative to competitors such as ASP.NET and JSP. PHP is an expert in most of the aspects; also it's used on the WAMP platform (Windows, Apache, PHP, MySQL). This wonderful combination of programmes together represents an economic value (lowest development and maintenance cost to other competitors), it has a quick database response time, is completely steady, and is a better option for the state of many databases read and write process (Ezeonwumelu, Eunice, & Ezenugu, 2017). PHP is more than just a programming language, but it is an integrated development environment for the graphical interface. Moreover, PHP is characterised by its ease of use according to the professional programmers and can create websites that serve as user interfaces, can collect inputs, and present the output results in a coordinated and programmed manner ideally (Tatroe & MacIntyre, 2020).

HTML is the predominant mark-up language for web pages. It provides a means to create structure documents by denoting structural semantic for text such as headings, paragraphs, lists, etc. It can be used to develop interactive models in which pictures and objects are embedded. The CSS language is used to format the appearance of all pages and contents. It is the encoding scheme used to format a web document. A mark-up language is utilised to structure and organise text, documents, and multimedia, and to create hyperlinks between them. With CSS, the website will be friendlier to users (Alawar & Naser, 2017).

In addition to the JS as an object-oriented language for programming, it is used to develop a web application. JS helps to develop dynamic interactive websites. The emergence of JS enables web pages and users to achieve a real-time, dynamic, interactive relationship so that pages contain more active elements and more exciting contents (Brown, 2019).

Finally, MySQL is a database that is widely used when creating a system database, as there is a need for a security system to collect, organise, and retrieve data on time, quickly and effectively. MySQL is one of the most famous open-source database systems characterised by the speed and security of information and accuracy process. MySQL is a relational database management system that has the advantage of being able to store data in separate tables instead of accumulating data in a large storage room (Ohyver, Moniaga, Sungkawa, Subagyo, & Chandra, 2019).

The above selection reference reflects the development in recent years of both conceptual and practical applications of the web-based development for the industry. Fig. 9.2 (b) displays the dynamic website that we developed to monitor and manage the green highway real-time performance in Malaysia using a dynamic web system; it is developed using HTML, CSS, JS, PHP on the WAMP Platform.

5. ASSESSMENT OF VISUALISATIONS SOLUTIONS

Data visualisation is now a concrete way to use valuable data assets to create new revenue channels. This is true for telecommunication and media companies, retailers, financial institutions, communication service providers, and other industries as well. The main question for these companies is how to conform to privacy issues and regulations while making money with all that data. One of the major issues while developing a web-based system is to provide an attractive and easy-to-use interface to users. It is known that appearance is important. It can't be overpassed the importance of the first impact. As a result, selecting the way of design and using colours and pictures are important. A different user might have different preferences about which web browser to use. Web developers need to ensure that a web page will have the same appearance in any web browser, regardless of distinct features present in each browser.

Both solutions proposed are available to all. The dynamic web system from its name is dynamic (open system), means the developer can improve the programme and extend its features to the no limits. In contrast, Microsoft Power BI has limited functionality software (closed system); the developer can use it with limited abilities to innovation.

Furthermore, the dynamic web system has more popularity, availability, and ease of reach; globally these features are major aspects of its prosperity. Reliability, flexibility, functionality, efficiency, and testability need to be taken into consideration for better achievement by the utilisation of the dynamic web systems. To choose one of these solutions is the first and critical decision to be made to develop a web-based visualisation application. The selection decision will affect its prosperity and success. Therefore, the developer must review the sources and features and compare the solutions before beginning to develop the web-based application. Here, we made this comparison to clarify the pictures and facilitate the correct and appropriate solution; the comparison between both solutions is shown in Table 9.1. Each of these solutions is a viable choice, and each carries its own set of pros and cons. It is difficult to say which one is better, so the company needs will determine the one to be used.

As mention in Table 9.1, we have two options for the web server; Internet Information Services (IIS) is tightly integrated with the Windows operating system and is only available on that platform. Meanwhile, Apache is open source and is available on both the Linux and Windows platforms. Apache is more secure than IIS; it does not cause security problems because it does not install any Apache modules. On the other hand, when using Windows with IIS, it will install an external dynamic-link library (DLL) files in addition to the FrontPage Server Extensions. IIS also allows system-wide access; as a result, the user with permission can access, modify, and remove any file in the system. On the other hand, the Apache elements when installed will act as a non-privileged user, so in the event of a buffer overflow, the damage is minor (Chitra & Satapathy, 2017). A comparison of IIS and Apache can be seen in Table 9.1.

When creating web sites generally two popular languages are selected. One of them is ASP and the other is PHP. The ASP language works with Windows as OS and IIS as a server, which means an extra cost. On the other hand, PHP works with any OS and Apache server with MySQL database which is open source and free. Some plug-ins and libraries are free for PHP but paid for ASP. PHP code runs in its own memory space; on the other hand, ASP is built on COM-based architecture, which is an overhead for the server (Sönmez, Bayat, Altuğlu, & Duru, 2015). A comparison of ASP and PHP can be seen in Table 9.1.

Database management is essential to enhance the efficiency of data controlling. There are many types of data and it has wide formats and features that need to be stored in different shapes in different databases. The most common and securable options are MySQL and SQL Server. MySQL has the ability and possibility to run on any OS and platform (Arleo, Didimo, Liotta, & Montecchiani, 2017). Meanwhile, SQL Server runs only on Windows-based platforms (Jeong et al., 2016). It is difficult to compare SQL Server and MySQL about their performance. Both of them nearly show the same performance. Comparison of SQL

Table 9.1. Comparison of Visualisation Solutions, Servers, Languages, and Databases.

	Comparison of Visualisation Solutions	
	Dynamic Web System	**Power BI**
Open Source	Yes	NO
Cost	Very Low	High
Security	High Secure	Secure for Pro-version
Storage	Unlimited	1GB for the free version and more for Pro-version
Dealing Big data	Easy	Hard
Sharing to the outside of the domain	Can	Cannot
Integrating	Easily integrating with other software	Limited and small integration
Flexibility	Flexible user interface and live editing	Limited flexibility and non-editable reports
Content	Flexible adding and manipulation of Text, image, table, figure, and buttons	Restricted addition
Social Connecting	Can send mail, notification, forms, and statistics to many users	Can share alerts and email only to the developer only
	Comparison of Web Servers	
	IIS	**Apache**
Open Source	No	Yes
Software Price	Free	Free
Security	Weak	Strong
Platform	Windows	Any
	Comparison of Server-Side Languages	
	PHP	**ASP**
Open Source	Yes	No
Software Price	Free	Free
Platform Price	Free	$$$
Speed	Strong	Weak
Platform	Any	Win32 (ISS only)
	Comparison of Databases	
	SQL Server	**MySQL**
Open Source	No	Yes
Free	No	Yes
Performance	Good	Good
Platform	Windows-Based Platforms	Any
Security and Reliability	Mid	High

Server and MySQL can be seen from Table 9.1. Today MySQL is one of the most popular databases used by many. It is characterised by its speed and ease of use with usability for small and large applications (Agrawal & Gupta, 2014). For a web-based system, we need to save a huge data and information into the database. MySQL's characteristics make system process data efficiently.

The dynamic web system is developed on different platforms, these platforms consist of key elements which are the operating system, web server, database, and programming languages. There are four types of platforms in use today which are WISA, LAMP, WIMP and WAMP. According to the features that are explained for each element of the solutions stack, a comparison table has been created as seen from Table 9.2.

The last aspect of the assessment discusses the usual challenges and barriers that still exist in sharing data between different organisations and consolidating internal and external data. Data integration applied to data visualisation initiatives raises a whole new set of issues:

- How to share data while keeping control of it?
- How to ensure that security and privacy requirements are clearly defined and followed?
- How to manage the appropriately granular level of access rights?
- How to ensure that the governance framework and tools can effectively define what is and is not acceptable, control how data is shared and monitor how it is used?
- How to speed up data integration to allow near-real-time decision-making?

Those challenges call for us to rethink our existing data integration paradigms and toolsets. Analyses and visualising big data provide a large volume of knowledge that can be used in many ways for the betterment of individual, society, nation, and even the world. Nowadays there is a shift in terms of the participation and openness of people's ideas to others in the world. As a result, there are risks of misusing these ideas and information as the people who use them bear the responsibility to protect the data and prevent any misuse of it. To visualise the big data is a big risk, the most important of which is related to security and privacy, and we can divide it into four major elements and subelements, infrastructure (secure structure, best process), privacy (maintaining the privacy of data mining, analyses, access control, cryptography), data management (secure data storage, granular audit, data provenance), and integrity (security and accuracy control, verification, and liquidation of operations).

Table 9.2. Comparison between the Platforms.

	Development Platforms			
	Operating System	**WEB Server**	**Database**	**Server-side Script**
WISA	Windows	IIS	SQL Server	ASP
LAMP	Linux	Apache	MySQL	PHP
WIMP	Windows	IIS	MySQL	PHP
WAMP	Windows	Apache	MySQL	PHP
	Comparison between the Platforms			
	LAMP	**WISA**	**WIMP**	**WAMP**
Open Source	Yes	NO	Just PHP and MySQL	yes
Cost	Very Low	Very High	High	Very Low
Security	High Secure	Secure	Secure	High Secure

6. CONCLUSION

Nowadays big data represents an important player and a big wave in the field of data management, and it is a very broad wave that must be studied and taken into consideration given its importance. Big data is a large data ocean that is difficult to process, analyse, store, and manage to reach the desired benefit. This data is extensively present not only in the field of digital computing but also in various fields of science and engineering of all kinds, economics, government, environment, and society. There are many types of processing mechanisms to handle big data efficiently and effectively. These processing mechanisms are utilised based on their features and characteristics. Moreover, different types of storage drivers also appear, for example, file systems and object storage systems. As a consequence, Big Data Analytics and visualisations tools are needed.

Web-based applications have provided a platform for monitoring from manual to web-based, to obtain the information required to evaluate the process or projects, and to help in speeding and smarter important decision-making that improves the organisation's performance in many aspects. This innovation is making the management and monitoring process more user-friendly and efficiency, reduce data complexity, easy data collaboration, and data integrity.

The two solutions (Microsoft Power BI and the Dynamic Web System) that have been presented have proven their effectiveness, usability, and functionality to be widespread because such technologies have met the company's requirements in terms of cost, security, support, maintenance, and interactive interface. The adoption and implementation of these solutions have to go through a methodological process to assure the success of the developed web-based system. The visualisation software has several beneficial characteristics such as high-performance estimation and multidimensional visualisation of big data.

The output results from the visualisation will help the organisation to strengthen the big data implementation to achieve their objectives (confidentiality, integrity, and availability). While data visualisation can display interactive performance and worthy reports that would help the management to fully understand big data performance and impact in the organisation.

ACKNOWLEDGEMENTS

The authors would like to thank the participants, the anonymous reviewers, the Editors, and Universiti Teknologi Malaysia for supporting with financial grant, Cost Centre No: Q.J130000.2551.21H52 to conduct the research.

REFERENCES

Agrawal, S., & Gupta, R. D. (2014). Development and comparison of open source based Web GIS Frameworks on WAMP and Apache Tomcat Web Servers. *The International Archives of Photogrammetry, Remote Sensing and Spatial Information Sciences*, *40*(4), 1.

Ajayi, A., Oyedele, L., Delgado, J. M. D., Akanbi, L., Bilal, M., Akinade, O., & Olawale, O. (2019). Big data platform for health and safety accident prediction. *World Journal of Science, Technology and Sustainable Development*, *16*(1), 2–21. https://doi.org/10.1108/WJSTSD-05-2018-0042.

Alawar, M. W., & Abu Naser, S. S. (2017). CSS-Tutor: An intelligent tutoring system for CSS and HTML. *International Journal of Academic Research and Development*, *2*(1), 94-98. Retrieved from https://hal.archives-ouvertes.fr/hal-01496882

Ali, S. M., Gupta, N., Nayak, G. K., & Lenka, R. K. (2016). Big data visualization: Tools and challenges. Paper presented at the 2016 2nd international conference on contemporary computing and informatics (IC3I).

Aouad, G., Kagioglou, M., Cooper, R., Hinks, J., & Sexton, M. (1999). Technology management of IT in construction: a driver or an enabler? *Logistics Information Management*, *12*(1/2), 130–137.

Arleo, A., Didimo, W., Liotta, G., & Montecchiani, F. (2017). Large graph visualizations using a distributed computing platform. *Information Sciences*, *381*, 124–141. Germany: Würzburg. Retrieved from http://barc-research.com/research/big-data-use-cases-2015

Bange, C., Grosser, T., & Janoschek, N. (2015). *Big data use cases: Getting real on data monetization.* Würzburg: Business Application Research Center (BARC).

Bilal, M., Oyedele, L. O., Qadir, J., Munir, K., Ajayi, S. O., Akinade, O. O., … Pasha, M. (2016). Big Data in the construction industry: A review of present status, opportunities, and future trends. *Advanced Engineering Informatics*, *30*(3), 500–521.

Brown, E. (2019). *Web development with node and express: Leveraging the JavaScript stack*. California, CA: O'Reilly Media.

Carlisle, S. (2018). Software: Tableau and Microsoft Power BI. *Technology|Architecture+ Design*, *2*(2), 256–259.

Chitra, L. P., & Satapathy, R. (2017). Performance comparison and evaluation of Node. js and traditional web server (IIS). Paper presented at the 2017 international conference on algorithms, methodology, models and applications in emerging technologies (ICAMMAET).

Erraissi, A., & Belangour, A. (2020). An approach based on model driven engineering for big data visualization in different visual modes. *International Journal of Scientific & Technology Research*, *9*(1), 198–206.

Ezeonwumelu, A. N., Eunice, A. B., & Ezenugu, I. A. (2017). Development of sales and inventory workflow management information system web portal for Petrospan Integrated Services, Eket, Akwa Ibom State, Nigeria. *Mathematical and Software Engineering*, *3*(1), 57–66.

Ferrari, A., & Russo, M. (2016). *Introducing Microsoft Power BI*. Redmond, Wash.: Microsoft Press.

Foote, K. D. (2019). Big data integration, the fundamentals of data integration. Retrieved from https://www.dataversity.net/the-fundamentals-of-data-integration/

Gara, J. A., Zakaria, R. B., Aminudin, E., Adzar, J. A., & Yousif, O. S. (2021). The Development of Real-Time Integrated Dashboard: An Overview for Road Construction Work Progress Monitoring. *Journal of Hunan University Natural Sciences*, *48*(5). Retrieved from https://johuns.net/index.php/journal/article/view/590.html

Geno Armstrong, C. G., & Max, K. (2019). Future-ready index, global construction survey 2019. Retrieved from https://home.kpmg/xx/en/home/insights/2019/04/global-construction-survey-future-ready.html

Gowthami, K., & Kumar, M. P. (2017). Study on business intelligence tools for enterprise dashboard development. *International Research Journal of Engineering and Technology*, *4*(4), 2987–2992.

Han, K. K., & Golparvar-Fard, M. (2017). Potential of big visual data and building information modeling for construction performance analytics: An exploratory study. *Automation in Construction*, *73*, 184–198.

Harenberg, M. (2017). 5 ways to boost construction productivity, Retrieved from https://www.planradar.com/construction-productivity/.

Himschoot, P. (2019). *Blazor revealed: Building web applications in. NET*. Berkeley, CA: Apress. https://doi.org/10.1007/978-1-4842-4343-5_1.

Hussien, N. S., Sulaiman, S., & Shamsuddin, S. M. (2016). Management system prototype for intelligent mobile cloud computing for big data. *Jurnal Teknologi*, *78*(12-2), 19–28.

Jeong, S., Zhang, Y., O'Connor, S., Lynch, J. P., Sohn, H., & Law, K. H. (2016). A NoSQL data management infrastructure for bridge monitoring. *Smart Structures and Systems*, *17*(4), 669–690.

Kung, S.-Y. (2015). Visualization of big data. Paper presented at the 2015 IEEE 14th international conference on cognitive informatics & cognitive computing (ICCI* CC).

Lachev, T., & Price, E. (2018). *Applied Microsoft Power BI: Bring your data to life!* Atlanta, GA: Prologika Press.

Li, D., Mei, H., Shen, Y., Su, S., Zhang, W., Wang, J., … Chen, W. (2018). ECharts: A declarative framework for rapid construction of web-based visualization. *Visual Informatics*, *2*(2), 136–146.

Madanayake, U. H., & Egbu, C. (2019). Critical analysis for big data studies in construction: Significant gaps in knowledge. Built Environment Project and Asset Management, *9*(4), 530–547. doi:10.1108/BEPAM-04-2018-0074.

Microsoft. (2020). Microsoft Power BI (Business Intelligence). Retrieved from https://powerbi.microsoft.com/.

Negru, V. (2018). Power BI: Effective data aggregation. *Quaestus*, *13*, 146–152.

Ohyver, M., Moniaga, J. V., Sungkawa, I., Subagyo, B. E., & Chandra, I. A. (2019). The comparison firebase realtime database and MySQL database performance using Wilcoxon signed-rank test. *Procedia Computer Science*, *157*, 396–405.

Patgiri, R. (2018). Taxonomy of big data: A survey. arXiv preprint arXiv:1808.08474.

Rosen, L., & Shklar, L. (2009). *Web application architecture: Principles, protocol and practices*. West Sussex: John Wiley & Sons Ltd.

Sklar, D. (2016). *Learning PHP: A gentle introduction to the web's most popular language*. Sebastopol, CA: O'Reilly Media, Inc.

Sönmez, Y., Bayat, O., Altuğlu, T. B., & Duru, A. D. (2015). Performance comparison of php-asp web applications via database queries. Paper presented at the proceedings of the international conference on engineering & MIS 2015.

Storey, V., & Song. (2017). Big data technologies and management: What conceptual modeling can do. *Data and Knowledge Engineering*, *108*, 50–67.

Su, Li-kai. (2019). A real-time futures information processing strategy based on multi-level cache and multi-threading cooperation. International Conference on Power, Energy, Environment and Material Science (PEEMS 22-23 Dec 2019), Sanya, China

Taivalsaari, A., Mikkonen, T., Pautasso, C., & Systä, K. (2017). Comparing the Built-In Application Architecture Models in the Web Browser. IEEE International Conference on Software Architecture (ICSA), (3-7 April 2017), 51-54, doi: 10.1109/ICSA.2017.23.

Taleb, I., Dssouli, R., & Serhani, M. A. (2015). Big data pre-processing: A quality framework. Paper presented at the 2015 IEEE international congress on big data.

Tatroe, K., & MacIntyre, P. (2020). *Programming PHP: Creating dynamic web pages*. Sebastopol, CA: O'Reilly Media, Inc.

Wagner, M., Fischer, F., Luh, R., Haberson, A., Rind, A., Keim, D. A., & Aigner, W. (2015). A survey of visualization systems for malware analysis. Paper presented at the eurographics conference on visualization (EuroVis).

Woldesenbet, A., Jeong, H. D., & Park, H. (2016). Framework for integrating and assessing highway infrastructure data. *Journal of Management in Engineering*, *32*(1), 04015028.

Xu, H. (2017). *Location based educational web system design and implementation*. Kent, OH: Kent State University.

Yahaya, J. H., Ibrahim, A. A., & Deraman, A. (2017). Software process model for dynamic website development towards quality product. *Journal of Telecommunication, Electronic and Computer Engineering (JTEC)*, *9*(3–3), 39–44.

Yousif, O. S., Zakaria, R. B., Aminudin, E., Yahya, K., Mohd Sam, A. R., Singaram, L., . . . Shamsuddin, S. M. (2021). Review of Big Data Integration in Construction Industry Digitalization. *Frontiers in Built Environment*, *7*(159). doi:10.3389/fbuil.2021.770496

PART B

IMPACT AND ASSESSMENT

CHAPTER 10

CREATING THE SUSTAINABILITY ENVIRONMENT FOR STUDENTS WELL-BEING: THE AWARENESS LEVEL OF VICTIMS AFTER FIRE INCIDENT IN PRIVATE ISLAMIC SCHOOL

Norehan Norlida Mohd Noor, Nadira Ahzahar, Intan Bayani Bin Zakaria, Siti Zubaidah Binti Hashim and Norazura Mizal Azzmi

ABSTRACT

Almost every year the nation was shocked by the fire incident at school and hostel. The Fire and Rescue Department of Malaysia (2020) recorded 216 fires that have occurred at the private Islamic religious schools from 2015 until 2019, where several fires have killed many students, such as accidents in 1985, 1998, 2013, 2014 and 2017. As a result, the public began questioning the level of awareness among the school administrators. Addressing these issues, a survey has been conducted on the private Islamic religious schools that had experienced fire incidents in order to identify the awareness level among the administrators and students and to investigate whether aspects of compliance with fire safety procedures are enhanced. Four groups of respondents were selected, in which the Department of Fire and Rescue acts as a focus group.

Sustainability Management Strategies and Impact in Developing Countries
Community, Environment and Disaster Risk Management, Volume 26, 121–133

Published under exclusive licence by Emerald Publishing Limited
ISSN: 2040-7262/doi:10.1108/S2040-726220220000026010

The other three groups are the victims who have faced the fire itself in their respective schools. The findings highlighted that the awareness level among victims towards the fire prevention practices is very low. Evidence has revealed there is no periodic supervision towards fire safety equipment, and only 35% comply with the standard procedure. Experts suggest sustainable school building should introduce to meet the criteria in performance-based fire management solutions. This reflects the fact that building continuity and fire safety can be complementary, not contradictory, if the two disciplines engage in meaningful dialogue at the beginning of the design process.

Keywords: Fire incident; private Islamic school; awareness; fire victim; fire prevention practices; sustainable school building

1. INTRODUCTION

Extreme hot climate, attitude, and knowledge of fire safety resulted in a lot of consequences in Malaysia. Not to mention, many fire incidents involve premises that house children, teenagers, and the elderly recently. According to McNamee et al. (2019), the world today is facing hard challenges in terms of access to global resources, due to the increasing and diversifying of population, culture, and climate change. Therefore, the main agenda of the International Association of Fire Safety Science 2030 (IAFSS) (McNamee et al., 2019) put a major target on the current and outlook on the growing fire problem as an issue that urgently needs to be addressed. The IAFSS (McNamee et al., 2019) said the important area that is currently often missing in discussions of societal grand challenges is the impact of fire on health, safety, climate, community resilience, and the economy. During a fire event, building materials are damaged, the property is lost, water is wasted, and pollutants are released into the environment through the air and water.

Lambie, Best, Tran, Ioane, and Sherperd (2015) recorded about 1,240,000 fire cases occurred in the United States in 2013, causing 15,925 injuries and 3,240 deaths. Meanwhile, in New Zealand, fire incidents achieved 70,907 cases between year 2012 and 2013 (Lambie et al., 2015) and in the same year, Britain attended 192,600 fire incidents (New Zealand Fire Service Annual Report, 2013). Most of these fire incidents have happened in residential locations. Statement by The World Health Organisation (WHO) revealed 180,000 global burn deaths annually. Sadly, most of these cases are from the circle of low- and middle-income countries (Ahrens, 2013). Lambie et al. (2015) also disclose the most fire victims are adolescents and children.

In a similar key area, this study is carried out concerning fire accidents that occurred in the private Islamic secondary schools, where most of the victims are students. In addition, this study also aims to explore the importance of sustainable elements that can be applied in the process of secondary school hostel development, which is one of the measures to minimise fires. Flynn (2010) claims that the most vulnerable groups to fire injuries are adolescents in the age range of

18–24 years. This age group is also 50% more likely to be injured in a cooking incident than the public. In other views, the United States Fire Administration (2010) highlighted 13.7% of all fire injuries, and 108.6 fire injuries per million are those aged between 15 and 24 years, between 2000 and 2011. Again, within the same period (2000–2011), adolescents and children aged between 15 and 25 years also accounted for 5.2% of fire deaths and 8.4 fire deaths per million (United States Fire Administration, 2010). Flynn (2010) states although these statistics maybe 'not be too high' but it still shows clear evidence that groups within this age range are highly vulnerable to fire risk. Indeed, many materials published on fire safety but very few have conducted studies on respondents among this adolescent age and had to experience fire incidents. To cultivate awareness and knowledge, this research focuses on school respondents, consisting of students who stay in a hostel and another group are teachers and office staff in a private Islamic school.

2. THE GROWTH OF THE ISLAMIC PRIVATE SCHOOLS IN MALAYSIA

As an alternative to a vernacular school known as a national school, Malaysia introduced a formal Islamic education beginning in 1966 (Deviyati, 2016; Murihah, Abdul-Hafiz, Arieff-Salleh, & Mohd-Faeez, 2015). This independent school or known as private Islamic religious schools adopted the national curriculum, but a major focus on religious studies (Deviyati, 2016; Nordin, 2015). The notable majoring are the Quran studies and Tahfiz, and Qiraat Studies (Nordin, 2015; Wan-Muhammad, 2003). The formal Islamic schools are divided into two categories, managed by the Government or private parties. While Azmil (2018) reported that since 1956, many of the traditional Islamic schools or 'sekolah pondok' have consistently changed their curriculum as directed by the government, as a step to make their institutions formal schools in Islamic studies. Moreover, this action is also as following the changes and demands of modern society, as well as the opportunity to apply for government funds.

Presently, the formal Islamic education in Malaysia can opt in four options (Azmil, 2017; Deviyati, 2016); three types are national religious schools which are mostly (i) national religious secondary school; state Religious schools that can be divided into (ii) primary; (iii) secondary; and (iv) private Islamic religious schools. The Islamic schools managed by Federal Government (National) are directly under the jurisdiction of the Ministry of Education (MOE) while state religious schools fall under the purview of State agencies (Deviyati, 2016). On the other hand, the private Islamic schools differ in terms of management, skills, sources of funding, and maybe, curriculum. These schools are owned and governed by independent management and only receive partial funding from the Government together with private donations, as well as funded by student fees.

By the 1970s, the highly demanded by the public had spurred the rapid growth of Islamic private schools (Solahuddin, 2015; Wan-Muhammad, 2003). This demand is due to the national educational reforms that took place from 1970 to the 1980s (Rosnani, 1994). Unfortunately, this phenomenon led to the new construction of classrooms, dormitories, and other facilities that do not comply with the defined specifications or ignoring the standard operating procedure. This situation is associated with poor and unstable financial resources to implement the effort adequately. Many schools failed to provide the building with learning facilities and satisfactory study areas (Rosnani, 2004). This statement is supported by Azmil (2018) who claimed most of these schools had poor infrastructure, old building structures, and obsolete facilities. Rosnani (1994) claimed the movement of transformation from traditional Islamic school (or popular as 'Pondok' school) to formal Islamic curriculum is evolved after the Independence. However, it is not in line with efforts to upgrade all available facilities. Due to neglecting the rules, or loose regulation, most private Islamic schools do not have a complete package or insufficient precautions against the safety and health of their students (Annual Report of Fire and Rescue Department of Malaysia, 2018). This scenario contributed to the fire incident for decades in private Islamic schools. The Fire and Rescue Department of Malaysia (2018) disclosed fire incidents become more frequent between 2015 and 2017 recorded 211 cases. Table 10.1 shows the data that has been acknowledged by the Department of Fire and Rescue Malaysia shown a list of serious fire cases that had occurred at the private Islamic schools, from 1989 to 2020.

In 1989, a fire case in northern Peninsular was a shocked society with 27 students dead in the fire, including destroying eight hostels. Once again, in 1998, three students are fatal due to a fire in the dormitory. Then, 2007 witnessed three cases of fire, followed by 2010 with two cases resulting in death. From 2012 to 2017, cases of fire in private Islamic schools are increasing every year, involving the loss of property, school premises, and even injuries. In fact, there is a school that has lost almost 70% of its building in 2015. In addition, in 2016 cases increased to six, whereas 10 cases occurred in 2017 including a case that saddens the public involving 23 student deaths. There have also been cases where the same school suffered two fire incidents in the same year.

2.1. Fire Safety System in School

Kobes, Helsloot, deVries and Post (2010) express that the most important aspect in building safety is being able to escape during a fire incident. They also claimed in many fire incidents have shown that a safe escape from a burning structure is not always possible for everyone. Groner (2016) argues that building fire emergencies are a major threat to the safety of its occupants. The most crucial aspect of a building's safety in the face of fire is the possibility of safe escape. An important precondition is that its fire safety facilities enable independent and adequate fire response by the building's occupants. Ebenehi et al. (2017) define fire safety as regular practices intended to decrease the destruction caused by fire. While the term fire safety refers to fire prevention, limiting the spread of fire and smoke, extinguishing a fire and the chance of a quick and safe exit, which intended to decrease the destruction caused by fire (Kobes et al., 2010). Fire safety policies reflect how people think about this issue in both societies at large and the political arena.

Table 10.1. Chronology of Fire Cases That Have Occurred in Private Islamic Schools in Malaysia.

Year	No. of Cases	Cases	Location	Severe Loss/Damaged, Death and Injury Due to Fires at Private Islamic School
1989	1	8 Blocks hostel	Kedah	27 Students died
1996	1	1 Block of female hostel	Kedah	
1998	1	2 Block hostel	Kedah	3 Students died
2006	1	1 Block of female hostel	Kelantan	
2007	3	1 Block school building	Pahang	
		40 Nos. of classroom	Kedah	Totally burnt
		Hostel building for 96 students	Kelantan	96 Rooms severe damaged
2009	1	1 Block two-storey school building	Sabah	
2010	2	The oldest religious school – 3 block educational	Kelantan	
		1 Block classroom	Selangor	1 Student died
2011	1	1 Block two-storey school building	Kedah	
2012	2	1 Block hostel – three times facing fire (1996, 2005, 2012)	Kedah	
		Second Floor of double storey school building	Terengganu	
2013	2	Hostel building	Kedah	1 Students died and two injured
		Hostel building	Sabah	
2014	1	Hostel and classroom buildings	Pahang	
2015	5	Administration building and food store	Terengganu	1 Injured
		Hostel building	Selangor	
		Hostel building	Kedah	3 Injured
		Hostel building	Johor	
		Whole school buildings	Sabah	70% Burnt
2016	6	1 Block two-storey school building	Selangor	
		Hostel building	Selangor	
		Hostel and three-storey shoplot	Selangor	Totally burnt
		1 Block two-storey school building	Penang	
		Hostel building – two fires occurred in the same year	Kelantan	Twice facing fire
		Administration and classrooms building	Kelantan	
2017	10	Hostel building	Pahang	1 Injured
		Hostel building	Pahang	
		Hostel building	Pahang	
		40 Nos. of dorms for 100 student	Kelantan	100 Students lost their dorm.
		10 Nos. of dorms	Kelantan	10 Dorms totally burnt
		Hostel building	Kelantan	
		Hostel building	Perak	
		18 Nos. of dorms	Kelantan	Totally burnt
		2 Blocks hostel	Selangor	Totally burnt
		Hostel building	Kuala Lumpur	23 Died
2019	2	Hostel building	N.Sembilan	
		Hostel building	Sabah	
2020	1	Hostel, hall, and classroom	Pahang	

Source: From research data.

Currently, the Department of Fire and Rescue Malaysia (2018) states that the fire safety procedures can be defined as a written set of procedures which is relating the actions to be taken in the event of a fire emergency and assigning responsibility for each action. Each set of plans needs to be modified and the recommended actions and responsibilities will not be the same as they are depending on the facility, the type of work being done there, the types of materials used, and the people present. Fire Safety Procedures (2018) state by having effective fire safety procedures and proper training, will decrease the injuries and damage caused by a fire. If there are no fire safety procedures, or if the procedures are not prepared properly or poorly tailored to the facility, the result will likely be a disorganised evacuation or emergency response, which will lead to misunderstanding, injury, and also increased property damage. Therefore, this research attempts to investigate the situation in private Islamic schools where fires often occur. As a first step, this survey would like to review and scrutinise fire safety measures at private Islamic schools, whether they have a plan or policy, or procedure on fire prevention.

Ebenehi et al. (2017) suggest that fire safety policies should comprise certain aspects starting from the building construction process or applied to an existing structure. Ndetu and Kaluyu (2016) acknowledge that student safety can be protected if staffs and students know what to do before, during and after fire incidents. This can be reached when staff, students, and stakeholders are aware of the risk and willing to receive the appropriate training in fire risk preparedness (Chan et al., 2018). Besides, Nadzim and Taib (2014) believe face-to-face-based education intervention focussing on raising the awareness, knowledge, risk perception, and response towards fire risk prevention is very effective. Therefore, for the same reason, this research is conducted in private Islamic schools as (i) to identify the awareness level among the school administrators and students and (ii) to investigate whether aspects of compliance with fire safety procedures are enhanced. As an expert agency in dealing with fires in Malaysia, the Fire and Rescue Department is invited as a judgemental group.

The Fire and Rescue Department of Malaysia (2018) has developed the Fire Prevention Action Plan as a standard operation procedure for school safety. This action plan consists of 26 procedures that have been formulated and directed to be implemented in all schools. Meanwhile, as a guideline to school administrators or educators (Nadzim & Taib, 2014) recommends that every school should have complete equipment of fire prevention system, including manuals of the fire alarm and fire extinguishers uses. The Fire and Rescue Department of Malaysia stress out that:

(i) A total of 495 registered private Islamic schools are at risk of fire due to failure to comply with requirements.
(ii) There are a total of 1,267 registered private Islamic schools in whole, that have undergone inspections with the remaining 772 premises are confirmed as safe areas.
(iii) Most private Islamic school officials are not well trained or lack knowledge in dealing with fire safety issues.

(iv) School does not have a fire safety committee.
(v) Insufficient firefighting system equipment.

3. IMPLEMENTING SUSTAINABLE BUILDING MEASURES IN PRIVATE ISLAMIC SCHOOL

In line with the aspirations of the Sustainable Development Goals (SDGs) in promoting sustainable health and well-being in their SDG agenda 3, Malaysia is one of the countries involved in promoting the SDGs through the new branding of development. Crawford (2011) suggested a dialogue or campaign between the two disciplines of knowledge, building sustainability and fire safety should be expedited in helping to make buildings safer and more sustainable. While Schoonmaker (2019) stressed that when adopting the concept of sustainable design, we should also think about the people who use the building and what happens in the event of a fire disaster. Recently, some argument occurred in order to create a sustainable environment for student's well-being, especially in schools or hostels.

Kennedy (2020) highlights in the twenty-first century, greater awareness of energy conservation and living in a sustainable concept is no longer a theory. Vice versa, it is a concept that must be made a daily practice, starting from the education system. That's why it is very encouraging to see the interest of many private schools moving fast in making progress towards creating sustainable schools (Kennedy, 2020).

How will these new technologies and systems affect the fire protection industry? Vecchiarelli (2019) states for decades of experience in the construction industry with traditional building materials have resulted in well-established building and life safety codes and standards. When new materials and systems are added to the built environment, the solution to the fire safety equation changes. Vecchiarelli (2019) also suggests a sustainable fire safety practice as a solution to reduce the amount or severity of fires, as can reduce wasted materials, pollution, and save money.

The manual of sustainable fire safety practice should present guidelines regarding potential fire hazards related to sustainable materials and technologies and include several mitigation strategies that may include operational criteria, code requirements, or both. This also includes a discussion of how fire safety can be considered a sustainable practice (Vecchiarelli, 2019).

4. METHODOLOGY

As mentioned before, the Fire and Rescue Department of Malaysia (2018) recorded 39% of private Islamic schools have critical problems that are the main cause of fire incidents in Islamic schools, namely:

(i) There is no periodic fire safety monitoring and inspection system.
(ii) Maintenance or repair work on wiring and electrical equipment is not carried out.

Meanwhile, previous studies as announced by the Minister of Urban, Housing and Local Government (1Media.my, 2017) claimed lack of awareness and knowledge of fire safety system contribute to increase in fire incident.

4.1. Case Study Approach and Study Subjects

The selection of case study locations is in the private Islamic schools. Major criteria of selection are schools had damage and loss their property due to fire incident; and school peoples those experiencing or facing the fire tragedy. Respondents were divided into three groups:

- Group 1 – Wardens and students who stay in a school hostel.
- Group 2 – Teachers, staffs, headmasters, and stakeholders.

These two groups are categorised as fire victims who directly faced the fire itself in their respective schools, which lost friends, hostel or dormitories, classrooms and school buildings, etc.

- Group 3 – The Local Department of Fire and Rescue Malaysia – acts as a focus group and judgemental group.

There are six schools are chosen in five States that fulfil the criteria with a total population of 338. Overall, the total number of respondents who answered the survey is 122, which means 36.1% of them have response to the survey. Firstly, survey assessment was undertaken in detail using the 'naked-eye' on forensic observation at the sites where that has been destroyed by fire, debris, cracks, or collapse (photographs were taken as part of the research evidence but cannot be shown here as they are prohibited documents). The purpose of forensic observation is as a critical indicator of the fire level, whether 'severe case', or 'moderately destroyed', or 'small fire'. Secondly, site observation and questionnaire survey are adopted to investigate the availability of fire prevention equipment, whether compliance with fire safety procedures is enhanced after the fire incident. Lastly, the level of destruction and experience of being a fire victim will be used to identify the impact or response to fire awareness among respondents.

5. FINDINGS ANALYSIS

5.1. The Critical Assessment of Fire Level

The naked-eye observation adapts critical indicators of fire level with marked as (S1) 'severe case'; (S2) 'moderately damage'; and (S3) 'small fire'. The benchmark of 'severe case' (S1) is a 'total burn' in which none of the building structures survived. The percentage of severe cases is between 70% and 100% burns. Moderate damage (S2) is categorised between 50% and 69% burns; meaning there are still structures or internal facilities that can be salvaged. While 'small fires' (S3) represent a burn percentage below 50%, where building structures and internal facilities are not affected and can still be used.

The establishment of the most dominant critical indicator of fire level is measured by compilation of the 'severe case' plus 'moderate case'. The overall score for S1 recorded 32%, followed by S2 28%, and S3 totalled 40%. The 'severe case' plus 'moderate case' shown total scoring both are 60% show the fire incident level as 'very serious' in a private Islamic school.

5.2. Findings of Availability of Fire Prevention Equipment

The Local Fire and Rescue Department has listed 26 procedures as gazetted as a major guideline for school. Also, the survey consists of four parts which are floor plan of the school, general requirement, active requirement, and passive requirement. The Local Fire and Rescue Department as a focus group had acknowledged doing a pre-inspection and follow-up checking towards fire prevention equipment within a year before the incident. But only 40–50% fulfilled the requirement. The Local Fire and Rescue Department suggested the site observation conducted by this research could be considered as post-inspection, to confirm the existence of the equipment. As a result, based on the availability of fire prevention equipment as displayed in Table 10.2 recorded:

- Location Cases 1 and 4 – only comply 9 of 26 procedures, total availability 35%.
- Location Case 2 – only 8 of 26, total availability 31%.
- Location Case 3 – totally 15 of 26, total availability 58%.
- Location Case 5 – 6 of 26, total availability (23%).
- Location Case 6 – comply only 12 out of 26, total availability 46%.

Table 10.2. The Availability of Fire Prevention System in Private Islamic School.

No	Fire Safety Procedure	L1	L2	L3	L4	L5	L6	Total (%)
	Section B (1): Floor Plan of the School							
1	Fire hydrant is locate in the layout plan and at the building itself		/	/		/		50
2	Fire hydrant is in good condition		/			/	/	50
3	Gradient of road for fire appliance access should be not less than 1:12	/		/	/	/	/	83
4	Height of clearance should less than 5 meters	/						17
5	Distance between buildings must comply with the 6th schedule of the UBBL 1984			/	/		/	50
	Section B (2): General Requirements							
6	All electrical wiring for emergency system should in metal conduit or cable	/	/	/	/		/	83
7	All structural elements should contain fire resistance period, as stated in the UBBL 1984			/	/	/	/	67
8	Ventilation system for emergency stair, either conventional or mechanical	/						17

(*Continued*)

Table 10.2. (*Continued*)

No	Fire Safety Procedure	L1	L2	L3	L4	L5	L6	Total (%)
	Section B (2): General Requirements							
9	Signage for fire safety should comply with MS 982:1985			/	/			33
10	All graphic design of floor plan must white colour as background, which include staircase, safety route, escape route, and firefighting equipment							0
11	Three sets of logbook as directed by Bomba must available		/	/		/	/	67
12	Scale in layout plan should comply with UBBL clause 9		/		/		/	50
	Section B (3): Active Requirements							
13	Type of glass brake (fire alarm) should comply with Bomba requirement							0
14	Heat detector/smoke detector system must meet the requirement			/				17
15	Public address system and its installation must comply with the requirements	/		/				33
16	Fire extinguisher unit including installation must according to MS 1539: Part 1: 2002 as in the plan		/		/	/	/	67
17	The warning system installation should directly connected to the emergency line of nearby Bomba							0
18	Installation of gas equipment must accordance with the requirements	/		/				33
19	EXIT route to emergency power supply must indicated in floor plan			/			/	33
	Section B (4): Passive Requirements							
20	Fire resistant door – should available at least 1 hour rated as marked in the plan				/			17
21	Brick wall for storage room should be 100 mm thick	/	/	/	/		/	83
22	Break-point apparatus must be located outside of building – the Bomba to carry out the operation			/				17
23	Select glass type for exterior wall as allowed by Bomba	/						17
24	All service shafts should covered as directed	/						17
25	All internal/partition wall shall be ½ hour fire resistance						/	17
26	Road and limitation shall comply with UBBL		/	/			/	50
	Total	9	8	15	9	6	12	
	% Compliance	35%	31%	58%	35%	23%	46%	

These findings were distributed among focus groups, with the majority agreeing that scores below 70% clearly show the level of compliance is 'very bad' to create a safe environment. In relation, schools with a percentage below 50% are considered 'not in compliance with the procedures at all' and 'will not be approved'. In conclusion, totally all of the case studies or these six schools consider as none of them fulfil the procedures demanded.

5.3. Investigate the Fire Awareness Level

Nineteen questions related to awareness level among fire victims are mapped and were tested including individual fire knowledge prevention awareness. The answer 'Yes' means 'know, care and take precautionary measures regarding fire safety'; while the answer 'No' represents 'do not care at all or ignorant'. For the third answer 'Not Aware' means 'uncertain, doubtful or lack of knowledge'. The results show that the answer of 'Yes' and 'Not Aware' are equal that is 32%, while for an answer 'No' recorded 36%, as shown in Table 10.3.

Table 10.3. To Identify the Impact or Response to Fire Awareness among Respondents.

No.	Question	Yes (%)	No (%)	Not aware (%)
1	Escape Plan Basics	0	50	50
2	Smoke Alarm Basics	5	95	0
3	Used candle indoor.	80	20	0
4	Cooking – have a safe cooking area in hostel	43	39	17
5	Had smoked in hostel/premises	61	0.39	0
6	Replace/repair frayed/loose damaged cords all electronics	44	56	0
7	Your cooking area is free from items that easy to catch on fire, such as curtains, papers, dry area, etc.	11	0	89
8	Multi-USB charger is commonly used in hostel/office	83	0	17
9	Electricity extension cord always used as a replacement for permanent wiring	72	9	19
10	The school has allocated a sum of funds for the fire prevention system		5	95
11	School takes responsibility to upgrade/install fire prevention equipment in the whole school buildings	6	29	65
12	School takes the lead and create awareness and knowledge in regards to fire prevention	3	50	47
13	Experienced in fire make school leaders understand the importance of fire safety procedures to protect their valued staffs and students	8	44	48
14	School had start created the communication around fire safety on a regular basis	22	20	58
15	Staffs or students are exposed to fire safety training	46	15	39
16	Staffs or students understand the fire safety regulation	6	83	11
17	Schools have their own fire safety plan	3	81	16
18	Every employee and student is instructed to aware of his or her safety responsibilities	93	0	7
19	Fire Awareness Leadership – School has appointed a leader in organising fire safety programs and procedures	7	77	16
	Total	32%	36%	32%

Source: From research data.

Significantly, when the total of 'No' and 'Not Aware' are added, the percentage recorded is 68%. In principle, the awareness level among the respondents or victims in private Islamic schools – which was recorded as 32% – is categorised as 'very low' or 'disappointing'. This revealed that experiencing in fire did not influence their response and views towards more proactive measures on fire safety aspects.

6. DISCUSSION

The results show that awareness of the need for knowledge, ability to operate equipment, and concern about the availability of fire safety systems in this school is very low or very weak.

The expert group recommends:

(i) All six schools of this case study were labelled as failed. Therefore, it is suggested that a re-inspection and further in-depth study should be continued immediately. The Local Fire and Rescue Department should be referred to as a part of the policyholder who has the right to endorse the findings.
(ii) Experts argue legislation on structural requirements, established construction methods, internal services regulation and manufacturer specifications that are perceived to be among the fire-triggering factors, should be tightened and further enhanced.
(iii) Enforcement of compliance should be implemented immediately.
(iv) Fine or lawsuits should be issued against premises that fail to comply with or violate school fire safety procedures.
(v) Besides that, the attitude among school administrators should be forced to change to be more disciplined towards their own safety.
(vi) Knowledge, training, and explanation from time to time must be allocated and implemented so that the occupants know how to act and cope when a fire occurs.
(vii) Expert groups believe this is the only way how a culture of awareness can be nurtured and practiced. Schools should be a safe place to gain knowledge, start education and chasing the future, not a dangerous place.

REFERENCES

1Media.my. (2017). 1 Sekolah tahfiz terbakar setiap 5 hari? Retrieved from https://www.menara.my/1-sekolah-tahfiz-terbakar-setiap-5-hari/. Accessed on September 14, 2017.

Ahrens, M. (2013). *Home structure fires*. Quincy, MA: National Fire Protection Association.

Azmil, T. (2017). State Islamic orthodoxies and Islamic education in Malaysia and Indonesia. *Kajian Malaysia*, *35*(2), 1–20.

Azmil, T. (2018). Islamic education in Malaysia. In E. Aslan (Ed.), *Handbook of Islamic education* (pp. 16–19). Berlin: Springer.

Chan, E. Y. Y., Lam, H. C. Y., Wun, P. P., Huang, C. Z., Yung, T. K. C., Ling, K. W. K., ... Chiu, C. P. (2018). Risk perception and knowledge in fire risk reduction in a dong minority rural village in China: A health-EDRM education intervention study. *International Journal of Disaster Risk Science*, *9*, 306–318. Retrieved from www.ijdrs.com. https://doi.org/10.1007/s13753-018-0181

Crawford, A. (2011). Fire safety and sustainability: The perfect combination? Retrieved from https://www.ifsecglobal.com/uncategorized/fire-safety-and-sustainability-the-perfect-combination/

Department for Communities and Local Government. (2013). Fire statistics monitor, England. April 2013 to March 2014. Fire & Rescue Statistical Release Publication, July 2, 2014. Retrieved from firestatistics@communities.gsi.gov.uk.

Department of Fire and Rescue Malaysia. (2018). Laws of Malaysia: Fire Safety Procedure Act 341: Fire Safety Procedure Act 198. Retrieved from https://.bomba.gov.my/wp-content/uploads/2021/07/Act_341_fire_services_act_1988.pdf.

Deviyati, A. (2016). *IMAN research: The potential of independent religious schools in Malaysia. A case study of Al-Amin.* Kuala Lumpur: Ideas' Publications.

Ebenehi, I. Y., Mohamed, S., Sarpin, S., Masrom, M. A. N., Zainal, R., & Mohd Azmi, M. A. (2017). The management of building fire safety towards the sustainability of Malaysian public universities. *IOP Conference Series: Materials Science and Engineering, 271*, 012034. doi:10.1088/1757-899X/271/1/012034.

Fire and Rescue Department of Malaysia. (2018). Annual report year 2018. Retrieved from https://www.bomba.gov.my.

Flynn, J. D. (2010). *Characteristic of home fire victims.* Quincy, MA: National Fire Protection Association.

Groner, N. E. (2016). A decision model for recommending which building occupants should move where during fire emergencies. *Fire Safety Journal, 80*, 20–29. https://doi.org/10.1016/j.firesaf.2015.11.002.

Kennedy, R. (2020). Sustainable schools. *Boarding School Review.* Retrieved from https://www.boardingschoolreview.com.

Kobes, M., Helsloot, I., deVries, B., & Post, J. G. (2010). Building safety and human behaviour in fire: A literature review. *Fire Safety Journal, 45*, 1–11.

Lambie, I., Best, C., Tran, H., Ioane, J., & Sherperd, M. (2015). Risk factors for fire injury in school leavers: A review of the literature. *Fire Safety Journal, 77*, 59–66.

McNamee, M., Meacham, B., Van Hees, P., Bisby, L., Chow, W. K., Coppallee, A., … Weckman, W. (2019). IAFSS agenda 2030 for a fire safe world. *Fire Safety Journal, 110*, 102889. https://doi.org/10.1016/j.firesaf.2019.102889.

Murihah, A., Abdul-Hafiz, A., Arieff-Salleh, R., & Mohd-Faeez, I. (2015). Pendidikan Tahfiz di Malaysia: Satu Sorotan Sejarah. *International conference on Islamic education and social entrepreneurship*, Tanjung Malai, Langkawi, October 12–14 ISBN: 978-967-10160-9-1.

Nadzim, N., & Taib, M. (2014). Appraisal of fire safety management systems at educational buildings. *Sustainable built environment symposium (SBES 2014) SHS web of conferences.* doi:10.1051/shsconf/20141101005.

Ndetu, D. K., & Kaluyu, V. (2016). Factors influencing fire disaster management preparedness: A case of primary schools in Makueni County, Kenya. *European Journal of Education Studies, 2*(6) ISSN: 2501-1111 ISSN-L: 2501-1111. doi:10.5281/zenodo.159722.

New Zealand Fire Service. (2013). *Annual report.* 30 June 2013.

Nordin, A. (2015). Memperkasa darul quran ke arah memartabatkan pendidikan tahfiz di Malaysia. *Simposium Pendidikan Tahfiz Nusantara Dan Multaqa Huffaz kali Ke IV. Darul Quran. Jabatan Kemajuan Islam Malaysia (JAKIM). Institut Latihan Islam Malaysia (ILIM)*, Bangi, Selangor, 1–3 June.

Rosnani, H. (1994). Educational dualism in Malaysia: Progress and problem towards integration. *Muslim Education Quarterly, 11*(3). Cambridge: The Islamic Academy.

Rosnani, H. (2004). *Educational dualism in Malaysia: Implications for theory and practice.* Kuala Lumpur: The Other Press.

Schoonmaker, R. (2019). Green buildings and sustainable fire safety technology – Moving ahead. Retrieved from https://www.pcimag.com/articles/106512.

Solahuddin, I. (2015). *Pembangunan dan perubahan pendidikan Islam di Malaysia: Satu kajian kes di Kedah, 1800M – 2012M.* PhD thesis, Unpublished, Universiti Kebangsaan Malaysia, Bangi.

US Fire Administration. (2010). USA fire loss data sets. Retrieved from http://www.usfa.fema.gov/data/statistic/order_download_data.htmi.

Vecchiarelli, T. (2019). Fire safety in a sustainable world. *National Fire Protection Association (NFPA).* Retrieved from https://www.nfpa.org/News-and-Research/Resources/Emergency-Responders/Job-tools-and-resources/NFPA-and-sustainability/

Wan-Muhammad, A. (2003, June). Pengurusan ma'ahad tahfiz al-Quran; Pengalaman darul quran. Jurnal Darul Quran. *Jabatan Kemajuan Islam Malaysia (JAKIM), 3.*

CHAPTER 11

ASSESSING THE CRITERIA OF ECO-INDUSTRIAL PARK SITE SELECTION FOR THE SUSTAINABLE DEVELOPMENT GOALS INITIATIVES

Steven Kuba Nuhu, Mohd Nadzri Md Reba, Zainuddin Abd Manan, Sharifah Rafidah Wan Alwi and Fatin Nabihah Syahira Ridzuan

ABSTRACT

The United Nations Industrial Development Organisation (UNIDO) proposed the development of eco-industrial parks (EIP) related to the 9th, 12th, and 13th of the sustainable development goals (SDGs) for ensuring green industrial practice to deal with climate change. The first approach to EIP is choosing a suitable site, however, it is not a simple task, because it involves spatial factors and is always impaired by uncertainties that require more than one decision module. There is a fewer study in objectively assessing the criteria for the selection of suitable sites for EIP development to contribute to the SDG initiative. This study provides an integrated process for assessing a consistent weight of criteria for EIP site selection. Nine steps were used in the fuzzy-analytical hierarchy process namely criterion identification, hierarchical structure construction, triangular fuzzy number matrix, geometric ratio, fuzzy relative weight, defuzzification, normalisation, sensitivity analysis (SA) and

Sustainability Management Strategies and Impact in Developing Countries
Community, Environment and Disaster Risk Management, Volume 26, 135–148

Published under exclusive licence by Emerald Publishing Limited
ISSN: 2040-7262/doi:10.1108/S2040-726220220000026011

weight ranking. When tested using spatial and non-spatial criteria for EIP site selection, results show transportation infrastructure (13%), raw materials (12%), water bodies (12%), climate (10%), labour (9%), land use (9%), markets (9%), governmental policies (8%), existing industries (7%), urban settlement (6%), and restricted areas (5%). The SA verified that any evaluation error of 2% or 5% on the criteria weight is insignificant, but for 10% error, results can be distorted. The study has developed a consistent, simple approach integrating hierarchical and uncertainty modules for choosing EIP locations, and it is proposed as a guide for selecting suitable greenfield or brownfield EIP sites for sustainable industrial practices.

Keywords: Fuzzy-analytic hierarchy process; criteria assessment for consistent weight and ranking; suitable eco-industrial park site selection; brownfield EIP site selection; sustainable development goals; industrial symbiosis and sustainability

1. INTRODUCTION

The United Nations Industrial Development Organisation (UNIDO) was established by the United Nations (UN) as a specialised agency to focus on industrial development (Stucki et al., 2019). The goal is to manage and assist the emerging nations and economies to achieve viable manufacturing growth, environmental sustainability, and increased access to clean energy. This obligation corresponds with sustainable development goals (SDGs) 9, 12, and 13, which can assist participating countries to attain Inclusive Sustainable Industrial Development (ISID) (Beers, Flammini, Meylan, & Stucki, 2019).

To achieve the SDGs, it is necessary to strategically plan and effectively transform traditional industrial parks into eco-industrial parks (EIP) to provide an effective opportunity to achieve the 2030 agenda (Torabi-Kaveh, Babazadeh, Mohammadi, & Zaresefat, 2016). EIP is an area for industrial use at a suitable location, ensuring sustainability by incorporating social, economic, and environmental quality aspects into its siting, planning, operations, management, and decommissioning (UNIDO, 2016). EIP can be greenfield or brownfield. The greenfield EIPs are used for completely new EIPs, while the transformation of an abandoned or underutilised existing industrial park into EIPs is considered brownfield (UNIDO, 2017). International best practices show that the EIP concept varies greatly and far exceeds the benefits of traditional industry cases (Rikalovic, Cosic, Labati, & Piuri, 2018). The concept of EIP is to be in a favourable area for industry cluster synergy, reduce operating costs and increase productivity by identifying environmental factors, green supply and value chain, mitigating climate change, material efficiency, and reducing industry risks. (Tian et al., 2014) Environmental and social issues that are vital to communities and governments can be resolved by the EIP model to ensure long-term greenhouse gas (GHG) mitigation and job provision.

EIP site selection is a complex spatial criteria process, and therefore requires multicriteria decision analysis (MCDA). The traditional process of industrial site selection has subjective features and may be accompanied by uncertainty, leading to inappropriate industrial site selection (Ubando, Felix, Gue, Promentilla, & Culaba, 2020). MCDA provides a basis for selection, organisation, and priority, and facilitates overall evaluation. It can construct an assessment of complex issues based on judgments and consistent procedures. Decision-making usually involves inaccuracy and uncertainty, and this can be effectively managed by hierarchical and fuzzy logic decision-making techniques (Chang et al., 2015).

The location of an industrial site depends on geographical conditions such as the type of land use, which leads to the spatial and non-spatial data multiple criteria problems. These data make the EIP site selection a complex process. Allah-Bukhsh, Stipanovic, Hartmann, and Klanker (2019) informed that decision-making module, such as the fuzzy-analytical hierarchy process (F-AHP), which is an MCDA, is highly recommended for site selection. The F-AHP performs better in solving location suitability and planning challenges criteria ranking due to the combination of fuzziness and analytic hierarchy process in the analysis (Muhsin, Ahamed, & Noguchi, 2018). The fuzziness covers a large boundary of values to decompose the uncertainty of spatial and non-spatial criteria involved in site selection processes for a better decision. Schmidt and Huenteler (2016) pointed out that F-AHP allows different alternatives to be evaluated on many criteria based on its wide margin weight acceptance, and these criteria weights often guide decision-makers to make wise site selections. Several studies have used different MCDA in the site selection process. For example, Rikalovic, Cosic, and Lazarevic (2014) used the AHP, WLC, and F-AHP to select industrial zones and utilised the basis for assigning weights to rank the criteria and compared for limitations of the techniques.

Before the MCDA, the traditional approach to industrial site selection based on the environmental impact assessment (EIA) was done manually taking a long time to produce results. Besides, inadequate data acquisition and lengthy processing time, less accurate outcomes due to the countless dependent, independent, physical, and incomplete acquisition of variables were the challenges to perform the accurate characteristics of the process (Kolhoff, Driessen, & Runhaar, 2018). Balfors et al. (2018) opined that the EIA only considers technical and social factors and thus, it becomes expensive from the non-automated process. However, the application of MCDA has made these processes more accurate, easier, and cheaper, and the adequate acquisition and analysis of spatial and non-spatial information have allowed the MCDA to find a suitable or unsuitable site for EIP location. Loomis and Dziedzic (2018) have reiterated that EIA was initially a gateway to site selection with time-consuming and inaccurate results, but the advent of MCDA provided major changes to the results. With the hybrid modules (such as F-AHP), the results of EIP site selection would be more accurate and faster. Multicriteria analysis (MCA) of industrial site selection was never performed and this is one of the reasons the abandoned and underutilised industrial parks manifested and are known as brownfields (Reisi, Afzali, & Aye, 2018). Salari, Shariat, Rahimi, and Dashti (2019) restated that when industrial site selection is improperly conducted the derived spatial and non-spatial criteria are inaccurate resulting in abandonment or underutilisation of the industries. To avoid this issue, the MCDA was suggested in assessing suitable locations for EIP and sustainability.

The dependable EIP should consider appropriate locations that hold the most suitable criteria in the EIP design. The EIP depends on the site, industrial ecology and symbiosis, comprehensive understanding of environmental impact, reduction of the required energy, water, waste, heat, and pollution output for better sustainable growth (Susur, Martin-Carrillo, Chiaroni, & Hidalgo, 2019). EIP sites should be driven by MCDA hybrid criteria selection methods to find suitable options to support green infrastructure interconnected with multifunctional mixed-use landscapes (Rikalovic et al., 2015). Global climate change has made the EIP site selection demanding to support the increasing efforts to reduce energy use, toxic emissions, and improve material efficiency. EIP must keep the balance between economic, social, political, technical, and ecological aspects to maximise human comfort. The latest research (Beers et al., 2019) shows most industrial cities such as Pasir Gudang in Johor, Malaysia, have been initiating efforts to achieve EIP. EIP sustainability technologies are life solutions inspired and supported by nature and provide benefits at the same time and help develop resilience.

The suitable location of EIP becomes an important attribute of EIP and one of the key requirements in industrial activities for EIP practice and thus renders sustainable industrialisation to occur in any upcoming industrial development. Therefore, the EIP site selection issues should be fully addressed to give a reliable structure and consistent results. EIP aims to manage sustainable industrial activities with the following considerations of best practices. The first step is to evaluate the site by using a reliable MCDA method to weigh and rank the criteria for suitable site selection. EIP sites with suitable solar, wind, water, and rainfall will switch to RE sources (sunlight, wind, and water) to minimise utility bills, industry's dependence on fossil fuels, and eliminate carbon emissions and other GHGs. By investing in utility-scale solar, wind, and green hydrogen projects, it helps the world transition to 100% renewable energy (RE). As industrial sector is a huge source of air, water, land, and sound pollution, posing a serious hazard to the environment, for example, by-products of chemicals, such as solvents, heavy metals, alkalis and acids, can have harmful effects on the ecosystem (Jangid et al., 2016). Also, traditional industries do not use environmentally friendly constituents and packaging materials, which are not conducive to product sustainability and recycling. Therefore, EIP located in suitable sites permits industrial clusters that produce various products and can adopt symbiosis to prevent pollution to achieve a sustainable future.

The study on the quantitative assessment of criteria for the selection of suitable sites for EIP to support the SDG program is limited. Therefore, the goal of this study is to present a hierarchical and fuzzy approachable structure for assessing stable criteria weights of importance to resolve uncertainties in EIP location selection. An integrated hierarchy-fuzzy logic, geometric ratio, defuzzification, normalisation, and sensitivity analysis (SA) will be employed to accomplish this.

This structure will serve as a guide for researchers and EIP developers in determining a reliable weight of criteria to use in choosing suitable sites for EIP to achieve the SDGs 9, 12, and 13 to reduce GHG emissions, promote industrial symbiosis, cleaner production, and address climate change.

2. METHODOLOGY

2.1. Data Collection

Spatial and non-spatial criteria based on some works of literature (Kanniah et al., 2015) were identified, collected, and analysed. A total of 11 suitable criteria were accepted for the analysis of the weight percentages and importance for EIP site selection.

2.2. Method

The F-AHP-MCDA structure was designed where the goal, criteria, and alternatives hierarchy levels were defined. The pairwise comparison matrix provided for triangular fuzzy numbers (TFNs) by Zadeh (1975) was adopted using the lower, middle, and upper (*l*, *m*, *u*) weights technique. For each level, the order of the matrix was based on the number of criteria on the level associated with it (i.e. *n* x *n*). Microsoft Excel spreadsheet was used to assess the criteria weight of importance for accuracy. Therefore, Equations (1)–(9) (Saaty & Vargas, 2013) are used and the geometric ratio, relative weights, defuzzified weights, normalisation, SA, and alternatives weights parameters are determined.

$$\tilde{A} = \begin{bmatrix} 1 & \tilde{\alpha}_{12} & \cdots & \tilde{\alpha}_{1n} \\ 1/\tilde{\alpha}_{21} & 1 & \cdots & \tilde{\alpha}_{2n} \\ \vdots & \vdots & \cdots & \vdots \\ 1/\tilde{\alpha}_{n1} & 1/\tilde{\alpha}_{n2} & \cdots & 1 \end{bmatrix} \tag{1}$$

where $\tilde{\alpha}$ = fuzzy triangular number; $\tilde{A}$ = decision matrix.

The upper or lower triangular matrix can be used to evaluate the criteria and alternatives weights of importance considering 1, 3, 5, 7, and 9, which corresponds with 'equal in importance', 'moderately more important', 'strongly more important', 'very strongly more important', and 'extremely more important', respectively (Saaty & Vargas, 2013). The weight value is assigned according to the importance of the criteria, and the diagonal elements are put at 1, 1, 1. The upper or lower triangle takes the reciprocal of all values, depending on which triangle was used for the decision but starts with *u, m, l,* as shown in Equation (2).

$$\tilde{A}^{-1} = (l, m, u)^{-1} = \frac{1}{u}, \frac{1}{m}, \frac{1}{l} \tag{2}$$

Using Equation (3), the geometric mean can be calculated from the assigned weights of the lower (l), middle (m), and upper (u) values.

$$\tilde{r}_i = (l_1 \times l_2 \ldots \times l_n)^{1/n};$$
$$\tilde{r}_i = (m_1 \times m_2 \ldots \times m_n)^{1/n}; \tag{3}$$
$$\tilde{r}_i = (u_1 \times u_2 \ldots \times u_n)^{1/n}$$

where $\tilde{r}$ = geometric mean value, l = lower value, m = middle value, u = upper value.

In this process, the product of each criterion (l) value is increased to the reciprocal of the criteria number. In the same way, the product of the (m) and (u) values for each criterion can be determined. Obtain the sum of l, m, u, and the average value, respectively, and then arrange them in ascending order corresponding to l, m, u.

To calculate the fuzzy relative weight using equation (4), each geometric mean is multiplied by its corresponding ascending value. Then, the fuzzy weight is defuzzified using equation (5), in which the average value of each criteria weight in l, m, u is evaluated, and a non-fuzzy (defuzzified) value is obtained.

$$\tilde{w}_i = \tilde{r}_i \otimes \left[\sum(\tilde{r}_1, \tilde{r}_2, \ldots, \tilde{r}_n)\right]^{-1} \text{ or } \tilde{w}_1 = \tilde{r}_1 \otimes (\tilde{r}_1 \otimes \tilde{r}_2 \otimes \ldots \tilde{r}_n)^{-1} \tag{4}$$

$$M_i = \frac{l_i + m_i + u_i}{3}, \quad i = 1, \ldots, n \tag{5}$$

where M_i = crisp value.

By equation (6), the normalisation of the defuzzified value can be obtained by dividing each weight by the total value. The normalised value must give a unit value, otherwise, the comparison matrix needs to be readjusted. F-AHP summarises the calculation of the consistency ratio (CR) in the fuzzy matrix and the geometric ratio. For the F-AHP weight to be used, the sum of the normalised total weight must equal 1.0 or 100%.

$$N_i = \frac{w_i}{\sum_{j=1}^{n} w_j}, \quad j = 1, \ldots, n \tag{6}$$

where $\sum_{i=1}^{n} N_1 = 1$, $i = 1, \ldots N$

Using the same F-AHP process, a pairwise comparison matrix of alternatives for each criterion can be formed. The weights of the alternatives are calculated based on each criterion. The overall criteria weight of importance is then assessed. The total weight value of each criterion is determined by multiplying the criteria weight of importance by the weight of the corresponding alternative based on each criterion and by the goals. The resulting value becomes the F-AHP weight for each criterion.

An SA can be performed using some chosen percentages on all or a few of the criteria to evaluate for any change if there will be an error in the criteria weight assessment (Saaty & Vargas, 2013). As shown in equations. (7)–(9), the chosen percentage values are y_1, y_2, and y_3 of the criteria weight, respectively.

$$\text{SA}(1):\ W_x = W_1 + (y_1 \times W_1) \tag{7}$$

$$\text{SA}(2):\ W_x = W_1 + (y_2 \times W_1) \tag{8}$$

$$\text{SA}(3):\ W_x = W_1 + (y_3 \times W_1) \tag{9}$$

where W_x = new weight and W_1 = previous weight.
y_1, y_2, y_3 = numerical value in percent

3. RESULTS AND DISCUSSION

The F-AHP flow process in this study is shown in Fig. 11.1a where nine steps are involved. The decision-making problem is structured in a hierarchical structure, which constitutes the goal, main criteria, and alternatives as shown in Fig. 11.1b. This was decomposed to a TFN pairwise comparison matrix. Results show that the weight in the pairwise comparison matrix ranges from equal to strongly more important. For example, government policies are as important as urban settlements but less important to labour, restricted areas, land use, and markets. Urban settlements are equally important to waterbodies, existing industries, labour, raw

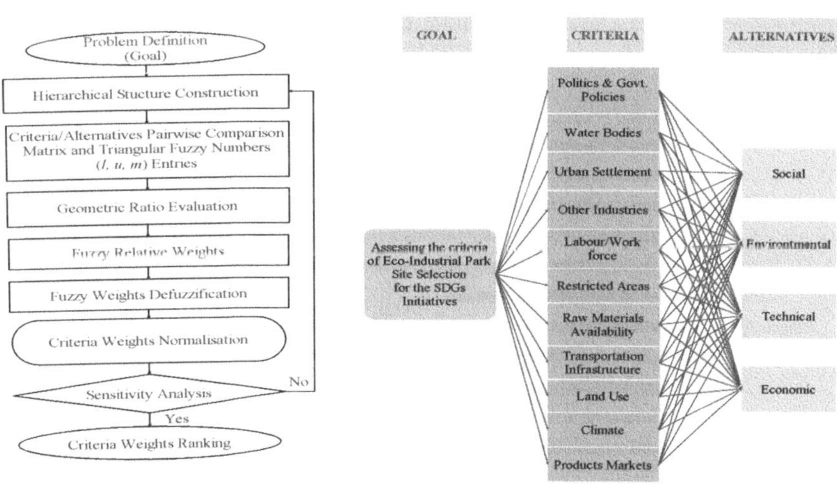

(a) (b)

Fig. 11.1. (a) Fuzzy Analytic Hierarchy Process Flow Sheet. (b) EIP Site Selection Criteria Structure.

materials, and transportation infrastructure. The market is strongly more important than waterbodies, urban settlements, and climate.

The geometric mean was computed in the form of *l, m. u*, where the average values, the inversed average values were determined, rearranged in ascending order, multiplied with the corresponding geometric ratio, and obtained the fuzzy relative weights. The average of the fuzzy relative weights for each criterion was defuzzified. If the summation of the defuzzified values is more than 1, normalisation must be performed to get the consistent weight values and their summation must also be 1 otherwise, the comparison matrix must be revised. The normalised values show transportation infrastructure has the highest weight importance of 13%, followed by water bodies and raw materials with 12% each. The criteria with the least weight of importance are the restricted area with 5%.

The alternatives were also evaluated with respect to each criterion. To obtain the overall criteria weight of importance, the criteria priority vectors were multiplied by the weights of the criteria based on the goal and by the alternatives with respect to each criterion. Results, as presented in Fig. 11.2, show the overall weight importance of transportation infrastructure and raw materials account for 13.2% and 12.4%, respectively. The top criteria that follow in importance are the water bodies and the climate conditions with 11.88% and 10.06% in that order. Workforce and land use account for 9.3% and 9.3%, respectively. Others include market, political/government policies, existing industries near EIP sites, urban settlement, and restricted areas corresponding with 8.7%, 7.8%, 6.8%, 5.8%, and 4.6%.

The SA was implemented considering 2%, 5%, and 10% error, respectively. The results indicate that the alteration in the overall criteria weight by 2%, and 5% error for political/government policies, waterbodies, restricted areas, raw materials, transportation infrastructure, climate, and markets are insignificant and would not cause any negative impact on the criteria ranking. The assessed weight of water bodies is 11.88%, but increases to 12.12% and 12.47 % when 2% and 5%

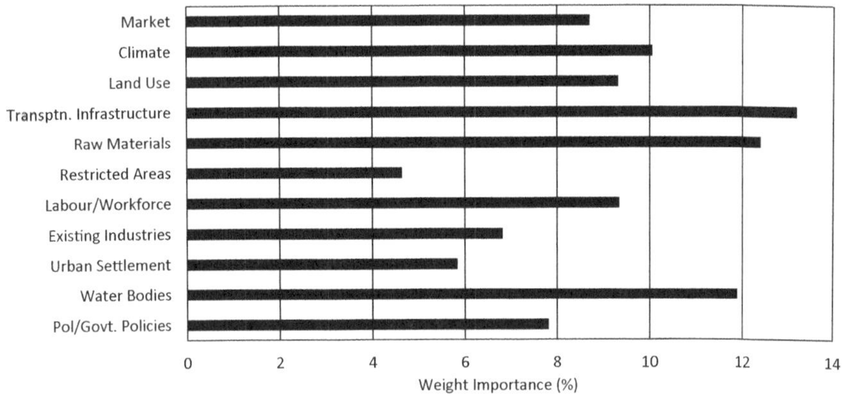

Fig. 11.2. Fuzzy-analytic Hierarchy Process Overall Criteria Weight Importance for EIP Site Selection.

calculation errors are implemented, respectively this implies that the alterations are still within the integer range. However, if a 10% calculation error occurs, the weight change will be greater than the criteria weight by a whole number, causing a significant change in the weight ranking. For instance, water bodies increased by 1.19% when 10% error of the criteria weight was evaluated. Although Rikalovic et al. (2015) stated that the perturbation of the assessment of criteria weights is a characteristic of multicriteria problems but the increase should not be more than 0.85% in error. Therefore, in this study, decisions can be made with the initial criteria weights or with the error weights changed by 2% or 5% error.

From the alternative perspective, the economic weight percent is the highest, at 35.8%. This means that to choose a site for EIP, economic aspects (accessibility of raw materials, urban settlements, available labour, ready markets, and developed infrastructure and utilities) must primarily be considered. The environmental aspect is 30.3%, indicating EIP site must have environmentally friendly features (existing industries that can be used for industrial symbiosis to reduce or eliminate toxic emissions, different transportation infrastructural systems that will prevent carbon emissions, and vast land that can accommodate many industrial clusters). The social aspect followed closely behind with 18.5%. In this regard, the presence of urban settlements close to the EIP site provides both skilled and unskilled labour. The last alternative is the technical aspect, which measures 15.4%. If the site has a high proportion of slopes and peaks, it makes it difficult to construct roads and industrial buildings, thereby increases cost. The alternative weights ranking is observed to agree with the importance of the criteria.

The accuracy of the importance of the criteria weights selected by the EIP site depends on the SA of the weighted results and the outcomes of the alternatives (calculated following equations (1)–(9) but with respect to each criterion) from the related criteria weights. Feyzi, Khanmohammadi, Abedinzadeh, and Aalipour (2019) reported that to consider a certain location for EIP activities, the economic, environmental, social, and technical aspects need to be assessed and each must not be less than 10% weight importance.

Each criterion analysed in this study for a suitable EIP site selection is essential in many ways. The climate conditions such as rainfall, temperature, and wind speed/direction of an area are important factors to siting an EIP. For instance, the rainfall helps in the continuous provision of water bodies for transportation, industrial cleaning and cooling, and domestic use. Solar radiation determines the temperature of a particular area, which defines the speed/direction of the wind. The temperature generated by solar radiation is used on photovoltaic (PV) panels to produce solar power. Wind with good speed drives wind turbines for the generation of wind power. The annual average rainfall, temperature, and wind speed of an area suitable for an EIP site should be 1,778–3,302 mm, 15°C–25°C, and 12–14 km/h, respectively (Ahmadipari, Hoveidi, Jafari, & Pazoki, 2018). This study is recommending 15°C–28°C for temperature for effective RE power generation. These RE sources can increase the EIP's power supply and reduce costs. Urban settlements (which accommodate banks, telecommunications, schools, hotels, entertainment centres, utilities, hospitals, and worship centres) should be within walking distance of not more than 5 km (Abdulhasan et al., 2019). Due to the expansion of industries in the EIP, 8–10 km is proposed for the distance of urban areas to the EIP site. All these ensure the welfare and good life of workers. For instance, banks and other financial organisations close to EIP provide sufficient capital flow for transactions and obtain investment funds. Research institutions easily conduct investigations for innovation on products to reduce costs and promote production (Noorollahi, Yousefi, & Mohammadi, 2016), and therefore, should be close to an EIP site at a distance not greater than 5 km in radius (Rikalovic et al., 2014). However, this study proposes a 10 km in radius to meet the distance of urban settlement from the EIP site.

EIP is required to be close to existing industries not exceeding 0.25 km (Susur et al., 2019). The industries help in exchanging various commodities (such as materials, energy, treated wastewater, and by-products) and providing technical services within the EIP. EIPs can thrive well in areas free from natural or man-made-restricted areas such as faults or mining camps. Mining camps are characterised by flying rocks caused by explosions, and ground deformation is caused by vibrations and faults that easily trigger earthquakes. Taibi and Atmani (2017) proposed the distance from restricted areas to the EIP site not to be less than 10 km. Envisaging the danger of faults and mining camps, it is recommended that the proximity of the restricted areas to the EIP site be 15 km and above. There should be a politically stable country (Rikalovic et al., 2014) to promote the development of EIP. Government policies and regulations include permissions, rules, and certain administrations. Some governments use tax incentives or policies to promote industries for cleaner production (Ghobadi & Ahmadipari, 2018), and others grant cuts and exemptions (Gao, Gao, Song, Ye, & Dong, 2019b) after affirming already established areas for special economic zones. Sustainable transportation infrastructure is one of the bases of modern-day industrial siting and development. The existence of park piping railways, airports, seaports, and main roads near EIP sites is critical. The distance from the railway and airport to the EIP site should be 0.2 and 1–2 km, respectively (Rahmat et al., 2017), while from the seaport and major road to the EIP site be 0.5 km and $\leq$1 km (Muhsin et al., 2018), in that order. The key goal is to find a joint transportation system close to EIP, as well as the lowest possible cost and the best requirements.

The EIP site needs to provide all possible usable land and provide the lowest land cost for the future development of industrial companies. Wetlands, economic mangroves or forests, and agricultural land near EIP will negate the prospects for industrial growth. Studies have shown that with anticipation of future development, the distance from EIP to any accessible wetland, forest or agricultural land must not be less than 20 km (Kamali et al., 2017). The water bodies' criterion includes oceans, rivers, and streams, which are essential for the transportation of raw materials and finished products to and from EIP. Water is also important for domestic use, industrial washing, and cooling of machinery. Gao et al. (2019b) projected that the distance from the water bodies to the EIP site be 1.6 km. Babalola (2018) described that the number of skilled and unskilled labour necessary in urban settlements near the EIP should be 50% and 30%, respectively. This encourages the selection of EIP sites to ensure a satisfactory and reliable supply of the requisite workforce. Skilled and unskilled attitudes and the educational level of the labour force can decide the labour cost in industrial operations. The accessibility of raw materials is required to be guaranteed for regular supply for sustainable production. According to Akther, Ahamed, Noguchi, Genkawa, and Takigawa (2019), the distance between raw materials to the EIP site must be between 10 and 15 km, which is essential for maintaining inventory in the industries. A readily available market for raw materials and finished goods steady flow encourages the development of EIP and the wealth of a country.

It is noticed that assessing many criteria contributes to the wider coverage of the factors, which help in the decision-making as to whether to select a site for EIP or not. The criteria assessment by the F-AHP indicates the strength of each criterion required in the selection of EIP sites. It also shows how important are the alternatives such as economic, environmental, and social, which usually support the criteria to achieve the EIP goal. The SA also verifies the stability of the F-AHP, which if a significant evaluation error occurs in the criteria weight, it will affect the EIP site selection analysis.

4. CONCLUSION

In this study, the technique for assessing a consistent weight percent importance of criteria for EIP site selection was designed using an F-AHP hybrid of the TFNs process. The hierarchy-fuzzy logic, geometric ratio, relative weights, defuzzification, normalisation, and SA were used. The analysis identified 11 criteria for the selection of suitable EIP sites.

The results according to criteria weight importance show that the availability of transportation infrastructure measures 13.2%, the availability and accessibility of raw materials account for 12.4%, the presence of water bodies weighs 11.9%, the climate of the region/country takes 10.1%, the availability of labour attracts 9.3%, and land use grabs 9.3%. Others are markets for raw materials and finished goods get 8.7%, politics/government and policies of the host country obtain 7.8%, existing industries near the park carries 6.8%, urban settlement holds 5.8%, and restricted areas take 4.6%. The first 10 criteria are very important to either greenfield or brownfield EIP development similar to some reported works of literature. The reported distances, percentages, and other boundaries by literature and suggested by this study can be used to maximise the EIP site selection goals. It is expected that when a hybrid, technical, and reliable approach is used and proper site selection is conducted, an analysis of the regional industrial resource flow, a list of facilities and infrastructure areas and specific locations, data on existing business, and production activities in the community will be provided. Similarly, data on material flows (such as raw materials, by-products), and the vicinity of EIP sites waste from existing industries supplied. Accurate EIP site selection will identify the end-users of the by-products and waste generated in the community and create an energy profile for production, demand, price, and environmental aspects. It will also determine the list of natural resources available for development and local supplies and services.

Finally, the best industrial locations can be identified by assessing its criteria with the F-AHP TFNs method to give a consistent criteria weight importance to achieve EIP site selection. Also, the 9th, 12th, and 13th SDGs mandate to promote local and regional economic development reduce GHGs, control resources, clean production, and provide employment can be reached. The SA has proven the F-AHP to be a stable and dependable technique which within 2% and 5% criteria weight evaluation error, the results can still be used. Therefore, this study can be used as a guide for evaluating suitable EIP site selection criteria. It is recommended that these results can be used for the evaluation of the brownfield of Tanjung Langsat Industrial Area and other brownfield to further test the efficacy of the framework.

ACKNOWLEDGEMENTS

This study was supported by the UTM-TDR grant (vote no: Q.J130000.3509. 05G95). We are thankful to the Universiti Teknologi Malaysia for providing the facilities for this research.

REFERENCES

Abdulhasan, M. J., Hanafiah, M. M., Satchet, M. S., Abdulaali, H. S., Toriman, M. E., & Al-Raad, A. A. (2019). Combining gis, fuzzy logic, and AHP models for solid waste disposal site selection in Nasiriyah, Iraq. *Applied Ecology and Environmental Research, 17*(3), 6701–6722. https://doi.org/10.15666/aeer/1703_67016722

Ahmadipari, M., Hoveidi, H., Jafari, H. R., & Pazoki, M. (2018). An integrated environmental management approach to industrial site selection by genetic algorithm and fuzzy analytic hierarchy process in a geographical information system. *Global Journal of Environmental Science and Management, 4*(3), 339–350. https://doi.org/10.22034/GJESM.2018.03.007

Akther, A., Ahamed, T., Noguchi, R., Genkawa, T., & Takigawa, T. (2019). Site suitability analysis of biogas digester plant for municipal waste using GIS and multi-criteria analysis. *Asia-Pacific Journal of Regional Science, 3*(1), 61–93. https://doi.org/10.1007/s41685-018-0084-2

Allah-Bukhsh, Z., Stipanovic, I., Hartmann, A., & Klanker, G. (2019). Evaluation and application of AHP, MAUT and ELECTRE III for infrastructure management. *Life-cycle analysis and assessment in civil engineering: Towards an integrated vision – Proceedings of the 6th international symposium on life-cycle civil engineering,* pp. 1467–1474.

Babalola, M. (2018). Application of GIS-based multi-criteria decision technique in exploration of suitable site options for anaerobic digestion of food and biodegradable waste in Oita City, Japan. *Environments, 5*(7), 77. https://doi.org/10.3390/environments5070077

Balfors, B., Wallström, J., Lundberg, K., Söderqvist, T., Hörnberg, C., & Högström, J. (2018). Strategic environmental assessment in Swedish municipal planning. Trends and challenges. *Environmental Impact Assessment Review, 73*, 152–163. https://doi.org/10.1016/j.eiar.2018.07.003

Beers, D. van, Flammini, A., Meylan, F. D., & Stucki, J. (2019). Lessons learned from the application of the UNIDO eco-industrial park toolbox in Viet Nam and other countries. *Sustainability (Switzerland), 11*(17), 1–18. https://doi.org/10.3390/su11174687

Chang, P. Y., Lin, H. Y., Fataei, E., Erdi, M. A., Farhadi, H., Mohammadian, A., ... Piuri, V. (2015). A comprehensive method for industrial site selection: The macro-location analysis. *IEEE Systems Journal, 8*(5), 1547–1575. https://doi.org/10.3384/lic.diva-105942

Feyzi, S., Khanmohammadi, M., Abedinzadeh, N., & Aalipour, M. (2019). Multi-criteria decision analysis FANP based on GIS for siting municipal solid waste incineration power plant in the north of Iran. *Sustainable Cities and Society, 47*, 101513. https://doi.org/10.1016/j.scs.2019.101513

Gao, C., Gao, C., Song, K., Ye, Z., & Dong, J. (2019b). Regional water ecosystem risk assessment based on GIS and pollutant diffusion model: A case study of Shenzhen eco-industrial park. *Process Safety and Environmental Protection*, *130*, 182–189. https://doi.org/10.1016/j.psep.2019.08.004

Ghobadi, M., & Ahmadipari, M. (2018). Environmental planning for wind power plant site selection using a fuzzy PROMETHEE-based outranking method. *Geographical Information System*, *2*, 75–87. https://doi.org/10.22097/eeer.2018.148760.1041

Jangid, J., Bera, A. K., Joseph, M., Singh, V., Singh, T. P., Pradhan, B. K., & Das, S. (2016). Potential zones identification for harvesting wind energy resources in desert region of India - A multi-criteria evaluation approach using remote sensing and GIS. In *Renewable and Sustainable Energy Reviews*. 65, 1–10. *https://doi.org/10.1016/j.rser.2016.06.078*

Kamali, M., Alesheikh, A. A., Alavi Borazjani, S. A., Jahanshahi, A., Khodaparast, Z., & Khalaj, M. (2017). Delphi-AHP and weighted index Overlay-GIS approaches for industrial site selection case study: Large extractive industrial units in Iran. *Journal of Settlements and Spatial Planning*, *8*(2), 99–105. https://doi.org/10.24193/JSSP.2017.2.03

Kanniah, K. D., Sheikhi, A., Cracknell, A. P., Goh, H. C. Tan, K. P., Ho, C. S., & Rasli, F. N. (2015). Satellite images for monitoring mangrove cover changes in a fast growing economic region in Southern Peninsular Malaysia. *Remote Sensing*, *7*, 14360–14385.

Kolhoff, A. J., Driessen, P. P. J., & Runhaar, H. A. C. (2018). Overcoming low EIA performance – A diagnostic tool for the deliberate development of EIA system capacities in low and middle-income countries. *Environmental Impact Assessment Review*, *68*, 98–108. https://doi.org/10.1016/j.eiar.2017.11.001

Loomis, J. J., & Dziedzic, M. (2018). Evaluating EIA systems' effectiveness: A state of the art. *Environmental Impact Assessment Review*, *68*, 29–37. https://doi.org/10.1016/j.eiar.2017.10.005

Muhsin, N., Ahamed, T., & Noguchi, R. (2018). GIS-based multi-criteria analysis modelling used to locate suitable sites for industries in suburban areas in Bangladesh to ensure the sustainability of agricultural lands. *Asia-Pacific Journal of Regional Science*, *2*(1), 35–64. https://doi.org/10.1007/s41685-017-0046-0

Noorollahi, Y., Yousefi, H., & Mohammadi, M. (2016). Multi-criteria decision support system for wind farm site selection using GIS. *Sustainable Energy Technologies and Assessments*. *13*, 38–50. https://doi.org/10.1016/j.seta.2015.11.007

Rahmat, Z. G., Niri, M. V., Alavi, N., Goudarzi, G., Babaei, A. A., Baboli, Z., & Hosseinzadeh, M. (2017). Landfill site selection using GIS and AHP: A case study: Behbahan, Iran. *KSCE Journal of Civil Engineering*, *21*(1), 111–118. https://doi.org/10.1007/s12205-016-0296-9

Reisi, M., Afzali, A., & Aye, L. (2018). Applications of analytical hierarchy process (AHP) and analytical network process (ANP) for industrial site selections in Isfahan, Iran. *Environmental Earth Sciences*, *77*(14), 1–13. https://doi.org/10.1007/s12665-018-7702-1

Rikalovic, A., Cosic, I., Aleksandar, R., Ćosillija, Ć., Rikalovic, A., & Cosic, I. (2015). A fuzzy expert system for industrial location factor analysis. *Acta Polytechnica Hungarica*, *12*(2), 33–51. https://doi.org/10.12700/aph.12.2.2015.2.3

Rikalovic, A., Cosic, I., Labati, R. D., & Piuri, V. (2018). Intelligent decision support system for industrial site classification: A GIS-based hierarchical neuro-fuzzy approach. *IEEE Systems Journal*, *12*(3), 2970–2981. https://doi.org/10.1109/JSYST.2017.2697043

Rikalovic, A., Cosic, I., & Lazarevic, D. (2014). GIS-based multi-criteria analysis for industrial site selection. *Procedia Engineering*, *69*, 1054–1063. https://doi.org/10.1016/j.proeng.2014.03.090

Saaty, T. L., & Vargas, L. G. (2013). Sensitivity analysis in the analytic hierarchy process. *International Series in Operations Research and Management Science*, *195*. https://doi.org/10.1007/978-1-4614-7279-7_15

Salari, M., Shariat, S. M., Rahimi, R., & Dashti, S. (2019). Land capability evaluation for identifying industrial zones: Combination multi-criteria decision-making method with a geographic information system. *International Journal of Environmental Science and Technology*, *16*(10), 5501–5512. https://doi.org/10.1007/s13762-018-1925-2

Schmidt, T. S., & Huenteler, J. (2016). Anticipating industry localization effects of clean technology deployment policies in developing countries. *Global Environmental Change*, *38*, 8–20. https://doi.org/10.1016/j.gloenvcha.2016.02.005

Stucki, J., Flammini, A., van Beers, D., Phuong, T. T., Anh, N. T., Dong, T. D., … Hieu, V. T. M. (2019). Eco-industrial park (EIP) development in Viet Nam: Results and key insights from UNIDO's EIP project (2014–2019). *Sustainability (Switzerland)*, *11*(17), 1–23. https://doi.org/10.3390/su11174667

Susur, E., Martin-Carrillo, D., Chiaroni, D., & Hidalgo, A. (2019). Unfolding eco-industrial parks through niche experimentation: Insights from three Italian cases. *Journal of Cleaner Production*, *239*, 118069. https://doi.org/10.1016/j.jclepro.2019.118069

Taibi, A., & Atmani, B. (2017). Combining fuzzy AHP with GIS and decision rules for industrial site selection. *International Journal of Interactive Multimedia and Artificial Intelligence*, *4*(6), 60. https://doi.org/10.9781/ijimai.2017.06.001

Tian, J., Liu, W., Lai, B., Li, X., & Chen, L. (2014). Study of the performance of eco-industrial park development in China. *Journal of Cleaner Production*, *64*, 486–494. https://doi.org/10.1016/j.jclepro.2013.08.005

Torabi-Kaveh, M., Babazadeh, R., Mohammadi, S. D., & Zaresefat, M. (2016). Landfill site selection using a combination of GIS and fuzzy AHP, a case study: Iranshahr, Iran. *Waste Management and Research*, *34*(5), 438–448. https://doi.org/10.1177/0734242X16633777

Ubando, A. T., Felix, C. B., Gue, I. H. V., Promentilla, M. A. B., & Culaba, A. B. (2020). A fuzzy analytic hierarchy process for the site selection of the Philippine algal industry. *Clean Technologies and Environmental Policy*, *22*(1), 171–185. https://doi.org/10.1007/s10098-019-01775-0

UNIDO. (2016). Global assessment of eco-industrial parks in developing and emerging countries: Achievements, good practices and lessons learned from thirty-three industrial parks in twelve selected emerging and developing countries. *World Evaluation of Eco-Industrial Parks Development*, *2*, 351–385.

UNIDO. (2017). In S. Braune & A. Anders (Eds.), *An international framework for eco-industrial parks*. Retrieved from www.worldbank.org

Zadeh, L. A. (1975). The concept of a linguistic variable and its application to approximate reasoning-III. *Information Sciences*, *9*(1), 43–80. https://doi.org/10.1016/0020-0255(75)90017-1

CHAPTER 12

CAUSAL FACTORS OF ACCIDENT RELATED TO DESIGN ASPECT IN CONSTRUCTION INDUSTRY

Herda Balqis Binti Ismail, Noor Nabilah Binti Sarbini, Hamizah Liyana Binti Tajul Ariffin, Izni Syahrizal Bin Ibrahim and Mohd Fairuz Bin Ab Rahman

ABSTRACT

The equability of environment, social and economic elements becomes a major issue to be achieved as to attain sustainability in the development of a construction project. As to cater to social sustainability, the Guidelines on Occupational Safety and Health in Construction Industry (Management) also known as OSHCIM has been introduced by the government to improve safety practices amongst Malaysia's construction practitioners. The basic principle adopted in OSHCIM is Prevention through Design (PtD), which enhances the elimination of hazards during project design stages. This concept is inspired from the implementation of Construction (Design and Management) (CDM) Regulations in the United Kingdom. The concept has also been adopted and practised in many developed countries including Australia and Singapore. The aim of this study is to identify the dominant accident causes in Malaysian construction industry. In this study, the secondary data were gathered from the Department of Occupational Safety and Health (DOSH) accident statistics. A content analysis and frequency distribution analysis were adopted to determine causal factors that contribute to the fatality. The findings show the existence of design-related causal factors, which is also incorporated with other

Sustainability Management Strategies and Impact in Developing Countries
Community, Environment and Disaster Risk Management, Volume 26, 149–164

Published under exclusive licence by Emerald Publishing Limited
ISSN: 2040-7262/doi:10.1108/S2040-726220220000026012

causes of accidents. This is true as every accident occurs due to more than one factor. Thus, these inputs will recommend further exploration to determine the design-related causal factors. This may help the industrial players, including stakeholders, practitioners and researchers, to have more focussed efforts and resources in ensuring the success of OSHCIM's implementation to reduce the accident statistics in Malaysia.

Keywords: Safety; design; causal; accidents; prevention through design (PtD); occupational safety and health in construction industry (management) (OSHCIM)

1. INTRODUCTION

Sustainable development in building design and construction is defined as a dynamic process to enhance and protect the health of the environment or the associated health and well-being of the building's occupants, construction workers, the general public or future generations using efficient resources and methods (Marjaba & Chidiac, 2016). As sustainable development is expected to yield environment, financial and social benefits, lifecycle safety was found to be a fundamental aspect of social sustainability (Karakhan, 2016b). This is supported by the discovery of Huemann and Ringhofer (2018), which emphasised that the risk assessment is also part of project sustainability. This is because projects are always complex and include uncertainty and risks, in the sense of positive or negative deviations. Therefore, balancing between risk reduction and taking risks is necessary as reduction of too many risks may at the same time minimise the project benefit and the benefit for project stakeholders. Study by Eskerod and Huemann (2013), which links sustainable development, projects and the role of stakeholders, discovered that there is a need to incorporate stakeholders and their interests in more project management activities. Therefore, this may imply the construction safety aspect.

In Malaysia, the construction sector has been identified as one of the industries with a higher rate of accidents from 2007 to 2015. As reported by the Department of Occupational Safety and Health (DOSH), the construction worksite fatality rate has been increasing from 2012 onwards. This incremental trend of accident rate has captured the Malaysia government's attention because it can cause losses of life and contribute to severe implication socially and economically to parties such as the employees, organisations and the country. Besides, the increment trend distracts from achieving the aims of the National Occupational Safety and Health Policy, which is highlighted in the Occupational Safety and Health Master Plan (OSHMP) (2016–2020). The aim is to protect workers' rights to a safe, healthy and conducive working environment. Therefore, in response to improve the occupational safety and health (OSH) performance specifically in the construction industry, the DOSH has introduced Guidelines on Occupational Safety and Health in Construction Industry (Management) or also known as OSHCIM early in 2017.

1.1. Occupational Safety and Health in Construction Industry Management

In general, the OSHCIM Guidelines is the latest valuable plan initiated by the Ministry of Human Resources, through the DOSH to combat issues related to construction safety. This is aligned with the mission of OSHMP (2016–2020) which emphasises on the inculcation of accident preventive culture which involves the building and infrastructure life cycle. Clearly, the Prevention through Design (PtD) concept has been integrated in this guideline. Its implementation embraces the thought that hazard and risk need to be eliminated or minimised during the preliminary planning and design phase of a project. Thus, this can reduce the likelihood of the accident occurrences throughout the project life cycle. In addition, the development of OSHCIM is recommended due to the success of the Construction (Design and Management) Regulations (CDM 2015) in the UK. It is reported that the annual average rate of construction fatality in the UK is 1.6 per 100,000 workers in 2016/2017 and 1.84 in 2020/2021 (HSE, 2021). This fatality rate is lower as compared to other countries including Malaysia.

Besides, PtD implementation has positive impacts to other aspects such as the schedule, morale, constructability, cost, quality (Karakhan, 2016a) and productivity improvement to the involved parties (Lam, Wong, & Chan, 2006). In addition, many countries are also adopting and practicing the PtD concept such as Australia, the United States, Hong Kong and in Europe countries such as Spain. As in Singapore, the PtD is known as Design for Safety (DfS) which the DfS Regulations have been enforced from August 2016 onwards (Goh & Chua, 2016). It shows that the PtD concept has been accepted globally as means to improve construction safety.

Currently, the OSHCIM Guideline is established and implemented on a voluntary basis. However, the government is in preparation to impose full implementation in the future. The enforcement is significant as to improve the OSH performance in Malaysia's construction industry. This action is aligned with previous discoveries in which the enforcement of regulations is very important to ensure the effectiveness of the regulations (Chong & Low, 2014). Hence, once OSHCIM has been enacted, it needs to be strictly complied by all duty holders.

1.2. Causal Factors of Accident

In Malaysian construction industry, the causes of occupational accidents and illness are four main elements consisting of human, worksite, management and external elements (Jaafar et al., 2018). The external and management elements are indicated as underlying causes, which contribute to the OSH issue, while human and worksite elements are more apparent causes of occupational accidents and illnesses. In addition, study by Hamid et al. (2019) reported that the main causes of fatal accidents in Malaysian construction site are mainly unsafe method, nature of the industry that is inherently dangerous, complex job site conditions, human errors, incompetent management, unsafe equipment and environmental factors.

However, based on global previous works, the findings show that there were relations between construction fatalities with design aspects. In the UK, analysis shows that 42% of fatal accidents are related to the design issues during the pre-planning stage (Behm, 2005). Haslam et al. (2005) reported that more than half of 100 accidents investigated can be prevented through a design change. The trade contractors revealed that 54% changes made to the design of a facility are proven to improve the construction accidents (Weinstein, Gambatese, & Hecker, 2005). Study conducted in Australia, which used local fatal accidents data sources also discovered that 37% of the 210 identified workplace fatalities are related to design issue (Driscoll, Harrison, Bradley, & Newson, 2008). In addition, the likelihood of accidents occurring in a workplace was related to the complexity of the design (Navon & Kolton, 2006). The work scope and design have become more complex and cramped project duration, the more the possibility of an accident tends to occur. This finding is aligned with Suraji, Duff, and Peckitt (2001) which discovered that accidents and injuries in the construction industry are caused by a wrong decision during the project planning, scheduling and design works.

The design safety issue has been discussed continuously and findings by Hallowell and Hansen (2016) show that approximately 25% of all hazards are latent in design. However, Gambatese and AlOmari (2016) suggested that the construction worker's safety can be controlled through careful design decisions. In addition, the assessment on the design-related causality accident factor and determining the inter-relationship between specific design features to the workers' injuries and illnesses has been recommended early by Gambatese, Behm, and Rajendran (2008). In general, the concern in early consideration to the design safety-related issues by designers might subsequently reduce the construction fatalities. Hence, in order to improve the designer hazard recognition skill, Lyon, Popov, and Biddle (2016) have further proposed to develop a PtD risk assessment tool in supporting decision-making during the design process. In respect to the OSHCIM implementation, exploring the root causes of construction accidents which are associated with the design-related aspect is significant. It was emphasised by Jamaluddin et al., (2018) that understanding of an injury and illness causality allows for redesigning the working environments, tools and systems and subsequently eliminating the associated hazards. Therefore, the aim of this study is to identify the dominant accident causal in Malaysia's construction industry related to the design aspects.

2. METHODOLOGY

In this study, a combination of qualitative and quantitative methods had been adopted. The secondary data obtained from the official website of the Department of Safety and Health (DOSH), Ministry of Human Resources were utilised to determine the objective. However, for the purposes of this study, the data used have been retrieved on 18 December 2020. In addition, the fatal accidents which were analysed are limited to the case, which is recorded between the years of 2016 and 2020. The type of information recorded for each case includes the date, title case, location, summary of case and focus of investigation.

All data were extracted from the database and tabulated in Microsoft Office Excel. The data were reviewed and scrutinised to ensure the details of each case were completed. Overall, the data collected based on the studied years comprise 179 cases. The non-numerical data process was implemented to gain better insights into the research. The data were analysed by conducting a content analysis. First, the data were screened according to the location. From this, the fatal accidents are sorted and classified based on the sector. Next, the fatal accidents which categories under the construction sector were further analysed. The keywords, terms and theme characteristics from the text of location, title case and summary case were defined in order to identify the project life cycle phase, either the accidents occurred during construction phase or post-construction phase. Moreover, each case was reviewed and examined to determine the causal factor, which contributed to the accident occurrences. Frequency analysis which focussed on the description of causal of accidents was counted and thus significant categories and factors which contribute to fatality in the construction sector were established. Finally, in-depth content analysis was conducted of all cases which classify under the construction sector. The keywords and terms related with the concept and design nature or structural failure were addressed. Hence, the causal factors of accidents related to design aspects in the construction industry are determined.

3. RESULTS AND DISCUSSIONS

3.1. Statistic of Fatal Accidents from 2016 to 2020

The total cases reported and published within the studied years were 179 cases, which include all sectors. From the content analysis, the total number of fatal accidents which occurred only in the construction sector is 95 cases. Fig. 12.1(a) shows the statistics of fatal accidents cases reported to DOSH in all sectors and refinement is made to the construction sector. In 2016, the total fatal accidents reported were 33 cases and 18 of the fatal cases were contributed by the construction industry. The number of fatal accidents in the construction industry decreased in the following year, 2017, where only 11 cases were reported. However, in 2018, the fatal accidents cases of all sectors were recorded the highest amongst the studied year which is 54 and the fatal accidents cases of the construction sector also recorded the highest within the 5 years with 35 cases (64.8%). Meanwhile, in 2019 the fatal accidents in the construction sector were reduced by almost 50%, which are 17 cases. The number of fatal accidents reported was kept on reducing in the year of 2020 with only 14 cases. The decrease of the statistics is most probably due to the reduced number of new project developments, which were affected by the Covid-19 pandemic.

In order to provide a better insight of fatal accidents in the construction sector, Fig. 12.1(b) shows the number of cases based on the project lifecycle phase, namely construction phase and post-construction phase. Most of the fatal accidents occurred during the construction phase with a total of 70 reported cases.

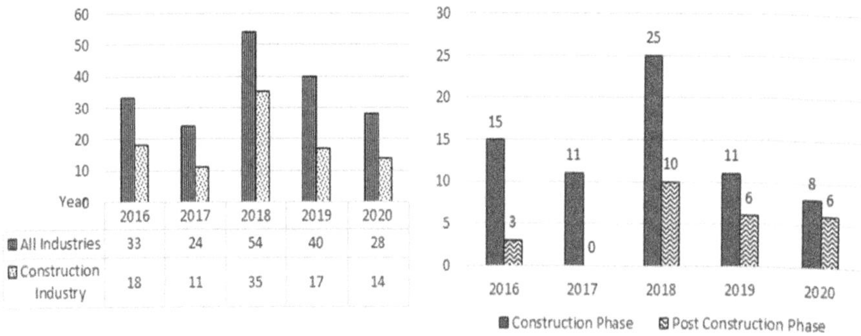

(a) (b)

Fig. 12.1. Statistics of Fatal Accidents in Malaysia Between 2016 and 2020. (a) Fatal Accidents in All Industries and Construction Industry; (b) Fatal Accidents According to the Project Lifecycle Phase.

This is aligned with findings by Jamaluddin et al., (2018), which discovered that the construction sites contribute to the higher rates of accidents which lead to permanent disability, loss of productivity and fatality. The highest number of fatalities occurred in 2018 with 25 cases and followed by 15 cases in 2016. In 2017 and 2019, the fatalities in accidents recorded are 11 cases. Meanwhile, in the year of 2020, the least fatal accidents were recorded, which are eight cases.

In comparison, the numbers of fatal accidents during the post-construction phase between 2016 and 2020 were 25 cases. The highest percentage of fatal accidents occurring during the post-construction phase was recorded in the year of 2020 with 42.9% from a total of 14 cases. For instance, workers face difficulties in accessing building's elements and components for regular inspection and maintenance due to improper accessibility which received lack of consideration during the design stage (Khalid, Abdullah, Hanafi, Said, & Hasim, 2019). Therefore, workers are prone to accidents during execution of maintenance works such as cleaning, servicing, re-painting or repairing works throughout the building lifespan.

3.2. Fatality Causal Factors in Construction Industry

In depth analysis on the accident's casualties of all cases which occurred in the construction sector, the causal factors were categorised into 10 categories. The fatality was due to either falls from height, hit by object, hit by vehicle, electrocution, being buried, asphyxiation, explosion, being trapped, drowning and stung by hornets. Each category was extracted based on the keywords and terms analysed from the secondary data. Fig. 12.2(a) shows the numbers of fatal accidents which occurred in Malaysia's construction sector between 2016 and 2020.

3.3. Falls from Height

In this study, falls from height is indicated as the most frequent accident which contributes to fatalities throughout the studied years. There were 52 cases

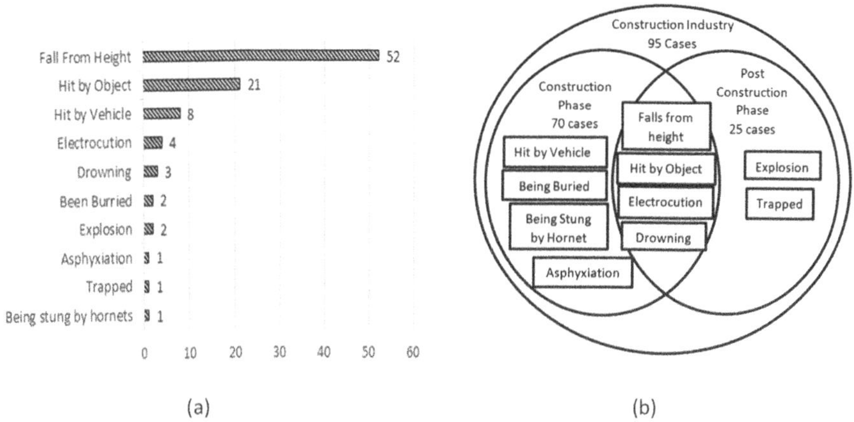

Fig. 12.2. Causal Factors of Fatality between 2016 and 2020. (a) Category of Fatal Accidents; (b) Fatal Accident During Construction Phase and Post-Construction Phase.

recorded which represented 54.7% of the total cases of fatal accidents where 40 cases identified occurred during the construction phase and 12 cases occurred during the post-construction phase. This finding is consistent as compared to other countries such as in the United States, as it is reported that fall accidents are the main cause of injuries and fatalities in the construction industry (Hu, Rahmandad, Smith-Jackson, & Winchester, 2011). In addition, developing countries like Pakistan (Zahoor, et al., 2015), also suffered from high fatality and injury rates due to the fall accidents.

During the construction phase, there are various physical tasks that need to be conducted depending on the type and size of the project. The victims were reported to have fallen due to few scopes of works such as installation and dismantling of temporary structures. The structures include formwork, platform, scaffolding and parapet wall. In addition, the installation work of permanent structures such as roof, air conditioning unit and utilities including pipe conduit, cable trunking and TV cable are prone to the same nature of working at height. Other scopes of works such as plastering and refining wall works and cleaning jobs on the cantilever platform also contribute to accidents due to the fall from a height. Besides, victims also reported to have fallen after being hit by moving objects while conducting lifting operations and being crushed by other objects. Meanwhile, working at height, such as while climbing the ladder, working on mobile scaffold and working in the elevator shaft, has also been recorded under this causal factor of fatal accidents.

From the analysis, there were various causes that contribute to fall from height accidents, which can be classified into human, management, technical and environmental factors. For the management factor, it is recorded that the employers failed to provide Standard Operation Procedure (SOP), failed to maintain the safe working system and failed to comply with the specification of temporary structure's installation. Failure to provide safe working areas such as lack of warning signs and lack of safety monitoring contribute to accidents due to open edges whereby the victims fell into the elevator pit, drain and sewer hole. The environmental factor is beyond human control as the accidents occurred when the victims were struck by lightning and fell from the working station. Moreover, human factors such as slipping during inspection works, improper use of the working platform, not wearing any personal protective equipment (PPE) such as safety harness have also been recorded as the causes of the accident. The heights of falling which are identified are in between 2 metres and approximately 120 metres which involve working at high-rise structures.

As for falls from height during the post-construction phase, nine cases were reported, which involve victims falling from a height while conducting works related to roof structures, which include renovation, repairing, cleaning, replacing, changing, measuring, fixing and removing works. Another two cases involved falling from height while the victims were handling pest control jobs and working in confined space at a sewer treatment plant. From the records, the heights of falling, which contribute to fatal accidents during the post-construction phase, are in between 3 and 12 metres. Moreover, the fatality is also contributed by human factors which can be controlled such as not wearing PPE and the victims were not properly attaching the safety gear even wearing the PPE. Besides, the accidents also occurred due to environmental factors such as victims losing control while working at height and falls after being crushed by other objects such as forklift buckets and broken roofs. In addition, management factors also contributed to the incidents where the employers failed to provide SOP and practiced poor supervision at the worksite.

3.4. Being Hit by Object

The second highest frequent factor of fatal accidents is due to being hit by an object. In this context of analysis, there are various terms and keywords used to categorise the causal of accidents, which includes 'being caught between objects', 'crushed by objects', 'hit by falling objects' or 'objects rolled on' the victims. This is aligned with the discovery by Yilmaz (2015) which highlighted 'being hit by dashing and flitting objects', 'being hit by objects', 'falling objects' and 'being stung by something' were the major construction accidents in Istanbul, Turkey. Besides, the word 'object' includes collapsed structures, construction materials, waste, debris and parts of components.

There were 21 cases, which represented 22.1% of the total numbers of fatal accident cases. During the construction phase, there were 14 cases reported throughout the studied years. The highest contribution of fatalities during this phase was due to being hit by falling objects (six cases). The objects that fell include construction materials (wooden block and brick) and broken tower crane's hook block. The second highest contributor is being hit by crushed structure (five cases) and being hit by debris of broken pipe (one case). Besides, one case was reported due to victims being caught in a concrete mixer while handling the machine and victims being caught between structures once the slab and wall structure collapsed due to landslides (1 case). During the post-construction phase, there were seven cases reported due to this causal. Five cases were reported due to victims being crushed by structures which collapsed during demolishing and repairing works. Besides, one case was reported due to victims being caught while conducting lift maintenance and one case involved a sewer line rolled onto the victim and caused fatality.

As for accidents that occurred during both phases, the management factor has been indicated which contributed to these incidents. Employers failed to provide the SOP to keep their workplace safe and cause harm to their workers. Besides, design factors had also been indicated when it was found that the brick wall work was not fully assembled and there was no stiffener to support the brick wall thus contributing to structure collapse. Therefore, the structure hit the victims and caused fatalities.

3.5. Being Hit by Vehicle

The third highest frequent factor of fatal accidents is due to being hit by vehicles. The keywords referred to classify the accidents under this category of causality are 'crushed by' and 'run over by'. This is because the conceptual and nature of incidents were almost the same. In this study, there were eight cases, which represented 8.4% of the total cases of fatal accidents. All cases recorded occurred during the construction phase as there are many movements of vehicles such as lifting, transporting and mobility of resources on and off site to complete the project. The vehicles involved in the reported accident include heavy vehicles and machinery such as lorry, mobile crane, four by four (4WD) vehicle, excavator and telescopic boom lift.

From the analysis, there were four sub-factors identified which contribute to the accident including lack of skills (incompetent driver; one case), unsafe action from worker (fail to park vehicle at the designated area; one case), driving exceed the speed limit (speeding; one case) and lack of safety awareness (rest at the entrance; one case). All these sub factors are classified as human factors. Besides, other four sub factors which are classified as management factors also have been addressed. one case is due to no supervision of traffic , two cases are due to the employer not providing standard or safe operating procedure (SOP) and one case is due to lack of compliance for lifting works.

3.6. Electrocution

Electrical contact or commonly referred to as electrocution contributes to 15% of all occupational fatalities amongst construction workers. There are various causation factors such as direct contact with the power supply, low voltage, working outdoors, and other mediums and environmental characteristics were associated with this accident's fatality (Kim et al., 2016). According to Shiau, Lo, and Ko (2020), electrocution constitutes a great risk factor for casualty accidents at construction sites.

In this study, four electrocution cases were recorded, which represented 4.2% out of the total fatal accidents cases. Three cases occurred during the construction phase and one case during the post-construction phase. From the analysis, two cases occurred due to management factors where the employer did not prepare the SOP (one case) and failed to identify electrical hazards before conducting any site work (one case). Besides, the accident also contributed due to the equipment factor. The equipment or machine which is used to execute works act as conductor once its body is touched or exposed to the power line or live wire in the surrounding area (one case). In addition, one case occurred due to human factors, which is the lack of communication between workers during work execution. According to Chong and Low (2014), poor communication and coordination between the employers and employees are said to be the causes of accidents because most of the workers came from various countries, and hence did not understand the local language.

3.7. Drowning

Drowning is one of the crucial causal factors that contribute to the fatal accident. According to Chan, Yang, and Darko (2018), the location of a working area above or near the sea will pose a high risk of drowning to the construction workers. Besides the surrounding work site that involves a water compartment or water body such as a tank, lake or river also prone to the similar risk. In this study, there were three cases of fatal accidents due to drowning throughout the studied years. During the construction phase, it is recorded that the victim drowned after falling into a hole containing water (one case) and into a river (one case). Besides, during the post-construction phase, the victim drowned in a water treatment plant tank (one case) while conducting cleaning work. All accidents are occurred due to management factors. This is because the employer failed to provide warning signs in the working area, practised poor supervision and failed to provide SOP to enter a confined space.

3.8. Being Buried

In general, there is a potential hazard that relates to the environmental aspect at the worksite as for example landslides. For these years, there were two cases recorded due to this incident. The victim was being buried when the landslide occurred while working on the utilities, electrical cables or hazardous materials underneath the soil (one case). In addition, the incident also occurred when the victim installed formwork boards on the trench wall (one case). The causal factors for both cases were classified under management factors as the employer failed to conduct a risk assessment and did not provide sufficient SOP for the special work and other related work activities.

3.9. Explosion

In line with the electrocution, the fatal accident due to the explosion also deals with the electrical power source. In this study, there were two cases recorded. It is reported that the victim was doing inspection work on the electric panel (one case) and unlocking the cabinet (one case). This task was conducted during the post-construction phase as part of a routine maintenance task in ensuring that the electrical power supply remained efficient. Victims died from burned injuries due to the explosion. The causes of accidents for both cases were mainly classified under the management factors because the employer did not provide the SOP to conduct the physical activities, which are prone to the electrical hazard at the worksite.

3.10. Being Trapped

Being trapped has also been identified as one of the factors contributing to the fatality in the construction industry. From the analysis, the victim was trapped in a manhole and died due to heavy water flowing (one case). This happened during the post-construction phase after the victim conducted maintenance work by clearing the waste that clogged the manhole. This incident happened due to management factors where the employer practised lack of compliance to a safety regulation and Industry Code of Practice for Safe Working in a Confined Space 2010 requirements.

3.11. Asphyxiation

From the analysis, the victim dies due to high concentration of nitrogen when cutting pipe in a confined space (one case). According to Watanabe and Morita (1998), the suffocation, strangulation and chemical exposure could be acknowledged as part of asphyxiation. Therefore, this incident is categorised as asphyxiation as the victims suffocate in the space and die. The incident happened during the construction phase due to management factors where the employer practised lack of compliance to a safety regulation and Industry Code of Practice for Safe Working in a Confined Space 2010 requirements.

3.12. Being Stung by Hornets

Besides, one fatality case was recorded within the studied year whereby the victim was killed after being stung by a swarm of hornets when installing a culvert. The installation work was conducted during the construction phase. Due to uncertainty of the situation or condition, the cause of this fatal accident may be classified as an environmental factor.

Moreover, even an accident due to being trapped and asphyxiation were isolated cases as only one incident was reported for both categories throughout the studied years, these factors should be taken into consideration as to prevent similar incidents from occurring in the future. In general, both types of accidents are prone to occur during the post-construction phase when maintenance or repairing works are required.

In general, Fig. 12.2(b) presents the existence of fatal accident's categories during the construction phase and post-construction phase in Malaysian construction industry between 2016 and 2020. It shows that the fatal accidents that occurred during the construction phase and post-construction phase mainly were due to falls from a height, hit by object, electrocution and drowning. Meanwhile, the fatal accidents that occurred only during the construction phase were identified as being hit by vehicles, being buried, stung by hornets and asphyxiation (suffocation). Besides, for the post-construction phase, there are only two categories of fatal accidents identified, which are due to explosions and being trapped. In general, the findings of this study are aligned with Hamid et al. (2019) discovery of the sub-causes that contribute to the fatal accidents include working at a height, incorrect work procedure, structural failure, unsafe work procedure, choosing not to wear PPE, equipment failure or defective tools, and lack of supervision.

The causes of accidents during the post-construction phase need to be explored which also form a substantial aspect of OSHCIM development. According to Zou, Zhang, and Wang (2007), the recognition of risk according to a project lifecycle may assist in prioritising the significance of influence in terms of cost, time, quality, safety and environmental sustainability. This also provides an important insight based on the duty holder's perspective and helps clear understanding about the duty holder's roles in eliminating construction hazards and risk as early as in the design and planning stages. A close involvement by the duty holders is a crucial process to promote less accident rate in the construction industry and improve cooperation between parties.

3.13. Design-Related Causal Factors in Construction Industry

From the analysis of 95 fatal accident cases, which have been classified in the construction sectors regardless during the construction phase or during the post-construction phase of the studied years, there were five cases that have been determined as the most design-related causal factors to the current study. In-depth analysis on the keyword and term used in the report description of the cases were related to the concept or nature of the design aspect. The word 'structure collapse' indicates structural failure, which is related to the design aspect. In the previous section, these cases were categorised under the category of hit by object accidents.

In the first case, the victims were killed after a structure collapsed while the victims were handling the pre-dumping work on the diagonal prop wall precast concrete (WPC). Meanwhile in the second case, the victims were killed after a structure collapse while repairing the retaining wall. The third case involved fatality incidents whereby the victim died after being hit by a collapsed structure of ribs while the victim was making measurements under the rib. In addition, the fourth case indicates that the particular brick wall was not fully assembled and there was no stiffener or support to the brick wall. Therefore, the brick wall collapsed and hit the victims which contributed to the fatality. And in the fifth case, it is recorded that the victim died after being hit by a collapsed mezzanine floor which was overloaded with excessive pallets. The summary of each case is presented in Fig. 12.3. The fatality of each accident was due to the consequences of victims being hit by collapsing structures which in this study is referred to as an object. As reported, the structure that has collapsed during the construction works includes the concrete panel, concrete wall, structure of T's ribs, brick wall and mezzanine floor.

In general, there were many confounding factors that exist due to the complexity of the construction process, multiple organisations involved, worksite

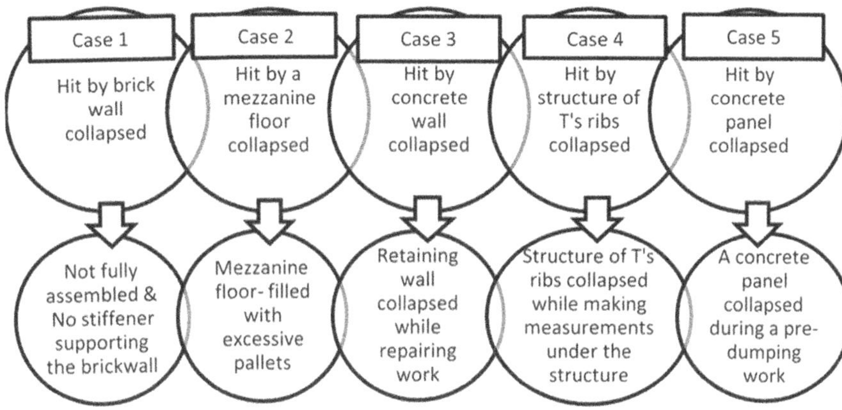

Fig. 12.3. Summary of Fatal Accident Cases.

conditions and human-related factors that complicate the investigations to determine the relationship between the accidents and the design risk (Gambatese, Michael Toole, & Abowitz, 2017). Therefore, researchers rely on the case studies, surveys, historical data analysis and document reviews to investigate potential design risks in PtD. This requires a thorough and systematic study to explore the causal factor of accidents to ensure the existence of design-related aspects, which interacts or influences the accidents occurrences. Therefore, the evaluation of the contributory factors of accident causation due to design aspect contributes to the considerable aspect of PtD principles of the development of OSHCIM guidelines. In addition, this study could facilitate the governor, policymakers and regulators to acknowledge the root causes of design safety issues and suitable measures to be adopted by the construction practitioners in preventing accidents.

5. CONCLUSIONS

In general, sustainable development is a comprehensive mission that aims to achieve intergenerational balance on the three key aspects namely environment, economic and social. As for the social sustainability in the construction sector, it involves a life-enhancing process to attain social equality amongst all construction stakeholders in terms of health, education, economic welfare and other human rights. Therefore, according to Marjaba and Chidiac (2016), for a project to be considered sustainable, these three pillars of sustainability must be equally achieved, where worker health and safety has been put as priority into the built environment.

Globally, there are everlasting efforts to identify the causal factors of accidents and prevention measurements to minimise the occurrences. Many studies and efforts are continuously conducted and explored due to the nature of the accidents, which may have contributed from many factors. This has caused complex interaction between the factors and it is hard to predict the actual reason of how such an accident or fatality happens. This is especially true when it is involved in court decisions. However, it is crucial to identify the root causes and understand the interaction factors as to understand and avoid such accidents from reoccurring.

As in Malaysia's context, the initiative taken by the Ministry of Human Resources, through the DOSH to improve the safety and health performance specifically in the construction industry by developing the OSHCIM Guidelines, is an excellent approach. Integrating the PtD principle into the guidelines has become an essential strategy to eliminate the construction hazards during design phase, as this can minimise the possibility of construction accidents throughout the project life cycle. However, it requires a comprehensive understanding of the connection or inter-relationship or interaction between design aspects with the fatalities, injuries or illnesses.

This study summarises the probable causes of Malaysia's construction accidents fatality. The fatal accidents cases between 2016 and 2020 show that the three main causal factors that contribute to fatality are fall from height, hit by object and hit by vehicle. In addition, this study also provides an insight into design aspect accident causation. The five individual cases have close interaction with the design aspects due to the structural collapse. The structures involved were concrete structure, brick wall and mezzanine floor. This was due to the improper assembling and non-adequate design. In addition, there was no supporting structure and the structure failed to cater the excessive load imposed.

By knowing the potential causes related to the design aspect, it will consequently prompt the duty holders to be more aware of the accidents that can occur in their building or structure at the initial phase of the project development. In addition, this study can assist the practitioners to prioritise preventive actions to combat the most likely causes for each accident mechanism at each construction phase. The safety issue is no longer solely the responsibility of the contractor anymore but needs to be shared amongst the duty holders of a respective project initiating the risks.

There are some limitations in this study where the accident cases are only focussed on the secondary data gathered from the official website of DOSH for the period between 2016 and 2020. In addition, there are also difficulties due to the ambiguity of words and terms used for reporting purposes, and the cases were not classified according to the project life cycle. However, the findings can assist further exploration for the key industrial players and government in implementing OSHCIM in the future construction project undertaking as this is also contributes to the sustainability.

ACKNOWLEDGEMENT

The authors wish to acknowledge the financial support received from Universiti Teknologi Malaysia through the research university grant (RUG) of UTM and Collaborative Research Grant (CRG) of Q.J130000.2451.08G56 and R.J130000.7351.4B519.

REFERENCES

Behm, M. (2005). Linking construction fatalities to the design for construction safety concept. *Safety Science, 43*(8), 589–611.

Chan, A. P. C., Yang, Y., & Darko, A. (2018). Construction accidents in a large-scale public infrastructure project: Severity and prevention. *Journal of Construction Engineering and Management, 144*(10), 05018010. doi:10.1061/(asce)co.1943-7862.0001545

Chong, H. Y., & Low, T. S. (2014). Accidents in Malaysian construction industry: Statistical data and court cases. *International Journal of Occupational Safety and Ergonomics, 20*(3), 503–513.

Driscoll, T. R., Harrison, J. E., Bradley, C., & Newson, R. S. (2008). The role of design issues in work-related fatal injury in Australia. *Journal of Safety Research, 39*(2), 209–214.

Eskerod, P., & Huemann, M. (2013). Sustainable development and project stakeholder management: What standards say. *International Journal of Managing Projects in Business, 6*(1), 36–50

Gambatese, J. A., & AlOmari, K. (2016). Degrees of connectivity: Systems model for upstream risk assessment and mitigation. *Accident Analysis & Prevention, 93*, 251–259.

Gambatese, J. A., Behm, M., & Rajendran, S. (2008). Design's role in construction accident causality and prevention: Perspectives from an expert panel. *Safety Science, 46*(4), 675–691.

Gambatese, J. A., Michael Toole, T., & Abowitz, D. A. (2017). Owner perceptions of barriers to prevention through design diffusion. *Journal of Construction Engineering and Management, 143*(7), 04017016.

Goh, Y. M., & Chua, S. (2016). Knowledge, attitude and practices for design for safety: A study on civil & structural engineers. *Accident Analysis & Prevention, 93*, 260–266.

Hallowell, M. R., & Hansen, D. (2016). Measuring and improving designer hazard recognition skill: Critical competency to enable prevention through design. *Safety Science, 82*, 254–263.

Hamid, A. R. A., Azmi, M. N., Aminudin, E., Jaya, R. P., Zakaria, R., Zawawi, A. M. M., ... Saar, C. C. (2019). Causes of fatal construction accidents in Malaysia. *IOP Conference Series: Earth and Environmental Science, 220*(1), 012044.

Haslam, R. A., Hide, S. A., Gibb, A. G., Gyi, D. E., Pavitt, T., Atkinson, S., & Duff, A. R. (2005). Contributing factors in construction accidents. *Applied Ergonomics, 36*(4), 401–415.

Health and Safety Executive. (2021). Workplace fatal injuries in Great Britain, 2021. Retrieved from https://www.hse.gov.uk/statistics/pdf/fatalinjuries.pdf Accessed on July 26, 2021.

Hu, K., Rahmandad, H., Smith-Jackson, T., & Winchester, W. (2011). Factors influencing the risk of falls in the construction industry: A review of the evidence. *Construction Management and Economics, 29*(4), 397–416.

Huemann, M., & Ringhofer, C. (2018). Challenge or potential? Risk identification in the context of sustainable development: A case study. In *Global business expansion: Concepts, methodologies, tools, and applications* (pp. 1318–1336). IGI Global. Retrieved from https://scholar.google.com/scholar?hl=en&as_sdt=0%2C5&q=Huemann%2C+M.%2C+%26+Ringhofer%2C+C.+%282018%29.+Challenge+or+Potential%3F+Risk+Identification+in+the+Context+of+Sustainable+Development%3A+A+Case+Study.+In+Global+Business+Expansion%3A+Concepts%2C+Methodologies%2C+Tools%2C+and+Applications+%28pp.+1318-1336%29.+IGI+Global.&btnG=

Jaafar, M. H., Arifin, K., Aiyub, K., Razman, M. R., Ishak, M. I. S., & Samsurijan, M. S. (2018). Occupational safety and health management in the construction industry: A review. *International Journal of Occupational Safety and Ergonomics, 24*(4), 493–506.

Jamaluddin, N., Yeoh, D., Ghani, A. H. A., Ayob, S. S., Ibrahim, M. H. W., Mohamad, N., ... & Ghafar, N. H. A. (2018). A case study of residential buildings subjected to cracking failures. *International Journal of Integrated Engineering, 10*(2), 118–122.

Karakhan, A. A. (2016a). Designer's liability: Why applying PTD principles is necessary. *Professional Safety, 61*(04), 53–58.

Karakhan, A. A. (2016b). LEED-certified projects: Green or sustainable? *Journal of Management in Engineering, 32*(5), 02516001.

Khalid, E. I., Abdullah, S., Hanafi, M. H., Said, S. Y., & Hasim, M. S. (2019). The consideration of building maintenance at design stage in public buildings: The current scenario in Malaysia. *Facilities, 37*(13–14), 942–960

Kim, H., Lewko, J., Garritano, E., Sharma, B., Moody, J., & Colantonio, A. (2016). Construction fatality due to electrical contact in Ontario, Canada, 1997–2007. *Work, 54*(3), 639–646.

Lam, P. T., Wong, F. W., & Chan, A. P. (2006). Contributions of designers to improving buildability and constructability. *Design Studies*, *27*(4), 457–479.

Lyon, B. K., Popov, G., & Biddle, E. (2016). Prevention through design: For hazards in construction. *Professional Safety*, *61*(09), 37–44.

Marjaba, G. E., & Chidiac, S. E. (2016). Sustainability and resiliency metrics for buildings – Critical review. *Building and Environment*, *101*, 116–125.

Navon, R., & Kolton, O. (2006). Model for automated monitoring of fall hazards in building construction. *Journal of Construction Engineering and Management*, *132*(7), 733–740.

Shiau, Y. R., Lo, F. Y., & Ko, P. C. (2020). Early intervention mechanism for preventing electrical shocks during construction projects: Portable electrical equipment. In *E3S web of conferences* (Vol. 186, p. 03004). EDP Sciences, Retrieved from https://www.e3s-conferences.org/articles/e3sconf/abs/2020/46/e3sconf_ceege2020_03004/e3sconf_ceege2020_03004.html

Suraji, A., Duff, A. R., & Peckitt, S. J. (2001). Development of causal model of construction accident causation. *Journal of Construction Engineering and Management*, *127*(4), 337–344.

Watanabe, T., & Morita, M. (1998). Asphyxia due to oxygen deficiency by gaseous substances. *Forensic Science International*, *96*(1), 47–59.

Weinstein, M., Gambatese, J., & Hecker, S. (2005). Can design improve construction safety? Assessing the impact of a collaborative safety-in-design process. *Journal of Construction Engineering and Management*, *131*(10), 1125–1134.

Yilmaz, F. (2015). Monitoring and analysis of construction site accidents by using accidents analysis management system in Turkey. *Journal of Sustainable Development*, *8*(2), 57.

Zahoor, H., Chan, A. P., Choudhry, R. M., Utama, W. P., & Gao, R. (2015). Construction safety research in Pakistan: A review and future research direction. In *7th International civil engineering congress (ICEC-2015) "Sustainable Development through Advancements in Civil Engineering"* June 12 (Vol. 13, pp. 1–8). Retrieved from https://www.researchgate.net/profile/Hafiz-Zahoor-Ahmad-Khan-2/publication/279195793_Construction_safety_research_in_Pakistan_A_review_and_future_research_direction/links/558e55dc08ae1e1f9bab35c2/Construction-safety-research-in-Pakistan-A-review-and-future-research-direction.pdf#page=8.

Zou, P. X., Zhang, G., & Wang, J. (2007). Understanding the key risks in construction projects in China. *International Journal of Project Management*, *25*(6), 601–614.

CHAPTER 13

COVID 19 AND ITS IMPACT ON MALAYSIAN WOMEN TRAVEL BEHAVIOUR

Masria Mustafa, Zanariah Abd. Rahman, Noor Azreena Kamaluddin and Takeru Shibayama

ABSTRACT

A comprehensive understanding of the pandemic impact on daily behavioural patterns of travellers' movement is crucial in creating safe and comfortable living environments. Since the Covid-19 pandemic has affected many countries in world, many countries have taken unusual steps of partial or full lockdowns. People's normal routine has been disrupted, which has made the transport system indirectly coming to a halt worldwide. Online options have been introduced to maintain the operations for offices, private and government agencies and universities and e-commerce businesses become a spotlight. The study is designed as an effort to understand the travel behaviour of Malaysian women affected by Covid-19 pandemic. An online survey to determine the travel behaviour impact was used as a data collection strategy. Analysis of the collected data reveals significant changes in various aspects of women's travel behaviour. The result will help to enable the policymaker in strategising the best solutions of travel options, which will also improve the women's traveller safety for better and equitable transportation.

Keywords: Covid-19; women; travel behaviour; online survey; Malaysia; equitable transportation

Sustainability Management Strategies and Impact in Developing Countries
Community, Environment and Disaster Risk Management, Volume 26, 165–178

Published under exclusive licence by Emerald Publishing Limited
ISSN: 2040-7262/doi:10.1108/S2040-726220220000026013

1. INTRODUCTION

During this pandemic situation, no industry will be left untouched by the virus and travel is one of the badly impacted sectors. To date, the Covid-19 pandemic has affected 200 countries with more than 100 million cases across the globe (Worldometers.info, 2021). In April 2020, Apple came out with the Mobility Trends Report, which produces the daily percentage of people driving, walking and using public transport (Apple, 2020). As expected, less volume of people travel during this pandemic time as compared to earlier months when lockdown was not yet imposed in most countries in the world. In Malaysia, Movement Control Orders (MCO) has been enforced while social distancing has been encouraged with many closure of gathering places such as large malls and offices. Burki (2020) reported that the lockdown measures and school closures affect girls and women differently across the world and may have long-term negative consequences. A comprehensive understanding of the pandemic impact on daily behavioural patterns of travellers' movement especially among women is crucial in creating safe and comfortable living environments. Since many countries have taken unusual steps of partial or full lockdowns, people's normal routine has been disrupted, which has made the transport system indirectly coming to a halt worldwide. Online options have been introduced to maintain the operations for offices, private and government agencies and universities and e-commerce businesses become a spotlight. It is essential to scrutinise their travel mode choices before and after the outbreak in order to ensure adequate travel choices for women as highlighted in Thombre and Agarwal (2021). Besides, much of our knowledge of gender impact during the pandemic comes from Carli (2020), who commented that the pandemic has generally created challenges for women's advancement. Some examples include more women than men have lost their jobs besides having to be burden by the household responsibility due to the increases in childcare and other responsibilities. The results of this study will help to enable the policy maker in strategising the best solutions of travel options, which will also improve the women's traveller safety for better and equitable transportation.

2. LITERATURE REVIEW

2.1. Covid-19 and Travel Behaviour

Due to the global threat of the Covid-19 pandemic outbreak, great numbers of research have focussed on the impact of the disease on the transportation industry, particularly on travel behaviour. Governments, policymakers and public health actors believe travel restriction could potentially reduce and control the rate of infection hence 'flatten the curve'. Consequently, the transportation sector is among the hardest hit. The introduction of non-pharmaceutical interventions (NPIs) such as social distancing, school closing, movement restriction and lockdown (Haug et al., 2020) like those applied in China to limit the spread of the virus has been adopted across the globe. The NPI could significantly affect and re-shape mobility pattern. However, travel restrictions may be less effective once the outbreak is more widespread (Kraemer et al., 2020). In general, the pandemic gives a huge impact on the mobility of the community as the effect of the travel restriction and threat of the Covid-19 itself. Sy et al. (2020) reported a reduction of more than 90% ridership of public transport in Southeast Asia countries. Several other countries also reported that the Covid-19 pandemic has reduced the mobility of people by more than 50% (Fatmi, 2020) either using a private or public mode of transports.

Kraemer et al. (2020) used real-time mobility data including travel history to elucidate the role of case importation in transmission in cities across China. Besides, the study was also conducted to ascertain the impact of control measures reported on the drastic control measures (i.e. travel restriction) implemented in China, which substantially mitigated the spread of Covid-19. Later, the changes of the mobility pattern studied by (Engle, Stromme, and Zhou, 2020) using the GPS data on the changes in average distance travelled by individual in the United States revealed the increment of local infection rate (i.e. from 0% to 0.003%) which has decreased individual mobility by 2.31% while the stay-at-home order could also reduce the individual mobility by 7.87%. Another study conducted by Bryant and Elofsson (2020) utilised mobility data from Google Mobility Changes Report (Google, 2020) in 11 European countries. The study reported the mobility pattern amid Covid-19 via five different categories, which are retail and recreation, grocery and pharmacy, transit stations, workplace and residential. They highlighted the importance of government action to play a major role in influencing population behavioural change. In addition, Fatmi (2020) shows results of their study on individuals' participation in outdoor activities, which was reduced by more than 50% in a region in Canada during the pandemic. The highest daily frequency of travel is found for routine shopping, followed by work-related travel. The effect of mobility habits in the spread of the Covid-19 in Italy was also studied by Carteni, Di Francesco, and Martino (2020) through a multiple linear regression model and concluded that mobility habits represent one of the variables that explain the number of Covid-19 infections, which the number of daily new cases was related to the trips performed three weeks earlier (i.e. Italian case study). Their findings claimed the underestimation of the mobility restrictions of 14-day quarantine as per incubation-based epidemiological considerations due to possibility of delays between contagion and detection. Based on the Google Mobility Changes Report (Google, 2020), Malaysian mobility pattern has changed as compared to baseline data (extracted during 5-week period from 3 January until 6 February 2020) with a reduction of –58% in the use of public transportation system, –45% in retail and recreation, –7% in visiting of supermarket and pharmacy, –49% to parks, –31% to workplaces and +17% to residential.

2.2. Travel Behaviour: Gender Perspective

Gender is a significant factor in accounting for differences in mobility and travel behaviour. Women's travel behaviour in day-to-day life differs from that of men;

for example, women are more likely to travel shorter distances and to stop more frequently than men during their journeys. The gender gap however is slowly closing. Gender differences in travel patterns are mainly accounted for by the division of roles in the labour market and in the family, as well as age and location. Gender travel behaviour patterns have been changing in recent years, reflecting the evolution of gender differences in socio-economic and demographic conditions (WIKI, 2020). Eurobarometer (2007) conducted a survey and provides gender disaggregated data on modal split in the European Union. It gives a clear indication of gender differences in relation to different modes of transportation. According to the data, a higher proportion of men travel by car and motorcycle than women, while women walk and use public transport and bicycles more than men. Women are more inclined than men to use low-carbon transportation modes such as public transport and walking, although existing conditions do not always take the specific needs and constraints of women into account. In addition, according to some studies, women and men perceive risks differently, including the environmental risk of climate change. Gender differences in socio-economic and demographic conditions are at the basis of women's lower ability to own and use a car. There is evidence to suggest that women travel in private cars more frequently as passengers rather than as drivers (Eurobarometer, 2007). This is also supported in other literature where several empirical studies conducted in both developed and developing countries have found that women tend to travel shorter distances, to chain trips, to spend more time travelling and to prefer public transport and taxi services to cars more than men (Gauvin et al., 2020). Previous studies also indicate that women often experienced fear of sexual harassment or street crimes on public transport and when walking in a public space. These depictions have created a gender socialisation that women are physically more vulnerable to street crime and assault which contribute to women's low perception of safety. Women often take walking or public transport due to less access to private vehicles and their travel behaviour is often constrained by cultural norms, limited financial capability and concern for personal safety (Hidayati, Tan, and Yamu, 2020).

Travel behaviour research swarms with evidence illustrating the difference between women's and men's transportation demands and realities. Although parameters like income, age, household size and structure, elder-child care responsibilities, ethnicity, employment status, degree of disability, location, class and education can produce significant differences among women's mobility patterns, certain key observations were also found to contribute that women spend more time on household maintenance activities and less time on leisure than men, with the result that women make more frequent but short trips. Other than that, it was also found that women adjust their schedules to accommodate their full-time employment with little or no adjustments from their male partners. Women are also less able to adjust their schedules and travel patterns to accommodate alternative schedules or transportation modes (Uteng, 2012). Multiple studies have shown that women have different patterns, needs and behaviours. Woman's travel behaviour is characterised by trip-chaining and time poverty. The main reasons for this are that women do 75% of the world's unpaid care work, the gender pay gap and women's physical condition. Women have a smaller range when travelling the same amount of time. Women carry luggage and accompany people, more often on public transport and by foot. These facts were largely confirmed in a workshop with 40 women professionals in Berlin, Germany, conducted in the summer of 2019 (Bellmann, Ypma, and Polack, 2020). In addition, many other projects in developing countries are also aiming to encourage access for women to services and means of transport and to improve the participation of women in transport-related jobs. The development agencies are supporting a varied range of efforts to take account of gender issues in transport and to develop tools that can be used by transport planners, policymakers and practitioners. Thus in developing countries, it was found that women made more trips than men, with a greater variety of routes, but within a more restricted geographical area. Furthermore, women generally use less expensive modes of transport than men. It is also important to stress that women, in their choices of modes of travel, are far more sensitive than men to environmental issues (Duchène, 2011).

3. METHODOLOGY

3.1. Survey Design

The Malaysian Government Movement Control, commonly referred to as the MCO or PKP, is a cordon sanitaire implemented as a preventive measure by the federal government of Malaysia in response to the Covid-19 pandemic in the country on 18 March 2020. Under MCO, residents are urged to stay at home, with some other restrictions such as only one person per household authorised to leave their residences to buy essential goods. For the purpose of this study, a questionnaire survey has been distributed online since end of March 2020 to acquire information on the demographic characteristics of the respondents such as age and gender, the purpose of travelling before and during Covid-19 and their travel mode to the destination. Besides, questions to describe their choices of transportation mode in terms of, especially, the frequency of travels and the trend of personal trips such as shopping for groceries. This subjective method of data collection is important to evaluate the background of respondents and their daily activity before and during Covid-19. The same method was also adopted in the study of Przybylowski, Stelmak, and Suchanek (2021) to identify travel behaviours with special regard to the level of safety and comfort of passengers. The Research Center of Transport Planning and Traffic Engineering, Vienna University of Technology, Austria distributed the survey with the assistance of other researchers in more than 10 countries as highlighted in Shibayama, Sandholzer, Laa, and Brezina (2021) including from Universiti Teknologi MARA, Malaysia. The questionnaire was available in more than 20 languages including Malay and has been distributed to more than 20 countries around the world including Malaysia and other ASEAN countries such as Thailand and Indonesia. The details on the metadata of the raw data set can be found in Brezina et al. (2020). Fig. 13.1 depicts the lockdown policy of Malaysia and the number of responses and lockdown policy for other countries associated with this study can be found in Shibayama et al. (2021).

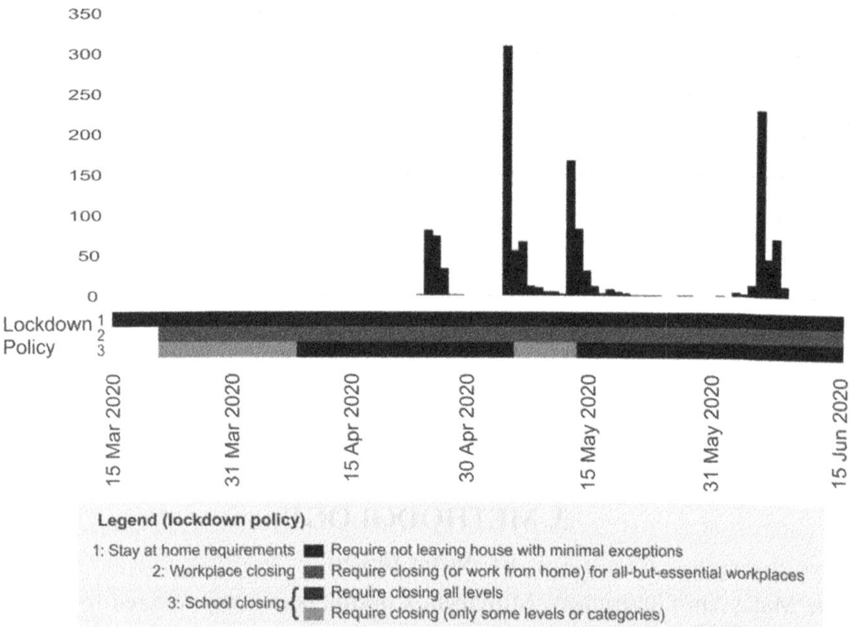

Fig. 13.1. Lockdown Policy for Malaysia.

4. RESULTS AND DISCUSSIONS

4.1. Demographic Analysis

Table 13.1 shows the demographic variables of respondents from the survey. In total, there were 1,361 respondents with 788 female respondents. The respondents were primary female while male respondents represent 42.1% of the total percentage of respondents. Majority of the respondents were between 19 and 29 years old for female and 30 and 39 for male with 63.3% and 68.7% were employee for female and male respondents, respectively. Majority of them were university graduate. 36.9% and 46.8% of the respondents were couple with children below 18 years old for female and male respondents. In addition, the majority of survey female respondents worked at university or school and the male respondents work at the office. Approximately 39.2% of female respondents and 44.2% of male respondents have their children staying at home. In addition, 43.6% and 39.3% of the children stayed at home with the parent for female and male respondents, respectively, due to the fact that parents stay at home due to Covid-19.

4.2. Travel Analysis for Work, Education and Groceries Trip

Commuting to workplace and education (school and university) is considered as primary travel purpose. As refer to Fig. 13.2(a), by looking at the mode choice among women and men, those who work and going out to buy groceries use private car as their main mode of transportation (84.94%). The findings resemble

Table 13.1. The Demographic Variables of Respondents.

Variables	Women (%)	Men (%)	No Info (%)
Age	***N*=788**	***N*=547**	***N*=26**
Under 18	0.0	0.4	0.0
19–29	38.2	30.3	26.9
30–39	32.9	34.0	34.6
40–49	19.5	18.8	15.4
50–59	8.4	15.2	0.0
60–69	0.5	1.1	0.0
70 or older	0.1	0.0	0.0
Prefer not to say	0.4	0.2	23.1
Occupation	***N*=788**	***N*=547**	***N*=26**
In school (up to high school)	0.0	0.5	0.0
A student (university and similar), not working	28.9	21.9	30.8
A student, also working part-time	2.3	1.8	0.0
An employee	63.3	68.7	61.5
A trainee, an apprentice or in internship	0.5	0.5	0.0
A self-employed	0.8	1.8	0.0
Volunteering, in civil or military service	0.1	0.2	0.0
Houseman, housewife	0.9	0.0	0.0
Unemployed	0.8	0.5	3.8
A pensioner/retired	0.5	1.3	0.0
Other (please specify)	1.9	2.6	3.8
Level of Education	***N*=663**	***N*=476**	***N*=19**
Mandatory education	0.3	0.6	0.0
High school	7.5	16.2	15.8
Apprentice, vocational education	0.5	2.1	0.0
University	88.2	76.5	63.2
Other	3.5	4.6	21.1
Household Size	***N*=558**	***N*=442**	***N*=19**
Single-person	15.6	17.6	10.5
Single-parent	5.4	2.3	0.0
Shared flat	4.3	2.9	0.0
A couple without children or without children under 18	11.5	10.2	10.5
A couple with children under 18	36.9	46.8	31.6
Extended family (3 generations or more)	13.1	8.1	0.0
Other	13.3	12.0	47.4
Type of Workplace	***N*=484**	***N*=374**	***N*=13**
Company office	29.5	31.8	30.8
Shop, store, restaurant, ticket counter, service centre)	5.2	7.2	15.4
Production site (e.g. factory)	0.4	2.1	7.7
Place to take care of other sick, old or disabled persons (e.g. hospital)	4.8	1.9	7.7
Task to visit places of different customers (e.g. delivery staff)	3.7	3.7	0.0
Particular site of my company (e.g. construction site)	1.2	5.9	0.0
Particular outdoor site of my own or my company (e.g. agricultural field)	0.0	0.3	0.0
A moving vehicle (e.g. driver, conductor)	0.0	1.3	0.0
A lecture room (school, university)	41.5	27.0	30.8
A civil protection service (e.g. police)	1.7	8.8	0.0
Is at home. I work from here	5.6	5.1	7.7
Others	6.4	4.8	0.0

Table 13.1. (*Continued*)

Variables	Women (%)	Men (%)	No Info (%)
Have Children at Home	***N*=684**	***N*=491**	***N*=19**
Yes	39.2	44.2	31.6
No	60.8	55.8	68.4
How Children Spent Time	***N*=259**	***N*=214**	***N*=6**
At home alone	1.5	0.9	0.0
At home with the parent (e.g. housewife)	21.2	38.8	0.0
At home with the parent. It became possible because parents stay at home due to Covid-19	43.6	39.3	33.3
At a family member other than the parents (e.g. older siblings)	19.3	14.0	66.7
At my workplace, but without particular childcare facility	0.8	0.0	0.0
At schools other than they usually go	0.4	0.0	0.0
Others	13.1	7.0	0.0

the results in the study of Johansson, Henriksson, and Envall (2019) where car is an important resource to manage everyday life for many informants, and private vehicle plays an important role in their lifestyles, shaping the locations of their homes, jobs, leisure activities and projects, such as renovating and socialising. For the students, walking contributed the highest user as many of them stayed in the campus. Fig. 13.2(b) and (c) depicts the status of commuting during Covid-19 for work and education trip. Since the lockdown was imposed, the women who work and study stayed at home because their workplace introduced obligatory teleworking and all courses and learning were held online. The Covid-19 pandemic has open doors to teleworking, which has been used, by companies and government offices worldwide to ensure their employees' safety and to provide continuity to economic activity (Belzunegui-Eraso and Erro-Garcés, 2020). Fig. 13.2(f) depicts the childcare situations by workplace types. In case of women presence become essential or when home office is possible, less percentage of children stayed at home could be observed. As highlighted by Mallett, Marks, and Skountridaki (2020), the working mother especially has been impacted by home-based working during the lockdown which also lead to the household work was unequally distributed, burdening women more than men.

For groceries shopping depicted by Fig. 13.2(d) and (e), throughout the data before the Covid-19 pandemic, it is apparent that the women and men respondents tend to buy large quantity of groceries in stores once or twice a week or less often. Very few of them tend to buy the groceries delivered on a regular basic or pre-ordered weekly. Besides, there are no behavioural changes around the way people are buying groceries. The men respondents in Malaysia reported that their trend of grocery shopping during the pandemic did not change at all. However, changes occurred for women as more than 20% of them stated that they were helping out the other people to buy groceries. Due to MCO restrictions, such as only one people per household authorised to leave their residences to buy essential goods, the respondents who normally fampooling (family member drive) to buy groceries reduce their travel and some of them even did not go out to buy

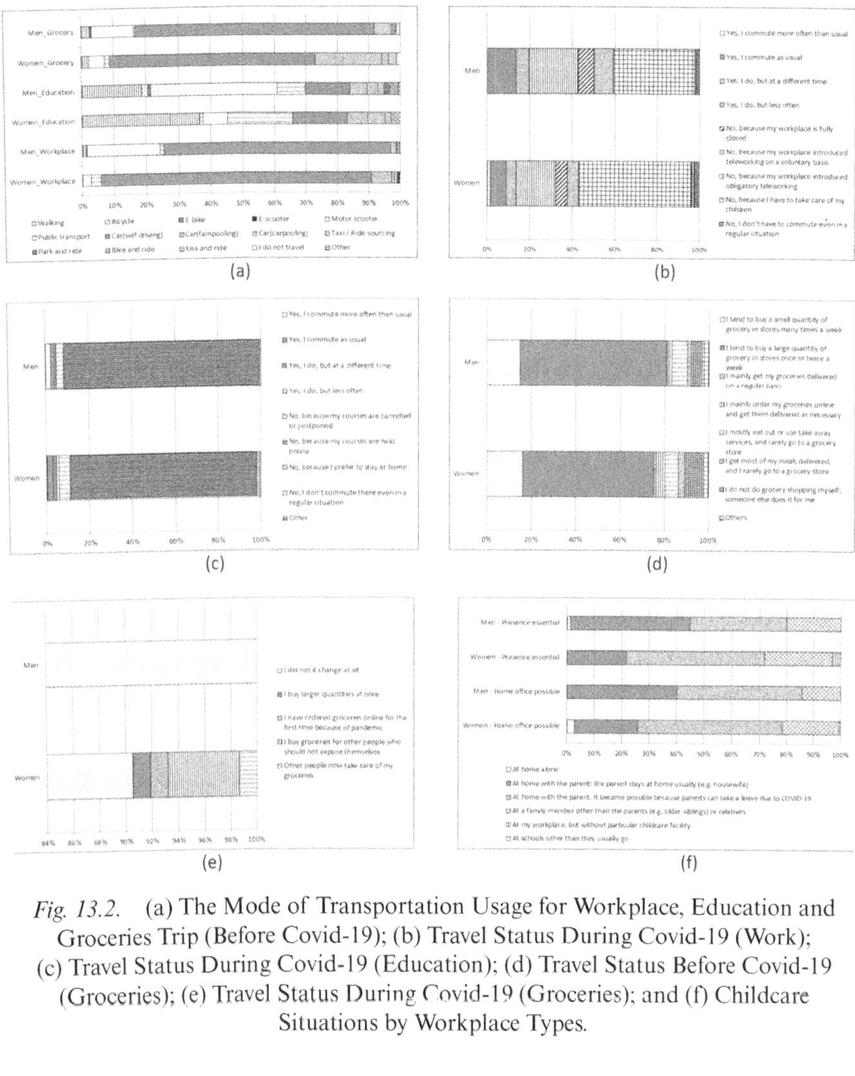

Fig. 13.2. (a) The Mode of Transportation Usage for Workplace, Education and Groceries Trip (Before Covid-19); (b) Travel Status During Covid-19 (Work); (c) Travel Status During Covid-19 (Education); (d) Travel Status Before Covid-19 (Groceries); (e) Travel Status During Covid-19 (Groceries); and (f) Childcare Situations by Workplace Types.

groceries but order online instead which increase the number of private vehicles for delivery services. In addition, women always take the responsibility for the household shopping as it has been suggested that men do not enjoy, or are unwilling, in the shopping task (Mortimer and Clarke, 2010). With E-shopping growing rapidly, the impact of E-shopping on shopping travel has been the focus of many researchers. A study by Koch, Frommeyer, and Schewe (2020) reported that during the current pandemics, customers are spending more time online, and it was found that hedonic motives exert the strongest influence on generation Y and Z consumers' behavioural intentions to shop online. The trends established during this crisis may remain stable into the future, inflicting serious consequences on physical stores due to a rapid increase in e-commerce. Other study conducted by Shi, De Vos, Yang, and Witlox (2019) highlighted some important issues that should be considered on the effect of E-shopping to the transportation system. The study reported that for some intangible activities such as, E-shopping can hardly replace the personal trips because the consumer has to travel to collect or conduct the activities. Other issues are on the trip making. It is also possible that delivery services cause additional urban congestion as more often people buy online, the higher demand for delivery service it will contribute.

4.3. Discussions

Gender inequality is one of the issues that rose during the pandemic as policies and public health efforts have not addressed the gendered impacts of any outbreak (Smith, 2019). Women act as the front-line at home; therefore, the Covid-19 gives a significant long-term negative consequence on them. They are among the group of people that should mentally and emotionally support during this fragile situation. This statement is backed-up by numerous studies that reported the increment number of domestic violence cases amid the Covid-19 (well elaborated in Burki (2020)). The restriction movement order could also cause women to become vulnerable to criminal targets. In economic perspective, women are usually employed by the informal sector; thus, they tend to lose their job during the pandemic (Burki, 2020). Furthermore, it has been reported that travel restriction causes financial challenges and uncertainty for most commuter women foreign domestic workers who travel in Southeast Asia (Carvalho, Cheung, and Siu, 2020). The analysis made by the United Nation and UNDP's Global Covid-19 Gender Response Tracker across 206 countries found that women have been discriminated against by most of the world's nations in protecting the rights of women and girls due to the Covid-19 crisis (UNDP, 2020). Taking experiences from past outbreaks such as the Ebola virus and the Zika virus, gender inequality does exist (Wenham, Smith, and Morgan, 2020).

Previous studies have shown the disadvantages women during the pandemic outbreak as most women working as front-liners such as nurses, doing groceries shopping for household survival during the pandemic and using public transport more often than their counterparts. UN Women reported that approximately 65% of women lost their accessibility to the transit as women less likely to own vehicles as compared to men (UN Women and Women Count, 2020). A case study in Belgium confirmed the challenges faced by women particularly among the working-age population as they are among the public transportation users that are vulnerable to virus exposure (Assoumou Ella, 2021). In Belgium, women recorded among the highest confirmed cases and they shared a large portion of the country essential and front-liners. In contrast, during the first restriction MCO in March 2020, the Malaysian government and other countries (e.g. The Philippines as in (UN Women and Women Count, 2020) only allowed the head of the family (i.e. men – father figure) to do all grocery shopping apparently to reduce the shopping time and exposure to the virus among women. An exploratory study conducted in the Netherlands by combining several mobility databases (e.g. Apple, Google and Translink) about changes in mobility patterns found that the impact of the virus on mobility patterns is significant among women especially those with lower education background and single mother (Kloof and Kensmil, 2020). Longitudinal study conducted by Dekhtyar, Weber, Helgertz, and Herlitz (2018) found that women and men tend to pursue their career following their initial academic strength. Nevertheless, women are more likely to avoid career demanding the technical or numerical skills. Women are reported more involved in humanities and social sciences field as compared to engineering filed of work. Wright, Eaton, and Skagerberg (2015) reported men are more likely than women to enter fields based on their empathising and systemising skills.

At the beginning of the pandemic, there were hope that the global shift to home-working or work from home could mean childcare and house chores would be divided more equally within couples. According to an article from Savage (2020), numerous studies of working parents' lives during Covid-19 have shown that a disproportionate share of the burden is still falling on women. In Australia, provisional results of a survey by the University of Melbourne suggest that in households with children, parents are putting in an extra 6 hours a day of care and supervision, with women taking on more than two-thirds of the extra time. Besides, Krentz, Kos, Green, and Alonso (2020) found that working women currently spend an average of 15 hours a week more on unpaid domestic labour than men. With schools and day-care centres closed, parents have become full-time childcare providers and home-school teachers, even as they try to meet their work responsibilities. Parlak, Cakiroglu, and Gul (2020) explored the Covid-19 experiences of Turkish female academics in term of gender roles by aiming on how these women distribute the load between domestic and academic responsibilities. The results reveal that the pandemic has deepened existing inequalities, along with gender inequalities and the academic life of women academics has changed in terms of academic productivity. The results were supported by Feng and Savani (2020) who highlighted during the lockdown, lower work productivity and job satisfaction were reported among women as compared to men despite have to undertake most of the responsibilities of the household and childcare.

5. CONCLUSIONS AND OUTLOOK

The current study has demonstrated how the pandemic has impacted the travel behaviour of Malaysian women. In light of the on-going Covid-19 pandemic worldwide, majority of workplaces such as companies and government offices have introduced work-from-home culture and the education sectors increase the online learning opportunity. Moreover, private vehicles are also one of the most frequented modes of transportation to be used as there are increased in terms of health risk confidence among the commuter. In addition, E-commerce sectors increase and most people travel only if they need to travel. Malaysian Government has announced variety stimulus packages to deal with coronavirus fallout. Therefore, in case of women, they have to engage more often in multi-modal travel, shifting their means of transportation. If trip-chaining is the norm, we can improve offerings towards more ease and efficiency in planning and executing multi-stop routes as highlighted by (Ypma, Bellmann, and Polack, 2020) for women's safety and convenient. In addition, we can also take the advantages of communities' relationship in a wide variety of situations such as picking up neighbours' kids from school. In general, the study sets a ground for future research, which will include a larger sample size, and to cover sub urban area nationwide.

ACKNOWLEDGEMENT

The authors appreciate the supports from Research Center of Transport Planning and Traffic Engineering, Vienna University of Technology and Universiti Teknologi MARA (UiTM).

REFERENCES

Apple. (2020). *Mobility trends reports. Apple and CDC.* [2020-04-29]. Retrieved from https://www.apple.com/covid19/mobility

Assoumou Ella, G. (2021). Gender, mobility, and Covid-19: The case of Belgium. *Feminist Economics*, *27*(1–2), 66–80. doi:10.1080/13545701.2020.1832240

Bellmann, F., Ypma, L., & Polack, D. (2020). Women move differently – What everyone working in mobility should know. Retrieved from https://www.weforum.org/agenda/2020/01/mobility-in-2020-a-female-perspective/. Accessed on March 1, 2021.

Belzunegui-Eraso, A., & Erro-Garcés, A. (2020). Teleworking in the context of the Covid-19 crisis. *Sustainability*, *12*(9), 3662.

Brezina, T., Takeru, S., Leth, U., Sandholzer, F., Laa, B., Kapfenberger, M., … Emberger, G. (2020). *International survey on covid-19 lockdowns and mobility behaviour* Version V1). doi: 10.17632/hkb3923nj3.1

Bryant, P., & Elofsson, A. (2020). Estimating the impact of mobility patterns on COVID-19 infection rates in 11 European countries. *PeerJ*, *8*, e9879. doi:10.7717/peerj.9879

Burki, T. (2020). The indirect impact of COVID-19 on women. *The Lancet Infectious Diseases*, *20*(8), 904–905. doi:10.1016/S1473-3099(20)30568-5

Carli, L. L. (2020). Women, gender equality and COVID-19. *Gender in Management: An International Journal*, *35*(7/8), 647–655. doi:10.1108/GM-07-2020-0236

Carteni, A., Di Francesco, L., & Martino, M. (2020). How mobility habits influenced the spread of the COVID-19 pandemic: Results from the Italian case study. *Science of The Total Environment*, *741*, 140489. doi:10.1016/j.scitotenv.2020.140489

Carvalho, R., Cheung, E., & Siu, P. (2020, 18 February). Hong Kong families await return of thousands of stranded domestic helpers as The Philippines lifts travel ban. *South China Morning Post*. Retrieved from https://www.scmp.com/news/hong-kong/health-environment/article/3051077/coronavirus-domestic-helper-tests-positive-taking?module=perpetual_scroll&pgtype=article&campaign=3051077

Dekhtyar, S., Weber, D., Helgertz, J., & Herlitz, A. (2018). Sex differences in academic strengths contribute to gender segregation in education and occupation: A longitudinal examination of 167,776 individuals. *Intelligence*, *67*, 84–92. doi:10.1016/j.intell.2017.11.007

Duchène, C. (2011). *Gender and transport*. International Transport Forum Discussion Paper, No. 2011–11, Organisation for Economic Co-operation and Development (OECD), International Transport Forum, Paris. http://dx.doi.org/10.1787/5kg9mq47w59w-en

Engle, S., Stromme, J., & Zhou, A. (2020). Staying at home: Mobility effects of COVID-19. *SSRN Electronic Journal*. https://doi.org/10.2139/ssrn.3565703

Eurobarometer. (2007). Attitudes on issues related to EU transport policy: Analytical report, the gallup organization. *E. Commission*. Retrieved from https://renewable-carbon.eu/news/media/news-images/20070810-03/fl_206b_en.pdf

Fatmi, M. R. (2020). COVID-19 impact on urban mobility. *Journal of Urban Management*, *9*(3), 270–275. doi:10.1016/j.jum.2020.08.002

Feng, Z., & Savani, K. (2020). Covid-19 created a gender gap in perceived work productivity and job satisfaction: implications for dual-career parents working from home. *Gender in Management: An International Journal*, *35*(7/8), 719–736. doi:10.1108/GM-07-2020-0202

Gauvin, L., Tizzoni, M., Piaggesi, S., Young, A., Adler, N., Verhulst, S., ... Cattuto, C. (2020). Gender gaps in urban mobility. *Humanities and Social Sciences Communications*, *7*(1), 11. doi:10.1057/s41599-020-0500-x

Google. (2020). *COVID-19 community mobility reports. See how your community is moving around differently due to COVID-19*. Retrieved from https://www.google.com/covid19/mobility/. Accessed on October 5, 2020.

Haug, N., Geyrhofer, L., Londei, A., Dervic, E., Desvars-Larrive, A., Loreto, V., . . . Klimek, P. (2020). Ranking the effectiveness of worldwide COVID-19 government interventions. *Nature Human Behaviour*, *4*(12), 1303–1312. https://doi.org/10.1038/s41562-020-01009-0

Hidayati, I., Tan, W., & Yamu, C. (2020). How gender differences and perceptions of safety shape urban mobility in Southeast Asia. *Transportation Research Part F: Traffic Psychology and Behaviour*, *73*, 155–173. doi:10.1016/j.trf.2020.06.014

Johansson, F., Henriksson, G., & Envall, P. (2019). Moving to private-car-restricted and mobility-served neighborhoods: The unspectacular workings of a progressive mobility plan. *Sustainability*, *11*(22), 1–19. doi:10.3390/su11226208

Kloof, A. v. d., & Kensmil, J. (2020). The effects of Covid-19 measures on the mobility of men and women. Retrieved from https://mobycon.com/wp-content/uploads/2020/06/Effect-of-covid-19-measures.pdf

Koch, J., Frommeyer, B., & Schewe, G. (2020). Online shopping motives during the COVID-19 pandemic – Lessons from the crisis. *Sustainability*, *12*(24), 1–20. doi:10.3390/su122410247

Kraemer, M. U. G., Yang, C. H., Gutierrez, B., Wu, C. H., Klein, B., Pigott, D. M., ... group, o. C.-d. w. (2020). The effect of human mobility and control measures on the COVID-19 epidemic in China. *medRxiv*. doi:10.1101/2020.03.02.20026708

Krentz, M., Kos, E., Green, A., & Alonso, J. G. (2020). Easing the Covid-19 burden on working parents. Retrieve from https://www.bcg.com/publications/2020/helping-working-parents-ease-the-burden-of-covid-19

Mallett, O., Marks, A., & Skountridaki, L. (2020). Where does work belong anymore? The implications of intensive homebased working. *Gender in Management: An International Journal*, *35*(7/8), 657–665. doi:10.1108/GM-06-2020-0173

Mortimer, G., & Clarke, P. (2010). Gender differences and store characteristics: A study of Australian supermarket consumers. In P. Ballantine & J. Finsterwalder (Eds.), *Proceeding of the Australian and New Zealand marketing academy conference 2010* (pp. 1–6). New Zealand: University of Canterbury.

Parlak, S., Cakiroglu, O. C., & Gul, F. O. (2020). Gender roles during COVID-19 pandemic: The experiences of Turkish female academics. *Gender, Work & Organization*, *28*(2), 461–483. doi:10.1111/gwao.12655

Przybylowski, A., Stelmak, S., & Suchanek, M. (2021). Mobility behaviour in view of the impact of the COVID-19 pandemic – Public transport users in Gdansk case study. *Sustainability*, *13*(1), 1–12. doi:10.3390/su13010364

Savage, M. (2020). How Covid-19 is changing women's lives. Retrieved from https://www.bbc.com/worklife/article/20200630-how-covid-19-is-changing-womens-lives

Shi, K., De Vos, J., Yang, Y., & Witlox, F. (2019). Does e-shopping replace shopping trips? Empirical evidence from Chengdu, China. *Transportation Research Part A: Policy and Practice*, *122*, 21–33. doi:10.1016/j.tra.2019.01.027

Shibayama, T., Sandholzer, F., Laa, B., & Brezina, T. (2021). Impact of COVID-19 lockdown on commuting: A multi-country perspective. *European Journal of Transport and Infrastructure Research*, *20*(1), 70–93.

Smith, J. (2019). Overcoming the 'tyranny of the urgent': integrating gender into disease outbreak preparedness and response. *Gender & Development*, *27*(2), 355–369. doi:10.1080/13552074.2019.1615288

Sy, S., Rahemtulla, H., & Carrasco, B. (2020). Using urban mobility and big data to track the pandemic. Retrieved from https://blogs.adb.org/blog/using-urban-mobility-and-big-data-to-track-the-pandemic. Accessed on September 28, 2020.

Thombre, A., & Agarwal, A. (2021). A paradigm shift in urban mobility: Policy insights from travel before and after COVID-19 to seize the opportunity. *Transport Policy*, *110*, 335–353. doi:10.1016/j.tranpol.2021.06.010

UNDP. (2020). *COVID-19 global gender response Tracker*.

UN Women, & Women Count. (2020). Unlocking the lockdown: The gendered effects of COVID-19 on achieving the SDGS in Asia and the Pacific. Retrieved from https://data.unwomen.org/publications/unlocking-lockdown-gendered-effects-covid-19-achieving-sdgs-asia-and-pacific

Uteng, T. P. (2012). *Gender and mobility in the developing world.*

Wenham, C., Smith, J., & Morgan, R. (2020). COVID-19: the gendered impacts of the outbreak. *Lancet*, *395*(10227), 846–848. doi:10.1016/s0140-6736(20)30526-2

WIKI, C. (2020). Gender equality and mobility: mind the gap! *CIVITAS*. Retrieved from https://civitas.eu/sites/default/files/civ_pol-an2_m_web.pdf

Worldometers.info. (2021). Covid 19 coronavirus pandemic. Retrieved from https://www.worldometers.info/coronavirus/. Accessed on July 31, 2021.

Wright, D. B., Eaton, A. A., & Skagerberg, E. (2015). Occupational segregation and psychological gender differences: How empathizing and systemizing help explain the distribution of men and women into (some) occupations. *Journal of Research in Personality*, *54*, 30–39. doi:10.1016/j.jrp.2014.06.004

Ypma, L., Bellmann, F., & Polack, D. (2020). *5 ways urban transport could step up a gear for women.* Retrieved from https://www.weforum.org/agenda/2020/03/urban-transport-mobility-women/. Accessed on January 4, 2020.

CHAPTER 14

CRITICAL SUCCESS FACTORS OF CONTRACTORS IN AFFORDABLE HIGH-RISE PUBLIC HOUSING IN MALAYSIA

Ainarull Assikin Abdul Hadi, Syuhaida Ismail, Nur Izzati Ab Rani and Nur Fatin Syazwani Abu Bakar

ABSTRACT

In Malaysia, there seems to be no mutual and general agreement among construction industry players and researchers on what the critical success factors (CSFs) of construction projects are since characteristics of construction projects vary across various projects complexity. This chapter thus examines the CSFs for affordable high-rise public housing projects in Malaysia through a thorough review of the literature on the CSFs, which were then contextually customised via a pilot study and presented in the form of Relative Importance Index (RII). Primary data were collected via administration of questionnaire surveys to 170 construction stakeholders of affordable high-rise public housing projects in Malaysia. The findings of this study revealed that the top 10 ranks are good management and supervision at site, good personal behaviour by all participants, good implementation in safety management and practice, high commitment in quality control by management, competent manager/supervisor, good communication and coordination, good and enough material and equipment, experience worker, clear objective and goals and good support by

Sustainability Management Strategies and Impact in Developing Countries
Community, Environment and Disaster Risk Management, Volume 26, 179–194

Published under exclusive licence by Emerald Publishing Limited
ISSN: 2040-7262/doi:10.1108/S2040-726220220000026014

senior employee/management, whereby it is crucial in ensuring the project success of affordable high-rise public housing projects in Malaysia. This chapter provides clear guidelines for the contractors of affordable high-rise public housing projects to be more competitive in the construction industry by illustrating the important factors to be considered while delivering the projects to their respective clients.

Keywords: Critical success factors; contractors; affordable high-rise; public housing; Malaysia; construction

1. INTRODUCTION

From an estimated 7.7 billion people worldwide in 2019, the medium-variant projection indicates that the global population could grow to around 8.5 billion in 2030, 9.7 billion in 2050, and 10.9 billion in 2100 (UN Habitat, 2019). Numerous studies have demonstrated the critical nature of housing for the human race, but an estimated 1 billion of the world's 7 billion inhabitants live in decaying structures (Branch, 2011). According to the United Nations (2018), by 2050, the world's population will have grown by 2.5 billion people, with 68% of the world's population living in cities; Asia and Africa will account for 90% of this growth.

In Asian cities, more than 500 million inhabitants live in slums, and almost 408 million people without access to improved sanitation facilities (Asian Development Bank & Inter-American Development Bank, 2014). The population of Malaysia in 2020 in fact is 32.7 million compared to 32.5 million in 2019, with an annual growth rate of 0.4%.

In Malaysia, low-cost housing is a government-introduced housing initiative to ensure that the low-income group continues to supply many low-cost homes. A low-cost house is also known as an affordable house where government financing for the house is supported or subsidised and maintained by local housing agencies (Ganisen, Hakim Mohammed, Jawahr Nesan, & Kanniyapan, 2015; Simm, 2013). A low-cost house can be described as a supply of housing that meets the masses' basic needs while remaining within their financial means without sacrificing construction quality (Ganisen et al., 2015). The low-cost housing programmes built by Malaysia's government mainly involve laminated properties such as low-rise flats or affordable high-rise flats. Successive Malaysian governments have made several attempts to make low-cost housing accessible and affordable, especially for the poor and disadvantaged. Statistics show that in 2015, Malaysia had 4,831,791 residential units, an increase of 2.2% from 4,725,109 in 2013 (Olanrewaju, Aziz, Tan, Tat, & Mine, 2016). The housing sector is very volatile hence to alleviate housing shortages (Ebekozien, Abdul-Aziz, & Jaafar, 2018).

However, lack of understanding of this aspect has made many construction projects do not fulfil their goals. Therefore, contractors have to come up with an excellent strategy to achieve a good result. As more than one discipline is involved in the construction project, comprehensive project management is therefore essential. Besides, there has been a lack of extensive and dedicated research on the critical success factors (CSFs) of contractors carried out by previous researchers for these affordable high-rise public housing projects in Malaysia (Gunduz & Almuajebh, 2020). Therefore, this study aims to examine the CSFs for affordable high-rise public housing projects in Malaysia.

2. LITERATURE REVIEW

The concept of project success is still evolving. The Iron Triangle is a visual representation of the most basic criteria for project success: if the project is completed on time, on budget and to a predetermined degree of quality, performance or scope (Albert, Balve, & Spang, 2017; Pinto, 2017; Pollack, Helm, & Adler, 2018). The Iron Triangle, also known as the Triple Constraint or the Project Management Triangle, is a basic notion in this paper understanding of project success (Gomes & Romão, 2016; Hassan, Adeleke, & Taofeeq, 2019; Rugenyi, 2016). This project management triangle process, which provides direction or guidance for any construction project, aids in the enhancement or improvement of the project's success.

The construction sector is extremely dynamic due to the constant occurrence of new obstacles and uncertainties in technology, budget and development approaches. Nowadays, residential construction projects, particularly those involving in affordable high-rise public housing, are inefficient and challenging. There are currently different construction building methods used for affordable high-rise public housing worldwide (Ee & Danesh, 2016). With the rising demand for affordable high-rise public housing and today's focus on sustainable growth, it is crucial that sustainable, affordable high-rise public housing is identified as an effective solution although in Malaysia, 55% of construction projects experienced cost overruns, and, astonishingly, private projects performed worse than public projects (Shehu, Endut, Akintoye, & Holt, 2014).

2.1. Affordable

The definition of affordable housing usually includes 'households should pay no more than 30% of their income, including utilities' (Chen, 2001; Cox & Pavletich, 2016; Yap & Ng, 2018). A study on affordable housing in Malaysia was undertaken by several studied in order to suggest a realistic solution to the demand-supply imbalance. Nonetheless, home affordability issues have never been addressed subtly, and little research has been conducted on housing affordability (Ebekozien et al., 2018).

The affordable housing implication, which has been commonly used in Malaysia by housing developers, is mostly their selling point without alluding to any settled facts or index as a base point (Chan et al., 2016). The scarcity of affordable house, along with the uneven rate of rise in housing prices and income, has made home ownership unaffordable (Yap & Ng, 2018). This is consistent with Samad, Zainon, Rahim, and Lou (2017), which concluded that there is disparity between affordable housing demand and supply. Another problem is loan availability, with approximately 60% of loan applications being rejected because they do not qualify (Ghouse, 2014).

The value of land has also increased dramatically across the country as a result of the high cost of property (Malaysian Insider, 2015). The high cost of construction materials increased with freight expenses and material costs (Ong, 2013), and abrupt increases in demand, but supply is inelastic (Syed Abdul Kader, 2011).

Apart from this, there are also CSFs of contractors that influence the project performance, which are the project size, appropriate experience, technical and professional capacity, project manager expertise, materials and equipment, project team member competency, sufficient funds/resources, project planning, quality problems, and also the contractor experience (Musarat & Ahad, 2016).

2.2. High-Rise Buildings

The International Conference on Fire Safety in High-Rise Buildings defined a high-rise as 'any structure where height can have a significant effect on evacuation', and no internationally agreed definition exists for 'high-rise building'. The National Fire Protection Association described a high-rise as one with a height of more than 75 feet (23 metres) or seven stories in the United States (Li & Chen, 2018). In China, according to the Technical Specification for Concrete Structures of High Buildings, high-rise buildings are residential buildings with a height of 10 or more floors or 28 metres or more, and other commercial buildings with a height of more than 24 metres, like mega-high-rise buildings (commercial buildings with a height of at least 100 metres) (NFPA, 2016). This study adopts China's local concept, which is a wide range of tall buildings containing mega-high-rise buildings.

Previous studies of safety management systems have failed to recognise variations between high-rise buildings and medium-rise and low-rise buildings. Common influential factors and CSFs for high-rise building construction have yet to be identified (Li, Ning, & Chen, 2018).

2.3. Critical Success Factors

CSFs will specify the requirements that will allow an organisation to succeed (Pakseresht & Asgari, 2012), and if the CSFs criteria are not met, the organisation will not achieve its objectives, which is to complete the project within cost, time and quality. CSFs, according to Moraveck (2013), are defined as criteria that aid project management practice in completing projects and can even improve project delivery. CSFs are also areas of operation that should receive continuous and careful management attention (Li et al., 2018).

CSFs are also important to ensure project completion and improve project delivery through the project management. Many studies attempted to capture the CSFs for the construction industry. According to research, due to different interpretations of success or failure by different participants in construction projects, classification of a project into a good project or a failure project is difficult.

Previously numerous researchers have examined (CSFs) in projects and have been discussed in details, namely Tamgadge and Shinde (2018), Durdyev, Eng, and Cheng (2018), Ofori-Kuragu, Baiden, and Badu (2016), Gunduz and Almuajebh (2020), Rajasekaran and Valli (2014) and Yong and Mustaffa (2013).

Tamgadge and Shinde (2018) claimed that 10 CSFs are good leadership, decision-making for project, safety at work place, quality of work delivered, communication with clients/contractors, coordination with clients/contractors, supervision, control over subcontractors, competent project team, site management, plan and schedule followed by clients/contractors, timely completion of work, well-defined scope, monitoring project, project execution getting done, top management support, speed of information flow, cost/cost control, organising of project, clients/contractors type and experience, knowledge of construction project organising and design team experience.

Each project is managed by a team of experienced construction management professionals that have a proven track record of delivering experience, value, innovation, high-quality construction and client satisfaction. In any construction project, any user expects high-quality work, on-time or on-schedule deliveries, and a reasonable budget. The intended procedure, on the other hand, will differ from the actual activity. As a result, the project team is coping with some challenging but unexpected events. At the absolute least, CSFs can help to organise or reduce the incidence of unanticipated occurrences in projects. CSFs will also improve the effectiveness and efficiency of construction activity if resources are available in adequate quantities. Regardless of their relative importance, all of these criteria are critical to the project's success. Tamgadge and Shinde (2018) also highlighted that one of the industry's biggest issues is finding skilled and reliable labour, and that effective project management is essential to solve this. Project management will provide direction or guidance to any construction project, so assisting in the advancement or improvement of project success.

Durdyev et al. (2018) claimed that complexity of a project, social/cultural environment, ability to make timely decision, client confidence in construction team, contractor's cash flow, client influence, project size, site management, contractor's experience, project planning, realistic schedule/urgency, professional capability, technical capability, contractor's competence, technology and skill availability, leadership and organisational, construction methods skills, physical work environment, clear and precise scope and objectives, resource availability (manpower, material, machinery), administrative approvals and motivating skill are the criteria needed for the CSFs. Clearly, each country has its own cultural characteristics, which have an impact on human behaviour. Due to the labour-intensive nature of construction projects, these culturally influenced attitudes have an impact on project performance, and thus on a contractor's overall performance. Contractors are one of the most significant stakeholders in both off-site and on-site project operations, and their performance can determine whether a project succeeds or fails.

Quality and zero defects culture, organisational design, work culture and work environment, client satisfaction, strategy, leadership, measurement, analysis of information and knowledge management, and implementation of lean principles were identified by Ofori-Kuragu et al. (2016) as 10 out of 16 CSFs. Contractors with little or no benchmarking expertise can leverage the effect of the generated CSFs to compare their performance to best practises or implement improvement programmes. Contractors should strive to provide exactly what the client wants and avoid the need for rework by adopting an organisational structure that allows for maximum productivity, creating a work environment that promotes production, aiming to satisfy their clients, developing an effective strategy, ensuring effective leadership, measuring performance, and promoting a learning environment. This is an important first step towards achieving business excellence for such organisations. Contractors with little experience in these areas might use the CSFs as a starting point for benchmarking and general performance improvement. These characteristics will not automatically lead to increased performance; rather, they will serve as a means to an end by highlighting the areas in which organisations aiming to enhance their performance should concentrate their efforts and seek to improve. Organisations with effective integration of these into their management and business practises have the potential to boost performance.

Gunduz and Almuajebh (2020) emphasised, on the other hand, that it is vital to identify CSFs that affect the construction process. Project-related factors, company- and work-related factors, client-related factors, project management factors, design-team-related factors, contractor-related factors and project-manager-related variables are among the 40 CSFs divided into 7 groups. The majority of the significant factors, according to the findings, were financial issues (payment mechanisms, project funds/resources), administrative issues (influence of client/representative, client's availability of experienced managers and skilled workforce) and government approval mechanisms (statutory approvals environment).

According to Rajasekaran and Valli (2014), 17 CSFs are identified as project success factors and ranked according to importance, including quality in construction, project completion on time, meeting specifications, satisfied users, technical performance, project completion within budget, efficiency of the project management process, functionality or fitness for purpose, and project management process efficiency. The study found that all three groups agreed that the quality of project construction, as well as the other 16 elements for project success, needed to be improved. The top five ranking factors for each group are remarkably similar, which is an intriguing finding. They are construction quality, project completion on time, fulfilling specifications, project users are satisfied or their needs are met, and technical performance. Because quality in construction has become a severe concern for government construction projects, the three groups identified the factor 'quality in construction' as the most critical factor for project success.

Furthermore, Yong and Mustaffa (2013) stated that, while substantial research on CSFs for construction projects has been conducted, very little of this study incorporates information particular to the local context. The major goal of this project was to obtain a better knowledge of the rising trend of CSFs, which was being discussed by numerous players in the local industry. The stakeholders appear to prefer a more balanced approach to CSFs, as seen by the 40 CSFs.

Apart from the 'hard' factors, project stakeholders are unanimous in their assessment of the relevance of human-related 'soft' components. According to the findings, the high-scoring variables are largely related to three major aspects: project staff, commitment and communication, and site administration and monitoring. In the face of a persistent adversarial mentality in the sector, human-related components will help to establish a climate of trust among stakeholders.

Contractor competence and experience, project funding, team leader competence, project consultant competence, and site management and supervision are the top five crucial success criteria for construction projects. The majority of these elements are related to the project stakeholders' capacity to keep their promises, which has a direct impact on overall project performance.

An extensive literature review was used to create all of the CSFs. Cost, time, quality, safety and health, environment, productivity and management are the seven groups of CSFs. This is based on their personality traits, with various success factors in each category. The weighted scale was created and comprised of 1–5 ratings, with 1 indicating that the project has no major impact on project success and 5 indicating that the project has the greatest impact.

Cost factors were identified as the first group of CSFs for construction projects. Several studies have identified that cost is one of the CSF (Durdyev et al., 2018; Gunduz & Almuajebh, 2020; Ofori-Kuragu et al., 2016; Rajasekaran & Valli, 2014; Tamgadge & Shinde, 2018; Yong & Mustaffa, 2013). Based on previous studies, this study identified six criteria of cost factors, which are experience worker, good communication and coordination, good management and supervision at site, good viability of sources and good and enough material and equipment. In general, a project must stay within the tender summary price budget. Cost overruns in building projects are possible as a result of poor performance in terms of timeliness. If the cost exceeds the budget, the clients and consultants will look into it and request that the contractors produce a detailed cost proposal for approval.

As for the second CSFs is time. This study identified six criteria, which are good competency of project participant, good procedure of change practice, skills worker, motivation, clear objective and goals and fast decision-making (Durdyev et al., 2018; Gunduz & Almuajebh, 2020; Ofori-Kuragu et al., 2016; Rajasekaran & Valli, 2014; Tamgadge & Shinde, 2018; Yong & Mustaffa, 2013). One of the most essential CSFs for a successful building project is time. Contractors must finish the project according to the specifications outlined in the Letter of Award. Some contractors failed to consider time as one of the CSFs for completing the job. This is due to the contractors' application of an extension of time (EOT) to the client. The client does not want a project to be delayed or not completed on schedule. However, contractors may be entitled to an extension of time for a specific reason, such as during Covid-19 and due to the Movement Control Order (MCO).

Quality factor was identified as a third group in CSFs, as stated earlier it is also one of the triple constraints in project completion. Several studies have identified quality is one of the CSFs (Durdyev et al., 2018; Gunduz & Almuajebh, 2020; Rajasekaran & Valli, 2014; Ofori-Kuragu et al., 2016; Tamgadge & Shinde, 2018; Yong & Mustaffa, 2013). Five criteria has been considered base on the previous six authors under the quality factor, which are, good organisational quality assurance, good monitoring and feedback by participant, good quality of raw material and equipment, good availability competent staff and high commitment in quality control (QC) by management. Despite the fact that past studies have acknowledged that quality is one of the CSFs in completing a project, there are still complaints and issues related to quality. One of the conditions for the contractor to follow during the tender submission stage is construction quality. In QLASSIC, passing ratings for quality are 75% and above. Achieving these quality levels will lead to increased client satisfaction, which is critical for construction companies' long-term success (Patel & Pitroda, 2021). ISO 9001 Quality Management System is a set of ISO 9000 standards that gives guidance on how to build up a quality management system for procedures that affect their goods or services. If the contractor has an ISO 9001 Quality Management System, it is also a requirement and a benefit during the tendering process.

The fourth CSFs of the group is safety and health, whereby the previous studies claimed that this factor is also one of the CSFs in construction project which the criteria were good coordination, control, and management practice on health and safety, good implementation in safety management and training, good conduct on-site inspection and good personal behaviour by all participants (Gunduz & Almuajebh, 2020; Tamgadge & Shinde, 2018; Yong & Mustaffa, 2013).

The fifth group of the CSFs is environment. Several studies have been identified environment as CSFs (Durdyev et al., 2018; Rajasekaran & Valli, 2014; Yong & Mustaffa, 2013). Based on these studies, the author identified three criteria in environment, which are proper site layout, use environmental friendly material and use environmental friendly equipment.

The sixth group of the CSFs is productivity. Several studies have been identified productivity as CSFs (Durdyev et al., 2018; Gunduz & Almuajebh, 2020; Ofori-Kuragu et al., 2016; Rajasekaran & Valli, 2014; Tamgadge & Shinde, 2018; Yong & Mustaffa, 2013). Based on these studies, this study identified seven criteria, which are competent manager/supervisor, competent skilled worker, well schedule and on time inspection, good change order practice, offer training to workers, good efficiency equipment and up-to-date technology.

Management has been identified as the seventh and final CSFs. Several studies have identified management as one of the CSFs for project completion (Durdyev et al., 2018; Gunduz & Almuajebh, 2020; Ofori-Kuragu et al., 2016; Rajasekaran & Valli, 2014; Tamgadge & Shinde, 2018; Yong & Mustaffa, 2013). Based on previous studies, this study identified four criteria, which are good attitude among employee, enough training for employee, legal requirement and good support by senior employee/management.

From these studies, the questionnaire survey is developed.

3. RESEARCH METHODOLOGY

This chapter began with a comprehensive literature review on CSFs of Contractors in Affordable High-Rise Public Housing in Malaysia, which subsequently led to questionnaires that underwent a pilot study on 30 professionals from the construction industry. Through the pilot study, the Cronbach's alpha coefficient value should be greater than 0.70. The Cronbach's alpha results generated via pilot study to test the questionnaires reliability were recorded between 0.719 and 0.920 as shown in Table 14.1, which indicates that the questionnaire survey was appropriate and reliable for the actual questionnaire survey. Content validity was

Table 14.1. Reliability Analysis.

Critical Success Factors of Contractors in Affordable High-Rise Housing in Malaysia	Cronbach's Alpha (α) value
Overall items	0.939
Cost	0.789
Time	0.877
Quality	0.908
Safety & Health	0.920
Environment	0.719
Productivity	0.918
Management	0.878

performed to ensure that the measurement implies an adequate and representative set of items according to the concept.

Mean and standard deviation were also utilised in this study. In this study, evaluation criteria (mean) or average is the weighing to each factor of the respondent. For example in the score interval (mean) range between 1 and 5 , which is 1–1.79 the evaluation criteria is categorise as very low level, 1.80–2.59 categorise as low level, 2.60–3.39 categorise as medium level, 3.40–4.19 categorise as high level and lastly 4.20–5.00 categorise as very high level. As for the standard deviation, it provides an indication of how far the individual responses to a question vary or deviate from the mean. Finally, hypotheses were evaluated by determining inter correlation values between variables.

In this study, Relative Importance Index (RII) method is used to determine the relative importance of the criteria in CSFs. RIIs are calculated for each factor as in Eq. (1):

$$\mathrm{RII} = \frac{\sum W}{(A * N)} \tag{1}$$

where RII = relative importance index; W = weighting given to each factor by respondents (ranging from 1 to 5); A = highest weight (i.e. 5 in this case); and N = total number of respondents. The RII value had a range of 0–1 (0 not inclusive); the higher the RII, the more important the CSFs. The RII were then ranked, and the results are shown in Table 14.2. Based on Table 14.2, CSFs of contractors in affordable high-rise public housing in Malaysia have been identified based on the findings. Those CSFs are cost, time, quality, health and safety, environment, productivity and management.

4. ANALYSIS AND RESULT

Three hundred Grade G7 construction workers from Kuala Lumpur and Selangor were chosen from Construction Industry Development Board (CIDB) Malaysia database. Grade G7 are those who engaged in the large-scale construction business with no financial constraint. By removing invalid and incomplete responses, 173 completed questionnaires were taken into account, with a total 58% of response rate, which shows adequacy for analysis and reporting as above. Thus, the current percentages of feedbacks are adequate enough for a meaningful analysis.

Table 14.2 is demonstrated by calculating the mean of RII value for each CSF. The rank is done based on RII, where the most important criteria should consider for project success to increase contractors' performance.

The cost factor group was the most important group of CSFs. This was mainly due to the factors' good management and supervision at site (RII=0.963), good communication and coordination (0.896), and good enough material and equipment (RII=0.894).

The second most important group was time factor, with clear objective and goals (RII=0.889), good competency of project participant (RII=0.884) and skill workers (RII=0.881).

After the time factor group, the quality group came in as the third most important group. The significance criteria were high commitment in QC by management (RII=0.908), good availability competent staff (RII=0.875), and good monitoring and feedback by participant (RII=0.860).

Following the quality, the safety and health group of CSFs ranks as the fourth most important group. The notable factors were good personal behaviour by all the participants (RII=0.931), good implementation in safety management and practice (RII=0.917), and good coordination, control and management practice on health and safety (RII=0.834).

The fifth most important group was environment. The prominent criteria were proper site layout (0.887), use environmental friendly material (RII=0.845) and use environmental friendly equipment (RII=0.775).

The sixth most important group of CSFs was productivity. The significant criteria were competent manager/supervisor (RII=0.905), competent skilled worker (RII=0.888), and well schedule and on time inspection (RII=0.879).

The management group was the last and least important CSF group. The criteria were good support by senior employee/management (RII=0.889), good attitude amongst employee (RII=0.877) and enough training for employee (0.855).

5. CONCLUSION AND RECOMMENDATIONS

A project can be completed when all the critical success factors (CSFs) criteria are met. The aim of this study was to identify the CSFs of contractors in affordable high-rise public housing in Malaysia because many projects having the same problem such as delay, cost overrun, the quality is not as per specification, not implementing safety and health at site, abuse of environment rules, throwing oil into the river, using illegal foreign workers and the current problem now is Covid-19, how do the contractor handle and manage the situation, and it is considered to be a serious problem in the construction industry. Through a detailed literature review and survey questionnaires, a total of 35 different criteria for CSFs were identified and categorised into seven CSFs as follows: cost, time, quality, safety

Table 14.2. Results on Critical Success Factors (CSFs) of Contractors in Affordable High-Rise Public Housing in Malaysia.

No	CSFs of Contractors in Affordable High-Rise Public Housing in Malaysia		RII	Mean	Std. Deviation	Rank
1	Cost	Good management and supervision at site	0.936	4.682	0.467	1
		Good communication and coordination	0.896	4.480	0.577	2
		Good and enough material and equipment	0.894	4.468	0.566	3
		Experience worker	0.889	4.445	0.543	4
		Less wastage	0.880	4.399	0.598	5
		Good viability of sources	0.562	4.410	0.580	6
2	Time	Clear objective and goals	0.889	4.445	0.623	1
		Good competency of project participant	0.884	4.422	0.601	2
		Skilled worker	0.881	4.405	0.636	3
		Fast decision-making	0.869	4.347	0.832	4
		Motivation	0.857	4.283	0.661	5
		Good procedure of change practice	0.852	4.260	0.687	6
3	Quality	High commitment in quality control by management	0.908	4.538	0.605	1
		Good availability competent staff	0.875	4.376	0.593	2
		Good monitoring and feedback by participant	0.860	4.301	0.733	3
		Good quality of raw material and equipment	0.859	4.295	0.665	4
		Good organisational quality assurance	0.857	4.283	0.728	5
4	Safety and health	Good personal behaviour by all participants	0.931	4.509	0.625	1
		Good implementation in safety management and practice	0.917	4.584	0.581	2
		Good coordination, control and management practice on health and safety	0.834	4.491	0.625	3
		Good conduct on-site inspection	0.757	4.520	0.712	4
5	Environment	Proper site layout	0.887	4.434	0.622	1
		Use environmental friendly material	0.845	4.225	0.639	2
		Use environmental friendly equipment	0.775	3.873	0.334	3
6	Productivity	Competent manager/supervisor	0.905	4.526	0.774	1
		Competent skilled worker	0.888	4.439	0.795	2
		Well schedule and on time inspection	0.879	4.393	0.826	3
		Good change order practice	0.864	4.318	0.827	4
		Good efficiency equipment	0.857	4.283	0.832	5
		Up-to-date technology	0.847	4.237	0.775	6
		Offer training to workers	0.845	4.225	0.870	7
7	Management	Good support by senior employee/ management	0.889	4.445	0.742	1
		Good attitude amongst employee	0.877	4.387	0.766	2
		Enough training for employee	0.855	4.277	0.824	3
		Legal requirement	0.817	4.087	0.855	4

and health, environment, productivity and management. The author created the seven groups of CSFs based on all criteria that have been collected and identified from the six previous authors as mentioned before. The paper then quantified the RII and ranking the criteria according to their importance level of CSFs. The aim of this study was achieved through the result and findings. According to the computed RIIs, all criteria and factors were ranked.

When all of the CSFs are met, a project is completed. The purpose of this study was to identify the CSFs of contractors in affordable high-rise public housing in Malaysia, because many projects are experiencing the same issues, such as delays, cost overruns, poor quality, failure to implement safety and health on site, violations of environmental regulations, oil spills in rivers, the use of illegal foreign workers, and the current issue is Covid-19. A total of 35 different criteria for CSFs were found and identified into seven CSFs based on a rigorous literature study and survey questionnaires: cost, time, quality, safety and health, environment, productivity and management. The author constructed the seven CSF categories based on all of the criteria gathered and defined by the previous studies, as previously stated. The RII was then quantified, and the criteria were ranked according to the importance of CSFs. The results and findings of this study helped to attain the paper's goal. All criteria and factors were ranked using the computed RIIs. The study focussed on the most important CSF criteria and variables. The ranking results were used to determine the most and least CSFs.

According to the findings, based on the top 10 RII ranking in criteria, the following recommendations can be given as measures to decrease the bad performance of contractors for construction projects: good management and supervision at site (cost factor), good personal behaviour by all participants (safety and health factor), good implementation in safety management and practice (safety and health factor), high commitment in QC by management (quality factor), competent manager/supervisor (productivity factor), good communication and coordination (cost factor), good and enough material and equipment (cost factor), experience worker (cost), clear objective and goals (time), good support by senior employee/management (management factor).

The most significant CSFs criteria in the completion of a construction project are good management and supervision (cost factor) on site. At the job site, the contractors must have strong management and supervision who can appropriately monitor the situation. Poor management and supervision will be unable to adequately design and manage projects, which may have negative repercussions.

The second highest-ranking CSF requirement is good personal behaviour by all participants (safety and health factor). In construction, safety always comes first. To avoid an accident or incident, the contractor must ensure that all site personnel, including the client, consultants, contractors, subcontractors and suppliers, obey the safety and health guidelines. This is why all of the individuals' personal behaviour is ranked second in CSFs.

The third rank goes to a good implementation in safety management and practice (safety and health factor at the job site. While ISO 9001:2015 is for Quality Management Systems, and ISO 45001:2018 is for Occupational Health and Safety

Management Systems. This worldwide standard will provide enterprises around the world with a foundation for improving employee safety, reducing workplace dangers and creating better, safer working environments.

The fourth rank goes to high commitment in QC by management (quality factor). QC is a technique by which organisations assess the consistency of all factors involved in output. QC is defined by ISO 9000 as a section of quality management geared at meeting quality requirements. QC examines if a job has been completed correctly and seeks to determine whether a project has been completed in compliance with the stated requirements.

Competent manager/supervisor is ranked fifth (productivity factor). It is critical for the contractor to ensure that they have a capable project manager and supervisor on site. Without a competent project manager or supervisor, the project will face numerous issues. For example, if the project manager fails to plan for materials delivery, the project will be delayed; similarly, if the supervisor does not know how to check or study the construction drawings, the project will almost certainly face additional difficulties in method of statement or site supervision. In construction, the project manager is in charge of overseeing all of the employees and labourers on the job site. As a result, the contractor must hire a capable manager, project manager or supervisor.

The sixth criterion in the CSFs is good communication and coordination (cost factor). Contractors, clients, consultants and subcontractors are among the many stakeholders engaged in construction projects. It is critical to have strong communication and coordination with them in order for the project to be completed on time. A skilled project manager will know how to communicate and coordinate effectively with the project team, which includes the client, consultants and subcontractors. Failure to complete the project will be due to a lack of communication.

The seventh place in CSFs is good and enough material and equipment (cost factor). A contractor must understand that before they enter the tender, they already know how much profit they can expect from the project. They normally have ready suppliers for the project to execute when it comes to financial project planning. In most cases, the ready supplier has a long-term business relationship with the contractors, and the contractor will receive a lower price than other contractors. In construction, it's better if the contractor has adequate materials and equipment on hand to complete and operate the task on the job site. For example, if a contractor orders a material from a supplier with whom he or she does not have a solid working relationship and the supplier is unable to deliver the material to the contractor's site, the project will be delayed.

In CSFs, the experience worker (cost factor) is ranked eighth. Foreigners from Indonesia, Myanmar, Pakistan, China, and Vietnam make up the majority of construction workers. Experienced (skilled) workers and non-experienced workers are the two sorts of workers. Contractors will require these two categories of workers in the construction industry since they will not be able to hire all of the experienced workers, for example, to clean the project site. A contractor must hire an experienced worker to ensure that the job does not have a defect or require redo in the future, incurring additional costs. As a result, in order to avoid an increase in costs, the contractor must hire an experienced worker.

Clear objectives and goals are ranked ninth in CSFs (time factor). Uncertain objectives and goals are one of the problems that many contractors encounter. If the contractor lacks defined objectives and aims, he or she will be unable to perform and complete the project according to the client's expectations.

The 10th position in CSFs indicates good support by senior employee/management (management factor). In construction projects, good support from senior employees/management is particularly important, as the workplace can sometimes have a bully culture based on seniority. When it comes to younger employees or new hires, senior management tends to overload them with work and expects them to accomplish it by the deadline. This will cause the junior employee to become stressed, and they will resign and seek employment elsewhere, causing a delay in finding a new candidate.

As a conclusion, the contractor must implement the top 10 CSFs identified in this paper in order to execute the project on time, on budget, and with good quality for Malaysia's affordable high-rise public housing. Other projects, such as hospital projects, school projects, residential projects, tunnel projects, and a variety of others, could also use the CSFs mentioned in this study. These 10 CSFs should also be considered in the CIDB's appraisal system in order to ensure that the existing key performance index is improved in order to offer the relevancy of contractors' performance in high-rise construction projects.

ACKNOWLEDGEMENT

The authors would like to express their appreciation for the support of Razak Faculty of Technology and Informatics of University Technology Malaysia and Construction Industry practitioner in Malaysia.

REFERENCES

Albert, M., Balve, P., & Spang, K. (2017). Evaluation of project success: A structured literature review. *International Journal of Managing Projects in Business*, *7*(1), 133–143.

Asian Development Bank & Inter-American Development Bank. (2014). *Sustainable urbanization in Asia and Latin America*. Springer.

Branch, M. P. (2011). The future is now. *American Scientist*, *99*(2), 163–164.

Chan, A. P. J., & Lee, B. H. C. (2016). A study on factors causing the demand-supply gap of affordable housing. *INTI Journal Special Edition – Built Environment*. 6–10.

Chen, E. (2001). Housing workshop for lower income group in Malaysia. Retrieved from http://www.epu.gov.my/c/document_library/get_file?uuid=8c3ff18f-58ca-4b80-9daed435fa39f201&groupId=283545

Cox, W., & Pavletich, H. (2016). *12th annual demographia international housing affordability survey*. Belleville, IL: Demographia.

Durdyev, S., Eng, H. T., & Cheng, K. Y. (2018). Quantification of critical success factors of contractors in Cambodia: AHP approach. *Journal of Management, Economics, and Industrial Organization*, *2*(2), 51–61.

Ebekozien, A., Abdul-Aziz, A. R., & Jaafar, M. (2018). Low-cost housing leakages in Malaysia: The unexplored dimension. *Pacific Rim Property Research Journal*, *24*(3), 249–264.

Ee, L. C., & Danesh, Z. A. (2016). Construction methods commonly used for affordable housing in Malaysia. *INTI International University INTI Journal Special Edition – Built Environment*, 2016, 1–3. Retrieved from http://rmk11.epu.gov.my/pdf/strategy

Ganisen, S., Hakim Mohammed, A., Jawahr Nesan, L., & Kanniyapan, G. (2015). Critical success factors for low cost housing building maintenance organization Jurnal Teknologi full paper critical success factors for low cost housing building maintenance. *Jurnal Teknologi*, *2*(May), 31–40.

Gomes, J., & Romão, M. (2016). Improving project success: A case study using benefits and project management. *Procedia Computer Science*, *100*, 489–497.

Gunduz, M., & Almuajebh, M. (2020). Critical success factors for sustainable construction project management. *Sustainability (Switzerland)*, *12*(5).

Hassan, A. K., Adeleke, A. Q., & Taofeeq, D. M. (2019). The effects of project triple constraint on Malaysia building projects. *Social Science and Humanities Journal*, *3*(5), 1222–1238.

Li, Y., Ning, Y., & Chen, W. T. (2018). Critical success factors for safety management of high-rise building construction projects in China. *Advances in Civil Engineering*, June 2018, 1–15.

Malay Mail Online. (2016). Over 50% of affordable housing loan bids reject REHDA says.

Moraveck, C. (2013). Critical success factors and project success. *Unmasking Project Management*, June, 195–202.

Musarat, M. A., & Ahad, M. Z. (2016). Factors affecting the success of construction projects in Khyber Pakhtunkhwa, Pakistan. *Journal of Construction Engineering and Project Management*, *6*(4), 1–6.

National Fire Protection Association (NFPA). (2016). High-rise building fires. Retrieved from http://www.nfpa.org/News-and-Research/Fire-statistics-and-reports/Fire-statistics/Fires-by-propertytype/High-Rise-Building-Fires

Ofori-Kuragu, J. K., Baiden, B., & Badu, E. (2016). Critical success factors for Ghanaian contractors. *Benchmarking: An International Journal*, *23*(4), 843–865.

Olanrewaju, A., Aziz, A. R. A., Tan, S. Y., Tat, L. L., & Mine, N. (2016). Market analysis of housing shortages in Malaysia. *Procedia Engineering*, *164*, 315–322.

Ong, T. S. (2013). Factors affecting the price of housing in Malaysia. *Journal of Emerging Issues in Economics, Finance and Banking*, *1*(5), 414–429.

Pakseresht, A., & Asgari, G. (2012). Determining the critical success factors in construction projects: AHP approach. *Interdisciplinary Journal of Contemporary Research in Business*, *4*(8), 383–393. 2 diagrams.

Patel, C. S., & Pitroda, J. R. (2021). Quality management system in construction: A review. *Reliability: Theory and Applications*, *16*(SI1), 121–131. doi:10.24412/1932-2321-2021-160-121-131

Pinto, J. K. (2017). Linking project management. *Project Management Achieving Competitive Advantage*, *5*, 88–97.

Pollack, J., Helm, J., & Adler, D. (2018). What is the iron triangle, and how has it changed? *International Journal of Managing Projects in Business*, *11*(2), 527–547.

Rajasekaran, A. G., & Valli, P. (2014). Analysis of the success factors influencing in construction project. *International Journal of Engineering & Applied Sciences*, *6*(3), 21.

Rugenyi, F. (2016). Assessment of the influence of project management competence on the triple constraint in projects in Nairobi. *International Journal of Academic Research in Business and Social Sciences*, *6*(4), 295–309. doi:10.6007/ijarbss/v6-i4/2108

Samad, D., Zainon, N., Rahim, F. A. M., & Lou, E. (2017). Malaysian affordability housing policies revisited. *Open House International*, *42*(1), 44–51.

Shehu, Z., Endut, I. R., Akintoye, A., & Holt, G. D. (2014). Cost overrun in the Malaysian construction industry projects: A deeper insight. *International Journal of Project Management*, *32*(8), 1471–1480.

Syed Abdul Kader, S. Z. (2011). Disputes and issues relating to sale and purchase of land in Malaysia. *Law and Commerce: The Malaysian Perspective*, 345–365.

Tamgadge, V., & Shinde, D. K. (2018). Analysis of critical success factors for construction projects, *International Research Journal of Engineering and Technology (IRJET)*, *5*(9), 414–417.

The Malaysian Insider (2015) IMbi Deal Could Set Record Price for Land in KL. Retrieved from http://www.themalaysianinsider.com/citynews/greater-kl/article/imbi-deal-could-set-record-price-for-landin-kl/imbi-deal-could-set-record-price-for-land-in-kl#sthash.xAnnauEf.dpuf. Accessed on February 12, 2016.

Uluocak, B. (2013). Critical success factors (CSFs) affecting project performance in Turkish IT sector. Paper presented at PMI® Global Congress 2013—EMEA, Istanbul, Turkey. Newtown Square, PA: Project Management Institute.

UN Habitat. (2019). Making affordable housing a reality in cities. *World Economic Forum*, June, 1–60. Retrieved from http://homeguides.sfgate.com/student-hous

United Nation. (2018). Retrieved from https://unstats.un.org/sdgs/report/2018

Yap, J. B. H., & Ng, X. H. (2018). Housing affordability in Malaysia: perception, price range, influencing factors and policies. *The Electronic Library*, *34*(1), 1–5.

Yong, Y. C., & Mustaffa, N. E. (2013). Critical success factors for Malaysian construction projects: An empirical assessment. *Construction Management and Economics*, *31*(9), 959–978. doi:10.1080/01446193.2013.828843

CHAPTER 15

GREEN ROOF SYSTEM: IMPLEMENTATION AND CHALLENGE IN COMMERCIAL BUILDINGS

Nazhatulzalkis Jamaludin, Siti Zubaidah Binti Hashim, Intan Bayani Bin Zakaria, Nadira Binti Ahzahar and Mior Alhadi Mior Ahmad Ridzuan

ABSTRACT

Sustainability issues have become crucial to mitigate urban heat islands (UHIs) and reduce the global warming effect. The climate change news is frequently heard lately due to the extreme weather to the extent that the increasing earth's temperature often causes disaster and loss of property and life. New adaptation needs to new climate context and limits the on-going effects. One of the ways is adopting green roofs on buildings. Implementing sustainable practices such as green roofs will help mitigate this adverse effect in urban areas. Green roofs provide many benefits such as enhancing the aesthetical quality of the built environment, reduce UHIs, reduce energy consumption, improve storm-water attenuation, roof longevity, and reduce noise pollution. However, only a few buildings in Malaysia have considering green roofs as a main green feature element. There is barely number of buildings that have green roof design even though it offers benefits to the community and environment. This chapter has emphasised the types of green roof systems that are potentially suitable in Malaysia climate and obstacles associated with the green roof system.

Sustainability Management Strategies and Impact in Developing Countries
Community, Environment and Disaster Risk Management, Volume 26, 195–207

Published under exclusive licence by Emerald Publishing Limited
ISSN: 2040-7262/doi:10.1108/S2040-726220220000026015

The study found the barriers to implementing green roofs in Malaysia, especially during the stage of building operation in maintaining the green roof system. The survey has been done, which revealed nine factors that hinder the green roof application. This study also highlights the challenges to overcome the barriers of implementing green roofs in Malaysia.

Keywords: Greenspace; global warming; green roof; commercial building; urbanisation; maintenance

1. INTRODUCTION

In urban development, more buildings were constructed to fulfil high population needs and rapid economic growth. United Nations report the increase of 68% of people living in the city by 2050 (UNDESA, 2018). Urbanisation modified the natural environment into human-made structures such as buildings and infrastructures, left little space for vegetation. These man-made alterations induced changes in urban temperature and disrupted surface energy balance in the urban area. Densely populated urbanisation will lead to numerous environmental problems like decreasing of green space, urban heat island (UHI), greenhouse gas emission, air pollution, destruction of natural elements, and energy crisis. Buildings sector alone accountable for nearly 40% of global energy use and contribute to 36% of carbon dioxide (CO_2) emission (European Commission, 2007; Hassan, Mohamad Zin, Abd Majid, Balubaid, & Hainin, 2014; Zakaria, Foo, Mohamad Zin, Yang, & Zolfagharian, 2012). Reduction of green space and increasing of hard surface in the cities exposed the urban area to more direct warming that raised the frequency and intensity of heat waves. Higher outdoor temperature experienced in the city is called as UHI effect (Oke, 1995).

Recent studies show that the temperature keeps increasing (Susca, Gaffin, & Dell'osso, 2011) in the city area with less vegetation and now becoming a threat to the environment (Emmanuel, 2017) and human health (Semenza, 2014). In urban spaces, vegetation could be found mostly in parks or recreational areas. A study on urban morphology in selected urban areas in Malaysia recorded higher outdoor temperature as high as 40.7°C (Syed Othman Thani, Nik Mohamad, & Syed Abdullah, 2013) and this will lead to higher energy consumption for the indoor thermal environment (Shaharuddin, 2011). Integration of vegetation within buildings fabric such as roofs and walls can reduce the urban temperature inside human habitats themselves (Jones, 2008). A green roof is also one of the approaches in designing an energy-efficient building as it helps to reduce the amount of electricity for air-conditioning units in the building. It is one of the practical strategies in sustainable building design, especially in urban areas to combat the reduction of open space for green areas and natural landscaping in cities (Abdullah, 2012).

Yet in Malaysia, implementing green roof systems is still at the early stage due to obstacles that obstructed the progressive development of this system (Ismail, Abdullah, Hashim, & Rani, 2018). The studies on the obstacle of green roofs system also have been found in many other countries and have their own hindrance. Hence identifying the factors will help to overcome with appropriate strategies. In Malaysia, the green roof concept is not very familiar in the construction industry and a little number of building applied green roof systems might be due to problems associated with the green roofs system. Despite some successful green roof projects, the trend of green roofs in Malaysia is not much favourable and several factors keep back the application of green roofs in Malaysia (Ismail, Aziz, Nasir, & Taib, 2012). This chapter will indicate the obstructions implementing the green roofs in selected commercial building during the maintenance stage.

2. LITERATURE REVIEW

2.1. Green Roof Overview

The green roof is a roof consisting of vegetation that can take many different forms. The term green roof can be defined as either a rooftop garden with ornamental planting or a fertile vegetation space, which has been designed to develop naturally, and with a substrate on a man-made structure, of at least one floor (Grant, 2006.). Rowe (2006) described green roof as a vegetated roof system with growing media, supporting layers such as root barrier, roof membrane, and drainage to recover the loss of green space. Most of the man-made structure with vegetation layers and habitable space beneath the structure can be considered as green roofs. Advanced in building materials, evolving the green roof design techniques, and emerging ideas to make the built environment more sustainable and humane (Rowe, 2006). Nowadays, there are many terms used to represent the green roof such as rooftop garden, Ecoroof, Bioroof, Living roof, Brown roof, and Green Roof Infrastructure (Abdul Rahman & Ahmad, 2008). A green roof is a vegetated system where plants are planted on the roof with an engineered growing medium laid on certain layers of the system (Tan, 2008). A green roof is principally a flat or sloping roof covered and layered with vegetation to maximise the use of green space, especially in urban areas (Shaharudin, Khalil, & Salleh, 2019).

There are generally two types of green roofs which are extensive and intensive which are determined by the depth, layers or media component and maintenance required. In Malaysia, the most common types found were intensive green roofs system with the thoughts of many professionals, extensive green roofs had a limitation on plant selection and less aesthetic value than extensive green roof systems (Abdul Rahman, Ahmad, & Rosley, 2013). Even though the scenario of green roofs in Malaysia is still at an introductory stage, the country has already initiated a green roof project, but the numbers are not inspiring (Shaharudin et al., 2019). Previous research on perception and awareness of various parties on the green roof in Malaysia (Abdul Rahman et al., 2013; Ismail, Ahmad, Kamarudin, & Ithnin, 2014; Ismail et al., 2018; Md. Zahir, Raman, Mohamed, Jamiland, & Nopiah, 2014) found respondents disagreed on the economic value of green roof or rooftop gardens and need improvement on the level of acceptances, local guideline, policy and campaign, local materials, and quantify of benefits on maintenance. Hence, it is crucial to consider the green implementation in practice and obstacles must be addressed for more development of the green roof in the Malaysian built environment.

2.2. Classification of the Green Roofs

There are two types of green roofs classified as intensive green roofs and extensive (Abdul Rahman, Ahmad, Mohammad, & Rosley, 2015; Osmundson, 1999) which are determined by the depth, layers or media component and maintenance required. An intensive green roof is also known as a roof garden of which the plants comprise of trees and shrubs and needs regular maintenance, the system requires specific support from the building as it is generally heavy (Abdul Rahman et al., 2013). Malaysia has several intensive green roofs compared to the extensive green roofs and are mostly found in commercial and urban residential areas (Abdul Rahman et al., 2015; Ismail et al., 2018; Shaharudin et al., 2019). Intensive green roofs require the deepest soil and have the greatest impact on the structural design, but they also accommodate all types of plantings including large shrubs and trees. Maintaining an intensive roof can be quite involved and needed periodically with skilled labours (Chow & Abu Bakar, 2016). Because they have larger plants need to be cared for and attention on walkways or other occupied zones for visitors' safety. Extensive green roofs are considered lighter than the intensive green roofs in terms of loading. An extensive green roof develops on the existing building's rooftop, made up of a very thin layer of soil or other planting medium with shallow-root plants like sedum, mosses, and grasses (Chow & Abu Bakar, 2016). The less maintenance required for the extensive green roof is lower compared to the other types and selection of plants is rather limited than intensive green roof has limited in its plant's selection and functional purposes; therefore, it requires less maintenance (Dunnet & Kingsbury, 2004). Climatic conditions, especially rainfall and extreme temperatures, may restrict the use of certain species or dictate the use of irrigation.

An extensive green roof system comprises the thin soil layer and features with limited plants, such as grass, sedum, succulents, bushes, and shrubs. It has a shallow substrate with a depth between 2 and 20 cm. Substrate depths of 7–15 cm can support a more diverse mixture of grass or perennial plant, more drought-tolerant but hospitable for undesirable weeds (Oberndorfer, 2007). The construction is lightweight and easy to install with less maintenance is required. This type of system is suitable for covering large surface areas; therefore, stressful conditions for plants require low-growing drought-resistant species (Bass, 2013). The purpose is practically for storm-water management, thermal insulation, and fireproofing. This type of roof is not accessible to the public because of the shallower substrate depth but need access for the maintenance work.The irrigation system is requiring and can be minimal.

An intensive green roof system requires a thicker soil layer, with the average depth of substrate between 20 cm and more. This type of system is also known as a roof garden of which the plants comprise trees and shrubs and needs regular maintenance (Abdul Rahman et al., 2013). The species of vegetation are not restricted other than those imposed by substrate depth, climate, building height and exposure, and irrigation facilities provided. The landscape appearance of intensive system offers a variety of plants and they appear as conventional ground-level gardens, and supplement living and recreation space in densely populated urban areas. The construction required planning during the design stage for the structural engineering system or roof system to withstand additional load (Oberndorfer, 2007). A proper irrigation system also is important. The purpose of an intensive green roof system is functional and aesthetic built environment feature and typically accessible for the occupants or visitors.

2.3. Benefits of the Green Roof in Commercial Buildings and Urban Areas

Green roofs bring benefits to the environment, social, and economic especially in urban areas with many adverse effects instead of rapid development and economic growth. Research on green roofs around the world with varieties of climatic condition provides extensive knowledge on the systems choice and outcome (Besir & Cuce, 2018; Li & Yeung, 2014; Shafique, Kim, & Rafiq, 2018; Theodosiou, 2009). Among the benefits are storm water management, thermal insulation regarding energy consumption, improve air quality, noise reduction, reduce UHI effects, positive impact to urban communities, displaying building aesthetic values and economic value for a longer term. Vegetation over the built space of the urban fabric is very much helpful in lowering the temperature, not within the human habitats as well as the parks or the green space. The potential benefits of roof greening for air quality have yet to be documented, except for indirect assessments of the impact of energy savings on emissions (Bass & Baskaran, 2003).

The installation of green roofs in urban areas helps in the reduction of energy use. A study by Susca et al. (2011) found that an energy saving of approximately 40–110%. The vegetation surface on the roof cools the air masses and contributes to the reduction of the temperature from 1 to –2°C directly decrease energy distribution (Herath, Halwatura, & Jayasinghe, 2018). A field measurement by Wong, Chen, Ong, and Sia (2003) found that the heat transfer through a green roof in Singapore over a typical day was less than 10% of that of a reference roof. Green roofs diminish the amount of heat transferred through the roof, thus reducing the energy demands of the building. Although, the economic benefits of green roofs are determined numerous factors like the selection of green roof systems and by the plant's types, the research findings provide useful data on the economic value of green roofs system.

2.4. Barriers and Challenge

Vast studies on the green roofs convey broad spectrums of this green design aspect. Wide-ranging issues were emphasised and recorded; as a result, positive or negative impacts contribute an international body of knowledge to green roofs development. Obstacles of the green roofs' implementation vary in different countries, but the findings are likely in the same context. Lack of interest in inventory strategy or feedback report on green roof demand hindered the barrier of the green roof market (Tsang & Jim, 2013). A study in Australia found that without government support and policies the private sector was unwilling to participate in the green roofs project (Tassicker, Rahnamayiezekavat, & Sutrisna, 2016). A legislative mechanism will further assist the government to be able to highlight that green roofs viability. Installation of green roof system is a complicated issue concerning many aspects such as motivations and pressure, supporting techniques and performance, investment and policy, and design, construction and maintenance, as well as the involvers and their pursuits (Zhang & He, 2021).

In Malaysia, the recent assessment model of green roof installation displays the risk on the technical aspect (Tabatabaee, Mahdiyar, Durdyev, Mohandes, & Ismail, 2019). The most affecting risk is the probability of damage including roof leakage. The result provides an insight into the green roof installation in the city with tropical climate conditions. In the meanwhile, a previous study conducted by Ismail et al. (2012) found nine obstacles come across in implementing green roofs in Malaysia. These factors are including complicated installation methods and high cost, fear of unknown risk, past failure, hard to maintain, limited local expertise, lack of scientific research, higher cost of materials supply, no design standards, and guidelines, and believe that green roof is susceptible to fire. The questionnaire survey and data analysing showed the main obstacle is lack of local expertise and professionals, higher material costs, and lack of studies on the green roofs.

3. METHODOLOGY

The research aims to determine the barriers in the implementation the green roofs in Malaysia. From the previous research (Ismail et al., 2012, 2018; Tabatabaee et al., 2019), many factors obstruct the implementation of a green roof. This research will focus on discovery of factors that impede the application of the green roof at the commercial building. The data were collected from the literature reviews, questionnaire surveys, and case studies. The questionnaire survey targets the respondent of building maintenance staffs from case studies using a set of questionnaire surveys. This is to determine views of the target group the barriers that cause the problem in implementing green roofs during the maintenance phase or building operation. According to Ismail et al. (2012, 2018), the nine factors were adopted as the barriers in implementing green roofs. These barriers were formulated in a set closed-ended questionnaire. The respondents work and involved in maintaining the green roofs in the commercial buildings selected during the survey done. Each case study has different number of respondents based on the number of maintenance staffs of the selected building. The site questionnaire survey was distributed at the same time during the interview session in each case study involving discussion between the maintenance staffs and the facility manager who have been in charge to obtain the effective response (Zhang, Shen, Tam, & Lee, 2012). The respondents were encouraged to give their judgement on the relative significance of each barrier to obstruct the implementation of intensive green roof systems for the existing buildings they involved. The age of the respondents ranges between 18 and 55 years old with working experience within 5–15 years. Three selected commercial buildings with the rooftop garden were chosen as our case studies to investigate the factors that could be challenges for the green roofs' implementation in Malaysia.

The data was collected from the respondents who are the maintenance department's staffs of the three different case study studies, which is focussed on the shopping mall building. The case studies are located at Petaling Jaya (CS1), Kuala Lumpur (CS2), and Subang Jaya (CS3). These case studies were selected because they are implementing similar intensive green roof system, which also act as recreational outdoor area. The green roofs located at the fifth-floor level, seventh-floor level, and twelfth-floor level accordingly to CS1, CS2, and CS3 and accessible to public. The case studies selected are in the central region of Malaysia the most urbanised area and densely populated to reflect with this study.

Likert's scale was used to measure the level of agreement of respondents. This scale represents the agreement of respondents towards which factors that appear as barrier and challenges that contribute to the difficulties of implementing green roofs practices in Malaysia. The factors that have been focussed on the past failure of green roof, difficult and high cost, complicated and hard to maintain, limited local expertise and inexperienced green roof professionals, lack of scientific research, fear of unknown risk, higher cost of material supply, design standards and guidelines, and susceptible to fire. The interview session was also conducted with the officer that responsible to maintain the green roof of the case study buildings such as the Facilities Manager or the Maintenance Department.

Descriptive analysis is used for this research to analyse the Likert scale questions. Zhang et al. (2012) used the Relative Importance Index (RII) to determine the relative importance of the various benefits and constraints on green roofs in Hong Kong. Thus, the RII was adopted in this study because of the similar method use to investigate the data and to rank the barriers and challenges of implementing green roofs at a commercial complex. The equation used is:

$$\text{Relative importance index (RII)} = \frac{\sum W}{AN}, \quad (0 \leq \text{RII} \leq 1) \tag{1}$$

Where, W is the weighting scores given by the respondents ranging from 1 to 5 where is strongly disagrees and 5 is strongly agrees A is the possible highest score for each factor (in this case is 5) and N is the total number of responses concerning those factors. RII analysis in SPSS helps us to identify the rank of the challenge from the most significant barrier to the least significant.

4. RESULT AND DISCUSSION

Case studies selected implement the intensive green roof system suited the purpose of functional, aesthetic and increased the living space to the building occupants and visitors. The basis of layers or substrate thickness is more than 20 cm and the design has a variety of plants or trees similar ground-level landscapes, high water-holding capacity, high capital and maintenance costs, and larger weight. The questionnaire was structured consisting of two sections of questions, which are divided into sections A and B. Each case study has a different number of respondents based on the number of maintenance staffs of the building. Section A of the questionnaire is about the demographic information of the respondents. There were 30 respondents involved during the survey conducted. For case study 1 located at Petaling Jaya has larger areas of the green roof area than the other two case studies, hence the respondents' participation was the highest. The age of the respondents' range 25–34 years old has a higher percentage of 54%. As for the working experience as shown in Fig. 15.1, the majority have working experience within 5–9 years with a percentage of 46%. This reflects with the age of the buildings they work in. A survey conducted by Shaharudin et al. (2019) with the working experience of the respondents between 1 and 10 years in green roof involved in the maintenance of the green roof in high-rise residential building. Moreover, only a small number of buildings in Malaysia have adapted green roof for the past 15 years (Ismail et al., 2012). Most of the respondents were involved in green roof systems during the building operation or the maintenance stage of the green roof as shown in Fig. 15.1, where 90% were responsible in planning and execution of the green roof maintenance and 10% involved during the construction. The experience of the respondents during maintenance is important in this study to seek the barriers from their perception in maintaining the green roof system. Effective strategies during operation and maintenance of green roof are crucial to mitigate misperceptions in implementing this system in Malaysia (Ismail et al., 2018; Tabatabaee et al., 2019).

Section B of the questionnaire is about the response to the barriers to implementing green roofs on commercial buildings in Malaysia at the selected case studies. The result of the RII of the barriers to implement the green roof during

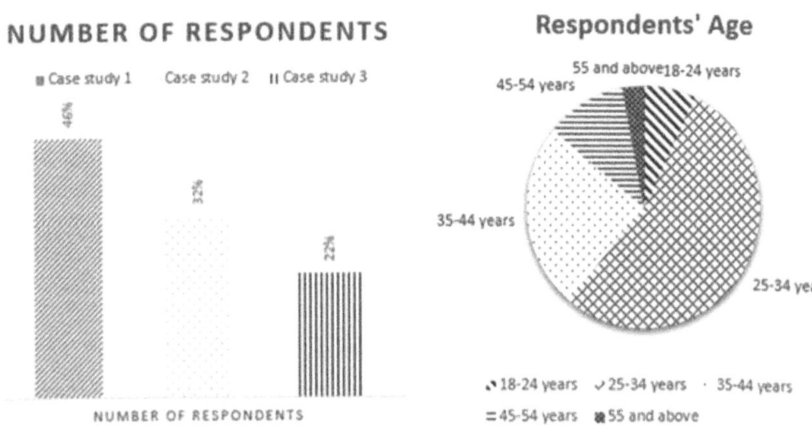

Fig. 15.1. Respondents' Working Experience in Years and Their Involvement in the Green Roof System Stage in the Building.

Table 15.1. Ranking of the Barriers That Become a Challenge in Implementing Green Roof during the Building Operation Stage in Maintaining the Green Roof System.

Nos.	Barriers	RII	Rank
1	Limited local expertise and inexperienced green roof professionals	0.896	1
2	Lack of scientific research on the green roof in a warm and humid climate	0.871	2
3	High maintenance cost	0.871	2
4	Higher cost of material supply	0.864	3
5	Fear of unfamiliar threat	0.857	4
6	No design Standards & Guidelines for the green roof in Malaysia	0.843	5
7	Past failure of green roof	0.840	6
8	Complicated and hard to maintain	0.836	7
9	The green roof is susceptible to fire.	0.593	8

the maintenance stage is summarised in Table 15.1. The significant or major challenge found is 'limited local expertise and inexperience professionals' in handling green roof systems. Almost 90% of respondents agree with this issue. Expertise and experience are crucial in installing and maintaining the green roof system (Chow & Abu Bakar, 2016; Ismail et al., 2012, 2018), if not this barrier will lead to poor maintenance work and failure of the green roofs system. Green roof design consists of several components from top to bottom: vegetation (landscape materials), growing medium (substrate), filter, drainage material (moisture retention), root barrier, water-proofing membrane, insulation layer, and structural layer (Townshend, 2007). Each of this component must carefully maintain and it needs knowledge and skilled in handling the system. Both 'Lack of scientific research on the green roof in local climate'and 'High maintenance cost' being ranked as the number two most significant barrier to implementing green roofs system as experienced by the respondent. These barriers will impede the development of green roofs to be adopting in the Malaysian built environment (Ismail et al., 2012, 2018). Some additional components of the green roofs are depending on climatic conditions like irrigation systems and the resistance of the selected vegetation. Ismail et al. (2012) suggested more research to identify obstacles from various parties involved such as policy maker, developers, and contractors to find key factors for further development of green roof in Malaysia. This indicates that to promote green roof more scientific research in the Malaysia climate context the maintenance cost such as require a regular check on the plant, drainage, and substrate of the green roof longevity. A suitable installation and well-maintained green roof system will further extend the utility and life span of the roof for 45 years (Shafique et al., 2018; Zhang & He, 2021).

The third rank is 'higher initial cost and material supply' due to the limitation of green roof suppliers and specialist contractors in Malaysia. This also depends on many factors such as location, labour costs, green roof types, and materials. According to the studies done by Ismail et al. (2018) and Tabatabaee et al. (2019), higher initial costs and material supply of green roofs installation among the main barriers in green roofs construction. A comprehensive study by

Li and Yeung (2014) found the costs vary between local and imported materials as claimed by the local suppliers in Hong Kong. 'Fear of unfamiliar threat' is ranked at number five, the green roof is not properly placed on the roof, and the risk for the roof leakage and structural building failure becomes high (Shafique et al., 2018). Although study by Kosareo and Ries (2007) found the green roof offers energy benefits in the life-cycle assessment, but the fear of high cost of installation and maintenance especially the repairing cost for leakage because of faulty design or poor workmanship is highly concerned to adopt the system in this country. Followed by the sixth-ranked which is 'no design standards and guidelines for the green roof system' – local standards and guidelines in Malaysia needs to be established to achieve success in adapting the green roofs system. For this more effort need for the co-operation and collaboration between different fields for the application and management of green roofs. Shafique et al. (2018) indicate the lack of collaboration and co-operation between different fields (architects, civil engineers, environmental engineers, and resident) in the management of the green roofs that arise in the maintenance phase. They suggest every person involved need to discuss and divide the task to overcome these issues.

'Past failure of the green roof' ranked number seven, when the stakeholders or building owner are not aware of the green roof benefits, for that reason it is important to share information of the benefits of the green roof and overall encouragement (local authorities, practitioners, building owner, and others). Past failure is the risk associated with green roof installation (Ismail et al., 2018; Tabatabaee et al., 2019), more participation from various stakeholders during installation process including for a better understanding of the maintenance and the implication of this risk. Next is the eight ranked is 'complicated & hard to maintain' in as much as the lack of knowledge and technical difficulties. It demands more work to find a more efficient local substrate for the green roof, Eco-friendly green roof components that can enhance the natural environment (Shafique et al., 2018). This factor requires huge effort for the application and management of the green roof. Final factor number nine which is 'green roofs is susceptible to fire' is ranked as least significant in this finding. A survey by Ismail et al. (2018) found the believe that green roofs are susceptible to fire is one of the barriers in adopting green roof. This factor is likely to occur on bitumen exposed roof (ABG Ltd, 2013; Ismail et al., 2018), as an alternative, a green roof more probable to prevent fire from occurring.

5. CONCLUSION

This research is conducted to investigate the barriers to implement green roofs on commercial buildings in Malaysia. The intensive green roof system requires extra cost, knowledge, and skill in maintaining the plants and building system involves, despite it has more advantages to the environment and humans. There are various barriers in implementing green roofs in the form of the perception of the maintenance staff in commercial buildings. The top three are 'limited local expertise and inexperience professionals', 'lack of scientific research on the green roof in local climate', and 'high maintenance cost'. Many of these barriers related to lack of expertise, experience professional, technical knowledge, and information that finally affect the cost to implementers hinder lacking interest in the green roof system. These barriers are challenging and need further research to provide extending knowledge and information on the technical and management of the green roofs system in the local context. Record and retain comprehensive descriptions of the routine and problem solving during the operation and maintenance very much help for future references. The findings of this study are limited to a few case studies of commercial buildings; the results may vary for another type of commercial building depending on its function. These findings contribute to the knowledge of the maintenance phase for the intensive green system in the commercial building. A further study is recommended on the implementation of an extensive green roof system which is simpler and less expensive than benefit in combatting environmental problems in the cities and greener Malaysia envisioned to be sustained in the future.

ACKNOWLEDGEMENTS

The authors would like to express their sincere appreciation to the anonymous reviewers for their valuable and constructive suggestions. The authors also wish to acknowledge the support from Universiti Teknologi MARA, Perak Branch.

REFERENCES

Abdul Rahman, S. R., & Ahmad, H. (2008). *Green roofs as urban antidote: A review on aesthetic, environmental, economic and social benefits. 6th South East Asian Tech. Univ. Consort. Symp, 6*, 93–97.

Abdul Rahman, S. R., Ahmad, H., Mohammad, S., & Rosley, M. S. F. (2015). Perception of green roof as a tools for urban regeneration in a commercial environment: The secret garden Malaysia. *Procedia Social Behavioral Science, 170*, 128–136.

Abdul Rahman, S. R., Ahmad, H., & Rosley, M. S. F. (2013). Green roof: Its awareness among professionals and potential in Malaysian market. *Procedia – Social and Behavioral Sciences, 85*, 443–453.

Abdullah, N. T. (2012). Study of landscape gardens: Expectations and users. *Procedia – Social and Behavioral Sciences, 50*, 633–642.

ABG Ltd. (2013). *A guide to the design and specification of ABG Geosynthetics green roof systems, Creative geosynthetic engineering*. England: ABG- Geosynthetics Engineering.

Bass, B. (2013). City of Toronto: Guidelines for biodiverse green roofs. Retrieved from https://web.toronto.ca/

Bass, B., & Baskaran, B. (2003). *Evaluating rooftop and vertical gardens as an adaptation strategy for urban areas. Ottawa*: Institute for Research in Construction, National Research Council Canada.

Besir, A. B., & Cuce, E. (2018). Green roofs and facades: A comprehensive review. *Renewable and Sustainable Energy Reviews, 82*, 915–939.

Chow, M., & Abu Bakar, M. (2016). A review on the development and challenges of green. *International Journal of Civil, Environmental, Structural, 10*(1), 16–20.

Dunnet, N., & Kingsbury, N. (2004). *Planting green roofs and living walls*. Oregon: Timber Press.

Emmanuel, R. (2017). Performance standard for tropical outdoors: A critique of current impasse and a proposal for way forward. *Urban Climate*. doi:10.1016/j.uclim.2017.01.002

European Commission. (2007). Energy efficiency of buildings. European Commission. Retrieved from https://ec.europa.eu/energy/en/topics/energy-efficiency/buildings. Accessed on October 19, 2019.

Grant, G. (2006). Extensive green roofs in London. *Urban Habitats*, *4*, 51–65.

Hassan, J. S., Mohamad Zin, R., Abd Majid, M. Z., Balubaid, S., & Hainin, M. R. (2014). Building energy consumption in Malaysia: An overview. *Jurnal Teknologi [Sciences & Engineering]*, *7*(70), 33–38.

Herath, H. M. P. I. K., Halwatura, R. U., & Jayasinghe, G. Y. (2018). Modelling a tropical urban context with green walls and green roofs as an urban heat island adaptation strategy. *Procedia Engineering*, *212*, 691–698.

Ismail, W. Z. W., Abdullah, M. N., Hashim, H., & Rani, W. S. W. (2018). Perception An overview of green roof development in Malaysia and a way forward. *AIP Conference Proceedings*, 2016, 020058. doi:10.1063/1.5055460

Ismail, W. Z. W., Ahmad, S. S., Kamarudin, H., & Ithnin, Z. (2014). Green roofs benefits: Perception by Malaysian residential highrise end users. *The 2014 IEEE symposium on business, engineering & industrial applications (ISBEIA 2014)*.

Ismail, Z., Aziz, H. A., Nasir, N. M., & Taib, M. Z. M. (2012). Obstacles to adopt green roof in Malaysia. *IEEE colloquium on humanities, science &engineering (Chuser)*, *Chuser*, pp. 357–371.

Jones, E. A. (2008). Temperature decreases in an urban canyon due to green walls and green roofs in diverse climates. *Building and Environment*, *43*, 480–493.

Kosareo, L., & Ries, R. (2007). Comparative environmental life cycle assessment of green roofs. *Building and Environment*, *42*, 2606–2613.

Li, W. C., & Yeung, K. K. A. (2014). A comprehensive study of green roof performance. *International Journal of Sustainable Built Environment*, *3*, 127–134.

Md. Zahir, M. H., Raman, S. N., Mohamed, M. F., Jamiland, M., & Nopiah, Z. M. (2014). The perception of Malaysian architects towards the implementation of green roof: A review of practices, methodologies and future research. *E3S Web Conference*, *3*, 01022.

Oberndorfer, E. L. (2007). Green roofs as urban ecosystems: Ecological structures, functions and services. *BioScience*, *57*(10), 823–833.

Oke, T. R. (1995). The heat island of the urban boundary layer: Characteristics, causes and effects. *Wind Climate in Cities*, 81–107.

Osmundson, T. (1999). *Roof gardens: History, design, and construction*. New York, NY: Norton.

Rowe, K. L. (2006). The role of extensive green roofs in sustainable development. *Hortscience*, *41*(5), 1276–1285.

Semenza, J. (2014). Climate change and human health. *International Journal of Environmental Research and Public Health*, *11*, 7347–7353. http://dx.doi.org/10.3390/

Shafique, M., Kim, R., & Rafiq, M. (2018). Green roof benefits, opportunities and challenges – A review. *Renewable and Sustainable Energy Reviews*, *90*, 757–773.

Shaharuddin, A. N. (2011). The effects of different land uses on the temperature distribution of a humid tropical urban centre. *World Applied Sciences Journal*, *13*, 63–68.

Shaharudin, S., Khalil, N., & Salleh, A. A. (2019). Review of significant maintenance criteria for tropical green roofs in Malaysia. *International Journal of Technology*, *10*(1), 69–80.

Susca, T., Gaffin, S. R., & Dell'osso, G. R. (2011). Positive effects of vegetation: Urban heat island and green roofs. *Environment Pollution*, *159*, 2119–2126.

Syed Othman Thani, S. K., Nik Mohamad, N. K., & Syed Abdullah, S. M. (2013). The influence of urban landscape morphology on the temperature distribution of hot-humid urban centre. *Procedia - Social and Behavioral Sciences*, *85*, 356–367.

Tabatabaee, S., Mahdiyar, A., Durdyev, S., Mohandes, S. R., & Ismail, S. (2019). An assessment model of benefits, opportunities, costs, and risks of green roof installation: A multi criteria decision making approach. *Journal of Cleaner Production*, *238*, 1–13.

Tan, P. Y. (2008). *A selection of plants for green roofs in Singapore* (2nd ed.). Singapore: National Park Board.

Tassicker, N., Rahnamayiezekavat, P., & Sutrisna, M. (2016). An Insight into the commercial viability of green. *Sustainability*, *8*(7), 603. doi:10.3390/su8070603

Theodosiou, T. (2009). Green roofs in buildings: Thermal and environmental behaviour. *Advances in Building Energy Research*, *3*, 271–288.

Townshend, D. (2007). *Study on green roof application in Hong Kong.* Final Report. Hong Kong.

Tsang, S. W., & Jim, C. Y. (2013). A stochastic model to optimize forecast and fulfillment of green roof demand. *Urban Forestry & Urban Greening*, *12*, 53–60.

UNDESA. (2018). United Nation Department of Economic and Social Affair. Retrieved from https://www.un.org/development/desa/en/news/population/2018-revision-of-world-urbanization-prospects.html. Accessed on February 1, 2020.

Wong, N. H., Chen, Y., Ong, C. L., & Sia, A. (2003). Investigation of thermal benefits of rooftop garden in the tropical environment. *Building and Environment*, *38*, 261–270.

Zakaria, R., Foo, K. S., Mohamad Zin, R., Yang, J., & Zolfagharian, S. (2012). Potential retrofitting of existing campus buildings to green buildings. *Applied Mechanics and Materials, 178–181*, 42–45.

Zhang, G., & He, B. (2021). Towards green roof implementation: Drivers, motivations, barriers. *Urban Forestry & Urban Greening*, *16*(2012), 314–319.

Zhang, X., Shen, V., Tam, W., & Lee, W. W. (2012). Barriers to implement extensive green roof systems: A Hong Kong study. *Renewable and Sustainable Energy Reviews*, *16*, 314–319.

CHAPTER 16

IDENTIFICATION OF BARRIERS AND CHALLENGES FACED BY CONSTRUCTION KEY PLAYERS IN IMPLEMENTING THE GREEN BUILDING INCENTIVES IN MALAYSIA

Nadira Binti Ahzahar, Siti Zubaidah Binti Hashim, Intan Bayani Bin Zakaria, Norehan Norlida Mohd Noor and Nur Anis Bt Abdul Rahman

ABSTRACT

Malaysia is still very much lacking behind in green building developments as compared to other countries such as Australia, Japan, and Singapore. Nevertheless, in order to strengthen the development of green building in Malaysia, government has provided and offers several initiatives to the construction key players in implementing green building such as investment tax allowance for the purchase of green technology equipment and income tax exemption on the use of green technology services and system, etc. Despite of all the incentives introduce, the implementation of green building construction still does not boast as expected and still relatively low. Therefore, this study will identify barriers, issues, and challenges faced by construction key players in implementing green building concepts especially related to green building incentives in their project. The opinions and views of related parties in building

Sustainability Management Strategies and Impact in Developing Countries
Community, Environment and Disaster Risk Management, Volume 26, 209–218

ISSN: 2040-7262/doi:10.1108/S2040-726220220000026016

industry were obtained from structured interviews and questionnaires to key personnel in construction industry to give a clearer picture of the current situation. This study is succeeded in identifying the barriers and challenges, which mainly categorised into financial incentives, fiscal incentives, and structural incentives. The main issues identified are excessive cost of construction, tax exemption is limited and only for qualified person and legislative challenges. Nonetheless, this study also suggests various ways to overcome the barriers in promoting green building concept in Malaysia towards greener environment.

Keywords: Green building incentives; barriers and challenges; financial incentives; fiscal incentives; structural incentives; green construction

1. INTRODUCTION

Green building has been introduced in Malaysia in 2009 by Malaysian Green Technology Corporation, MGTC (wholly owned subsidiary of Pertubuhan Arkitek Malaysia (PAM), and the Association of Consulting Engineers Malaysia, ACEM). The purpose of green building is to excite all key players in construction to make a development of environmentally and sensitive building through building rating system that ranks a building's performance (Green Building Index. n.d). Committed to encourage the public and private sectors to invest in green development, the government then introduced a series of green building incentives (GBIs) such as the introduction of some incentives for green building development in Malaysia. The purpose of incentives is to drive the adoption of green buildings by building sector stakeholders such as developers, investors, owner of building involved in sustainable development to save the environment by utilise all the resources efficiently (Olubunmi, Xia, & Skitmore, 2016). Despite of all the incentives introduces, the implementation of green building construction still does not boast as expected and still relatively low. The numbers of Malaysian firms that obtain GBI certification to capitalise on the Malaysia Green Building tax incentives are significant, but not outstanding (Aliagha, Hashim, Sanni, & Ali, 2013). Shafiei, Abadi, and Osman (2017) share the same opinion as from their study; they have found that even though the concept of GBI has been introduced in Malaysia, there is a lack of interest among the building industry stakeholders. Therefore, the objective of this study is to identify barriers, issues, and challenges faced by construction key players in implementing green building concepts especially related to GBIs in their project. From the research done, there are three types of incentives identified; financial, fiscal and structural. Apart from that, there are also several barriers and challenges that arise in implementation of GBIs introduced by government and its also categorised according to types of incentives..

1.1. Financial Incentives

The financial incentives are direct monetary provided by government as a financial support for developers who propose or willing to involve in green development. There are various financial incentives provided such as grants, loans, fund, vouchers, rebates, etc. Below are some of barriers and challenges identified related to financial incentives:

i) *Lack of knowledge and expertise* – The contractor and design key players still lack knowledge and still using the traditional and standard construction. Hence, they need to be equipped with the current knowledge on the green construction method, techniques, and product used in construction of green building. It is very important to the construction industry workers to update their skill, knowledge, and capabilities (Aliagha et al., 2013; Sahat, 2012).
ii) *Higher in cost of construction* – Furthermore, the other challenges that arise in implementing GBIs to the key players are the cost of construction for green building, even government has introduced the incentives for green building, but the cost is still higher than conventional method. The financial constraint has become the most critical issues, even the concept of green construction is believed by many people to be economically, but the sustainable practices will increase the construction cost because higher capital upfront needed (Sahat, 2012; Wong et al., 2021).
iii) *Negative perception on the green construction* – There is a negative perception in the building industry that green building needs extra cost for construction expenditure even though the key players of construction are aware with the benefits in implementing for green building; they are still reluctant to adopt the green building concept in their future project (Yudelson, 2008).
iv) *Low investment and participation from government and private companies* – Due to the low investment and participation from private companies, it is has become one of the barriers to implement the green construction in Malaysia. Government and private companies should invest and support the green construction for the green development (Esa et al., 2011; Wong et al., 2021).
v) *Resistance from local agencies* – The approving agencies such as local authority and government agencies have not given positive feedback and showed some resistance to green building concept due to lack of understanding in the basis and concept.
vi) *Reluctant of bank to support the green construction* – Based on Organization for Economic Co-operation and Development (OECD), banks had reluctant to support green building because of a lack of understanding of green projects and doubts about the ability of loan holders to service their loan (OECD, 2013; Wong et al., 2021).
vii) *Lack of clarity and details on qualifying expenditure* – The lack of detail on qualifying expenditure as to what constitutes reference base cost for green assert as some green asserts were given reference base cost while others were not (Aliagha et al., 2013).

1.2. Fiscal Incentives

Fiscal is about less much common as financial incentives. However, it is not a direct monetary given by government to encourage developers like financial incentives. Fiscal incentive is like a privilege given by government, in term of exclusion from paying any tax, but only given to qualified project. Fiscal can be classified as profit-based, capital-investment-based, labour-based, sales-based, import-and-export-based, and based on other expenses. Fiscal is more neutral, more predictable for companies, wider reach, very low on administrative cost, and more accessible. Below are some of barriers and challenges identified related to fiscal incentives:

i) *Lack of knowledge and expertise* – Most construction key players do not have knowledge about the GBIs such as in the green building fiscal incentives (Wong et al., 2021).
ii) *Income tax only for qualifying person (limited target group)* – Only a person who incurs qualifying expenditure and commences his business at GBI building would qualify for GBI income tax incentives and property developers, private house owner who lease GBI residential properties to collect passive income and first property buyers would not qualify for GBI income tax (Aliagha et al., 2013).

1.3. Structural Incentives

Structural incentives are also known as administrative incentive, which is the indirect way of how developers could get their benefit from building green. Structural incentives are much common incentives offered by government because; it would not require expenditure of fund and not reduce the income of city and county. Below are some of barriers and challenges identified related to structural incentives:

i) *Lack of knowledge and expertise* – Construction key players do not have knowledge or aware of structural incentives that have been provided by government (Wong et al., 2021).
ii) *Dissatisfaction on the incidental cost* – Among challenges that may arise are the criticisms and dissatisfaction by the construction key players, such as on qualifying expenditure. The incidental cost likes green building fees, facilitator cost and consultancy cost are not included as additional capital expenditure to obtain the green building certification, due to that most of key players that involved in construction thinks that can cause additional in construction expenditure and refused to construct for green building (Aliagha et al., 2013).
iii) *Legislative challenges* – Apart from that, the other challenges in implementing for GBIs among construction key players is the legislative challenge. The inability of construction key players to regulate and to enforce the legislative framework especially for green technology and green growth (Rostami, Khoshnava, Ahankoob, & Rostami, 2014). Besides, for getting the green building certification to achieve the green building requirement, they need to face a lot of complicated and complex of legislative. Due to that factor, they reluctant to implementing for green building construction and more prefer to construct by using conventional method.

1.4. Other Related Issues

The other issues that arise besides the issues on the fiscal, financial, and structural incentives are:

i) *Limited sources of worker* – Construction of green building must be managed and involved by a personnel and worker who are fully trained and have adequate knowledge and experience since the construction method and techniques. Due to least number of qualified works, this factor becomes an obstacle in green building construction (Sahat, 2012).
ii) *Lack of awareness* – The challenges in implementing GBIs among the construction key players is lack of awareness. Even the initiatives have been introduced by the government to improve the development of green building, the lack of awareness even from the architects, contractor, consultant, and client have become barriers in development of green building and will cause the slow progress and development of green building in Malaysia (Esa et al., 2011; Wong et al., 2021).
iii) *Lack of technology* – Ineffective information technology and lack of system knowledge have become barriers to implement the green construction in Malaysia because to construct the green building it is need for special technology to construct it, and the advance of technology is needed (Samari, Godrati, Esmaeilifar, Olfat, & Shafiei, 2013; Wong et al., 2021).
iv) *Lack of government support* – In Malaysia, there is a lack on the government support especially at state level. Government should play a bigger role in promoting the green building construction for development through actions such as through strong enforcement of legislation, devising and new policy on the green building (Samari et al., 2013; Wong et al., 2021).
v) *Lack of strategy to promote green building* – Generally, the current tax incentives for green technology in Malaysia may not be sufficiently attractive to the public and private sectors as compared to those given by neighbouring countries (Aliagha et al., 2013; Samari et al., 2013).
vi) *Lack of statutory of green building rating system* – There is no element of mandatory clause or regulation making it mandatory for some class of new building to achieve at least a minimum certified level of GBI rating or mandatory regulation setting a realistic target such as for existing public building to undergo major retrofitting or either to gain certified or silver GBI rating level (Aliagha et al., 2013).
vii) *Lack of sustainable material to be obtained for green construction* – Sustainable materials are difficult to obtain in Malaysia. Prices of sustainable materials such as low volatile organic compounds (VOC) paints are higher than normal paints. Sourcing sustainable technology is difficult and expensive (Goh, Seow, & Goh, 2013).
viii) *Lack of enforcement* – The sustainable housing development in construction sectors does not being encourage by public policies and regulatory. As example, local authority only enforces the developers to install rainwater-harvesting systems in the semi-detached house and condominium. Although

the Malaysian government has encouraged for the green construction, there is still the lack of enforcement and monitoring of laws and legislations (Goh et al., 2013).

ix) *Lack of demand by stakeholders for green construction* – Usually, the stakeholders is involved of individuals and organisations that include of clients, government, contractors, and other. The lack of demand by stakeholders on green construction in Malaysia is derived from the green building construction or sustainability is not their priorities (Goh et al., 2013; Wong et al., 2021).

2. METHODOLOGY

This study achieves the objectives from the literature, with questionnaires, and also interviews. This study used two categories of data: primary and secondary data. Primary data are data obtained directly from actual work situation. Among the techniques used to obtain primary data is like using questionnaires and interviews. Secondary data are information from existing materials and can be obtained through reference library. It involves research texts, documents, papers, mass media, and so on. The technique chosen is quantitative where more than 30 sets of questionnaires posed to respondents that related to the green construction of building sector in Malaysia. The collected data were analysed using the Statistical for Social Science (SPSS). Frequency analysis is obtained from the SPSS output and average index method is adopted for analysis from the result of frequency analysis. The frequency and the percentage will be representing in the form of related table and chart.

3. FINDING AND ANALYSIS

3.1. Barriers and Challenges in Implementing Financial Incentives

Based on the findings shown in Table 16.1, the most occured barrier for financial incentives is higher in cost of construction where the green building construction may lead to the excessive cost of construction with 4.17 mean index value. It shows that the respondents mostly agreed with the issues. This may imply that the green building construction needs special materials and technology in achieving the green building standard. Therefore, these lead to extra capital cost and construction cost. This is supported by barriers ranked at second with 4.10 mean index value which are perception of construction cost for green building will add extra cost, perception that green construction is complicated and complex to construct, and the construction of green building is higher than conventional construction. Apart from that, all barriers and challenges listed under financial have scored more than 4.0 mean index each. This shows that financial barriers are main concerns to industry players. The financial barriers have become the most critical issues, even the concept of green construction is believed by many people to be economically, but the sustainable practices will increase the construction cost because higher capital upfront needed.

Table 16.1. Table of Rank for Barriers and Challenges in Implementing Financial Incentives.

Indicator	Financial Incentives	Mean	Index	Rank
F3a	Green building construction can lead to the excessive cost of construction	4.17	Agree	1
F2b	Perception of construction cost for green building will add extra cost.	4.10	Agree	2
F2a	Perception that green construction is complicated and complex to construct	4.10	Agree	3
F3b	The construction of green building is higher than conventional construction	4.10	Agree	4
F6	Approval agencies such as local authority and government agencies do not give positive feedback to construct green building	4.03	Agree	5
F3c	Green construction increases the project cost because higher capital upfront needed	4.00	Agree	6
F7a	Some of bank reluctant to support green projects due to the lack of understanding about green projects	3.90	Agree	7
F1a	Construction key players do not have expertise to apply for financial incentives	3.90	Agree	8
F7a	Lack of detail on qualifying expenditure as to what constitutes reference base cost for green assert as some green asserts were given reference base cost while others were not	3.87	Agree	9
F4	Some of banks have doubts about the ability of key players to service their loan for construction of green building	3.87	Agree	10
F1b	Most key players do not know what is financial incentives that have been provided by government	3.70	Agree	11
F5	Approval agencies such as local authority and government agencies do not give positive feedback to construct green building	3.57	Agree	12

Indicator	Fiscal Incentives	Mean	Index	Rank
FC2a	GBI income tax incentives only qualified for a person who incurs qualifying expenditure and commences his business	4.07	Agree	1
FC2b	First property buyers would not qualify for GBI income tax	4.07	Agree	2
FC1b	Most of key players do not know how to apply for fiscal incentives	3.93	Agree	3
FC1a	Most of key players do not have knowledge on what are fiscal incentives	3.80	Agree	4

Indicator	Structural Incentives	Mean	Index	Rank
S3b	Inability to regulate and enforce legislative frameworks for green building construction	4.90	Strongly Agree	1
S3a	Legislative to apply for green building incentives is complicated and complex	4.10	Agree	2
S1b	Most of key players do not know how to apply for structural/administrative incentives	4.07	Agree	3
S1a	Most of key players do not have knowledge on what is a structural/administrative incentive	3.90	Agree	4
S2a	The registration fee, facilitator cost, and consultancy are not included as additional capital expenditure incurred to obtain the green building certification	3.90	Agree	5
S2b	Higher or incidental cost to construct green building	3.83	Agree	6

3.2. Barriers and Challenges in Implementing Fiscal Incentives

For the fiscal issues as shown in Table 16.1, the income tax only for qualified person, GBI income tax incentives only qualified for a person who incurs qualifying expenditure and commences his business, and first property buyers would not qualify for GBI income tax with the mean of 4.07, are the most important barriers due to most of the government specification in commences for income tax such as qualified on the financial factors, experience, and technology that lead to the limited of parties that can beneficial from this incentives. For awareness and knowledge among key players, it seems to imply that the respondents may not be fully aware, or they have moderate knowledge on the incentives that provided by the local government.

3.3. Barriers and Challenges in Implementing Structural Incentives

The structural incentives issues in Table 16.1 show that the respondent are mostly agree with the issues of legislative challenges which is inability to regulate and enforce legislative frameworks for green building construction with the mean index of 4.23 is the most occurred barrier cause by lacking of statutory form the government to regulate the professional to construct green building and besides they need to face a complicated legislative procedure such as in getting permission and it requires longer time. Besides, for getting the green building certification to achieve the green building requirement, they need to face a lot of complicated and complex of legislative as it ranked at second with 4.10 mean index value. Due to that factor, they reluctant to implement green building construction and more prefer to construct by using conventional method.

3.4. Other Related Barriers and Challenges in Implementing GBIs

Based on Table 16.2, the most agreed barrier is lacking sustainable material to be obtained for green construction which the price of sustainable materials is higher compared to the prices for conventional materials with the mean index of 4.27. This is due to the material that being used are special material which environmentally friendly and resulting they refused to construct and used the incentives that have been provided. Low awareness among key players on the incentives that have been provided by government and low of support from government to train the skilled workers have become the second most important barriers with mean index 4.13. Some respondents had given feedback which agreed that there was a lacking on the government support especially at state level. Government at all levels should play a bigger role in promoting the green building construction for development through actions such as through strong enforcement of legislation, devising and new policy on the green building.

Table 16.2. Table of Rank for Other Related Barriers and Challenges in Implementing Green Building Incentives.

Indicator	Incentives	Mean	Index	Rank
O7a	Price of sustainable materials are higher compared to the prices for conventional materials	4.27	Agree	1
O2a	Key players do not aware the incentives that have been provided by government	4.13	Agree	2
01b	Low of support from government to train the skilled workers	4.13	Agree	3
O2b	Most of key players do not aware about the benefits of green construction	4.07	Agree	4
O8b	Lack of enforcement and monitoring by laws and legislations	4.07	Agree	5
O9	The stakeholders do not take the green construction or sustainability as their priorities in their needs	4.07	Agree	6
O3	Inadequate technology and inefficient green building technology	3.97	Agree	7
01a	Lack of skilled workers in green building cause limited sources of workers	3.93	Agree	8
O8a	Current policy and regulatory do not encourage construction key players to construct green building	3.93	Agree	9
O4	The incentives that have been provided by government do not enough and not attractive to pursue key players to construct a green building	3.93	Agree	10
07b	Sustainable materials are difficult to obtain in Malaysia	3.90	Agree	11
O6	There is no element of mandatory, clause or regulation making it mandatory for new building to achieve at least a minimum certified level of GBI rating	3.77	Agree	12
O5	Ineffective of green building promotion	3.67	Agree	13

4. CONCLUSION

There are many barriers and challenges identified based on three main categories of incentives namely financial, fiscal, and structural incentives. For financial incentives, most critical barrier is higher cost in green construction. For fiscal, the most critical issue is limited qualifying person in tax exemption and for structural incentive is legislative challenges which is inability to regulate and enforce legislative frameworks for green building construction. Apart from that, other related barriers are also identified such as lack of green materials, lack of awareness among key players, limited source of workers, and much more. From these reasons, some possibilities have been identified to solve the problem where it needs the involvement of various parties such as government, private sector, and key players themselves. Relevant efforts and measures should be implemented to improve the implementation of GBIs in Malaysia. The ways that can be suggested to overcome the issues are by promoting the usage of green technology to construction key players, impose mandatory policy for new building to achieve a realistic target or green building for example at least achieve for certified or silver of green building status, also allocate grant for training in gaining knowledge for green building construction and many others suitable ways in other to promote green building concept in Malaysia towards greener environment.

REFERENCES

Aliagha, G. U., Hashim, M., Sanni, A. O., & Ali, K. N. (2013). Review of green building demand factors for Malaysia. *Journal of Energy Technologies and Policy*, *3*(11), 471–478.

Esa, M. R., Marhani, M. A., Yaman, R., Hassan, A. A., Noor Rashid, N. R., & Adnan, H. (2011). Obstacles in implementing green building projects in Malaysia. Australian Journal of Basic and Applied Sciences, *5*(12), 1806–1812.

Goh, K. C., Seow, T. A., & Goh, H. H. (2013). Challenges of implementing sustainability in Malaysian housing industry. *International conference on sustainable built environment for now and the future (SBE2013) proceedings*, pp. 26–27.

Green building index (website), (n.d). Retrieved from http://new.greenbuildingindex.org/whatandwhy. Accessed on October 25, 2020.

Olubunmi, O. A., Xia, P. B., & Skitmore, M. (2016). Green building incentives: A review. *Renewable and Sustainable Energy Reviews*, *59*, 1611–1621.

Organization for Economic Co-Operation and Development (OECD). (2013). *OECD investment policy reviews Malaysia*. OECD Publishing.

Rostami, R., Khoshnava, S. M., Ahankoob, A., & Rostami, R. (2014). Green construction trends in Malaysia. *Management in Construction Research Association (MiCRA) postgraduate conference proceedings*.

Sahat, N. A. (2012). *The challenges of green building implementation in Malaysia*. Pahang: Faculty of Civil Engineering and Earth Resources, Universiti Malaysia.

Samari, M., Godrati, N., Esmaeilifar, R., Olfat, P., & Shafiei, M. W. M. (2013). The investigation of the barriers in developing green building in Malaysia. *Modern Applied Science*, *7*(2), 1–10.

Shafiei, M. W. M., Abadi, H., & Osman, W. N. (2017). The indicators of green buildings for Malaysian property development industry. *International Journal of Applied Engineering Research*, *12*(10), 2182–2189.

Wong, S. Y., Low, W. W., Wong, K. S., & Tai, Y. H. (2021). Barriers for green building implementation in Malaysian construction industry. *IOP Conference Series: Materials Science and Engineering*, 1101, 012029.

Yudelson, J. (2008). The green building revolution. *Journal of Real Estate Literature*, *16*(2), 253–255.

CHAPTER 17

LOCAL STAKEHOLDERS AND CONSUMER AWARENESS ON FLUOROCARBON GAS MANAGEMENT IN MALAYSIA

Nurul Nazleatul Najiha Mohd Nazif, Shazwin Mat Taib, Mohd Fadhil Md Din, Nurfarhain Mohammed Rusli and Dianah Mazlan

ABSTRACT

Fluorocarbon (FC) gas, which contributes to the ozone depletion and global warming, is commonly used especially in the refrigeration and air conditioning (RAC) equipment. In Malaysia, lifecycle management of FC gas is still lacking at all stages, especially at the downstream level (maintenance, service, recycle, recovery, and destruction). Thus, the aim of this study is to assess the level of awareness of local stakeholders and consumers regarding FC gas management. Furthermore, the level of awareness among the consumers has been identified based on their educational background. Two sets of questionnaires were developed based on the dichotomous question types (yes/no) and were distributed to local stakeholders and consumers by using convenience sampling in two different programmes. The data were statistically analysed using IBM SPSS software. Findings demonstrate that, in contrast to consumers, local stakeholders have high level of awareness in every section. Remarkably, all non-engineering respondents have a low level of awareness

Sustainability Management Strategies and Impact in Developing Countries
Community, Environment and Disaster Risk Management, Volume 26, 219–231

Published under exclusive licence by Emerald Publishing Limited
ISSN: 2040-7262/doi:10.1108/S2040-726220220000026017

about FC gas management. As a result, capacity building for consumers and service maintenance personnel who are heavily involved in middle steam and downstream lifecycle FC gas management is needed.

Keywords: Fluorocarbon gas; fluorocarbon gas management; awareness level; climate change; local stakeholders; consumers

1. INTRODUCTION

As the earth is getting warmer due to the climate change, the demand for refrigeration and air conditioning (RAC) equipment is getting increased. RAC equipment is commonly used in food industry, to conserve the quality of the food, as well as maintaining thermal comfort at home, commercial building, public area, and others (Randazzo, De Cian, & Mistry, 2020). The RAC equipment is consuming fluorocarbon (FC) gas, which can contribute to the environmental impact due to its leakage from the refrigeration system into the atmosphere.

This anthropogenic emission of the FC gas has contributed to widespread depletion of the ozone layer in recent decades (Hossaini et al., 2017). In the 1970s, the first group of researchers from the University of California cautioned about the possibility of atmospheric ozone deterioration when they examined the effects of anthropogenic gas such as chlorofluorocarbons (CFCs) and halons in the atmosphere (Chipperfield et al., 2017). Chemicals containing in those elements are chlorine and bromine, which are halogens that cause ozone depletion. This anthropogenic element is stable enough to stay in the atmosphere until they got into the middle of the stratosphere, where it will dissociate in the presence of ultraviolet (UV) light, releasing chlorine atoms, which then go on to catalyse ozone destruction. In the gas phase, the Cl-catalysed ozone depletion can take place, but in the presence of polar stratospheric clouds (PSCs) it is significantly improved. These compounds, also known as ozone-depleting substances (ODS), are responsible for depleting the stratospheric thickness of the ozone layer, and allowing UV radiation to be directly reflected from the sunlight (Adeoye & Aina, 2019). Thus, nowadays RAC equipment have high potential for ozone depletion because the FC gas is directly released into the atmosphere through the leakage (Razzaq, Ahamed, Hossain, & Hossain, 2019).

FC gas is widely used in RAC equipment due to their thermodynamic properties in the refrigeration cycle. The common forms of the FC gas are CFCs, hydrochlorofluorocarbons (HCFCs), and hydrofluorocarbons (HFCs). Due to the high ozone depletion potential (ODP), which contributed nearly 70% of manmade ozone-depleting chemicals in the atmosphere, it has been fully phasing out CFC in 2010 for developing countries (Cardoso, Lamas, Gaspar, & Ribeiro, 2017). The alternatives of CFCs, which have low ODP have been introduced such as HCFC and HFC. Unfortunately, HCFC and HFC are determined to be powerful agents in climate change, often hundreds to thousands of time the power of CO_2 (Duan et al., 2018). For example, HCFC-22 contain 0.055 of ODP and it has relatively high 1,780 global warming potential (GWP). As a consequence, chlorine and fluorine elements exist 12 years in the atmosphere (Kudoma & Tekere, 2021). The phase out of CFCs and HCFCs is under the Montreal Protocol, which is an international agreement to protect the ozone layer by phasing out ozone depleting substance (ODS) development and use by 2030 (Adeoye & Aina, 2019; Reddy, Kumar, & Kumar, 2020). Then, HFC gases are the leading substitutes for CFC and HCFC refrigerants as a result of having zero ODP and have become important in all cooling equipment with highest GWP (Cardoso et al., 2017). The Kigali Amendment to the Montreal Protocol is to phase down globally HFC production along with consumption in 2050. Currently, the alternative of HFC is hydrofluoroolefin (HFO) and natural refrigerant (ammonia, carbon dioxide, and other), which has relatively low GWP (0-6 GWP) (Höglund-Isaksson et al., 2017). Cardoso et al. (2017) state that the alternatives for FC gas must consider five different properties, namely: GWP, system complexity and compatibility, boiling point, efficiency or coefficient of performance (COP), and safety.

Those properties need to be considered especially on the efficiency or COP. This is because electricity consumption of the RAC can increase when the COP decrease. The decrease of COP can be caused by the insufficient amount of FC gas in RAC equipment. Sawalha, Piscopiello, Karampour, Manickam, and Rogstam (2017) reported the leakage of FC gas in supermarket can be in between 3% and 22%. Duan et al. (2018) mention supermarkets undergo variety faults in components and system especially in RAC unit. The fault from the RAC equipment is the main reason for the FC gas leakage and increase in electricity consumption (Rogers, Guo, & Rasmussen, 2019). Thus, it will contribute to large portion of the indirect carbon emission from electricity consumption. The carbon emission is trigger by the burning of fossil fuel (Islam, Srinivasan, Thu, & Saha, 2017). According to Yusof, Muslim, Suhaimi, and Basrawi (2018), 50% of the electricity usage in a building is consumed by the air conditioning (Yusof et al., 2018). While in UK supermarket, 70% of electricity consumption is due to refrigeration equipment (Tassou, Ge, Hadawey, & Marriott, 2011). The environmental impact of the RAC equipment can be doubled up during the leakage of high GWP together with the increase in electricity consumption. This environmental impact occurs due to the improper lifecycle management of a refrigerant.

The lifecycle management of FC gas in Malaysia is starting from the production and consumption of FC gas. This FC gas has been controlled by the import and export licencing or permit from the Royal Malaysian Customs Department. As Malaysia is one of the manufacturer of air conditioning who export the equipment (Latif, Fahmy-Abdullah, & Sieng, 2019) and import the refrigerant from the China, India, Korea, Singapore, and USA (DOE & UNDP, 2017). Royal Malaysia Customs Department has established Customs (Prohibition of Exports) Order 2017 and Customs (Prohibition of Imports) Orders 2017 to control both activities through Approval Permit (AP) system that is managed by the Department of Environment (DOE). The DOE also establishes Environmental Quality (Refrigerant Management) Regulation 2020 and has been enforced in June 2020. This regulation has been covered on the production and manufacturing; maintenance and service; import and export;

recycling and disposal; and alternative of FC gas. Even though Malaysia is currently phasing out HCFC and phasing down HFC, the latest regulation is not including the HFC management, and the regulation is too generic without any specific guidelines for each sector in refrigerant lifecycle management. In a word, lifecycle management of FC gas in Malaysia is still lacking at each phase, especially at the midstream (service and maintenance) and downstream level (recycle, recovery and destruction). Thus, this study is to examine the awareness level of local stakeholders and consumers on refrigerant management. This is because to improve FC gas management in Malaysia, both target population needs to be identified with their level of awareness which is playing an important role to improve the lifecycle management of FC gas in Malaysia.

2. METHODOLOGY

2.1. Questionnaire Design

Two surveys were conducted in this study to measure the level of awareness on the leakage of FC gas and energy saving in RAC sector between local stakeholders and consumers. The questionnaires were developed based on the literature review and in-depth interview with the local stakeholders. In-depth interviews play a significant role in gaining a better understanding on the perspectives, practices, and problems of FC gas management in Malaysia (Agarwal et al., 2021). The interview is with local government and industry sector. From the output of the literature review and in-depth interview, two sets of questionnaires were developed based on the dichotomous question type (yes/no) and not on the Likert scale that is either nominal or ordinal scale (Bhupalam, 2019). The dichotomous question type is utilised when the problem under evaluation is most likely thought of in two alternative values (Tejedor, Cervi, Pérez-Escoda, & Jumbo, 2020). In addition, this type of question will give a direct answer rather than misunderstanding (Capik & Gozum, 2015). Survey content included Section 1 (demographic) and Section 2 (FC gas and effect to the environment; leakage and maintenance of FC gas; and electricity consumption).

2.2. Data Collection

Both surveys used a convenience sampling technique. Convenience sampling is a non-random sampling type where the target population meet certain criteria and are easily accessible to the researcher (Andrade, 2021; Etikan, Musa, & Alkassim, 2016). In this study, the population were conveniently accessible at the two different seminars. First seminar was 'International Seminar on Energy Saving and GHG Emission Reduction by Refrigerant Leakage Prevention Using IoT in Refrigeration and Air Conditioning Sector', population were invited to take part in this study because they are the local stakeholders who involved in FC gas management in Malaysia. The second seminar was 'The role of consumer in Ozone Layer Protection' which are representative sample of the consumers who used refrigeration and/or air conditioning equipment.

2.3. Statistical Analysis

The result from these surveys was descriptively analysed using Statistical Package for the Social Sciences (SPSS). This descriptive analysis included mean, standard deviation, variance, correlation, and percentage. The correlation was conducted only for the consumers in order to identify the relationship existing between the statement and educational background (Akoglu, 2018). The result would be summarised numerically in a clear and understandable way. Besides that, this kind of analysis can simplify large amount of data into a simpler summary. The data from this survey were interpreted in percentage for Sections 1 and 2.

3. RESULT

The population for this study were local stakeholders and consumers. The local stakeholders were the experts who had more than 5 years' experience in FC gas management in Malaysia. The local stakeholders were from different background, mostly from ministries and governance agencies (68%) followed by Industry (12%) and private (11%) sectors. Meanwhile, population categorised under consumers had different educational background and assumed that they consume refrigeration or/and air conditioning equipment. The consumers who involved in this study had educational background in engineering (64%), science (23%), network and security (7%), social science (4%), and library science (2%). The result was interpreted in percentage, and it gave positive feedback (yes) from the population. Table 17.1 shows the summary of the statistical analysis for local stakeholders and consumers.

3.1. FC and Effect on Environment

The statistical analysis of the FC gas and its effect on environment for the local stakeholders shows that 100% of the local stakeholders support the statement 'Each fluorocarbon gas possesses different ODP and global warming potential (GWP) value'. The statements 'fluorocarbon gas emission will cause ozone depletion' and 'GWP value of HFC is higher compared to CFC and HCFC' show 95% and 72% of the respondents are aware about these statements.

Based on the result in Table 17.1, 89% of the consumers were positively responded to the statement 'I have heard about fluorocarbon gas before' and this statement also shows the strong correlation, r of 0.763, between the variables (Fig. 17.1(a)). Meanwhile, the statements of 'all type of Fluorocarbon (FC) gas can contribute the same effect on ozone depletion and global warming, when its leaking to the atmosphere' and 'Malaysia is phasing out hydrochlorofluorocarbon (HCFC) gas and phasing down hydrofluorocarbon (HFC) gas' show the weak correlation, r of 204 and r of 0.363, between the variables. This is because respondents who are aware on both statements are from engineering and science background only, as shown in Fig. 17.1(b) and (c). Besides, only 50% of the consumers were aware on the statement 'Malaysia is phasing out hydrochlorofluorocarbon (HCFC) gas and phasing down hydrofluorocarbon (HFC) gas'.

Table 17.1. Statistical Analysis for Local Stakeholders and Consumers Awareness on FC Gas Management.

Population	Section	Question	Mean	SD	Variance	Percentage
Local Stakeholders	FC and Effect on Environment	Small amount of FC gas emission may not directly cause ozone depletion, but it still contributes to direct release to atmosphere	1.9474	0.2294	0.053	95%
		Each FC gas possesses different ODP and GWP value	2	0	0	100%
		GWP value of HFC is higher compared to CFC and HCFC	1.7895	0.41885	0.175	72%
	Leakage and Maintenance of FC	FC leakage might occur continuously because difficult to detect by naked eye and will increase the maintenance cost	2	0	0	100%
		The FC gas leakage detection equipment can only detect 50–80% of leakage occurrence	1.8235	0.39295	0.154	82%
		Optimum amount of refrigerant recharge is important to increase the efficiency of RAC operation system	1.9474	0.22942	0.053	90%
	Electricity Consumption	The RAC system is the main contributor to the increase in electric consumption	2	0	0	100%
		Increase in electricity consumption may contribute in global warming due to indirect carbon emission	1.8947	0.3153	0.099	90%
Consumers	FC & Effect on Environment	I have heard about FC gas before	1.886	0.32104	0.103	89%
		All types of FC gas can contribute the same effect on ozone depletion and global warming, when its leaking to the atmosphere	1.5	0.50578	0.256	70%
		Malaysia is phasing out HCFC gas and phasing down HFC gas	1.705	0.46152	0.213	50%
	Leakage & Maintenance of FC	Leakage of FC gas can reduce the efficiency of air conditioning or/and refrigeration unit	1.659	0.47949	0.23	66%
		It is important to manage air conditioning or/and refrigeration unit in a good manner	1.75	0.43802	0.192	86%
	Electricity Consumption	Electricity consumption can increase when the efficiency of the air conditioning or/and refrigeration unit reduce	1.773	0.42392	0.18	77%

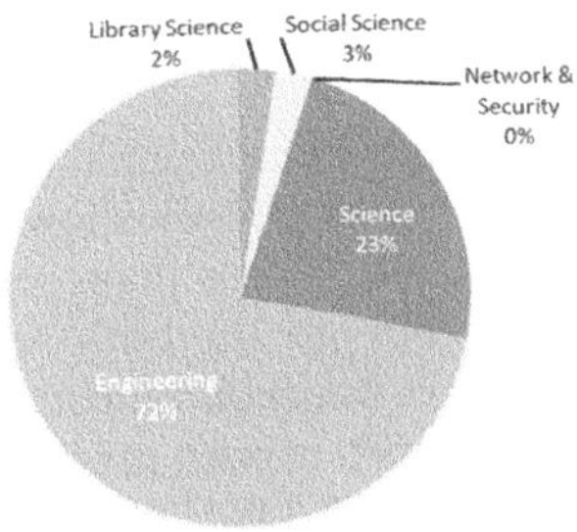

(a)
I have heard about fluorocarbon (FC) gas before

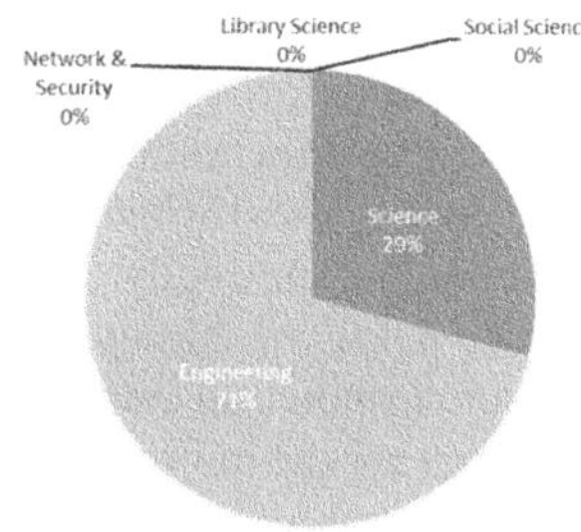

(b)
All type of Fluorocarbon (FC) gas can contribute the same effect on ozone depletion and global warming, when its leaking to the atmosphere

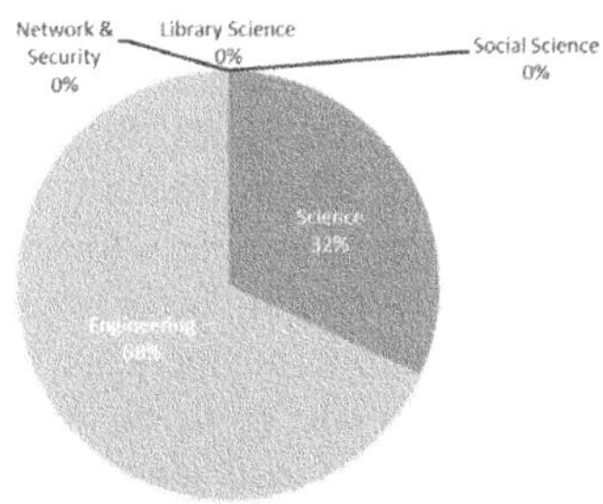

(c)
Malaysia is phasing out HCFC gas and phasing down HFC gas

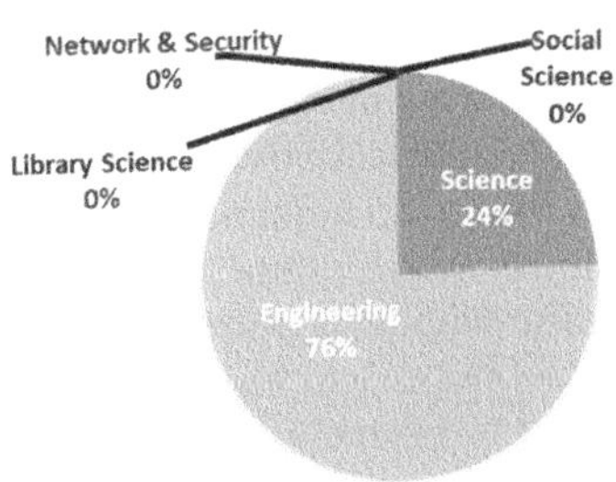

(d)
Leakage of fluorocarbon gas can reduce the efficiency of air conditioning or/and refrigeration unit

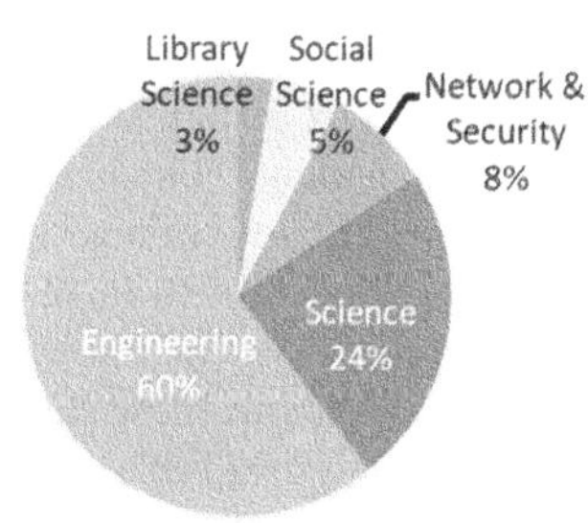

(e)
It is important to manage air conditioning or/and refrigeration unit in a good manner

Fig. 17.1. Percentage of Consumers Based on Education Background: (a) I Have Heard About FC Gas Before; (b) All Types of FC Gas Can Contribute the Same Effect on Ozone Depletion and Global Warming, When It's Leaking to the Atmosphere; (c) Malaysia Is Phasing Out HCFC Gas and Phasing Down HFC Gas; (d) Leakage of FC Gas Can Reduce the efficiency of Air Conditioning or/and Refrigeration Unit; (e) It Is Important to Manage Air Conditioning or/and Refrigeration Unit in a Good Manner.

Thus, consumers who had engineering and science education background showed high level of awareness on this section.

In short, local stakeholders show high level of awareness on the impact of FC gas on the environment when compared with consumers. This result shows that local stakeholders are ready to make a move for a better FC gas management in Malaysia. DOE of Malaysia has raised the awareness to the both sectors about the environmental impact of this FC gas. This is because, industry and private sectors are the majority that been involved in import, export, production, consumption, service, maintenance, and disposal of FC gas. DOE of Malaysia considers both sectors in any decision-making process for the future plan of FC gas in Malaysia, for instance, phasing out HCFC, phasing down HFC and substitution for low-GWP and natural refrigerants. However, the Government of Malaysia needs to put more effort to increase the awareness of the consumers regarding this matter. According to Shafqat and Fong (2020), the government agency and non-profit organisation, who are most involved at the community level, play an important role in communicating to the consumers regarding climate change or other environmental issues (Shafqat & Fong, 2020) in order to rise their awareness on this matter. There are many methods that can be used to raise the level of awareness among the consumers, for example Feygina et al. (2020) mention that local media is a trusted communicator to provide consistent and strong evidence on present climate information. In America, climate communication shows successful engaging with the weathercaster by involving some discussion with expert so that consumers can learn significant facts about the issues (Goldberg, van der Linden, Maibach, & Leiserowitz, 2019; Myers et al., 2020).

3.2. Leakage and Maintenance of FC

Based on the analysis in Table 17.1, it shows that 100% of the local stakeholders support the statement 'Fluorocarbon leakage might occur continuously because it is difficult to detect by naked eye and will increase the maintenance cost'. While the other two statements 'The Fluorocarbon gas leakage detection equipment can only detect 50%–80% of leakage occurrence' and 'Optimum amount of refrigerant recharge is important to increase the efficiency of refrigeration and air conditioning operation system' show positive response with 82% and 90% of the respondents aware about these statements.

The result analysis (Table 17.1) shows that 86% of the consumers were positively responded to the statement 'It is important to manage air conditioning or/and refrigeration unit in a good manner'. This statement shows the moderate correlation, r of 0.618, between the variables (Fig. 17.1(e)). Meanwhile, the statement 'Leakage of fluorocarbon gas can reduce the efficiency of air conditioning or/and refrigeration unit' shows the moderate correlation, r of 403, between the variables. This is because respondents who are aware on these statements are from engineering and science background as shown in Fig. 17.1(d). Hence, consumers who had engineering and science education background showed high level of awareness on this section.

Briefly, the result from this section also shows that the level of awareness of the local stakeholders is higher compared to consumers. This is because majority of the respondents have involved in FC gas management and in handling the FC gas for more than 5 years. Meanwhile for the consumers, it is hard for them to detect the occurrence of FC gas leakage because the gas is odourless and colourless. This situation will increase the emission of FC gas to the environment. In addition, even the small leakage of FC gas is also hard to detect by service and maintenance technician through direct method such as electronic detector, instance fluorescent detector, bubble detector, and so on. Yoo, Hong, and Kim (2017) said that the indirect detection of FC gas leakage is the most effective way that collects all the data, such as pressure and temperature, from the RAC systems. Also, the indirect method can provide real-time monitoring to the service and maintenance technician and facility manager regarding the condition of the equipment. The early response time can be taken to avoid direct release and increase in electricity consumption. Che-Ghani, Myeda, and Ali (2016) also recommend to maintenance administration to shorten the waiting time for the maintenance team to conduct the maintenance (Rogers et al., 2019). The delayed-response problem will cause equipment get worsen, initially minor damage then major damage (Nawi, Baharum, Ibrahim, & Riazi, 2017) to a level where it can cause the refrigeration system operates under optimum condition. Unfortunately, direct method is the common method used in Malaysia, and this method will detect 50–80% after leakage occurrence. During that time, the RAC equipment already shows the malfunctioning system and will raise the maintenance cost (Koronaki et al., 2012; Rogers et al., 2019).

In the governance level, DOE has taken some initiatives in conducting some training workshops for the industry and private sectors especially for service and maintenance. Since 2004, Certification Service Technician Programme (CSTP) has been implemented and has been made mandatory in Environmental Quality (Refrigerant Management) 2020 which requires every service and maintenance technician to be certified for the sake of handling the FC gas. The competent technician will be providing certificate and certified technician card that is issued by DOE. This programme has some value added to (DOE, 2016):

- Ensure the service and maintenance technician is competent in FC gas handling and apply good practice during servicing and the RAC system.
- Promote better job opportunity for the service and maintenance technician.
- Be the identity of the professional technician for RAC and ensuring competitive pay for the service provided.

However, there are still uncertified technicians in the field who are improper in handling FC gas and in conducting good practice during service, maintenance, and disposal. At the same time, there are unavailable data on the emission of FC gas, because the amount of FC gas during recharge, recycle, recovery, and destruction has not been recorded. The Government of Malaysia needs to develop a database in order to record every movement of the FC gas. Thus, it can be said that Malaysia still has poor downstream lifecycle management of FC gas (Hauashdh, Jailani, & Rahman, 2020) especially on the RAC equipment. However, by having high awareness level on the local stakeholders, there is a potential for Malaysia to improve the FC management.

3.3. Electricity Consumption

The analysis result from this section demonstrates that 100% of the local stakeholders support the statement 'The refrigeration and air conditioning system is the main contributor to the increase in electric consumption' (Table 17.1). While the other statement on 'Increase in electricity consumption may contribute in global warming due to indirect carbon emission' also shows positive response with 90% of the respondents aware about this statement. The analysis result from Table 17.1 presents 77% of the consumers were positively responded to the statement 'Electricity consumption can increase when the efficiency of the air conditioning or/and refrigeration unit reduce'.

In short, this section also presents that local stakeholders have high level of awareness on the effect of electricity consumption for the optimum amount of FC gas in refrigeration equipment when compared to consumers. The electricity consumption has been considered as a co-benefit for FC gas management. Mentioning FC gas management with the industry player they will show less interest this is because environmental saving is more visible compare to money value. Hence, it is suggested to pair with monitoring value saving like energy saving in order to attract attention especially from commercial and industry sectors who involved in RAC equipment. The increase in electricity consumption of the RAC equipment is related with the optimum amount of FC gas in the RAC system. Some studies have been reported that the residential air conditioners have operated 17% below their rated efficiency (Rogers et al., 2019). Thus, the amount of FC gas needs to be maintained in order to achieve COP of RAC equipment and reduce the indirect impact of increase in electricity consumption. Cascini, Gamberi, Mora, Rosano, and Bortolini (2016) said high energy consumption together with the FC gas leakage will double up the contribution to global warming due to the burning of fossil fuel.

4. CONCLUSION

Lifecycle FC gas management in Malaysia is still lacking in many aspects especially on leakage gas at RAC equipment. Thus, this study was conducted to examine the awareness level of local stakeholders and consumers on FC gas management. The findings from this study reveal that local stakeholders show high level of awareness on FC gas management when compared with consumers. Besides, among the consumers who have educational background on engineering and science show better awareness when compared with others who have background on network and security, social science and library science. Hence, there is a need to conduct a capacity building for the consumers and service maintenance especially in order to reduce the direct and indirect impact of the FC gas emission. This is because FC gas management in Malaysia is still lacking at middle stream and downstream lifecycle management which mostly involved consumers and service maintenance technician. The leakage of FC gas mostly occurs due to the faults from the refrigeration system (Rogers et al., 2019).

ACKNOWLEDGEMENTS

I would like to express my sincere appreciation to Dr Shazwin Mat Taib for encouragement, guidance, and critics. In addition, this work was financially supported by the Universiti Teknologi Malaysia under the Industry-International Incentive Grant Scheme (IIIG), (UTM Vote: Q.J130000.3051.01M43) from Universiti Teknologi Malaysia.

REFERENCES

Adeoye, O., & Aina, S. (2019). An appraisal of ozone layer depletion and its implication on the human environment. *JL Pol'y & Globalization, 83*, 6.

Agarwal, A., Ranjan, P., Rohilla, P., Saikaustubh, Y., Sahu, A., Dwivedi, S. N., … Kumar, A. (2021). Development and validation of a questionnaire to assess preventive practices against COVID-19 pandemic in the general population. *Preventive Medicine Reports, 22*, 101339. doi:10.1016/j.pmedr.2021.101339

Akoglu, H. (2018). User's guide to correlation coefficients. *Turkish Journal of Emergency Medicine, 18*(3), 91–93. doi:10.1016/j.tjem.2018.08.001

Andrade, C. (2021). The inconvenient truth about convenience and purposive samples. *Indian Journal of Psychological Medicine, 43*(1), 86–88. doi:10.1177/0253717620977000

Bhupalam, P. (2019). Yes or no 2.0: Are Likert scales always preferable to dichotomous rating scales? *International Journal of Pharmaceutical Investigation, 9*(3), 146.

Capik, C., & Gozum, S. (2015). Psychometric features of an assessment instrument with Likert and dichotomous response formats. *Public Health Nursing, 32*(1), 81–86. doi:10.1111/phn.12156

Cardoso, B. J., Lamas, F. B., Gaspar, A. R., & Ribeiro, J. B. (2017). Refrigerants used in the Portuguese food industry: Current status. *International Journal of Refrigeration, 83*, 60–74. doi:10.1016/j.ijrefrig.2017.07.013

Cascini, A., Gamberi, M., Mora, C., Rosano, M., & Bortolini, M. (2016). Comparative carbon footprint assessment of commercial walk-in refrigeration systems under different use configurations. *Journal of Cleaner Production, 112*, 3998–4011. doi:10.1016/j.jclepro.2015.08.075

Che-Ghani, N. Z., Myeda, N. E., & Ali, A. S. (2016). Operations and maintenance cost for stratified buildings: A critical review. *MATEC Web Conference, 66*, 00041. doi:10.1051/matecconf/20166600041

Chipperfield, M. P., Bekki, S., Dhomse, S., Harris, N. R. P., Hassler, B., Hossaini, R., … Weber, M. (2017). Detecting recovery of the stratospheric ozone layer. *Nature, 549*(7671), 211–218. doi:10.1038/nature23681

DOE. (2016). *Ozone bulletin 2016*. Putrajaya: A. D. Ozone Protection Section, Department of Environment.

DOE, & UNDP. (2017). *Malaysia HCFC phase-out management plan (HPMP Stage-2) (2017–2022)*. Putrajaya: DOE.

Duan, H., Miller, T. R., Liu, G., Zeng, X., Yu, K., Huang, Q., … Li, J. (2018). Chilling prospect: Climate change effects of mismanaged refrigerants in *China*. *Environmental Science & Technology, 52*(11), 6350–6356.

Etikan, I., Musa, S. A., & Alkassim, R. S. (2016). Comparison of convenience sampling and purposive sampling. *American Journal of Theoretical and Applied Statistics*, *5*(1), 1–4.

Feygina, I., Myers, T., Placky, B., Sublette, S., Souza, T., Toohey-Morales, J., & Maibach, E. (2020). Localized climate reporting by TV weathercasters enhances public understanding of climate change as a local problem: Evidence from a randomized controlled experiment. *Bulletin of the American Meteorological Society*, *101*(7), E1092–E1100.

Goldberg, M. H., van der Linden, S., Maibach, E., & Leiserowitz, A. (2019). Discussing global warming leads to greater acceptance of climate science. *Proceedings of the National Academy of Sciences*, *116*(30), 14804. doi:10.1073/pnas.1906589116

Hausahdh, A., Jailani, J., & Rahman, I. A. (2020). Building maintenance practices in Malaysia: a systematic review of issues, effects and the way forward. *International Journal of Building Pathology and Adaptation*, 38(5), 653–672.

Höglund-Isaksson, L., Purohit, P., Amann, M., Bertok, I., Rafaj, P., Schöpp, W., & Borken-Kleefeld, J. (2017). Cost estimates of the Kigali Amendment to phase-down hydrofluorocarbons. *Environmental Science & Policy*, *75*, 138–147. doi:10.1016/j.envsci.2017.05.006

Hossaini, R., Chipperfield, M. P., Montzka, S. A., Leeson, A. A., Dhomse, S. S., & Pyle, J. A. (2017). The increasing threat to stratospheric ozone from dichloromethane. *Nature Communications*, *8*(1), 15962. doi:10.1038/ncomms15962

Islam, M. A., Srinivasan, K., Thu, K., & Saha, B. B. (2017). Assessment of total equivalent warming impact (TEWI) of supermarket refrigeration systems. *International Journal of Hydrogen Energy*, *42*(43), 26973–26983. doi:10.1016/j.ijhydene.2017.07.035

Koronaki, I. P., Cowan, D., Maidment, G., Beerman, K., Schreurs, M., Kaar, K., … Cazauran, X. (2012). Refrigerant emissions and leakage prevention across Europe – Results from the RealSkillsEurope project. *Energy*, *45*(1), 71–80. doi:10.1016/j.energy.2012.05.040

Kudoma, B., & Tekere, M.(2021). Exploration of the environmental and socioeconomic implications of HCFC-22 phase-out for Botswana. *Advances in Climate Change Research, 12*(1), 108–118.

Latif, M. S. A., Fahmy-Abdullah, M., & Sieng, L. W. (2019). Determinants factor of technical efficiency in machinery manufacturing industry in Malaysia. *International Journal of Supply Chain Management*, *8*, 917–928.

Myers, T. A., Maibach, E. W., Placky, B. W., Henry, K. L., Slater, M. D., & Seitter, K. L. (2020). Impact of the climate matters program on public understanding of climate change. *Weather, Climate, and Society*, *12*(4), 863–876.

Nawi, M. N. M., Baharum, F., Ibrahim, S. H., & Riazi, S. R. M. (2017). A review study of maintenance and management issues in Malaysian commercial building towards sustainable future practice. Paper presented at the AIP Conference Proceedings.

Randazzo, T., De Cian, E., & Mistry, M. N. (2020). Air conditioning and electricity expenditure: The role of climate in temperate countries. *Economic Modelling*, *90*, 273–287. doi:10.1016/j.econmod.2020.05.001

Razzaq, M. E., Ahamed, J., Hossain, M., & Hossain, S. (2019). A review on hydrocarbon (HCs) as an alternative refrigerant: based on thermodynamic and environmental approach. *Mechanical Engineering Research Journal, 11*, 86–96.

Reddy, P. S., Kumar, P. R., & Kumar, M. R. (2020). Performance of air conditioner system by using various refrigerants. *International Journal of Applied Engineering Research*, *15*(2), 118–126.

Rogers, A. P., Guo, F., & Rasmussen, B. P. (2019). A review of fault detection and diagnosis methods for residential air conditioning systems. *Building and Environment*, *161*, 106236. doi:10.1016/j.buildenv.2019.106236

Sawalha, S., Piscopiello, S., Karampour, M., Manickam, L., & Rogstam, J. (2017). Field measurements of supermarket refrigeration systems. Part II: Analysis of HFC refrigeration systems and comparison to CO_2 trans-critical. *Applied Thermal Engineering*, *111*, 170–182. doi: 10.1016/j.applthermaleng.2016.09.073

Shafqat, B. Z., & Fong, Y. L. (2020). Climate change communication and the use of Facebook by non-governmental organisations: A case study in Malaysia. *Journal of Sustainability Science and Management*, *15*(7), 147–163.

Tassou, S. A., Ge, Y., Hadawey, A., & Marriott, D. (2011). Energy consumption and conservation in food retailing. *Applied Thermal Engineering*, *31*(2), 147–156. doi:10.1016/j.applthermaleng.2010.08.023

Tejedor, S., Cervi, L., Pérez-Escoda, A., & Jumbo, F. T. (2020). Digital literacy and higher education during COVID-19 lockdown: Spain, Italy, and Ecuador. *Publications*, *8*(4), 48. Retrieved from https://www.mdpi.com/2304-6775/8/4/48

Yoo, J. W., Hong, S. B., & Kim, M. S. (2017). Refrigerant leakage detection in an EEV installed residential air conditioner with limited sensor installations. *International Journal of Refrigeration*, *78*, 157–165. doi:10.1016/j.ijrefrig.2017.03.001

Yusof, M. H., Muslim, S. M., Suhaimi, M. F., & Basrawi, M. F. (2018). The effect of outdoor temperature on the performance of a split-unit type air conditioner using R22 refrigerant. Paper presented at the MATEC Web of Conferences.

CHAPTER 18

PUBLIC OPINION ANALYSIS FOR MANAGEMENT OF URBAN INFRASTRUCTURE SYSTEMS: SOCIAL MEDIA DATA MINING APPROACH

Nguyen Thanh Viet, Denver Banlasan and Do Tien Sy

ABSTRACT

Adequate, reliable, and efficient urban infrastructure systems (UIS) are fundamental to sustainable development, social mobility, and economic vitality. As communities continuously rely on basic infrastructure services to support their daily communal functions, major components of UIS are subject to heavy use, and thus rapidly deteriorate over time; hence, it is critical that efficient infrastructure management strategies practices are in place. As current strategies remain confronted with various limitations including adaptability to changing conditions, lack of public engagement, and cost-effectiveness, this study explores social media data mining as an approach to revitalise and support current urban infrastructure monitoring strategies by extracting valuable insights from public opinion. Twitter messages or 'Tweets' pertaining to public infrastructure in The Philippines were collected and analysed to identify recurring issues in public infrastructure, emerging topics in public discussions, and the overall perception of the public on infrastructure services. This study presents a topic model that extracts dominant topics from aggregated social media data and a sentiment analysis

Sustainability Management Strategies and Impact in Developing Countries
Community, Environment and Disaster Risk Management, Volume 26, 233–242

Published under exclusive licence by Emerald Publishing Limited
ISSN: 2040-7262/doi:10.1108/S2040-726220220000026018

model that determines public opinion sentiment in relation to different urban infrastructure components. The findings of this study highlight the potential of social media data mining to surpass the limits of conventional data collection techniques and the importance of public opinion as a key driver for a more user-involved decision-making in infrastructure management and as an important social aspect that can be utilised to support planning and response strategies in routine maintenance, preservation, and improvement of UIS.

Keywords: Data mining; infrastructure management; public opinion; urban infrastructure; social media; text mining

1. INTRODUCTION

Adequate, reliable, and efficient urban infrastructure systems (UIS) are fundamental to sustainable development, social mobility, and economic vitality (Sánchez-Silva, Frangopol, Padgett, & Soliman, 2016; P. Wang & Shi, 2018). Due to sustained use and continuous increase in demand, major components of UIS such as roads, light rails, and water supply networks are subject to heavy use throughout their operable life. As a result, the system deteriorates rapidly over time (Flintsch & Chen, 2004; Frangopol & Kim, 2011; Sánchez-Silva et al., 2016; Sánchez-Silva & Klutke, 2016). Under these anticipated situations, it is crucial that efficient infrastructure management strategies are in place to ensure that UIS components are maintained in excellent condition.

Management of UIS involves multi-faceted and complex decision-making processes throughout the life cycle of the project (Guillaumot, Durango-Cohen, & Madanat, 2003). Performance monitoring and evaluations are some of the core processes involved in this aspect (L. Chen, Henning, Raith, & Shamseldin, 2015; Mild & Salo, 2009), in which public engagement plays a pivotal role (Jiang, Lin, & Qiang, 2016; Seto & Sekimoto, 2019; Valentin, Naderpajouh, & Abraham, 2018). These activities are executed in many different forms: surveys, interviews, and visual inspections are commonly implemented by responsible authorities to assess the current condition of a UIS component and implement any maintenance and improvement strategies that it may require (Harris et al., 2017; Mishalani & Gong, 2009; Torres-Machi et al., 2018). These data collection techniques, however, remain confronted with various limitations. Preplanned inspections, for instance, are centralised within the functions of responsible authorities (Harris et al., 2017) and ignore public participation in assessing the performance of UIS. On the other hand, surveys and interviews, while affording public engagement to a certain extent, are inadequate in properly representing the population of interest and in eliminating biases (Martín, Cutter, & Li, 2020; Tang, Shen, Skitmore, & Wang, 2015; Tang, Zhang, Dai, Yoon, Song, & Sharma, 2017; Y. Zhang, Li, & Li, 2019). In addition, these methods are burdened with exhaustive labour and sizable use of resources, especially considering the scale of operations required for infrastructure management.

These identifiable flaws of current data collection techniques bring attention to the need to improve current urban infrastructure monitoring strategies; hence, this study explores the utility of social media data mining as a novel approach that is proactive, cost-effective, and provides an improved avenue for public engagement. Primarily, this study aims to extract meaningful information from user-generated social media data and derive actionable knowledge for the benefit of improving UIS.

2. LITERATURE REVIEW

In the aspect of infrastructure management, public opinion is regarded to be of significant importance (Jiang et al., 2016; Seto & Sekimoto, 2019; Valentin et al., 2018). This is particularly emphasised when dealing with UIS performance indicators that are qualitative and cannot be measured numerically (Khatri, Vairavamoorthy, & Akinyemi, 2012). On a similar perspective, public satisfaction is viewed to have a strong direct correlation with efficiency and quality of urban infrastructure services (Van Ryzin, Immerwahr, & Altman, 2008; P. Wang & Shi, 2018), which makes analysing public opinion an explorable channel for public agencies to improve infrastructure services and achieve desired levels of efficiency for UIS. Studies further substantiate that the general public is increasingly becoming an expedient source of valuable information needed for infrastructure development, and engaging them often leads to novel solutions that would otherwise not surface in an exclusive and centralised decision-making environment (Lakhani & Panetta, 2016; Nik-Bakht & El-diraby, 2016, 2020; von Hippel, 2005). Despite its recognised importance in UIS management, integrating public opinion in urban infrastructure management remains challenging, primarily due to shortfalls of data collection methods that are employed by public authorities. To bridge these inadequacies, contemporary research points to social media platforms as an emerging social environment that has been consistently gaining attention as an untapped repository of valuable data that has the potential to surpass the limits of conventional methods of public engagement.

The process in which raw data in social media is collected, analysed, and interpreted as actionable information is referred to as social media data mining (Zafarani, Abbasi, & Liu, 2014). Through this process, social media platforms act as databases from which data are extracted then processed using various statistical algorithms with the primary objective of uncovering latent information (Barbier & Liu, 2011; Zafarani et al., 2014). Its utility has evidently transcended multiple disciplines and subjects (Martín et al., 2020). Particularly, in the architecture, engineering, and construction industry, its prominence continues to evolve (Azhar, Riaz, & Robinson, 2019). Previously, social media data mining has been utilised to investigate the interdependence of human mobility and urban infrastructure (Q. Wang & Taylor, 2016); analyse public opinion pertaining to different construction projects and construction-related discussions and events (Jiang et al., 2016; Nik-Bakht & El-Diraby, 2020; Tang, Zhang, Dai, Yoon, & Song, 2018; D. Zhang et al., 2018; Y. Zhang et al., 2019); detect litigation risks in construction projects (Diao, Liang, Sharma, & Cui, 2020); and assess post-disaster impacts and damages (Y. Chen, Wang, & Ji, 2020; Yuan & Liu, 2020).

One promising aspect of social media is that it allows for massive generation of free-form and dynamic data which can be utilised for a wide range of purposes (Barbier & Liu, 2011; Han, Cook, & Baldwin, 2014). This abundance is perceived as an opportunity to uncover insights that have never been explored before, overcome the limits imposed on traditional data sources, and pave the way for finding solutions in a swift and cost-effective manner (Klašnja, Barberá, Beauchamp, Nagler, & Tucker, 2015; Tang et al., 2017).

Social media, irrefutably, presents a new breadth of possibilities unlike any other means. Despite its following however, the potential of social media as vault of valuable knowledge that can be utilised for management of urban infrastructures systems remains uncharted. This present study, thus, aims to bridge this gap by uncovering underlying insights in user-generated social media data as a response to the persistent challenges in management of UIS.

3. METHODOLOGY

3.1. Data Collection

The social media platform utilised for this research is Twitter primarily because of its unique features as a combined social and information network (W. J. Wang, Haase, & Yang, 2020), availability of data, and ease of data acquisition (Klašnja et al., 2015).

This study entailed collecting Twitter messages or 'Tweets' pertaining to urban infrastructure components in The Philippines. The UIS components of interest in the study were: roads, highways, and bridges; transportation; water supply, sewerage, and sanitation; and urban space. The responsible authorities considered for the study were: Department of Public Works and Highways, South Luzon Tollway Corporation, and North Luzon Tollway Corporation for Roads, Highways, and Bridges; Department of Transportation, Light Rail Manila Corporation, Metro Rail Transit Corporation, Light Rail Transit Authority, and Philippine National Railways for Transportation; Metropolitan Waterworks and Sewerage System, Maynilad Water Services, Manila Water Company for Water Supply, Sewerage, and Sanitation; and Metropolitan Manila Development Authority for Urban Space.

All Tweets mentioning the accounts of the authorities were collected by means of 'web crawling' (Klašnja et al., 2015); a python script was written to automate collection of Tweets from Twitter's webpage. After removal of duplicates and unrelated messages, a total of 70,131 Tweets were prepared for analysis.

3.2. Data Preprocessing

In its raw form, data collected from social media are characterised to be 'noisy', or containing unnecessary elements that have minimal to no research value (Azhar et al., 2019; Barbier & Liu, 2011; Q. Wang & Taylor, 2016; D. Zhang et al., 2018). This sequence of activities includes removal of embedded links, special characters, addresses, and irrelevant words (stop words) among many other things (Jiang et al., 2016; Tang et al., 2017; D. Zhang et al., 2018).

3.3. Data Analysis

To analyse unstructured text data, this study employed text mining or the process of extracting information from qualitative data (Marzouk & Enaba, 2019; F. Zhang, Fleyeh, Wang, & Lu, 2019). Text mining utilises natural language processing – a sub-discipline of artificial intelligence and computational linguistics that allows computers to comprehend human languages (Song, Kim, & Lee, 2018; F. Zhang et al., 2019). In line with the objectives of this research, topic modelling and sentiment analysis were the principal text-mining techniques performed.

3.4. Topic Modelling – Latent Dirichlet Allocation

Latent Dirichlet Allocation (LDA) is a three-level hierarchical Bayesian model that has gained vast attention in research. Topic models assume that a set of keywords represents a certain topic, and a set of topics, in turn, represent the entire document (Blei, Ng, & Jordan, 2003; Tang et al., 2017; Y. Zhang et al., 2019). Topic models allow extraction of dominant topics from a huge set of text documents. In the context of this research, a topic model was built to identify the common and recurring issues in UIS.

3.5. Sentiment Analysis

Sentiment analysis is a robust tool that aids in understanding the sentiment or emotion of textual data (Tang et al., 2017). In this study, the deep learning-based Natural Language Toolkit (NLTK) (Bird, Loper, & Klein, 2009) was used to perform sentiment analysis that will classify Tweets as either, positive, neutral, or negative. In this study, it is assumed that the underlying emotion of messages sent over by the public is representative of their individual perception on different UIS components and their attached services.

4. RESULTS AND DISCUSSIONS

4.1. Topic Modelling – LDA

A topic model was built to extract dominant topics for UIS component 'Water Supply, Sewerage, and Sanitation'. Upon optimising the parameters of the model, 4 dominant topics, including the 10 most frequent terms per topic were obtained. By principle of topic modelling, the 10 representative terms for each topic were grouped based on similarities in word patterns, relevance, and frequency. Appropriate topic labels that collectively describe the obtained keywords were then assigned by the researchers based on the context of the study and domain knowledge. Table 18.1 summarises the output of the topic model for water supply, sewerage, and sanitation along with the number of Twitter messages constituting each topic.

Table 18.1. Topic Model Output for UIS Component Water Supply, Sewerage, and Sanitation.

Topic Number	Tweet Count	Assigned Topic Label	Keywords
Topic 1	3,416	Billing and Payment Concerns	Bill, supply, account, customers, metro, interruptions, service, concern, billing, payment
Topic 2	3,014	Service Interruptions	Interruption, city, service, advisory, *brgy*, supply, update, scheduled, pressure, schedule
Topic 3	2,612	Maintenance and Repair Works	Leak, notice, new, fix, help, pipe, need, metre, work, number
Topic 4	2,565	Demands for Service Improvement	*mwss*, bills, *duterte*, problem, project, action, ask, government, issue, response

It is apparent that messages from the public pertaining to billing and payment concerns dominated the discussions on water supply services. The relatively high Tweet counts concerning service interruptions, repair works, and persistent calls for more reliable services also imply that these are major issues among the public. Mention of key phrases and words specific to the local context such as *brgy* (ward), *mwss* (Metropolitan Waterworks and Sewerage System – government authority regulating water supply services), and *duterte* (president of the Republic of The Philippines) were also evident, hinting at the relation of these words to issues such as localised water supply concerns and calls to government authorities to take action for service improvement.

From these results, many important insights can be drawn and utilised for improvement of UIS management practices. For instance, the predominance of messages pertaining to billing and payments points to the public's perceived inadequacy of current billing and payment systems by the water supply service providers, substantiating a need for improvement on this particular aspect. Meanwhile, the prevalence of messages concerning service interruptions may be indicative of the providers' failure to provide timely advisories and mitigating solutions for water supply interruptions, compromising the daily societal functions of the users.

Identifying recurring issues and gauging public's concerns on UIS components provides insight on critical areas for improvement that can be taken as more proactive in contrast to periodic monitoring of infrastructure components as it takes into account the interest of end users as direct stakeholders of UIS. The velocity and volume in which social media data are received also make it possible to understand the frequency and intensity of concerns which are both important dimensions that may not be acquired through conventional data collection techniques.

4.2. Sentiment Analysis

In line with the objective of determining the overall perception of the public on different UIS components and their attached services, the underlying sentiment

Table 18.2. Public Opinion Sentiment Distribution for all UIS Components.

	Public Opinion Sentiment		
UIS Component	**Positive**	**Neutral**	**Negative**
Roads, Highways, and Bridges	39%	37%	24%
Transportation	46%	29%	25%
Water Supply, Sewerage, and Sanitation	41%	22%	38%
Urban Space	39%	29%	32%

of collected messages were analysed using the built sentiment analysis model. Table 18.2 presents in detail the distribution of sentiments across all four UIS components.

The presence of considerable proportion of negative messages for all four UIS components was notable. Particularly for water supply services and urban space, the share of negative public opinion appears to be relatively higher, which may be reflective of how satisfactorily these UIS components serve the interest of the public. As the underlying sentiment prevailing in public opinion may be suggestive of the performance of UIS, it may be possible to translate and interpret such results quantitatively. For example, a specific set of public satisfaction benchmarks can be laid out by the government authorities which can be used to assess the performance of infrastructure components, in which measure of public opinion sentiment can be translated as rewards or penalties to service providers as a form of regulation. Similarly, the dynamic nature of public opinion sentiment can be leveraged to analyse the changing perspective of the using public in response to the changes on the performance and reliability of different UIS components.

From the perspective of infrastructure management, many insights can be gained from understanding how the public perceives the quality and reliability of infrastructure components and services. Specifically, since public satisfaction has been shown to have a strong correlation with the quality of urban infrastructure (Van Ryzin et al., 2008; P. Wang & Shi, 2018), understanding public sentiment plays a vital role in achieving the desired levels of performance of UIS.

5. CONCLUSIONS

This research explored the possibility of extracting valuable insights pertaining to UIS from user-generated social media data through various text-mining techniques. The topic model was able to extract dominant topics from unstructured collection of qualitative data which proved beneficial for understanding the present and emerging concerns of the public regarding UIS. Finally, with the goal of comprehending how the using public perceives the quality and reliability of UIS components and their attached services, sentiment analysis was performed as an evaluation measure of the overall public perception which can be used as a determining factor of the level of satisfaction of the users on the level of performance of UIS components.

In view of inherent limitations of current management strategies in UIS, particularly in performance monitoring and evaluation, this study sought a more proactive, user-involved, and cost-effective approach that can help support planning and response strategies in routine maintenance, preservation, and improvement of urban infrastructure components. This study also highlights public opinion as both an important social aspect and a potential key driver for a more user-involved decision-making in infrastructure management.

ACKNOWLEDGEMENTS

This research was funded by Japan International Cooperation Agency Project for ASEAN University Network/Southeast Asia Engineering Education Development Network (JICA Project for AUN/SEED-Net) in the framework of Collaborative Education Program (CEP) under Program Contract No. HCMUT CEP 2101.

REFERENCES

Azhar, S., Riaz, Z., & Robinson, D. (2019). Integration of social media in day-to-day operations of construction firms. *Journal of Management in Engineering*, *35*(1), 1–7. doi:10.1061/(ASCE)ME.1943-5479.0000660

Barbier, G., & Liu, H. (2011). Social network data analytics. *Social Network Data Analytics*, 1, 327–352. doi:10.1007/978-1-4419-8462-3

Bird, S., Loper, E., & Klein, E. (2009). *Natural language toolkit (NLTK) book*. O'Reilly Media Inc. O'Reilly Media. Retrieved from http://www.nltk.org/book/ch00.html

Blei, D., Ng, A., & Jordan, M. (2003). Latent Dirichlet allocation. In J. Lafferty (Ed.), *Journal of machine learning research* (Vol. *3*, pp. 993–1022). Elsevier. Retrieved from https://linkinghub.elsevier.com/retrieve/pii/B9780124115194000069

Chen, L., Henning, T. F. P., Raith, A., & Shamseldin, A. Y. (2015). Multiobjective optimization for maintenance decision making in infrastructure asset management. *Journal of Management in Engineering*, *31*(6), 1–9. doi:10.1061/(ASCE)ME.1943-5479.0000371

Chen, Y., Wang, Q., & Ji, W. (2020). Rapid assessment of disaster impacts on highways using social media. *Journal of Management in Engineering*, *36*(5), 1–11. doi:10.1061/(ASCE)ME.1943-5479.0000836

Diao, C., Liang, R., Sharma, D., & Cui, Q. (2020). Litigation risk detection using Twitter data. *Journal of Legal Affairs and Dispute Resolution in Engineering and Construction*, *12*(1), 1–9. doi:10.1061/(ASCE)LA.1943-4170.0000356

Flintsch, G. W., & Chen, C. (2004). Soft computing applications in infrastructure management. *Journal of Infrastructure Systems*, *10*(4), 157–166. doi:10.1061/(ASCE)1076-0342(2004)10:4(157)

Frangopol, D. M., & Kim, S. (2011). Service life, reliability and maintenance of civil structures. *Service Life Estimation and Extension of Civil Engineering Structures*, 145–178. doi:10.1533/9780857090928.2.145 Retrieved from https://www.sciencedirect.com/science/article/pii/B9781845693985500110

Guillaumot, V. M., Durango-Cohen, P. L., & Madanat, S. M. (2003). Adaptive optimization of infrastructure maintenance and inspection decisions under performance model uncertainty. *Journal of Infrastructure Systems*, *9*(4), 133–139. doi:10.1061/(ASCE)1076-0342(2003)9:4(133)

Han, B., Cook, P., & Baldwin, T. (2014). Text-based Twitter user geolocation prediction. *Journal of Artificial Intelligence Research*, *49*, 451–500. doi:10.1613/jair.4200

Harris, D. K., Alipour, M., Acton, S. T., Messeri, L. R., Vaccari, A., & Barnes, L. E. (2017). The citizen engineer: Urban infrastructure monitoring via crowd-sourced data analytics. In J. G. Soules (Ed.), *Structures congress 2017* (pp. 495–510). American Society of Civil Engineers. Reston, VA: Conference location is Denver, CO.

Jiang, H., Lin, P., & Qiang, M. (2016). Public-opinion sentiment analysis for large hydro projects. *Journal of Construction Engineering and Management*, *142*(2), 1–12. doi:10.1061/(ASCE)CO.1943-7862.0001039

Khatri, K. B., Vairavamoorthy, K., & Akinyemi, E. (2012). Framework for computing a performance index for urban infrastructure systems using a fuzzy set approach. *Journal of Infrastructure Systems*, *17*(4), 163–175. doi:10.1061/(ASCE)IS.1943-555X.0000062

Klašnja, M., Barberá, P., Beauchamp, N., Nagler, J., & Tucker, J. A. (2015). Measuring public opinion with social media data. In L. R. Atkeson & R. M. Alvarez (Eds.). *The Oxford handbook of polling and polling methods (Issue April 2018)*. doi:10.1093/oxfordhb/9780190213299.013.3

Lakhani, K., & Panetta, J. (2016). The principles of distributed innovation. *Successful OSS project design and implementation: Requirements, tools, social designs and reward* (pp. 7–26).Taylor and Francis. https://doi.org/10.1162/itgg.2007.2.3.97

Martín, Y., Cutter, S. L., & Li, Z. (2020). Bridging Twitter and survey data for evacuation assessment of Hurricane Matthew and Hurricane Irma. *Natural Hazards Review*, *21*(2), 1–14. doi:10.1061/(ASCE)NH.1527-6996.0000354

Marzouk, M., & Enaba, M. (2019). Text analytics to analyze and monitor construction project contract and correspondence. *Automation in Construction*, *98*(December 2017), 265–274. doi:10.1016/j.autcon.2018.11.018

Mild, P., & Salo, A. (2009). Combining a multiattribute value function with an optimization model: An application to dynamic resource allocation for infrastructure maintenance. *Decision Analysis*, *6*(3), 139–152. doi:10.1287/deca.1090.0143

Mishalani, R. G., & Gong, L. (2009). Optimal sampling of infrastructure condition: Motivation, formulation, and evaluation. *Journal of Infrastructure Systems*, *15*(4), 313–320. doi:10.1061/(ASCE)1076-0342(2009)15:4(313)

Nik-Bakht, M., & El-diraby, T. E. (2016). Communities of interest-interest of communities: Social and semantic analysis of communities in infrastructure discussion networks. *Computer-Aided Civil and Infrastructure Engineering*, *31*(1), 34–49. doi:10.1111/mice.12152

Nik-Bakht, M., & El-diraby, T. E. (2020). Beyond chatter: Profiling community discussion networks in urban infrastructure projects. *Journal of Infrastructure Systems*, *26*(3), 1–15. doi:10.1061/(ASCE)IS.1943-555X.0000555

Sánchez-Silva, M., Frangopol, D. M., Padgett, J., & Soliman, M. (2016). Maintenance and operation of infrastructure systems: Review. *Journal of Structural Engineering (United States)*, *142*(9), 1–16. doi:10.1061/(ASCE)ST.1943-541X.0001543

Sánchez-Silva, M., & Klutke, G.-A. (2016). *Reliability and life-cycle analysis of deteriorating systems*. Springer. doi:10.1080/13854049708407039

Seto, T., & Sekimoto, Y. (2019). Trends in citizen-generated and collaborative urban infrastructure feedback data: Toward citizen-oriented infrastructure management in Japan. *ISPRS International Journal of Geo-Information*, *8*(3). doi:10.3390/ijgi8030115

Song, J., Kim, J., & Lee, J.-K. (2018). NLP and deep learning-based analysis of building regulations to support automated rule checking system. – The International Association for Automation and Robotics in Construction. *IAARC*. Retrieved from https://www.iaarc.org/publications/2018_proceedings_of_the_35th_isarc/nlp_and_deep_learning_based_analysis_of_building_regulations_to_support_automated_rule_checking_system.html

Tang, L., Shen, G. Q., Skitmore, M., & Wang, H. (2015). Procurement-related critical factors for briefing in public-private partnership projects: Case of Hong Kong. *Journal of Management in Engineering*, *31*(6). doi:10.1061/(ASCE)ME.1943-5479.0000352

Tang, L., Zhang, Y., Dai, F., Yoon, Y., & Song, Y. (2018). What construction topics do they discuss in social media? A case study of Weibo in China. In C. Wang, C. Harper, Y. Lee, R. Harris, & C. Berryman (Eds.), *Construction research congress 2018: Construction information technology* (pp. 612–621). American Society of Civil Engineers. Reston, VA: Conference location is New Orleans, LA.

Tang, L., Zhang, Y., Dai, F., Yoon, Y., Song, Y., & Sharma, R. S. (2017). Social media data analytics for the U.S. construction industry: Preliminary study on Twitter. *Journal of Management in Engineering*, *33*(6), 1–15. doi:10.1061/(ASCE)ME.1943-5479.0000554

Torres-Machi, C., Osorio-Lird, A., Chamorro, A., Videla, C., Tighe, S. L., & Mourgues, C. (2018). Impact of environmental assessment and budgetary restrictions in pavement maintenance decisions: Application to an urban network. *Transportation Research Part D: Transport and Environment*, *59*, 192–204. doi:10.1016/j.trd.2017.12.017

Valentin, V., Naderpajouh, N., & Abraham, D. (2018). Impact of characteristics of infrastructure projects on public opinion. *Journal of Management in Engineering*, *34*(1), 1–11. doi:10.1061/(ASCE)ME.1943-5479.0000576

Van Ryzin, G. G., Immerwahr, S., & Altman, S. (2008). Measuring street cleanliness: A comparison of New York city's scorecard and results from a citizen survey. *Public Administration Review*, *68*(2), 295–303. doi:10.1111/j.1540-6210.2007.00863.x

von Hippel, E. (2005). *Democratizing innovation* (pp. 1–220). Cambridge, MA: The MIT Press.

Wang, P., & Shi, S. (2018). *Empirical analysis on how urban infrastructure influence residents' satisfaction. Wang 2008*, Charleston, SC, 82–88. Reston, VA: American Society of Civil Engineers.

Wang, Q., & Taylor, J. E. (2016). Process map for urban-human mobility and civil infrastructure data collection using geosocial networking platforms. *Journal of Computing in Civil Engineering*, *30*(2), 1–11. doi:10.1061/(ASCE)CP.1943-5487

Wang, W. J., Haase, T. W., & Yang, C. H. (2020). Warning message elements and retweet counts: An analysis of tweets sent during Hurricane Irma. *Natural Hazards Review*, *21*(1), 1–11. doi:10.1061/(ASCE)NH.1527-6996.0000351

Yuan, F., & Liu, R. (2020). Mining social media data for rapid damage assessment during Hurricane Matthew: Feasibility study. *Journal of Computing in Civil Engineering*, *34*(3), 1–14. doi:10.1061/(ASCE)CP.1943-5487.0000877

Zafarani, R., Abbasi, M. A., & Liu, H. (2014). Social media mining: An introduction. In *Social media mining: An introduction* (Vol. 9781107018853). New York, NY: Cambridge University Press. doi:10.1017/CBO9781139088510

Zhang, F., Fleyeh, H., Wang, X., & Lu, M. (2019). Construction site accident analysis using text mining and natural language processing techniques. *Automation in Construction*, *99*(June 2018), 238–248. doi:10.1016/j.autcon.2018.12.016

Zhang, Y., Li, D., & Li, C. (2019). Public transportation analysis based on social media data. *CICTP 2019*, 1517–1529. doi:10.1061/9780784482292.133

Zhang, D., Qiang, M., Jiang, H., Wen, Q., An, N., & Xia, B. (2018). Social sensing system for water conservation project: A case study of the south-to-north water transfer project in China. *Water Policy*, *20*(4), 667–691. doi:10.2166/wp.2018.141

CHAPTER 19

THE INFLUENCE OF LANGUAGE PROFICIENCY ON OCCUPATIONAL SAFETY OF FOREIGN WORKERS IN THE SUSTAINABLE CONSTRUCTION INDUSTRY

Hamzat Isah, Norhidayah Md Ulang and Norazura Mizal Azzmi

ABSTRACT

Malaysia is one of the developing countries which is progressing in terms of infrastructural facilities, but the country is facing a problem of having very low growth in population and this led to the frequent migration of workers with language proficiency to come to the country as foreign workers, language proficiency implications among which is causing injury to workers in the construction especially foreigners as they are getting it difficult to understand instruction during operations, safety guides and interpreting safety warning signs due to their low language proficiency. Because of this, the research aimed to reduce the rate of accident happening among the foreign workers and, therefore, the research sets three objectives: the research identified the common types of accidents faced by foreign workers due to language proficiency in construction sites, the research also investigated the extent to which language proficiency is affecting foreign workers and lastly provides an effective communication method that will help to minimise the rate of these

Sustainability Management Strategies and Impact in Developing Countries
Community, Environment and Disaster Risk Management, Volume 26, 243–252

Published under exclusive licence by Emerald Publishing Limited
ISSN: 2040-7262/doi:10.1108/S2040-726220220000026019

types of accidents. The research found that language proficiency is causing several types of accidents that comes with different injury cases ranging from non-severe, severe and fatal once of about 44% of the total accident cases happening in the Malaysian construction industries.

Keywords: Language; proficiency; foreign workers; sustainability; safety; construction

1. INTRODUCTION

Construction industries are considered as the sector that quickly booms the economy of both developed and developing countries. Research conducted in Malaysia shows that the construction industries make a significant role in the rapid growth of the Malaysian economy (Mohd Yazid Mohamad Yunus, 2017). He further figured out that more than 3% of the whole gross domestic product of Malaysia was drawn from the construction industries, which corresponds to RM 34.9 billion to the complete sum of GDP of RM 937.5 billion in 2012, and in 2014, the total cost of the contract given in the country is RM 120 billion. No one could argue on the impact of construction industries on the job opportunity and economic development in both developed and developing countries like Malaysia (Wem, 2021).

Robertson and Association (2009) mentioned that Malaysia is one of the developing countries that are progressing in terms of infrastructural facilities, but the country is facing a problem of having very low growth in population; the projected population growth of the country is 1.7% in 2008, which amounted to 25.27 million. Robert further stressed that 10.94 million was considered to be required as the workforce in the country. The need for foreign workers is seriously high annually, and this led to the frequent migration of workers who cannot understand English and Malaysian languages to come into Malaysia as foreign workers. This problem is affecting foreign workers especially in terms of health and safety of the workers on site.

2. LITERATURE REVIEW

2.1. Communication on Construction Site

Hoezen (2019), cited in Rogers and Kincaid in their study, defined communication as a method that parties involved create and share information among themselves to establish mutual understanding. Communication can also be described as a vital issue in the construction industry, and when the problem occurred in the construction industry, it is reported as a communication problem. Everette (2018) stated that any effort or mechanism used especially by a human being to solve the communication is termed to be a language that has explained this.

2.2. Method of Communicating with Foreign Workers on Construction Sites

Mei and Rashad (2019) reported that communication gap can cause any kind of occupational injury. Isah (2018) said that most site officers are using a third party (interpreter) to pass information to foreign workers with language proficiency problem.

2.3. Factors Influencing Communication

Some of the factors that influence communication in the construction industry were highlighted by Frank, Ribeiro, and Echeveste (2017) as follows: technical and systemic knowledge about the project, individuals' abilities (communication, proactivity, leadership, etc.), the delegation of responsibilities, leader behaviour, psychological safety to participate in projects, capacity to interpret messages, the inability of the stakeholders to emphasise with other parties involved in the project activity especially between the demand and supply parties as well as the principal officer that are not open-minded to the constructors and unbalance of stakeholder's power.

2.4. Languages Used in Malaysia

In Malaysia, there are three main languages used by the Malaysian, which makes the country to become a multilingual country. According to Chan and Abdallah (2016), these languages depend upon the tribe and upbringing of the individuals in the country. The languages include Bahasa Malaysia, English, Mandarin and Tamil. The Bahasa Malaysia was recognised by the country as its National language, which also serves as the national symbol of the country that is showing national unity and maintains the wisdom of cultural value and identity of Malaysia

2.5. Language Proficiency

Proficiency is the competent level of being proficient depending on a particular or profession. In terms of language, proficiency can be seen as the verbal or written ability of an individual. Divi et al. (2017) define language proficiency as the verbal performance of a given person. The findings of their research show that those who speak more than one language are mostly the once experiencing problem in language proficiency and this has become a disadvantage to them (Bialystok & Feng, 2019). Language proficiency can be considered as a factor that contributes immensely to the occurrence of accident among foreign workers in Malaysia and other English speaking countries.

2.6. Measuring Language Proficiency

To determine the level of proficiency of an individual, a variety of tools can be used but none was defined to be a 100% reliable especially when measuring language proficiency (Wolf et al., 2018). Hallen et al. (2017) highlighted the following as language proficiency measuring tools: Oral language screening tool (OLDS), comparable language assessments in both home language and second language, conceptual scoring (by developing items of assessment in both first and second language, correct or incorrect response to the items in whichever language they are given will be assessed.), diagnostic language testing and TOEFL. All of these measuring tools were to determine the strength or weakness of the once proficiency in terms of language.

2.7. Impact of Language Proficiency

Lo (2016) in his research cited the report of the Ecumenical Council for Corporate Responsibility, which shows that lack of language proficiency among foreign workers is a factor that can put foreign workers in unexpected danger of accident and risk. According to Nurul (2017), language proficiency is one of the factors that cause injury in construction in Malaysia as they are getting it difficult to understand instruction during operations, safety guides and interpreting safety warning signs. Language proficiency does not only affect foreign workers in the construction industry but also those in the other sectors such as agricultural, administrative, manufacturing, management, etc.; however, it does not only has an impact on causing an accident, it also has a great impact on foreign workers on issues like earning, inability to understand new and current labour policies and market characteristics (Budria & Pablo, 2018).

2.8. Foreign Workers

Foreign workers are usually found in most countries working in different sectors depending upon the opportunity and availability of the job around the workers. Joppe (2016) defines foreign workers as workers who have the freedom for a job in any country in the world (ILO, 2020).

2.9. Foreign Workers in Malaysia

Malaysia is a country that receives foreign workers from different countries especially from Asian and Middle East countries. Robertson and Association (2009) said that majority of foreign workers are trooping into Malaysia from 12 different Asian countries and most of them are from Indonesia followed by Nepal, Bangladesh, India, Pakistan, Vietnam, Cambodia, Thailand and the Philippines (Table 19.1). Robertson continues to figure out that Malaysia needs 10.94 million as its workforce, but unfortunately the indigenous citizens

Table 19.1. The Number of Foreign Workers from Different Countries to Malaysia.

S/No	Year	Number of World Migrant Workers	Percentage
1	1990	153 Million	2.9%
2	1995	161 Million	2.8%
3	2000	173 Million	2.8%
4	2005	191 Million	2.9%
5	2010	222 Million	3.2%
6	2015	244 Million	3.3%
Total		**1144**	**17.9%**

Source: International Organization for Migration (IOM, 2018).

of the country are not ready to accept valueless work that they called 3-D (Dirty, Difficult and Dangerous), and this gives room for foreign workers to complement the gap in construction and other sectors (Robertson and Association, 2009).

2.10. Foreign Workers in Malaysia Construction Industries

In 2017, it was reported in The Edge Market's statistical data that the population of migrants in Malaysia was 3.1 million and further said that the population of migrant workers in Malaysia continues to grow and become more than Indian Malaysians. Mohamed et al. (2015) said that 10% of the total foreign workers in Malaysia are working in Penang.

2.11. Issues with Foreign Workers

As foreign workers are playing a vital role and making a positive impact on the Malaysian construction industries, on the other hand, they also make a lot of negative impact on this sector. The most difficult life of foreign workers is the inability to get a job at the right time and the situation is worsening when the world is in an economic crisis, but still they temporarily solve the labour problem (Joppe, 2016). Mohd et al. (2016) highlighted some of the issues associated with foreign workers in Malaysia and these include cheap labour as their availability brings about the issue of cheap labour in the labour market, law productivity as most of the foreign workers are unskilled workers that cannot excellently perform, communication problem as they normally have a lower level of education and this makes them face language problem in terms of reading, writing and understanding work orders and safety rules, unable to fit or adjust they mostly found it difficult to change from traditional method modern way, on and off as most of the foreign workers are voluntarily withdrawing their offer from one organisation to another that has a better pay, socio-economic and political problems: the problem of foreign workers is not only to the construction industry but also to the general community in terms of spreading disease (such as malaria, HIV/aids, cholera etc.), prostitution and stealing.

2.12. Accident on Construction Sites

Abdulhamid et al. (2018) and Patel, Barot, and Shah (2018) said that the construction industry is being considered as one of the most dangerous working places as many cases of accidents were recorded ranging from severe to fatal injuries. Researchers continue to see the construction industry as 'one of the most hazardous industrial sectors wherein the construction workers are more prone to accidents' (Hadikusumo, 2016). A statistical report from the Department of Occupational Safety and Health shows that from January to July 2017, a total number of 124 accident cases were recorded from the Malaysian construction industries. This comprises an accident that causes permanent and non-permanent disabilities to the victims of their life (DOSH, 2017).

2.13. Causes of Accident on Construction Site

The result from research conducted by Abdul Rahim Abdul Hamid and Singh (2018) shows that various types of construction accidents exist ranging from fall from a high, accident due to falling object on the victim, struck by, stepping leg on an object that can cause an accident, caught in between, exposed to or contact, over-exertion or strenuous and others. An accident because of language proficiency, use of unsafe equipment, working condition, wrong method of operation, poor safety plan and management can now be categorised under another type of accident.

2.14. Accident in the Malaysian Construction Site

Previous studies show that accident in the Malaysian construction industry is still happening with a high number of victims that suffered in one way or the other. Construction accidents like other accidents it always causes damages to human life and properties, sometimes and loss of life. A statistical report from the Department of Occupational Safety and Health shows that from January to July 2017, a total number of 124 accident cases were recorded from the Malaysian construction industries. This comprises an accident that causes permanent and non-permanent disabilities to the victims of their life (DOSH, 2017). Abdul Rahman et al. (2018) also show a statistical report of accidents that happened in the Malaysian construction industry with only 14.12% as non-serious injuries. Also, the result shows 31% of the population study was recorded to have a serious injury while 66.75% with moderate injuries. From the frequent accident reports and the rising number of victims, the Malaysian government under the Construction Industry Development Board (CIDB) created a special training programme to arrest and minimise the rate of accident cases in the Malaysian construction industries (Salleh, Nifa, Zakaria, & Rashid, 2018).

2.15. Accident Investigation Method

To investigate the causation of accident, a human factor and organisation analysis method should be used for an in-depth interview that will enable the researcher to know the remote cause of the accident; this method has been used in Massachusetts Institute of Technology to investigate the human factor towards accidents in the aviation sector of country (Stringfellow, 2020). EHStoday is an online magazine of occupational health and safety, which published a statement made by Hartshorn in 2003 and published in EHStoday magazine (2017) on how to carry out an in-depth accident investigation and its remote. Hartshorn stated that an in-depth investigation of the accident should be made by asking the four basic 'W' question and obtained their answers; these for basic 'W' referred to who, what, where and when the accident happened. This method found to be useful as the same questions were put in place by the Canadian Centre for Occupational Health and Safety (CCOHS, 2017) under Occupational Safety Health (OSHA).

This method of the in-depth interview for investigating process has been carried out by Lo (2016) in the UK to investigate the role of language and communication problem for the migrant in the case study area.

2.16. Accident on Foreign Workers

Cheng and Wu (2017) said that most of the foreign workers are employed to operate in a very high-risk job; an accident can be seen as an injury that occurred undesirable to the injured person and it can be simple or complex; its result can also be severe or fatal. Research conducted by Loosemore in Australia shows that 25% of the total number of foreign workers in the country are speaking with their mother tongue instead of the Australian Language.

3. RESULTS AND FINDINGS

3.1. Rate of Accident to Foreign Workers Due to Language Proficiency

There are a significant number of foreign workers in the Malaysian construction industries with 66.67% of them facing a serious high risk of accident as a result of low-level language proficiency. However, Isah said that 44.71% of the total injury cases among foreign workers were due to language proficiency problem and causing serious injury that includes: amputation of finger, loss or damage to sight, electrocution, injury to both lower and upper limbs, skin injury, body paid, removal of a fingernail, broken borne and fracture, punctures as a result of body contact with sharp object, etc.

3.2. Effect of Accident Caused by Low-Level of LP on the Worker and His Performance

Each foreign worker has his/her differences that also make their problem differ from one person to another but at the same time, some problems were common to all especially to people with the same status of life (such as foreign workers with low level of LP). But the effect of these problems on all foreign workers can be broadly categorised into four groups: Practical Challenges, Low Productivity (they take a longer time to become familiar with the work given to them); Low Income and Sudden Absenteeism.

3.3. Effect of Workers' Accident on the Project

Low-level language proficiency is affecting not only the workers but also the company and the project itself in terms of poor workmanship, too much waste of working materials, extra expenditure and the making of too many errors. He further explained these in details as follows: Poor Workmanship, Too Much Waste of Working Materials, Extra Expenditure, Too Much Error.

3.4. Extent to Which Accident Due to Language Proficiency Is Affecting Foreign Workers

The research found that accident due to language proficiency problem is affecting foreign workers to the following extent: Loss of body part, temporary and permanent deformation, loosing of job, early retirement and loss of feature earning, psychological touch, drug addiction.

4. SUSTAINABLE METHOD OF MINIMISING RATE OF ACCIDENT TO FOREIGN WORKERS

Sustainability is not only an idea related to the effects of the environment in terms of minimising emission, energy consumption or recycling of waste materials but it also more than just becoming green but it is also about people who use the environment. To effectively sustain workers on any construction site, be it a foreigner or local one, he should be protected from all forms of injury including the one caused due to his/her inability of understanding the language used to pass instruction on safety rules and work orders. Some of the followings can be used to sustainably minimise the rate of accidents to foreign workers with low language proficiency.

4.1. Safety Drills and Regular Site Meetings

Safety drill is a practical way of preparing workers on construction site to know how to react to an emergency such as accident and its alike while the regular meeting is an official gathering usually hold between employer and his employee, or between site officers and their workers. Safety drill enables the foreign workers to have an idea of reacting quickly to rescue themselves in case of any event of an accident while the regular site meetings will make them have a room of interacting with their superior officers and share their feelings with them about health and safety.

4.2. Safety Workshops and Seminars

Safety workshops and trainings help to improve the working ability of the trainee and for safety workshop; it helps the company to reduce the rate of on the job accidents that can cause personal suffering, delay and low productivity. It also helps the company to qualify for an inspection to be conducted by government authorities as this form part of the requirements of OSHA. It also helps the company to attract more employees trying to join the company.

4.3. Computer-Generated Imagery

The research participants agreed that, using a live screening with customised animations generated from computer-generated Imagery (CGI) showing characters wearing the personal protective equipment (PPE) and the consequences of those that are not wearing them. Also, the screen will be customised to show a practical way of carrying out work safely step-by-step. In addition to this, an ordinary TV screen will be used to display the animated characters, which will be placed by the site huts.

4.4. On the Job Training and Knowledge Transformation

This is another effective way of minimising the rate of an accident happening among foreign workers in the Malaysian construction industries as the training will be more inclined to safety training. This will help in terms of:

i. Good training helps in the economical use of materials and machinery.
ii. It reduces supervision.
iii. It lowers the rate of accidents.
iv. It boosts the morale of employees to perform the task/job efficiently.

5. CONCLUSION

The research concludes that language plays a vital role in the conduct of project execution from inception to the completion stage; the success of any project lies in good communication between all the parties involved in the project. Therefore, for a successful and sustainable company, protection should be given to its energetic resource (worker) in terms of welfare, health and safety. The research, however, concludes that health and safety are equally same with other social responsibility components of sustainability that need to be administered in proactive and innovative strategies as recommended below for workers with low language proficiency. However, the research also concludes that lack of good communication is leading to several types of an accident such as power tool and machine accidents that normally occurred during operation, fall from a high working place such as a ladder, scaffold and roof work, contact with harmful working material such as cement, toxic materials explosive, etc., accident that is causing damage to the working material, caught in between objects, electrocution and hit by an object during operation.

REFERENCES

Abdul Rahim Abdul Hamid, M. Z. A. M., & Singh, B. (2018). Causes of accidents in construction. *Malaysian Journal of Civil Engineering, 20*(2) 242–259.

CCOHS. (2017). Accident investigation. Retrieved from www.ccohs.ca.

Chan, T. K. (2016). Measuring the performance of the Malaysian construction industry. *Construction Management and Economics, 27*(12), 1231–1244. doi:10.1080/01446190903233137

Department of Occupational Safety and Health Malaysia (DOSH). (2017). Retrieved from http://www.dosh.gov.my/index.php/en/

Everette, D. (2018). *Language: The culture tool.* Profile Book Ltd.

Frank, A. G., Ribeiro, J. L. D., & Echeveste, M. E. (2017). Factors influencing knowledge transfer between NPD teams: A taxonomic analysis based on a sociotechnical approach. *R&D Management, 45*(1), 1–22. doi:10.1111/radm.12046

Hadikusumo, K. D. a. B. H. W. (2016). Safety management practices in the Bhutanese construction industry. *Journal of Construction in Developing Countries, 11*(2).

International Labour Organization (ILO). (2020). *International labour migration: A rights-based approach*. Geneva: ILO.

International Organization for Migration (IOM). (2018). Retrieved from https://www.iom.int/

Joppe, M. (2016). Migrant workers: Challenges and opportunities in addressing tourism labour shortages. *Tourism Management*, *33*(3), 662–671. doi:10.1016/j.tourman.2011.07.009

Lo, L. (2016). The role of language and communication for the migrant community integration into host society. *GSTF International Journal of Law and Social Sciences (JLSS)*, *3*(2), 46–51. doi:10.5176/2251-2853_3.2.157

Malaysian Department of Statistic. (2016a). Pulau Penang geographical location. Retrieved from www.dosm.gov.my

Malaysian Department of Statistic. (2016b). Pulau Penang current population. Retrieved from www.dosm.gov.my

Mohd Yazid Mohamad Yunus, A. A. L. (2017). A review of safety management in Malaysian construction industry. *The Social Science*, *12*(4), 702–711.

Patel, R., Barot, U., & Shah, K. (2018). Accident on construction site: Identification & mitigation: A literature survey.

Rob, R. H. (2017). Study of human language. *Journal of Modern Language*.

Robertson, P. S. Jr., & Association, F. L. (2009). Migrant workers in Malaysia – Issues, concerns and points for action. *Journal of Advanced Research in Engineering, Science and Management*.

Salleh, N. A., Nifa, F. A. A., Zakaria, M. N. S., & Rashid, A. K. A. (2018). A study of im-smart safety courseware development for foreign workers in the safety course Malaysia construction industry. *Jurnal Teknologi*, *77*(5), 163–168.

Stringfellow, M. (2020). Accident analysis and hazard analysis for human and organizational factors. Retrieved from https://dspace.mit.edu

CHAPTER 20

UNDER-REPORTING OF OCCUPATIONAL ACCIDENTS IN THE NIGERIAN CONSTRUCTION INDUSTRY

Adetunji Kamoli, Razali Adul Hamid and Syamsul Hendra Bin Mahmud

ABSTRACT

Under-reporting of an occupational accident is commonly found at both organisational and individual levels. It interferes with the reality of health and safety in organisations and countries. It also hinders the ability to identify trends, recognise priorities, improve strategies, and allocation of resources for accident prevention. This study examined the reasons for the under-reporting of occupational accidents at the organisation level in the Nigerian construction industry. A review of the literature was conducted on the under-reporting of occupational accidents. Thereafter, a field survey with questionnaires was distributed to solicit information from the Nigerian construction professionals in the Federal Capital Territory, Abuja, Nigeria. 300 questionnaires were distributed, and 235 responses were received and analysed with Microsoft Excel and SPSS software by applied relative importance index and ranked. The study found that among the top-ranked reasons for under-reporting of occupational accidents by the organisation is to maintain a reputation. It is therefore important to increase awareness on the reporting of occupational accidents and its importance in accident prevention programmes by the regulatory bodies. Also,

Sustainability Management Strategies and Impact in Developing Countries
Community, Environment and Disaster Risk Management, Volume 26, 253–264

ISSN: 2040-7262/doi:10.1108/S2040-726220220000026020

more collaborative efforts, standards, and policies should be put in place by the governments for ensuring reporting and record-keeping of accidents in the Nigerian construction industry. Records of dangerous incidents are the key indicator for the organisation for the improvement in the prevention of hazards. The study, therefore, concludes that there should be proper recording and surveillance of occupational accidents, hazards, and their related background causes in reaction to quick and complex variations in work-life.

Keywords: Accident; health; occupation; organisation; under-reporting; safety

1. INTRODUCTION

Under-reporting of occupational accidents is a recognised issue, leading to a conclusion that national statistics sources are not adequate to dependably estimate the figure of occurrence of occupational accidents at the workplaces (Demers, Debono, Arrandale, & Keefe, 2019; Pollack & Keimig, 1987; Heuvel et al., 2017; Eurostat, 2015, 2020; Kurppa, 2015). The existent of under-reporting continues to be a concern for all stakeholders. Because construction operations will be unsuccessful without adequate record-keeping of accidents, which allows organisations, employees, and construction professionals to learn from previous experience and make adjustments for the future. Accurate reporting of occupational illnesses and injuries is essential to observe workplace safety and health and to recognise the most desirable interventions (Melius et al., 1989; pransky Snyder, Dembe, & Himmelstein, 1999; Public Health England Transition Team, 2012). The robust roles of employers and employees are important to guarantee the accurate and comprehensive collection of occupational accident data and to utilise this information to fulfil obligatory improvements of health and safety at the workplaces. State agencies equally play a significant function and complementary role in association with federal organisations (National Academy of Sciences, 2018). State agencies collect, examine, and communicate data from the local sources to direct preventive measures at the local and state levels, and provide statistics to federal organisations to be combined for national data for necessary policy formulation. Hence, there must be collaborative efforts of regulatory bodies, employees, employers, and all stakeholders in the collection of occupational accident data to improve health and safety in the construction industry.

The Nigerian construction industry is encircling with a high rate of accidents, and some researchers had pointed out that construction organisations do no keep precise data of accidents and also do not report to the regulatory bodies (Agwu & Olele, 2014; Idoro, 2008; Umeokafor, 2018), despite the existence of the obligatory requirement that mandated the notification of accidents that occurred in the workplace to be reported to the authority (The Federal Republic of Nigeria Factories Act, 1990). Although there was a penalty for non-reporting of the occupational accidents that occurred in the workplace, the amount levied (N1,000 = 2.63 dollar at the current exchange rate) is low and cannot serve as a deterrent for non-reporting of occupational accidents. With this scenario, health and safety in the workplaces cannot be improved.

Health and safety systems have mainly been established in response to a legal obligation and occupational health and safety reporting anchor generally on mandatory data related to accidents (Marosszeky et al., 2004). In many nations, the regulatory bodies are weak and organisations support regulations only superficially (Lee & Halpin, 2003) while Enshassi et al. (2008) and Kajiki et al. (2020) also establish that in many developing nations, the legislation managing OHS is limited. It was posited by Idubor and Oisamoje (2013) that the absence of strong enforcement of OSH rules supports non-compliance with health and safety regulations. Likewise, Diugwu, Baba, and Egila (2012) affirmed that the malfunction of the OSH system in Nigeria is a result of the non-function of provisions and OSH regulations. According to Ezenwa (2001), concealment and under-reporting of occupational accidents were found to be rampant in the workplace. Therefore, a better method is required for proactive efforts in dealing with the under-reporting of occupational accidents in the Nigerian construction industry with the factors responsible for them. Therefore, the study is conducted to identify the reasons for the under-reporting of occupational accidents in the Nigerian construction industry.

2. BACKGROUND

The figure for reported injuries might be extremely underestimated with what is truly experienced in the construction industry as different researchers have revealed that under-reporting of occupational injuries is extensively occurring (Abbas, Zalat, & Ghareeb, 2013; Dong et al, 2011). A reporting level of occupational accidents at work is referred to as the relation between the approximate figure of notifiable accidents covered by the statistics and the figure of accidents precisely notified (European Union, 2013). Under-reporting can be compromised at two levels. Establishment level under-reporting is occurring when the record of employees' illness and injuries are not recorded in the regulatory body log of work-related illness and injuries while individual level under-reporting is when workers fail to report illness and injuries that happen in the workplace (Eurostat, 2013; Probst, Bettac, & Austin, 2019). A further problem for under-reporting is that the self-employed are hardly report accidents to the regulatory bodies (Weerd et al., 2014). Weerd et al. (2014) and Wuellner, Adams, and Bonauto (2016) affirm that occupational injuries were under-reported by some organisations. Under-reporting has been found to differ by organisation characteristics. Some studies suggest that under-reporting is higher for injuries among smaller organisations (Morse et al., 2004) whereas it differs by sector (Rosenman et al., 2006). Research similarly suggests that occupational accident data among multi-organisation are more probably be missed than among single/organisations (Boden, 2014). Although in every nation, there were some kinds of legal responsibility to report occupational accidents, Heuvel et al., (2017) reveals that under-reporting is more frequent in nations with the absence of an insurance-based reporting system.

Insurance-based occupational accident reporting systems generally provide liberal monetary remuneration for the victims if an accident is reported, as against the systems in which victims are secure by common systems that do not differentiate among causes of the illness or accident.

According to ILO (2003), less than 20 per cent of construction accidents are reported. Similarly, Glazner et al. (1998) found that in the construction of Denver International Airport, the entire injury rate for employees doubled the published figure of the Bureau of Labour Statistics. Likewise, Probst et al. (2008) established that under-reporting of injuries between 2,400 construction personnel working on the semiconductor factory while linking the figure of injuries documented in the logbook of job-related illness and injuries with the figure of injuries stated to the Proprietor Controlled Insurance Program. Also, Probst (2006) found that unreported injuries happened at almost twice the rate of reported injuries; this implies that for every reported injury almost two went unreported. Equally Probst and Estrada (2010) found that employees failed to report 71 per cent of all job-related injuries to their establishment. Just as Probst and Graso (2010) highlighted that more than four health and safety cases went unreported for every single case reported to the organisation, signifying a failure to report more than 80 per cent of experienced events. It was opined by Dong et al. (2011) that construction organisations were most probable to under-report injuries; the survey of occupational injuries and illnesses information revealed that only 25 per cent of serious injuries between Hispanic employees were registered, and 60 per cent between white employees in small construction organisations.

Furthermore, Rosenman et al. (2006) found that the national surveillance system may omit 61 per cent of the occupational illness and injuries that occurred in Michigan from1999 to 2001. The figure represents 60 per cent and 67 per cent for injuries, 66 per cent and 69 per cent for illnesses, respectively. The study of under-reporting occupational accidents in the Sri Lanka construction industry by Silva and Rathnayake (2018) shows 80 per cent of construction accidents went under-reported. It was highlighted by Oleinick, Gluck, and Guire (1995) that under-reporting in Michigan in 1986 might influence the workplaces of 30 per cent of the employees and could result in a 20 per cent under-reported of work-related. A study conducted by Hadi, Guan, How, Rahman, and Tamrin (2017) found that a high record of non-reporting accidents exists in the construction industry; nearly 94.7 per cent of workers in the sector did not report an accident, while Mohsin and Mansour (2018) found that occupational accidents under-reporting was 77 per cent and 23 per cent reported occupational accidents. The result of the study by Klausen and Iversen (1979) found that less than 50 per cent of the occupational accidents within one year were reported. Similarly, Lipscomb et al. (2013) found that considerable proof of fear of reprisal for reporting occupational injuries was shown in their study where less than half of employees (46.4 per cent) reported that occupational injuries were reported at the workplace and over 30 per cent said they were virtually never or hardly report an accident.

The reporting of occupational accidents at work constitutes the best approach for accident prevention (Eurostat, 2013). Such reporting plays a significant role as it can be used for motives like inspection targeting, safety standards development, performance measurement, resource allocation, the identification of low and high hazardous sectors, and compilation of national surveillance programs (OSHA, 2018). Also, occupational accident data can equally be used for improving workers' and organisation understanding of occupational hazards, making policy decisions, and for research purposes (Tedone, 2017). Federal Ministry of Labour and Employment (2016) stated that under-reporting of occupational accidents is more pronounced in the workplaces in Nigeria. Therefore, understanding the reasons for the under-reporting of occupation accidents is important.

3. SYSTEM OF REPORTING OF OCCUPATIONAL ACCIDENTS

The standards for reporting and registration are quite diverse across the nations (Tedone, 2017). This is primarily due to variances in the legal description of an accident at work across the nations. In countries like Austria, Spain, Belgium, and Portugal, the injuries which happen on the way to and from work are considered to be injuries at work and recorded on the same database but classified as a special group. Whereas, in other nations like the UK, Germany, and Italy, they are categorised as commuting injuries rather than injuries at work. The European Union, (European Communities, 1989) unambiguously clarifies the obligation of the organisations to reports occupational injuries suffered by their employees and resulting in an absence from work beyond three days. Nations like Sweden, Portugal, Belgium, France, Denmark, and Spain record all accidents resulting in one or more days of absence from duties in addition to the day of injuries. Whereas, the UK, Ireland, Finland, Italy, Germany, Nigeria, and Austria utilised the standard beyond three days (Health and Safety Executive, 2013).

4. CURRENT REPORTING PROCEDURE OF OCCUPATIONAL ACCIDENTS IN NIGERIA ACCORDING TO FACTORIES ACT OF 1990

Every notice needed to be given under the rules and shall be in writing under section 51 of the Act, sent to the nearby inspector forthwith upon the occurring of the dangerous event. Report of accidents (1) where an accident happens in a factory which either (a) causes loss of life to an individual engaged in that factory or (b) incapacitates any such individual beyond three days from carrying out the obligations for which he was engaged, written notification of the accident, in the detailed form and complemented by the given specifics, shall forthwith be directed to the inspector of the area by the occupier of the factory. (2) Where any accident causing incapacitation is reported under the section, and after notice thereof results in the death of the individual incapacitated, notification in writing of the death shall be directed to the inspector of the area by the occupier of the factory, quickly as the death comes to his awareness. (3) Where any accident to which the section applies happens to an individual engaged and the occupier of the factory is not the real employer of the individual killed or wounded, the real employer shall if he fails to account the accident to the occupier instantly, be guilty of an offence. (4) Any employer or occupier of a factory who fails to report an accident under the section shall be guilty of an offence and shall on conviction be liable to a fine not beyond N1,000 (The Federal Republic of Nigeria Factories Act, 1990).

5. RENEWED FOCUS ON HEALTH AND SAFETY AND ACCIDENTS REPORTING FOR SUSTAINABLE DEVELOPMENT

It was emphasised by United Nations (1992) that human beings are central to sustainable development; they are entitled to a healthy and productive life in accord with nature. Thrive for a world with negligible occupational accidents and safety and health is considered as a basic human right (ILO, 2009). Establishing a healthy, safer, and hazard-free workplace might provide stronger, physical, and mental well-being of employees, greater productivity, and improve the competitiveness of the organisations. Further expansion of OSH policies and boosting existing measures are vital in actualising a healthy and safer workplace. An insight into the economic consequences of occupational accidents provides organisations and governments with important data for the purpose of establishing OSH policies and accidents prevention (Heuvel et al., 2017). The improved commitment to health and safety and accommodating milieu among employees and organisations have been connected with: quality services, product enhancements, improvement of morale, and better staffing in the workplace (OSHA, 2015).

Furthermore, many nations are nowadays giving greater precedence to OSH and preventing occupational accidents and ill health. There seem to be numerous motives for this trend. Possibly the utmost significant one is that globally, numerous stakeholders – employers, governments, and workers now admit that the problems of occupational ill health and accidents are much bigger than formerly believed. While accurate statistics for such occupational problems are still difficult to obtain on a local, state, national, and global scale (ILO, 2015). It is widely known that occupational accidents and illnesses can have a substantial influence on the competitiveness, productivity, and reputation of individual organisations, likewise on the livelihoods of employees and their families. Besides, at the country level, occupational accidents and ill health can create an intolerable economic burden, humanitarian and destroying any reputation and negatively affecting sustainable economic growth (ILO, 2014). Therefore, there is a need for integrated methods that involve promoting employees' health and safety, guarantee decent work, useful lives, and boost development. The hope that employees be able to work effectively without harm due to wealth-generating events is the symbol of a complete, responsible, and reasonable industry. G20 leaders recommend a decent safety and healthy working environment for all employees as part of a series of measures to support labour requests and nurture new and better job formation (ILO, 2013)

6. METHOD

The objective of the study is to identify the reasons for the under-reporting of occupational accidents at the organisational level in the Nigerian construction industry. A literature review was conducted to encapsulate reasons for the under-reporting of occupational accidents by organisations and employees. Thereafter, a questionnaire was developed, to solicit information for the reasons for under-reporting of occupational accidents by the organisations in the Nigerian construction industry. These questionnaires were sent to the population for this study consist of construction professionals in the Federal Capital Territory Abuja, Nigeria. The respondents' selections of answers to the questions were arranged on a five-point Likert scale from strongly disagree to strongly agree. Out of 300 questionnaires, 235 were returned, representing 78.33 per cent, therefore considered for the analysis of the study. The internal consistency of the questionnaire was tested and the Cronbach's alpha result of the data was 0.836. The results were greater than 0.6–0.70 of the standard guideline according to Ursachi, Horodnic, and Zait (2015). The data were afterward analysed with SPSS and Microsoft Excel. The mean score of the data was computed then ranked accordingly.

7. RESULT AND DISCUSSION

Table 20.1 shows that maintaining a reputation forms the topmost reason for organisations not to report an occupational accident. An organisation wants to maintain accident rates as low as possible since the health and safety performance of an organisation is judged by the accident rate. Similarly, according to Health and Safety Executive (2001), organisations want to maintain performance by not reporting occupational accidents that occurred in their construction sites. The fewer injuries reported, the higher the organisation's history and previous experience will look to be pure and free of injuries, leading to satisfactory experience ratings (Ziad Hamideh, 2013). Establishments may influence the reporting procedure to preserve their clean record of few serious occupational injuries and hence maintain an excellent position. Also from an employer's viewpoint, under-reporting is a tool for evading the cumulative cost of insurance premiums. The existence of real employees' compensation showed that organisations are very sensitive to increment in insurance rates, and so influencing injuries through under-reporting. Having fewer accidents ascribe to lower employees' compensation claims. Establishments incur extensive costs related to their workers, likewise, costs associated with the negligence to address the cause of occupational accidents (Pransky & Snyder, 1999). These expenditures may be complicated with government-levied fines and fines that come from such establishment under-reporting. Rantanen, Lehtinen, Valenti, and Iavicoli (2017) highlighted that inadequate competence and capability to appraise and manage H&S problems could be assumed to be among the reasons for the under-reporting of accidents. Failure to record and report occupational accidents could be attributed to reporting requirements by the nations (Welch, Carre, & Ringen, 2007). An organisation's absence of understanding of record-keeping could result in the under-reporting of occupational

Table 20.1. Reasons for Under-Reporting of the Occupational Accident at the Organisations Level.

Reasons	Mean	Std Dev	Rank
To maintain reputation	3.87	1.162	1
Administrative barrier and absence of effective recording system from the regulatory body	3.72	1.048	2
For avoiding the increasing cost of insurance premiums	3.7	1.168	3
Notions that organisations may be subject to disciplinary measures by the regulatory agency	3.64	1.102	4
Non deterrent penalties for poor record-keeping	3.6	1.252	5
Fear of contracts may be denied if the organisation injury rate is too high	3.45	1.254	6
Desire to avoid inspection by inspectorate officer	3.38	1.380	7
Employer's lack of understanding of the Importance of data and the need for reporting	3.32	1.309	8
Unrealistic recordable objectives set up by the safety department	2.98	1.178	9
Size of the organisation	2.96	1.073	10
Interchangeable relationship between employers and employees	2.89	1.155	11
lack of time to complete the necessary paperwork or online reporting process	2.74	1.231	12

accidents to the authorities (Lim et al., 2018). The absence of awareness on statutory, poor penalties for bad record-keeping levied on organisations and the problem of documentation of important paperwork was identified by Wai (2007) as among the reasons for under-reporting of occupational accidents. According to Workplace Safety and Health Council (2018), under-reporting could arising from general absence of awareness on the importance of reporting occupational accidents. While Federal Ministry of Labour and Employment (2016) pinpoint that under-reporting of occupational accidents could be attributed to the perception that organisations may be subjected to penalties as a result of the high recording of accidents because they ought to have taken necessary measures to prevent occupational accidents.

8. CONCLUSION

The study provides an overview of the reasons for the under-reporting of occupational accidents by organisations in the Nigerian construction industry. Reporting occupational accidents are effective methods that can be used for accident prevention. Ascertaining the causes should not only be the right step but also solving the problems. It, therefore, suggests that regulatory agencies should make reporting non-complicated and robust for the organisations. There should also be increasing in surveillance and inspection of workplaces by designated inspectorate officers. For the organisations, a non-punitive and constructive method should be employed to encourage them to report their injuries encountered in the workplace. Open communication concerning near misses and errors should be encouraged among the construction teams. A system that fosters better involvement from the workers, employers, and the regulatory bodies should be developed; this will enhance recording and reporting of occupation accidents. Electronic reporting rules should also be promulgated; this will help by providing data important for illness and injury surveillance not existing in the national occupational database. The rule will also offer new prospects to control and to offer mechanisms and support to organisations that need to recognise and solve hazardous problems at individual worksites. The outcomes of surveillance data should be used for the comprehensive field assessment of occupational safety and health issues because field identification and evaluation are essential first steps in the prevention method. Data should be used to recognise and prevent occupational accidents. Good data on workplace illnesses and injuries are to identify trends, to develop priorities for setting a standard and enforcement actions, and to appraise its effectiveness in the regulation of workplace safety and health. Nations need to develop an efficient collection of occupational accidents information systems; this is to improve the application of dependable data for reporting.

REFERENCES

Abbas, M., & Balkhyour, M. A. (2018). The trend of occupational accidents and their under-reporting estimations in the factories of Pakistan; 1993-2009. *Journal of King Abdulaziz University – Meteorology, Environment and Arid Land Agriculture Sciences*, *27*(2), 41–53. https://doi.org/10.4197/met.27-2.5

Abbas, R. A., Zalat, M. M., & Ghareeb, N. S. E. (2013). Non-fatal occupational injuries and safety climate: A cross-sectional study of construction building workers in Mit-Ghamr City, Dakahlia Governorate, Egypt. *Open Journal of Safety Science and Technology*, *3*, 69–79. https://doi.org/10.1177/0748233717733853

Agwu, M. O., & Olele, H. E. (2014). Fatalities in the Nigerian construction industry: A case of poor safety culture. *British Journal of Economics, Management & Trade*, *4*(3), 431–452. https://doi.org/10.9734/bjemt/2014/6439

Boden, L. I. (2014). Capture-recapture estimates of the undercount of workplace injuries and illnesses: Sensitivity analysis. *American Journal of Industrial Medicine*, *57*(10), 1090–1099. https://doi.org/10.1002/ajim.22247

Demers, P. A., Debono, N. L., Arrandale, V. H., & Keefe, A. R. (2019). Options for tracking occupational disease and exposure in Ontario. Occupational Cancer Research Centre, Cancer Care Ontario Toronto, Canada. Retrieved from https://www.occupationalcancer.ca/2020/ocrc-options-report/

Diugwu, I. A., Baba, D. L., & Egila, A. E. (2012). Effective regulation and level of awareness: An exposé of the Nigeria's construction industry. *Open Journal of Safety Science and Technology*, *02*(04), 140–146. https://doi.org/10.4236/ojsst.2012.24018

Dong, X. S., Fujimoto, A., Ringen, K., Stafford, E., Platner, J. W., Gittleman, J. L., & Wang, X. (2011). Injury underreporting among small establishments in the construction industry. *American Journal of Industrial Medicine*, *54*(5), 339–349. https://doi.org/10.1002/ajim.20928

Enshassi, A., Choudhry, R. M., Mayer, P. E., & Shoman, Y. (2008). Safety Performance of Subcontractors in the Palestinian Construction Industry. *Journal of Construction in Developing Countries*, *13*(1), 51–62.

European Communities. (1989). Council Directive 89/391/EEC: The introduction of measures to encourage improvements in the safety and health ofworkers at work. *Official Journal of the European Communities*. https://doi.org/2004R0726 – v.7 of 05.06.2013

European Union. (2013). *European statistics on accidents at work (ESAW)*. Luxembourg: European Union. https://doi.org/10.2785/40882

Eurostat. (2015). Accidents at work and other work-related health problems (Eurostat metadata). Eurostat, the Statistical Office of the European Union, pp. 1–10. Retrieved from https://ec.europa.eu/eurostat/cache/metadata/en/hsw_acc_work_esms.htm

Eurostat. (2020). Accidents at work statistics: Statistics Explained. Eurostat Statistics Explained, European Union, pp. 1–7. Retrieved from https://ec.europa.eu/eurostat/statistics-explained/index.php?title=Main_Page

Ezenwa, A. O. (2001). A study of fatal injuries in Nigerian factories. *Occupational Medicine*, *51*(8), 485–489. https://doi.org/10.1093/occmed/51.8.485

Federal Ministry of Labour and Employment. (2016). Nigeria country profile on occupational safety and health. Federal Ministry of Labour and Employment, Abuja, Nigeria. Retrieved from https://www.ilo.org/africa/countries-covered/nigeria/WCMS_552748/lang--en/index.htm

Glazner, J. E., Borgerding, J., Lowery, J. T., Bondy, J., Mueller, K. L., & Kreiss, K. (1998). Construction injury rates may exceed national estimates: Evidence from the construction of Denver International Airport. *American Journal of Industrial Medicine*, *34*(2), 105–112. https://doi.org/10.1002/(SICI)1097-0274(199808)34:2<105::AID-AJIM2>3.0.CO;2-W

Hadi, N. A. A., Guan, N. Y., How, V., Rahman, R. A., & Tamrin, S. B. M. (2017). Association between non-reporting of accident and contributing factors in Malaysia's construction industry. *Proceedings of The 2nd Asian Conference on Ergonomics and Design 2017*, *53*, 648–651. https://doi.org/10.5100/jje.53.s648

Hamideh, Z. (2013). *The under-reporting of injuries for hispanic workers in construction (University of Utah)*. Salt Lake City, UT: University of Utah. https://doi.org/10.1017/CBO9781107415324.004

Health and Safety Executive. (2001). A guide to measuring health & safety. *Health and Safety Executive*, 1–30. Retrieved from https://www.hse.gov.uk/opsunit/perfmeas.pdf

Health and Safety Executive. (2013). Reporting accidents and incidents at work: A brief guide to the Reporting of Injuries, Diseases and Dangerous Occurrences Regulations 2013 (RIDDOR). *Health and Safety Executive*, 1–5. Retrieved from http://www.hse.gov.uk/riddor/

Heuvel, S. van den, Zwaan, L. van der, Dam, L. van, Oude-Hengel, K., Eekhout, I., Emmerik, M. van, … Willlhelm, C. (2017). *Estimating the costs of work-related accidents and ill-health: An analysis of European data sources*. https://doi.org/10.2802/566789

Idoro, G. I. (2008). Management health and safety management efforts as correlates of performance in the Nigerian construction industry. *Journal of Civil Engineering and Management*, *14*(4), 277–285. https://doi.org/10.3846/1392-3730.2008.14.27

Idubor, E. E., & Oisamoje, M. D. (2013). An exploration of health and safety management issues in Nigeria's effort to industrialize. *European Scientific Journal*, *99*(1212), 1857–7881.

ILO. (2003). *Safety in numbers—Pointers for a global safety culture at work*. Geneva: International Labour Organization. Retrieved from https://www.ilo.org/wcmsp5/groups/public/---ed_protect/---protrav/---safework/documents/publication/wcms_142840.pdf

ILO. (2009). *Health and life at work: A basic human right*. Geneva: International Labour Organization. Retrieved from https://www.ilo.org/wcmsp5/groups/public/---ed_protect/---protrav/---safework/documents/publication/wcms_108686.pdf

ILO. (2013). *Safety and health in the use of machinery*. Geneva: International Labour Organization. Retrieved from http://www.ilo.org/wcmsp5/groups/public/@ed_protect/@protrav/@safework/documents/normativeinstrument/wcms_164653.pdf

ILO. (2014). *Safety and health at work: A vision for sustainable prevention*. Geneva: International Labour Organization. Retrieved from https://www.ilo.org/wcmsp5/groups/public/@ed_protect/@protrav/@safework/documents/publication/wcms_301214.pdf

ILO. (2015). *Good practices and challenges in promoting decent work in construction and infrastructure projects*. Geneva: International Labour Organization. Retrieved from http://www.ilo.org/wcmsp5/groups/public/---ed_dialogue/---sector/documents/publication/wcms_416378.pdf

Kajiki, S., Mori, K., Kobayashi, Y., Hiraoka, K., Fukai, N., Uehara, M., … Nakanishi, S. (2020). Developing a global occupational health and safety management system model for Japanese companies. *Journal of Occupational Health*, *62*(1), 1–13. https://doi.org/10.1002/1348-9585.12081

Klausen, H., & Iversen, L. (1979). Notification of occupational injuries from a place of employment. A problem of under-reporting. *Ugeskrift for Laeger*, *141*(20), 1353–1357. https://doi.org/10.1016/j.gmhc.2013.04.007

Kurppa, K. (2015). Severe Under-reporting of work injuries in many countries of the Baltic Sea Region: An exploratory semi-quantitative study. *Finish Institute of Occupational Health*. Retrieved from http://www.balticseaosh.net/wp/wp-content/uploads/2015/10/Severe-Under-reporting_final-report_Kurppa.pdf

Lee, S., & Halpin, D. W. (2003). Predictive tool for estimating accident risk. *Journal of Construction Engineering and Management*, *129*(4), 431–436. https://doi.org/10.1061/(asce)0733-9364(2003)129:4(431)

Lim, S. S., Yoon, J. H., Rhie, J., Bae, S. W., Kim, J., & Won, J. U. (2018). The relationship between free press and under-reporting of non-fatal occupational injuries with data from representative national indicators, 2015: Focusing on the lethality rate of occupational injuries among 39 countries. *International Journal of Environmental Research and Public Health*, *15*(12). https://doi.org/10.3390/ijerph15122856

Lipscomb, H. J., Nolan, J., Patterson, D., Sticca, V., & Myers, D. J. (2013). Safety, incentives, and the reporting of work-related injuries among union carpenters: "You're pretty much screwed if you get hurt at work." *American Journal of Industrial Medicine*, *56*(4), 389–399. https://doi.org/10.1002/ajim.22128

Marosszeky, M., Karim, K., Davis, S., & Naik, N. (2004). Lessons learnt in developing effective performance measures for construction safety management. In 12th Annual Conference of the International Group for Lean Construction-Helsingør, Denmark. Retrieved from http://iglc.net/Papers/Details/314/pdf%0Ahttp://iglc.net/Papers/Details/314

Melius, J. M., Sestito, J. P., & Seligman, P. J. (1989). IX. Occupational disease surveillance with existing data sources. *American Journal of Public Health*, *79*, 46–52. https://doi.org/10.2105/ajph.79.suppl.46

Morse, T., Dillon, C., Weber, J., Warren, N., Bruneau, H., & Fu, R. (2004). Prevalence and reporting of occupational illness by company size: Population trends and regulatory implications. *American Journal of Industrial Medicine*, *45*(4), 361–370. https://doi.org/10.1002/ajim.10354

National Academy of Sciences. (2018). *A Smarter National Surveillance System for occupational safety and health in the 21st century*. Washington, DC: National Academy of Press. https://doi.org/10.17226/24835

Oleinick, A., Gluck, J. v., & Guire, K. E. (1995). Establishment size and risk of occupational injury. *American Journal of Industrial Medicine*, *28*(1), 1–21. https://doi.org/10.1002/ajim.4700280102

OSHA. (2015). *OSHA safety and health program management guidelines*. U.S. Department of Labor-Occupational Safety and Health Administration. Retrieved from https://www.osha.gov/sites/default/files/SHPM_guidelines.pdf

OSHA. (2018). *Employer rights and responsibilities*. U.S. Department of Labor-Occupational Safety and Health Administration.

Pollack, E. S., & Keimig, D. G. (1987). *Counting injuries and illnesses in the workplace proposal for a better system*. Washington, D.C.: National Press Academy https://doi.org/10.17226/18911

Pransky, G., Snyder, T., Dembe, A., & Himmelstein, J. (1999). Under-reporting of work-related disorders in the workplace: A case study and review of the literature. *Ergonomics*, *42*(1), 171–182. https://doi.org/10.1080/001401399185874

Probst, Tahira M., Bettac, E. L., & Austin, C. (2019). Accident underreporting in the workplace. In *Increasing occupational health and safety in workplaces* (pp. 30–47). Cheltenham: Edward Elgar Publishing. https://doi.org/10.4337/9781788118095.00009

Probst, T. M., Brubaker, T. L., & Barsotti, A. (2008). Organizational injury rate underreporting: The moderating effect of organizational safety climate. *Journal of Applied Psychology*, *93*(5), 1147–1154. https://doi.org/10.1037/0021-9010.93.5.1147

Probst, T. M., & Estrada, A. X. (2010). Accident under-reporting among employees: Testing the moderating influence of psychological safety climate and supervisor enforcement of safety practices. *Accident Analysis and Prevention*, *42*(5), 1438–1444. https://doi.org/10.1016/j.aap.2009.06.027

Probst, T. M., & Graso, M. (2013). Pressure to produce = pressure to reduce accident reporting? *Accident Analysis and Prevention*, *59*, 580–587. https://doi.org/10.1016/j.aap.2013.07.020

Probst T.M. (2006). Job insecurity and accident underreporting. In *21st Annual conference of the society of industrial and organizational psychology, Dallas, TX.*

Public Health England Transition Team. (2012). *Public Health Surveillance: Towards a Public Health Surveillance Strategy for England*. PHE Transition Team 133-155. Retrieved from https://assets.publishing.service.gov.uk/government/uploads/system/uploads/attachment_data/file/213339/Towards-a-Public-Health-Surveillance-Strategy.pdf

Rantanen, J., Lehtinen, S., Valenti, A., & Iavicoli, S. (2017). *Occupational health services for all A global survey on OHS in selected countries of ICOH members*. Milan: International Commission on Occupational Health. Retrieved from http://www.icohweb.org/site/multimedia/pubblicazioni/ICOH global survey OHS for all.pdf

Rosenman, K. D., Kalush, A., Reilly, M. J., Gardiner, J. C., Reeves, M., & Luo, Z. (2006). How much work-related injury and illness is missed by the current national surveillance system? *Journal of Occupational and Environmental Medicine*, *48*(4), 357–365. https://doi.org/10.1097/01.jom.0000205864.81970.63

Silva, N. De, & Rathnayake, U. (2018). Under-reporting of construction accidents in Sri Lanka. *Journal of Engineering, Design and Technology*, *16*(6), 850–868. https://doi.org/10.1108/JEDT-07-2017-0069

Tedone, T. S. (2017). Counting injuries and illnesses in the workplace: An international review. *Monthly Labor Review*, (9), 1–24. https://doi.org/10.21916/mlr.2017.23

The Federal Republic of Nigeria Factories Act. (1990). Factories Act of 1990. *The Federal Republic of Nigeria. Factories Act*. https://doi.org/10.1002/j.1552-4604.1963.tb00067.x

Umeokafor, N. (2018). An investigation into public and private clients' attitudes, commitment and impact on construction health and safety in Nigeria. *Engineering, Construction and Architectural Management*, *25*(6), 798–815. https://doi.org/10.1108/ECAM-06-2016-0152

United Nations. (1992). Report of the United Nations conference on environment and development. United Nations, New York. https://doi.org/A/CONF.151/26/Rev.l (Vol. l)

Ursachi, G., Horodnic, I. A., & Zait, A. (2015). How reliable are measurement scales? External factors with indirect influence on reliability estimators. *Procedia Economics and Finance*, *20*(15), 679–686. https://doi.org/10.1016/s2212-5671(15)00123-9

Wai, A. L. S. (2007). *Critical causes of accident under reporting in Malaysia construction industry*. Malaysia: Universiti Teknologi Malaysia.

Weerd, M. de, Tierney, R., Duuren-Stuurman, B. van, & Bertranou, E. (2014). *Estimating the cost of accidents and ill-health at work: A review of methodologies*. Bilbao: European Agency for Safety and Health at Work. https://doi.org/10.2802/92605

Welch, L., Carre, F., & Ringen, K. (2007). Is the apparent decrease in injury and illness rates in construction the result of changes in reporting? *International Journal of Occupational and Environmental Health*, *13*(1), 39–45. https://doi.org/10.1179/oeh.2007.13.1.39

Workplace Safety and Health Council. (2018). *Improving workplace health management in Singapore*. Singapore: Workplace Safety and Health Council.

Wuellner, S. E., Adams, D. A., & Bonauto, D. K. (2016). Unreported workers' compensation claims to the BLS Survey of Occupational Injuries and Illnesses: Establishment factors. *American Journal of Industrial Medicine*, *59*(4), 274–289. https://doi.org/10.1002/ajim.22563

CHAPTER 21

GAS PERMEABILITY ASSOCIATED WITH CLEAT PATTERN IN A COAL BED OF LOW RANK COALS, SOUTH SUMATRA BASIN

Afikah Binti Rahim, Taslim Maulana, Ferian Anggara and Mohammed Hail Hakimi

ABSTRACT

Cleats are considered one of the significant permeability-related parameters in coalbed methane (CBM) growth. As critical parameters for CBM extraction, a complete characterisation of cleat distributions and orientation can provide a better tool to indirectly estimate porosity and permeability in coal reservoirs. This chapter presents the outcomes of the production of comprehensive research cleats within Miocene coal seams as part of CBM exploration and development. The majority of data (cross-section view measurement) were collected on mine's walls. Cleat data were gathered from 16 windows measurement locations with hundreds of cleats were measured from outcrops for several coal seams. Two primary cleat orientations; for face cleats, NNE-SSW and for butt cleats, ESE-WNW. The ratio of low permeability coals appears to have a smaller cleat aperture than high permeability coals. As critical parameters for CBM extraction, a complete characterisation of cleat distributions and orientation can provide a better tool to indirectly estimate porosity and permeability in coal reservoirs.

Keywords: Coal; permeability; enhance coalbed methane; South Sumatra Basin; cleat; subbituminous

Sustainability Management Strategies and Impact in Developing Countries
Community, Environment and Disaster Risk Management, Volume 26, 265–277

Published under exclusive licence by Emerald Publishing Limited
ISSN: 2040-7262/doi:10.1108/S2040-726220220000026021

1. INTRODUCTION

Indonesia's coal deposits, mainly in Sumatra and Kalimantan, typically have a low variety, from lignite to subbituminous. Recent research has confirmed that Indonesia has an estimated *in situ* reserve of coalbed methane (CBM) (Stevens & Hadiyanto, 2004) of more than 450 trillion cubic feet of gas (tcfg) of potentially CBM. Regional assessment indicates that the South Sumatera Basin comprises approximately 183 tcfg, which provides 54% of the estimated prospective resources of the total Indonesian CBM. In Indonesia, CBM is one of the possible types of unconventional energy. By referring to a preliminary assessment conducted by Advance Resource International Inc. (Stevens & Hadiyanto, 2004), Indonesia has 453 TCF of estimated prospective CBM resources within several basins. CBM is a coal seam reservoir formed from natural gas containing close to 100% methane (CH_4). At shallow depths, CBM is often produced and is often associated with large amounts of water produced. CBM is natural gas in a coal seam that is sourced and reserved (Fanchi & Christiansen, 2017; Sosrowidjojo, 2013; Stevens & Hadiyanto, 2004; Stevens, Sani, & Hardjosuwiryo, 2001).

Low-grade coals, such as coal formations in South Sumatra, were not considered as an acceptable candidate for CBM exploration and development in the past, as it was assumed that very low-grade (lignite-sub-bituminous) coals could not generate viable methane gas volumes. However, efficient development of CBM has been seen in similar low-grade coals in recent years, such as in the US Powder River Basin and has led the CBM industry worldwide to pursue these types of coals for commercial gas production. Low-rank coals in South Sumatran are suggested to have viable producing potential for CBM (Rahim, Surjono, & Amijaya, 2018). CBM from coal seams is known as an unconventional hydrocarbon. Indonesia thought that due to the declining supplies of conventional hydrocarbons, CBM would become one of the most significant energy contributions in the future.

As critical parameters for CBM extraction, a complete characterisation of cleat distributions and orientations can provide a better tool to indirectly estimate porosity and permeability in coal reservoirs. The sequences of low-ranking coals belonging to the Late Miocene Muara Enim Formation (Upper Palembang) in South Sumatra, Indonesia, are the domain of the work. This chapter describes the results of the analysis and permeability of cleats on selected coal samples and 16 windows located at three A1, A2 and B1 coal seams, measured at Tambang (Mine) Banko Barat, Tanjung Enim coalfield. The coalfield is owned by PT. Tambang Batubara Bukit Asam, Indonesia's state-owned coal-mining company.

As critical parameters for CBM extraction, a complete characterisation of cleat distributions and orientations can provide a better tool to indirectly estimate porosity and permeability in coal reservoirs. Indonesia thought that due to the declining supplies of conventional hydrocarbons, CBM would become one of the most significant energy contributions in the future. Cleats are considered one of the significant permeability-related parameters in CBM growth. As critical parameters for CBM extraction, a complete characterisation of cleat distributions and orientation can provide a better tool to indirectly estimate porosity and permeability in coal reservoirs.

The sequences of low-ranking coals belonging to the Late Miocene Muara Enim Formation (Upper Palembang) in South Sumatra, Indonesia, are the domain of the work. This chapter describes the findings of the study and permeability of cleats on selected coal samples and 16 windows located at three CS A1, A2 and B1 seams, measured at Tambang (Mine) Banko Barat, Tanjung Enim coalfield. The coalfield is owned by PT. Tambang Batubara Bukit Asam, Indonesia's state-owned coal-mining company.

2. GEOLOGY AND STRATIGRAPHY OF STUDY AREA

Study field at Muara Enim Members M2. Members M2 consists of looping claystone with sandy mudstone, and in the grab the seam Mangus (A), Suban (B), Petai (C) there are major coal seams. Samples taken from the study area of 16 undisturbed samples with information. A 3-channel sample of 3 seam from seams of coal, namely A1, A2, and B1. Five samples were taken on the roof and floor of A2 and B1, while on the roof (top) and on the floor (bottom) of A1.

3. METHODOLOGY

3.1. Scanline and Window Cleats Mapping

Field survey and field data collection, data sorting, statistical analysis and interpretation are the approaches used in this research. In the field survey and field data collection, fractures, butt and face cleats within the layer/bed are defined and the fracture characteristics (spacing, height, opening, and orientation) of each fracture and/or cleat are measured. In this analysis, there are two measurement methods used. The first approach is the method of scanning, where only the information that intersects the scanline has been calculated.

The calculated geometry is designed to be at least 3-m wide (parallel to the bedding plane) and the height depends on the thickness of the bed, so it is important to set the maximum height. The other approach is the method of sampling windows, where the geometry of the measured area is constructed to be a rectangle, usually with a dimension of 100 cm × 100 cm, but there are coalbeds that are only 25-cm thick, so the measured area is limited to a dimension of 0.25 m × 0.25 m. Many of the fractures and cleats in this region have been assessed.

For cross-section view, the scanline approach is widely used, while the windows technique (e.g. top of the coal seam) is used for plan view exposure. These conventions are used to define cleats: length is parallel to the surface of the cleat and parallel to the bedding; height is parallel to the surface of the cleat and perpendicular to the bedding; aperture is perpendicular to the surface of the fracture; spacing is the distance between two cleats and/or fractures at right angles to the surface of the cleat.

3.2. Coal Sampling

At the time of taking the field data is also sampling. There are three locations of samples were taken for proximate analysis. These samples were taken at each coal seam. This sampling mechanism itself first coal samples are taken evenly from the base up to the top, and then also taken samples at 20 cm below the base and 20 cm above the top of a coal seam.

3.3. Proximate Analysis

The analysis was conducted to determine the composition of moisture content, ash content, volatile matter content, and the carbon content are moored. This analysis can then be used to determine the rank of the coal. British Standard used for analysis on coal is a BS 1016 (Speight, 2005). In more detail for analysis of substances used on volatile matter BS 1016-1, for the analysis of substances used on volatile matter BS 1016-104.3, for analysis using BS 1016-104.4 ash content, for the analysis of calories using BS 1016-105 (Speight, 2005).

3.4. Calorific Value

The tool used for coal calorific value analysis is the calorimeter and bomb head. The working principle for the analysis of calorific value is to burn coal and calculate the amount of energy produced during coal combustion. Unlike the proximate analysis, the analysis of calorific value uses a computer system to calculate the calories produced. The workings of this calorie analysis by entering the coal samples which have been measuring 0.212 mm into bomb head with additional threads dangling above the sample, this thread serves to trigger the burning of coal. Bomb head input into the calorimeter and calorimeter in the process will occur automatically with oxygen for combustion, after burning is completed, caloric value will appear on the computer device.

4. RESULTS AND DISCUSSION

4.1. Coal Rank and Proximate Analysis

The determination of coal rank was done based on the value of moisture, the content of volatile matter and calorific values. The value of volatile matter obtained from laboratory analysis was found to contain air-dried basis (adb), while Teichmüller (1987) classification used dry ash free (daf) basis, where conversion needed to be done. The coal rank analysis based on those three parameters will be further explained in the following sections.

4.2. Moisture Content

Moisture content to determine the coal rank based on the Teichmüller (1987) classification is called bed moisture. Bed moisture is the moisture content of coal that still remained after the surface moisture has been lost (Speight, 2005). The term bed moisture in this proximate analysis research is also called as inherent moisture.

Table 21.1 shows the analysis for the determination of coal rank for every seam. Based on the table, coal ranks in research sites are Subbituminous A [5] (See Table 21.1). This is due to the value of inherent moisture, which is around 10–20%.

4.3. Calorific Value

Coal rank is determined based on the calorific values using adb. Calorific values are included in the Teichmüller (1987) classification. Table 21.1 shows the determination of coal rank for every seam based on the calorific values. Based on the calorific values, coal rank is discovered to be Subbituminous B. Further parameter used for the determination of coal rank needed to undergo basis conversion, the following equation is the method used for basis conversion. The first thing needed to be done in basis conversion is to calculate the conversion factor at every seam. The conversion from adb to daf is done based on the following equation:

$$\frac{100}{100-(\text{Mad}+\text{Aad})}$$

where,

Mad = moisture content in adb
Aad = ash content in adb

After conversion factor is known, volatile matter in adb is multiplied with the conversion factor; then the value of volatile matter content and fixed carbon content in daf basis is obtained.

4.4. Volatile Matter Content

Determination of coal rank is based on the value of volatile matter content using daf basis. The values of volatile matter content are included in the Teichmüller (1987) classification. Table 21.1 shows the determination of coal rank at every seam based on the value of volatile matter content. Based on Table 21.1, coal

Table 21.1. Coal Rank Analysis Based on the Inherent Moisture.

Layer	IM [a] % (adb)	Coal Rank (Taylor et al., 1998	GCV(Cal/gr)[a] (adb)	(ar)	Coal Rank (Taylor et al., 1998)	Coal Rank (Taylor et al., 1998)
A1middle	13.1	Subbituminous A	5,866.5	4,832	Subbituminous B	Subbituminous B
A2 top	13.85		5,809.5	4,768		Subbituminous B
A2 middle	13.3		5,777	4,773		Subbituminous C
A2 bottom	14.45		5,742.5	4,859.5		Subbituminous B
B1 top	11.35		6,081	5,072.5		Subbituminous C
B1 bottom	11.4		5,978.5	4,997.5		Subbituminous B

Notes: [a]IM = inherent moisture; Coal rank determination based on the inherent moisture.

ranks at several seams are varied. For example, the seams at A1, A2 middle, and B1 have Subbituminous B rank, while the seams at A2 top and A2 bottom have Subbituminous C rank. Based on the three parameters used for the determination of coal rank, the coal ranks in the research sites are discovered to be Subbituminous B. In conclusion, volatile matter, three layers representing group from Subbituminous B and C, and coal rank based on calorific value is Subbituminous B.

4.5. The Relationship Between Cleat Attribute and Permeability

The relationship between cleat attribute and permeability will be shown in graph form. Cleat attributes which will be compared with permeabilities are intensity, density, aperture, cleat length, and cleat spacing. The permeabilities which will be compared with the cleat attributes are permeabilities that used Robertson and Christiansen's (2006) formula which have been converted to Darcy unit. Robertson and Christiansen's (2006) formula were compared with the cleat attributes because this formula is a formula specifically used for calculating cleats on coal, while Lucia's (1983) formula is a formula fundamentally used in calculating permeability for carbonated rocks. The research for Lucia's (1983) formula is carried out by developing it into cubes and matchsticks. Based on Lucia's three formulas (carbonate, cubes, and matchsticks), carbonate has the largest value and matchsticks will produce the smallest value of permeability. The carbonate in Lucia's (1983) formula has a permeability value that is almost the same as the value in Robertson and Christiansen's (2006) formula.

Fig. 21.1(a) shows a graphic of the relationship between density and permeability. Based on Fig. 21.1(b), the relationship between density and permeability is directly proportional and has a slope instead of a straight line, the higher the density of the cleat, the larger the permeability value of the coal. Fig. 21.1(c) shows a graphic of the relationship between average length of cleat and coal permeability. Based on the graphic in Fig. 21.1(c), the relationship between the average length of cleat is found to be slanted and has a slope instead of a straight line when compared with the permeability. The higher the density of cleat, the larger the permeability value of the coal.

Aperture and cleat spacing is the cleat attribute that has a significant relationship with permeability value. Fig. 21.1(a)–(e) shows the graphic of a relationship between the average value of cleat aperture and the permeability based on the cleat calculation. The graphics in Fig. 21.1(a)–(e) show that the average cleat aperture is directly proportional to the permeability. Hence, the bigger the cleat aperture on the coal, the larger the permeability value of the coal.

Based on the relationship from five cleat attributes with the permeability, the density, cleat aperture and cleat length will be directly proportional with the permeability values, which means the higher the value of density, cleat aperture and cleat length, the larger the value of permeability. The relationship between cleat spacing and permeability will be inversely proportional, which means the larger the value of cleat spacing, the smaller the value of permeability.

Length, density, cleat aperture, and cleat intensity based on the research done by Apriyani et al. (2014) show a relationship that is directly proportional to the

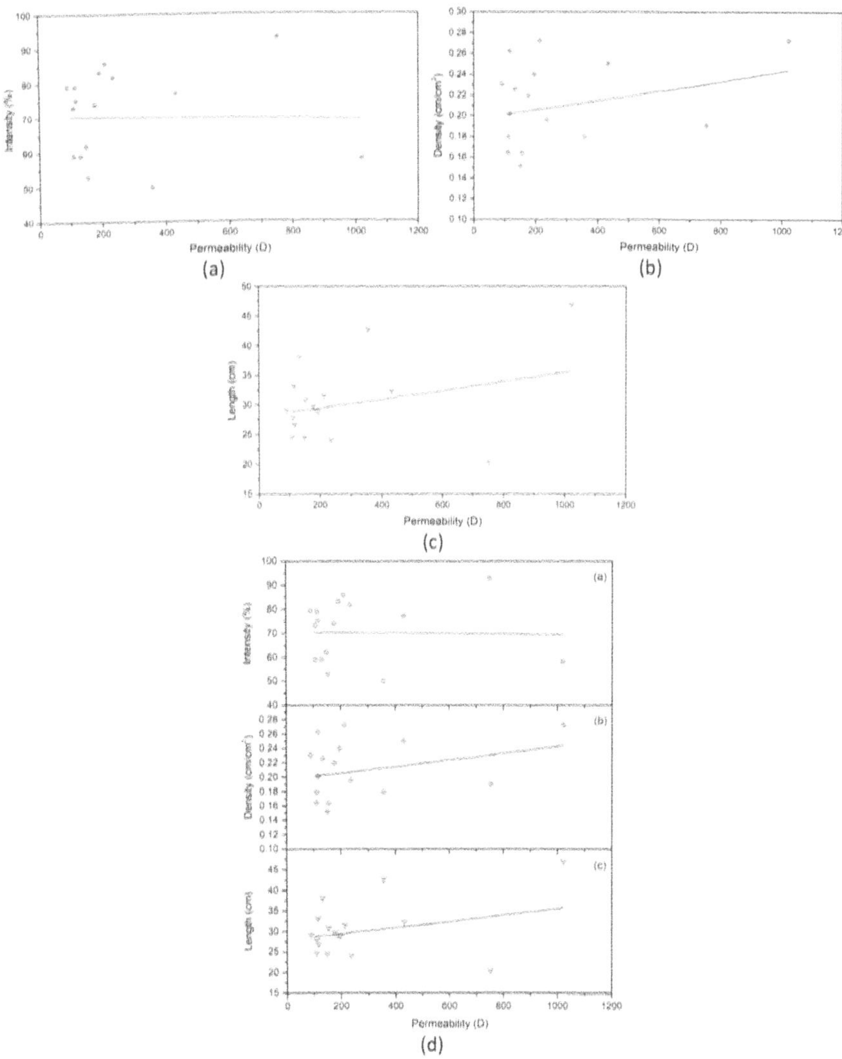

Fig. 21.1. Graphics Showing the Relationship between the Intensity (a), Average Density (b) and Average Length (c) with the Permeability. Graphic (d) Is the Combined Graphic of Intensity, Average Density and Average Length, (e) Relationship between Cleat Aperture and Permeability and (f) Relationship between the Cleat Spacing and the Permeability.

permeability, while cleat spacing has an inversely proportional relationship with permeability. In addition, the research done by Apriyani et al. (2014) is suitable with the research done by this researcher and the only difference is in the intensity, where the research done by the researcher shows a constant distribution.

The result from the research done by Apriyani et al. (2014) has an average value of cleat aperture around 0.015–0.053 cm with permeability value between

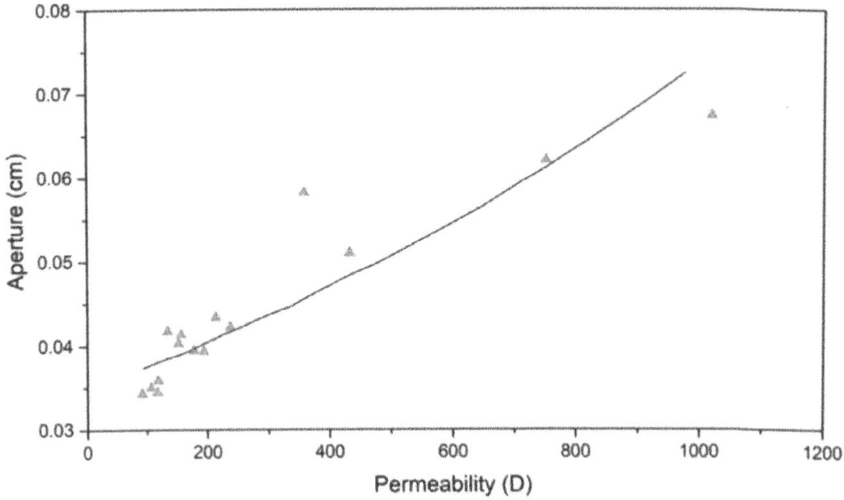

(e)

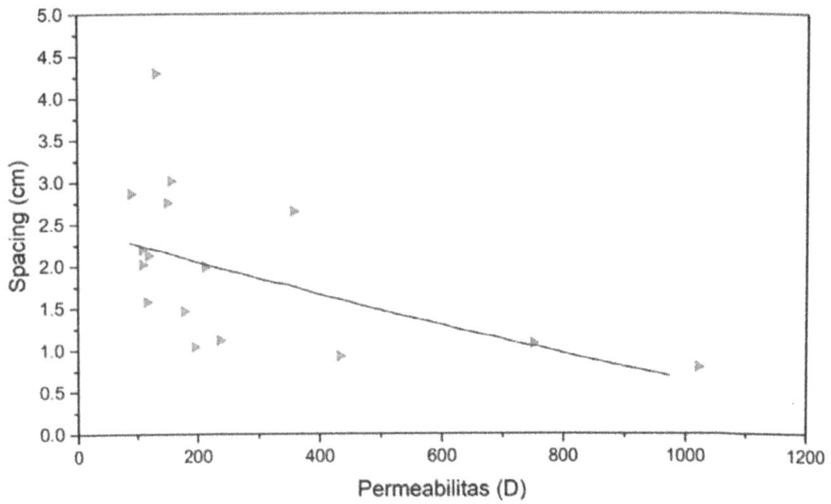

(f)

Fig. 21.1. (Continued)

0.062 and 6.67 D (cubes), while on this research the average value of cleat aperture is between 0.034 and 0.067 cm with permeability value around 2.06–45.81 D (cubes). Based on the comparison done on the value of permeability in this research and the research done by Apriyani et al. (2014), it can be concluded that the value of cleat aperture and the permeability on this research is larger than the value obtained in the research done by Apriyani et al. (2014) at Kutai Basin.

4.6. Comparison Between the Value of Cleat Permeability and Permeability in Drilling Reservoir

According to Sosrowidjojo (2006), it is known that coal permeability in drilling reservoir is around 2.60–9.66 mD. In relation to that, the permeability value based on the cleat measurement is around 1.55–1021 D. The data shown by Sosrowidjojo (2006) are based on the data obtained from five drilling reservoirs where samples were taken from the depth of 415.8–1,620.9 m. Permeability value shows an increase that reached 100,000 times more than the *in situ* permeability value.

Permeability data obtained based on cleat measurements and drilling reservoirs has a fairly wide range of results. This fairly wide range of results was due to the coal condition during measurement. The coal that had undergone cleat measurement was exposed on the surface with overburden pressure condition, which is nearly zero, and this causes the cleat aperture to experience dilation.

Permeability value from drilling resource has a value that is much smaller compared to the permeability based on the cleat measurements. This is because in the drilling reservoir, the coal seam which was at the shallowest part was at a depth of 451.8 m. The shallowest depth shows that there is an overburden and gives pressure as thick as 451.8 m above the coal layer, which caused the cleat aperture on the coal to have much smaller width compared to the condition on the surface.

The cause for the increase of coal permeability value other than the overburden factor is the matrix shrinkage of coal. The measured coal condition during this research is the coal that had been exposed at a period of time that is long enough. The exposed coal will experience the loss of moisture. The loss of moisture from this coal matrix will cause coal to shrink and the coal aperture will experience dilation that is in line with the shrinkage of the coal. This aperture dilation will cause the coal permeability to increase compared to the coal which has not been exposed.

This coal shrinking phenomenon caused the permeability in A2 and A1 seams to be much larger that B1 (Table 21.1), even though B1 seam has a rank that is much higher. B1 seam is the coal layer that had just undergone dredging when the cleat measurements were taken. A2 seam has permeability value that is much higher compared to A1 seam because the rank for A2 seam is much better.

The research done by Weniger et al. (2016) shows the comparison of permeability value based on the calculation of cleat system and the calculation of in-situ permeability. Based on the research, it can be observed that the cleat permeability value has a median of $3.7 \times 10–11$ m^2, while in-situ permeability has a value of $5.8 \times 10–16$ m^2, the range between these two permeability values are around 100,000 times. There is conformity between the increase of permeability values in the research done by Weniger et al. (2016) and the research done by the researcher.

Permeability value based on cleat measurement needs to undergo conversion on the condition that is below the surface; then equalisation can be carried out on the permeability value. Fig. 21.1 shows the comparison of permeability values in the research done by the researcher and the one carried out by Weniger et al. (2016) and the most productive CBM reservoir in USA.

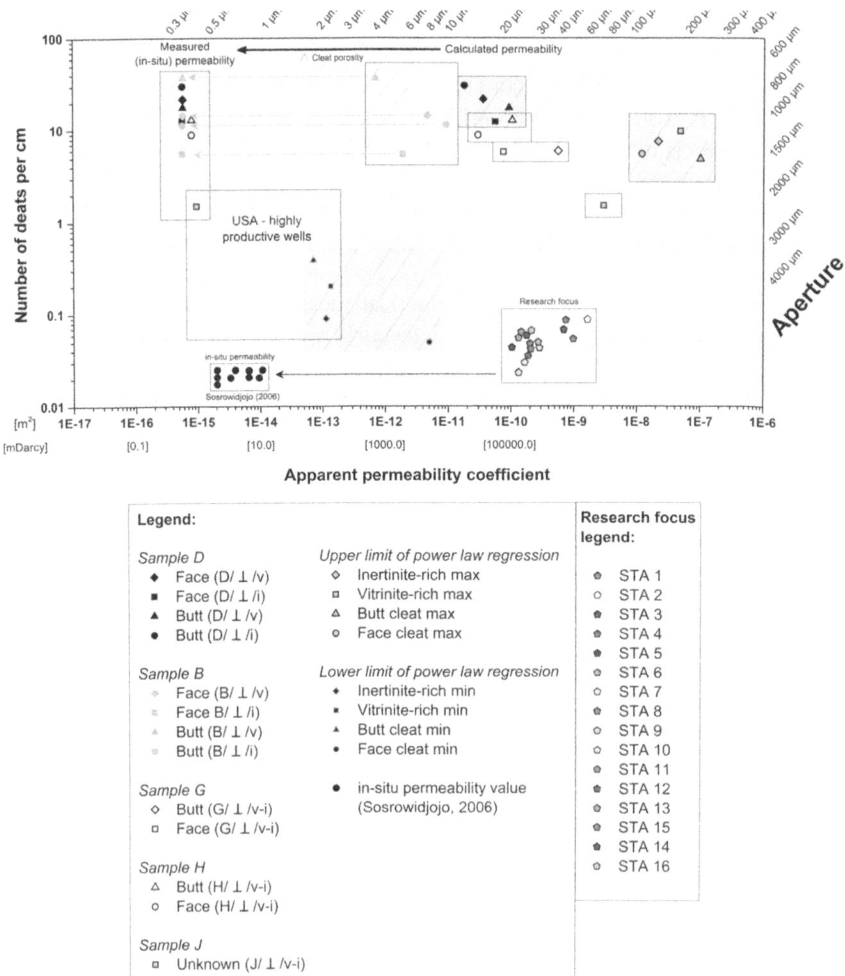

Fig. 21.2. Comparison of Permeability Values in the Research Done by the Researcher and Weniger et al. (2016), with Modifications.

Fig. 21.2 shows that the large value of permeability in this research is much larger compared to Weniger, Kalkreuth, Busch, and Krooss (2010). The *in situ* permeability values in the research conducted by Weniger et al. (2010) show that the values are much smaller compared to the ones in Cekungan Sumatera Selatan, while the in-situ permeability values in Weniger et al. (2016) is around 1 mD, while the ones in Cekungan Sumatera Selatan based on Sosrowidjojo (2013) are around 2–9 mD. In relation to that, the researcher's research has a larger permeability value when compared to the permeability in the most productive CBM reservoir in USA, which is around 100–10,000 times larger.

Table 21.2. Relationship Between the Cleats Attribute and the Permeability.

No	STA	Seam	Average Spacing	Average Aperture	Robertson and Christiansen (cm^2)	Robertson and Christiansen (Darcy)	Lucia (carbonat) (Darcy)	Lucia (cubes) (Darcy)	Lucia (match sticks) (Darcy)
1	Cleat 12	A1	3.65455	0.04032	1.495E-06	149.496265	151.4098	4.02675	3.02007
2	cleat 11	A1	2.94286	0.03443	1.156E-06	115.577957	117.0574	2.65823	1.99368
3	cleat7	A1	3.80851	0.04132	1.544E-06	154.371924	156.3479	4.26101	3.19576
4	cleat 4	A1	2.65	0.06204	7.51E-06	751.01995	760.633	31.1258	23.3444
5	cleat 8	A1	2.62361	0.0394	1.942E-06	194.23535	196.7216	5.11181	3.83385
6	cleat 6	A2	3.19737	0.04337	2.126E-06	212.645998	215.3679	6.1609	4.62067
7	cleat 5	A2	3.72388	0.0343	9.033E-07	90.3336597	91.48993	2.06999	1.55249
8	cleat 2	A2	2.48367	0.06724	1.02E-05	1020.07968	1033.137	45.8192	34.3644
9	cleat 1	A2	3.5925	0.0536	3.572E-06	357.204027	361.7762	12.7896	9.59221
10	cleat 3	A2	2.565	0.05104	4.32E-06	431.953364	437.4824	14.727	11.0453
11	cleat 16	A2	3.27692	0.03587	1.173E-06	117.334454	118.8363	2.81121	2.10841
12	cleat 15	A2	2.88462	0.03946	1.775E-06	177.494228	179.7662	4.67856	3.50892
13	cleat 14	B1	3.20769	0.03479	1.094E-06	109.435599	110.8364	2.54358	1.90769
14	cleat 13	B1	3.32692	0.03525	1.098E-06	109.751374	111.1562	2.58463	1.93847
15	cleat 10	B1	4.57692	0.04169	1.32E-06	131.975838	133.6651	3.67582	2.75686
16	cleat 9	B1	2.67333	0.04232	2.362E-06	236.217739	239.2413	6.67736	5.00802

4.7. Cleats Orientation

- Orientation cleat in the study area ranged northeast–southwest.

4.8. Length, Density, Aperture, and Spacing

- The average length ranges cleat 23.89–46.87 cm.
- The average aperture of the research area from 0.0343 to 0.067 cm.
- The average spacing ranging from 2.48 to 4.57 cm.
- The average density of cleats on research areas ranging from 0.163 to 0.272 cm/cm^2.
- The intensity of the cleat in the study area ranges from 53 to 93 cleat.

4.9. Permeability

The value of permeability among the sites based on a Robertson and Christiansen (2006) formula ranged from 90.33 to 1,020 Darcy. Permeability values using the formula Lucia (1983) cubes ranged from 2.07 to 45.82 Darcy (Table 21.2).

5. CONCLUSION

It is shown that the relationship between permeability in the highly cleated rock mass in the study area is good (1.55–1,020 D).

ACKNOWLEDGEMENTS

This work was supported by the Fundamental Research Grant Scheme (FRGS) awarded by the Ministry of Education of Malaysia entitle 'Enhanced Coalbed Methane Recovery Processes by Coupling Fluid Flow of Mukah-Balingian Coal Deposits' with the referral no. R.J130000.7851.5F371. This work was also supported by the Universiti Teknologi Malaysia Encouragement Research Grant (UTMER) awarded by Universiti Teknologi Malaysia entitle 'Diagnosis of Alkali-Aggregate Reaction – Polarizing Microscopy and SEMEDS Analysis' with the referral no. Q.J130000.3851.19J79.

REFERENCES

Apriyani, N., Suharmono, Momen, M., Djaelani, S., Sodli, A., Satria, A., & Murtani A. S. (2014). Integrated cleat analysis and coal quality on CBM exploration at Sangatta II PSC, Kutai Basin, Indonesia. *AAPG international conference & exhibition*, 14–17 September 2014, Istanbul, Turkey.

Fanchi, J. R., & Christiansen, R. L. (2017). *Introduction to petroleum engineering*. Hoboken, NJ: John Wiley & Sons, Inc.

Lucia, F. J. (1983). Petrophysical parameters estimated from visual description of carbonate rocks: A field classification of carbonate pore space. *Journal of Petroleum Technology*, *35*, 629–637.

Rahim, A., Surjono, S. S., & Amijaya, D. H. (2018). CO_2 adsorption the numerical simulations and the controlling factors to low rank coal. *IOP Conference Series: Earth and Environmental Science*, *212*, 012016.

Robertson, E.P., & Christiansen, R.L. (2006). A permeability model for coal and other fractured, sorptive-elastic media. Working Paper SPE 104380.

Sosrowidjojo, I. B. (2006). Coalbed methane potential in the South Palembang Basin. In *Proceedings of the international geosciences conference and exhibition, IPA, 33th annual convention*. Jakarta: CD publication.

Sosrowidjojo, I. B. (2013). Coal geochemistry of the unconventional Muaraenim Coalbed Reservoir, South Sumatera Basin: A case study from the Rambutan field. *Indonesian Mining Journal*, *16*(2), 71–81.

Speight, J. G. (2005). *Handbook of coal analysis*. Hoboken, NJ: John Wiley and Sons, Inc.

Stevens, S. H., & Hadiyanto, (2004). Indonesia: Coalbed methane indicators and basin evaluation. SPE 88630. SPE Asia Pacific oil and gas conference, Perth, Australia, 8 p.

Stevens, S. H., Sani, K., & Hardjosuwiryo, S. (2001). Indonesia's 337 Tcf CBM resource a low-cost alternative to gas, *LNG. Oil & Gas Journal*, *99*(43), 40–45.

Taylor, G. H., Teichmüller, M., Davis, A., Diessel, C. F. K., Littke, R., & Robert P. (1998). *Organic Petrology*.

Teichmüller, M. (1987). Recent advantages in coalification studies and their application to geology. In A. C. Scott (Ed.), *Coal and coal-bearing strata: Recent advantages (Geological Society Special Publication* 32, pp. 127–169).

Weniger P., KalkreuthW., BuschA., & Krooss B. M. (2010). High-pressure methane and carbon dioxide sorption on coal and shale samples from the Paraná Basin, *Brazil. International Journal of Coal Geology*, *84*, 190–205.

Weniger S., Weniger P., & Littke R. (2016). Characterizing coal cleats from optical measurements for CBM evaluation. *Int. J. Coal Geol.*,176–192.

CHAPTER 22

EVALUATION OF STRENGTH AND DEFORMABILITY OF JOINTED OF METASEDIMENTARY ROCK AT NATM-1, KARAK, PAHANG

Afikah Binti Rahim, Hareyani Zabidi and Najib

ABSTRACT

The correlations between mechanical behaviour, tensile strength, and rock parameters of metasedimentary rock samples in Karak, Pahang's New Austrian Tunnelling Method (NATM) were statistically evaluated from the rock mechanic laboratory works at the selected sections around 2,000 m of the tunnel (named as NATM-1). According to a statistical analysis, lithotypes, geological structures, and region geology have a significant impact on the mechanical behaviour of the metasedimentary rock. In the Brazilian test, the fracture behaviour of the disc specimens was highly related to the reliability and precision of the experimental data by validations of methods. In this work, the impact of different loading methods and rock lithotypes on the failure mechanism of Brazilian discs was examined utilising five different metasedimentary rock types and three different loading methods. During the loading operation, the strain and displacement fields of the specimens were recorded and evaluated using a computerised strain gauge system. The rock types, according to experimental data, have a significant impact on the peak load and deformation properties of Brazilian discs. With the method below, tensile strength point of a disc specimen is clearly regulated by the material stiffness and tensile–compression ratio. Seismic occurrences have had a substantial impact on changing

Sustainability Management Strategies and Impact in Developing Countries
Community, Environment and Disaster Risk Management, Volume 26, 279–295

Published under exclusive licence by Emerald Publishing Limited
ISSN: 2040-7262/doi:10.1108/S2040-726220220000026022

the rock and exerting forces that may affect its mechanical characteristics as well as its vulnerability to weathering effects or discontinuities. As a result, the goal of this study is to look into the connection between rock mechanics and metasedimentary rock stress analysis in NATM-1, Karak, Pahang.

Keywords: Tensile strength; rock mechanics; NATM; Pahang-Selangor raw water transfer; metasedimentary rock; tunnel geology

1. INTRODUCTION

Rock is a brittle material that can be used in a variety of geological formations and is used in geotechnical applications such as tunnelling, mining, and slope engineering (Howarth, 1987; Zabidi, Rahim, & Trisugiwo, 2019). Numerous laboratory experiments observed the significant part in the failure process of rocks to the procedures introduced (Hajiabdolmajid, Kaiser, & Martin, 2002; Kahraman, 2001; Lim & Martin, 2006; Mustaffa Kamal Shuib, 2000). The tensile strength is often substantially lower than the compressive strength. As a result, understanding the tensile mechanical properties of rock, particularly its tensile strength, is crucial. In general, either direct or indirect experimental procedures are employed to determine the tensile strength of a rock.

2. RESEARCH PROBLEM

In the previous work established by Akazawa (1943) and Carneiro (1943), a novel method to determine the tensile strength of concrete has been developed. Many researchers have conducted theoretical and experimental research on the Brazilian test's validity, which is intimately related to the dependability and correctness of the experimental outcomes. Commonly discussed methods as shown in Fig. 22.1 is typical Brazilian test with three loading configurations. They are (a) flat loading platens (Type I), (b) flat loading platens with two small diameter steel bars (Type II) – Chinese standard, and (c) the official International Society for Rock Mechanics (ISRM) standard method (Type III), which recommends that two steel loading

According to the planar elasticity theory and the Griffith criterion, the compressive diametral line originates in the middle of the disc and then propagates along the compressive diametral line. The location of fracture initiation was discovered to be largely away from the disc core. On the contrary, based on experimental and numerical rock investigations, some work figured out that the tensile failure of the Brazilian disc occurs in the middle (interior) of the disc and subsequently propagates to the top and bottom surfaces. The difference between the two phenomena could be attributed to inconsistencies in experimental or numerical study circumstances.

Standard measurement tools comprising of strain gauges, linear variable differential transformers (LVDTs), and extensometers, can be employed to discover

Figure 1(a): The Brazilian Tensile strength machine

(b)

Fig. 22.1. (a) Image of a Sample with the Image Analyser and (b) Laboratory Setting of Brazilian Tensile Test.

possible crack start areas in the experiment and to investigate the start of the failure as well as the strength values. These tools, on the other hand, are incapable of providing precise information regarding the specimen's fracture activity. Furthermore, the strain measurements made by these sensors are highly localised and are influenced by a range of parameters such as temperature, adhesives, and so on. This digital image is a non-destructive approach that helps to seek the failure mechanism and propagation of rock specimens as also to record the experiment in real time.

In addition, five distinct metasedimentary rocks with various texture indices were studied. Finally, using digitised image analysis, the effect of rock and texture on indirect tensile strength and crack patterns (including crack initiation and propagation) was examined in Brazilian disc experiments.

2.1. Pahang-Selangor Raw Water Transfer (PSRWT) Project

The Malaysian government has suggested a proposal, the Pahang-Selangor Raw Water Transfer (PSRWT) tunnel, to meet the water demands in the nation's commercial and industrial development centres. The transfer tunnel will be 44.6-km long and will cross the igneous rocks Titiwangsa Main Range granite batholith, some Semantan Formation and Jelebu Schist Formation, and metasedimentary rocks of the Karak Formation (Fig. 22.1). The contact zone between the Karak Formation and the Titiwangsa Main Range granite is located west of the Bentong-Raub suture, approximately 3.50 km from the inlet. The tunnel excavation is planned to be built in two stages: the tunnel will be excavated using a Tunnel Boring Machine (TBM) for 35 km, and the upper and lower ends will be excavated using the traditional New Austria Tunnelling Method (NATM) for roughly 10 km. The entire project is built with three TBM cutting faces and four NATM approaches.

As part of the PSRWT project, 16 samples of Karak metasedimentary rock were collected at NATM-1. From the inlet tunnel portal to chainage 3.82 km, the tunnel will pass through Karak Formation rocks with a metamorphism contact zone 2.4 km wide.

According to a study on geological inquiry and construction material investigation for PSRWT, from the outside edge in, there is a progressive shift from spotted slate to micaceous phyllite and schist to hornfels at the granite contact. Away from the contact line, the rocks are predominantly agrellites, with interbeds of conglomerate, chert, quartzite, and sub-greywacke, as well as quartz mica schist, intra-formational breccias, and quartz hornfels (Mustaffa Kamal Shuib, 2000). The Karak Formation metasedimentary rocks are located in the Sg. Telemong valley and trend in the same direction as the Main Range Granite batholiths (NW-SE) (Zabidi et al., 2019). From the inlet portal to chainage 3.82 km, the tunnel will cut through rocks of the Karak Formation. Due to the folded nature of the Karak Formation rocks, dips vary over a short distance.

2.2. Metasedimentary Rock Samples of NATM-1 (Karak, Pahang) Aligned to

The region rock units comprise of meta-sediments (calc schist and brecciated schist) from metasedimentary rock between the Karak Formation and the Main Range Granite. Carbonate pelagic strata and mafic crystalline rocks underwent high-pressure low-temperature metamorphism during the early stages of alpine orogenesis. Schists and serpentinite have a foliated texture. The geological map shows that the attitude of rock units in the tunnel is more or less consistent, ranging from N220–2701E/35–451 (dip direction/dip).

A 20-m-thick shear zone is encountered inside the tube. It's composed of massive blocks of brecciated schist embedded in a sheared matrix of chlorite

Table 22.1. The Curve Developed and the Physico-Mechanical Characteristics of the Tested Rock After Being Subjected to Tensile Tension.

No.	Sample No. and Rock Type	Stress versus strain curve graph and condition of rock after tensile strength test		Analysis of rock properties
1.	**SK1 Slate (SL)**	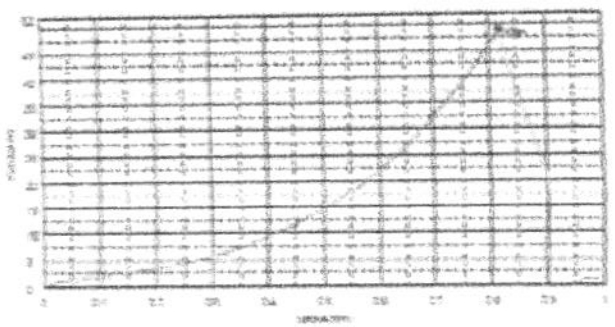		• Slatey cleavage with fine grain • Failure in two pieces due to fragmentation • Tensile strength: 10.66 kN/ m^2. • Brittleness, low stiffness, and low strength.
2	**SK2 Slate (SL)**	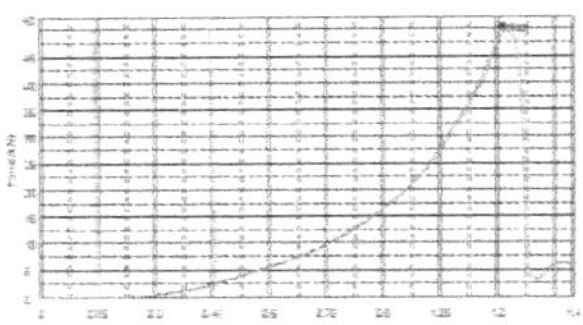		• Slatey cleavage with fine grain • Failure in two pieces due to fragmentation • The tensile strength is 10.97 kN/ m^2. • Brittleness, low stiffness, and low strength.
3	**SK3 Gneiss (G)**	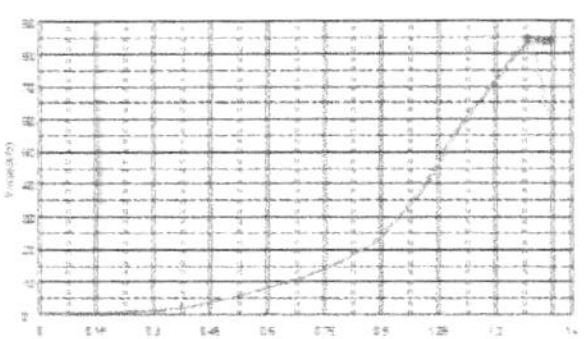		• Grain size ranges from medium to coarse. • Bending of gneissic • Failure in two pieces due to fragmentation • The tensile strength is 18.40 kN/ m^2. • Medium stiffness, strength, and brittleness.
4	**SK4 Gneiss (G)**	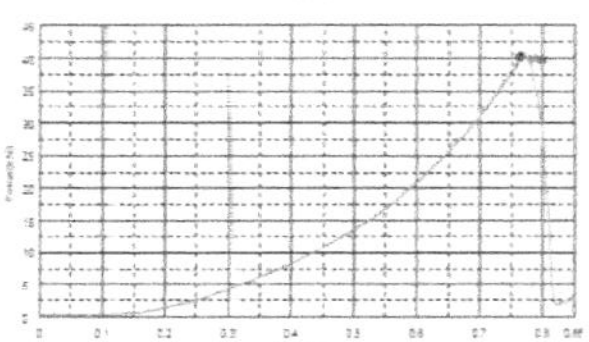	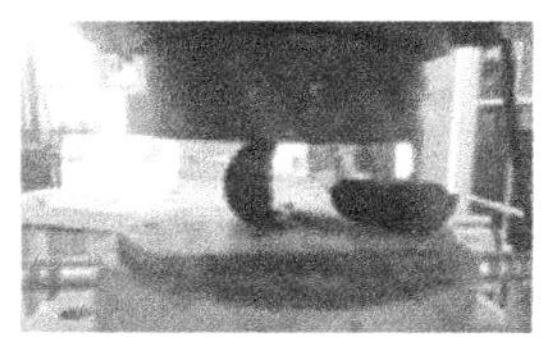	• Gneissic bending foliation with medium to coarse grain size • Symmetry and clean failure in two sections • Tensile strength: 8.78 kN/m^2. • Brittleness, low stiffness, and low strength.

Table 22.1. (*Continued*)

No.	Sample No. and Rock Type	Stress versus strain curve graph and condition of rock after tensile strength test		Analysis of rock properties
5	**SK5 Brecciated Schist (BS)**	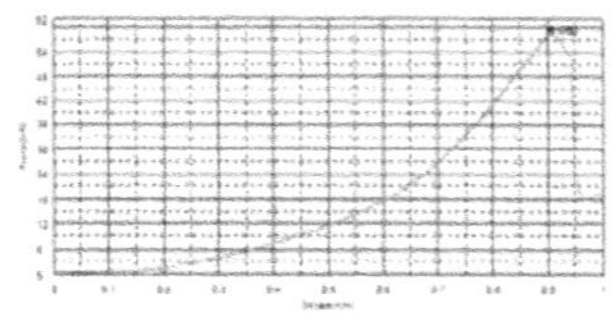		• Schistosity of fine-grained rock • In two sections, there is symmetry and clean failure. • The tensile strength of the material is 12.97 kN/ m^2. • Brittleness, stiffness, and weakness .
6	**SK6 Breccia (B)**	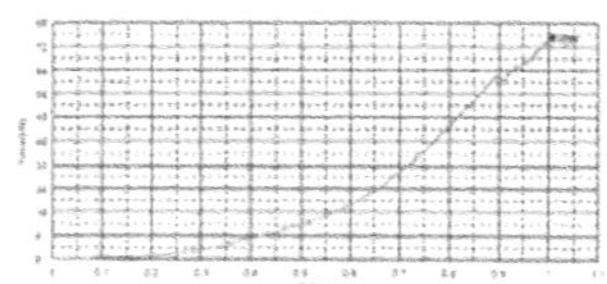		• Clasts in fine-grained rock • Foliation of schistosity • There was a clean failure in two sections, but there was no symmetry. • The tensile strength is 16.41 kN/ m^2. • Brittleness, low stiffness, and low strength.
7	**SK7 Brecciated Schist (BS)**	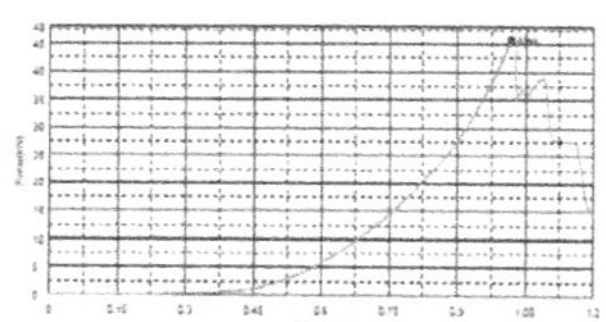		• Schistosity clasts in fine-grained rock foliation • In two sections, there is symmetry and clean failure. • 9.99 kN/ m^2 tensile strength • Brittleness, stiffness, and weakness
8	**SK8 Brecciated Schist (BS)**	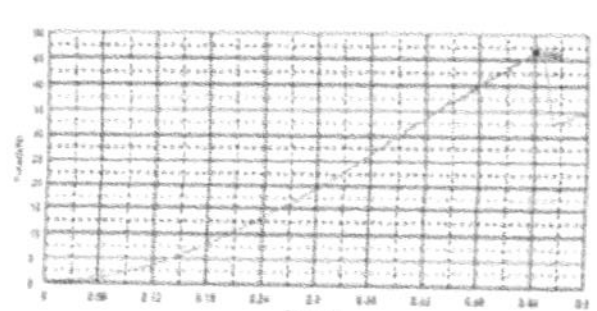		• Schistosity clasts in fine-grained rock foliation • Failure of a disc in three sections • 10.14 kN/ m^2 is the tensile strength. • Stiffness in the medium to high range, strength in the medium to high range, and brittleness in the medium to high range.

9	**SK9 Schist (S)**	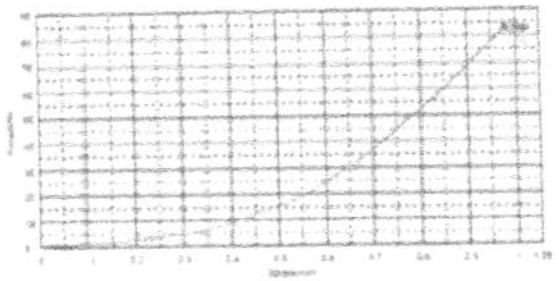		• foliation with schistosity and fine granularity • In two sections, there is symmetry and clean failure. • The tensile strength of the material is 18.14 kN/m². • Stiffness, strength, and brittleness are all medium .
10	**SK10 Brecciated Schist (BS)**	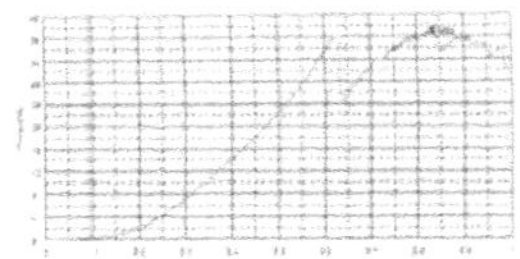		• Clasts in fine-grained rock • foliation of schistosity • Failure in fragments, as in pieces, and symmetry • Tensile strength: 8.09 kN/m². • Medium stiffness, strength, and brittleness
11	**SK11 Brecciated Schist (BS)**	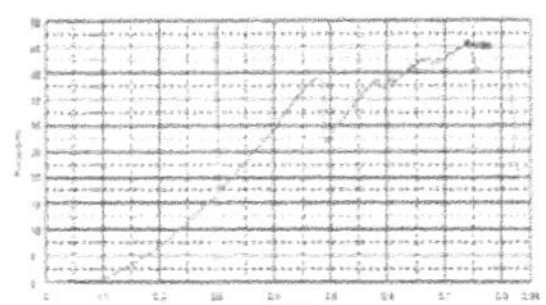		• Clasts in fine-grained rock • foliation of schistosity • There was a clean failure in two sections, but there was no symmetry. • Tensile strength: 9.94 kN/m². • Medium stiffness, strength, and brittleness.
12	**SK12 Schist (S)**	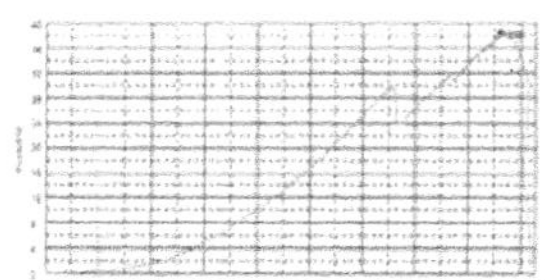		• Schistosity with fine grainedness • Disc failure in three pieces • Tensile strength: 8.38 kN/m² • Brittleness, low stiffness, and low strength
13	**SK13 Schist (S)**	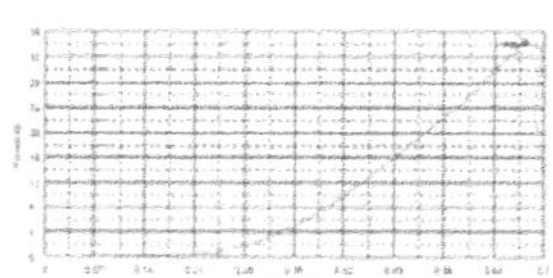		• Schistosity foliation with fine-grained schistosity • Symmetry and clean failure in two sections • Tensile strength: 7.47 kN/m². • Brittleness, low stiffness, and low strength

Table 22.1. (*Continued*)

No.	Sample No. and Rock Type	Stress versus strain curve graph and condition of rock after tensile strength test	Analysis of rock properties
14	**SK14 Brecciated Schist (BS)**	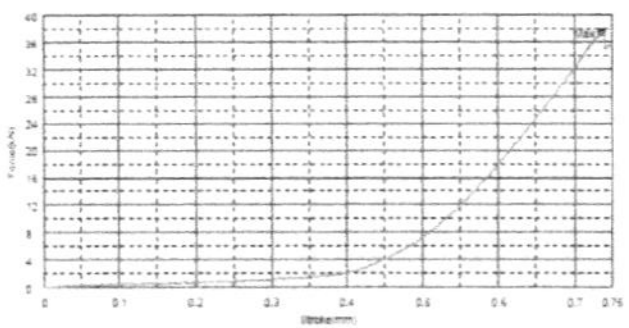 	• Schistosity foliation with fine granularity • There is no symmetry in a clean failure in two pieces • Tensile strength: 8.19 kN/m^2 • Brittleness, low stiffness, and low strength
15	**SK15 Brecciated Schist (BS)**	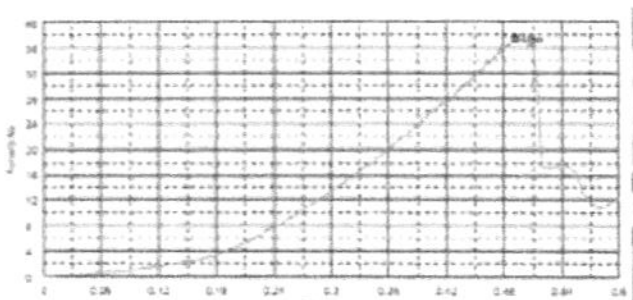 	• Schistosity foliation with fine granularity • Symmetry and clean failure in two sections • Tensile strength: 8.19 kN/m^2 • Brittleness, low stiffness, and low strength
16	**SK16 Schist (S)**	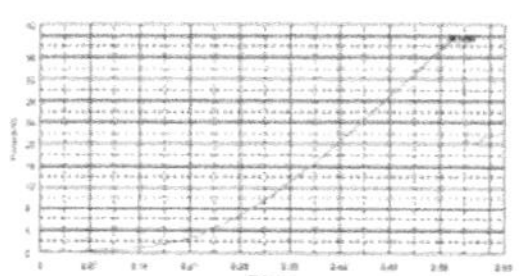 	• Exceptionally fine-grained foliation of schistosity • Symmetry and clean failure in two sections • Tensile strength: 8.61 kN/m^2 • Brittleness, low stiffness, and low strength

Note: [a]SK = Sample of Karak., Pahang.

schists with cataclastic bands, of which the rock samples in this study were a part. Despite the fact that geological research clearly indicated the fault zone, massive stones stopped the NATM during blasting as soon as the excavation neared the unfavourable stretch. Table 22.1 shows the critical power as measured by laboratory experiments on undamaged rock samples.

3. TECHNIQUES

3.1. Experimental Procedures for the Brazilian Tensile Strength Test

For this study, 16 metasedimentary rock samples were subjected to Brazilian tensile strength testing. Tensile strength in connection to rock characteristics core samples was tested on an average of five distinct types of rock for each TD. Slate (SL), Gneiss (G), Brecciated Schist (BS), Breccia (B), and Schist (Sc) in a variety of textures, including fine grained (F), medium grained (M), Very fine-grained rock with clasts (VFC), Very fine-grained rock with (VF).

Brazilian disc specimens of 50 mm × 25 mm were created (diameter × thickness). These specimens were collected from petrographically homogenous rock blocks from the same site with no obvious fissures or bedding planes. As a result, they can be considered almost isotropic. Because the Brazilian test employed a digital image, the speckle patterns were meticulously created to be non-repetitive, isotropic, and high in contrast, as illustrated in Fig. 22.2. For this study, 16 metasedimentary rock samples were subjected to Brazilian tensile strength testing. Tensile strength in connection to rock characteristics core samples was tested on an average of five distinct types of rock for each TD. Slate (SL), Gneiss (G), Brecciated Schist (BS), Breccia (B), and Schist (Sc) in a variety of textures, including fine grained (F), medium grained (M), Very fine-grained rock with clasts (VFC), Very fine-grained rock with (VF).

Brazilian disc specimens of 50 mm × 25 mm were created (diameter × thickness). These specimens were collected from petrographically homogenous rock blocks from the same site with no obvious fissures or bedding planes. As a result, they can be considered almost isotropic. Because the Brazilian test employed a digital image, the speckle patterns were meticulously created to be non-repetitive, isotropic, and high in contrast, as illustrated in Fig. 22.2. For this study, 16 metasedimentary rock samples were subjected to Brazilian tensile strength testing. Tensile strength in connection to rock characteristics core samples was tested on an average of five distinct types of rock for each TD. Slate (SL), Gneiss (G), Brecciated Schist (BS), Breccia (B), and Schist (Sc) in a variety of textures, including fine grained (F), medium-grained (M), Very fine-grained rock with clasts (VFC), Very fine-grained rock with (VF).

Brazilian disc specimens of 50 mm × 25 mm were created (diameter × thickness). These specimens were collected from petrographically homogenous rock blocks from the same site with no obvious fissures or bedding planes. As a result, they can be considered almost isotropic. Because the Brazilian test made use of a digital image, the speckle patterns were carefully created to be non-repetitive, isotropic, and high in contrast, as illustrated in Fig. 22.1(a).

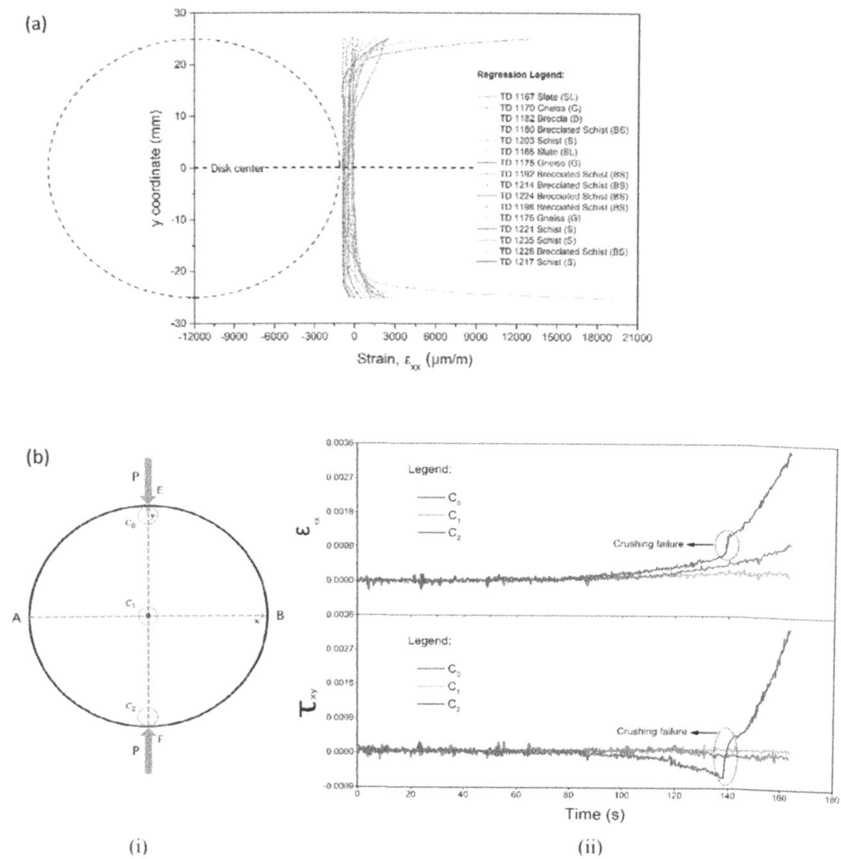

Fig. 22.2. (a) In Type II Tests, Strain Patterns over the Loaded Diameter Right before the Peak Load; (b) (i) Three Positions of a Sample Showing the Failure Mechanism; (ii) Failure of Mechanism between Tensile and Shear Strains in These Areas (i).

4. EXPERIMENTAL SETTING AND LABORATORY METHOD

The main experimental equipment in the Brazilian study was a loading device (MTSLandmark servo-hydraulic loading system) and an image acquisition device (Point Grey-GS3-U3-123S6M-C), as illustrated in Fig. 22.1(a) and 1(b). Loading was accomplished at a rate of 0.2 mm/min using displacement capacity. The specimens failed in about 5 minutes, which was within the suggested time frame of 1–10 minutes. During loading, two cameras captured photos at 50 ms intervals (20 fps). Two cameras with fixed focal lengths of 50 mm were set in front of the specimen, with their axes at a 20° angle to the specimen's axis, as illustrated in Fig. 22.1(b). The two cameras were also linked to a computer, which analysed the images using three-dimensional visual image correlation software (VIC-3D). Correlated solutions goes into greater detail about camera arrangement. Two LED lamp sources were installed on opposite sides of the specimen to guarantee that the specimen surface was sufficiently illuminated. Prior to testing with the 3D-DIC, image calibration was also performed.

5. RESULT AND DISCUSSION

In the Brazilian test, a circular disc is symmetrically squeezed along its diameter, resulting in a constant tensile stress perpendicular to the loading direction in the specimen's central section. The maximum tensile stress criterion (MPa) is as follows: σ_t (MPa) according to the maximum tensile stress criterion is:

$$\sigma_t = \frac{2P}{\pi Dt} = 0.636\frac{P}{Dt}$$

where P signifies the failure load (N), and D and t denote the diameter and thickness of the specimen, respectively (mm). However, it is believed that rock material qualities and load conditions have a significant impact on determining indirect tensile strength and rock fracturing. To put it another way, an invalid Brazilian test can be caused by any of the internal or external causes described in the introduction. In this investigation, crack initiation was found in several rock specimens away from the disc centre. As a result, the results of this conventional formula do not adequately represent the tensile strength of specific rock types, and the equation shown here is solely for comparison.

The complete stress–strain curve in tensile compression is the most valuable single definition of mechanical behaviour. The stroke–force curve, which also serves as a stress-strain curve, can be used to demonstrate all of the rock properties for the 16 samples. The curve established and the physic-mechanical properties of the tested rock after tensile force are shown in Table 22.1. The description of strain–stress curve patterns and their associated rock properties is shown in Table 22.2.

The stroke–force curve, which is similar to the stress–strain curve, is used to explain the impact of rock microstructure (stroke or stress) and background on mechanical behaviour (force or strain). The horizontal axis represents the strain, which is the relative change in length of the specimen, and the vertical axis represents the stress, which is the load per unit area, as seen here. The variety of microstructures that exist and the effect that they have on the form of the curve, in combination with the applied loading conditions and loading speeds, are variations on this theme. The intact rock would have characteristics such as homogeneity and anisotropy, as shown by the tensile strength rating. In terms of rock fracturing, the tensile strength value is the product of producing a geometrical framework of fractures forming rock blocks. Table 22.2 summarises how all rocks are classified into Groups 1, 2, and 3 based on their type of rock, texture, grain size, and failure mode.

Table 22.2. The Classification of Strain–Stress Curve Pattern and Their Relevant Rock Properties.

No	Brazilian Strength (MPa)	Analysis of rock properties					
1	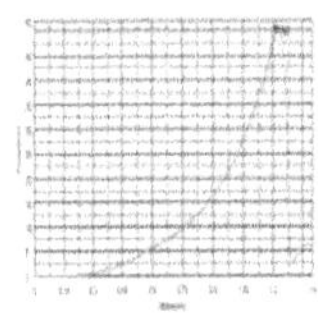	SK1	SK2	SK3	SK4	SK5	SK7
		SL	SL	G	G	BS	BS
		F	F	M	M	VFc	Fc
		III	III	III	I	I	I
2	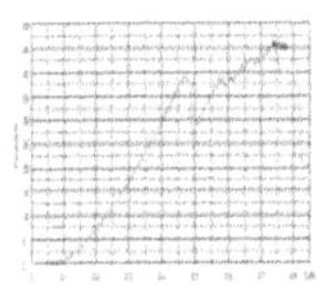	SK6	SK10	SK11	SK12		
		B	BS	BS	BS		
		Fc	Fc	Fc	F		
		II	III	II	IV		
3	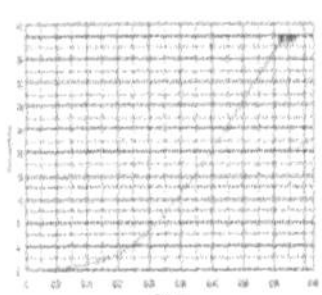	SK8	SK9	SK13	SK14	SK15	SK16
		BS	Sc	Sc	BS	S	BS
		Fc	F	F	Fc	F	VF
		IV	I	I	II	I	I

Legend:
SL: Slate; **G**: Gneiss; **BS**: Brecciated Schist; **B**: Breccia; **Sc**: Schist;
F: fine grained; **M**: Medium grained; **VFc**: Very fine-grained rock with clasts; **Fc**: Fine-grained rock with clasts; **VF**: Very fine grained;
I: Clean failure in two pieces & symmetry; **II**: Clean failure in two pieces & not symmetry; **III**: Fragmented failure in two pieces; **IV**: Failure in 3 pieces disk

Table 22.1 shows the macroscopic view of the deformed samples up to $t =$ 18.40 MPa. At 7–9 MPa confining strain, the deformed samples showed incohesive fracture with smaller sub-fractures, with Group 1 and 2 being the most affected. The samples split into two or three fragmented discs and failed. The sample remains cohesive at 10 MPa confining strain, and visual inspection reveals that the main fracture accommodated a significant portion of the deformation. At pressures ranging from 10 to 18.40 MPa, most rocks fall into Group 3, with the rock breaking into two parts and symmetry, and a clean failure.

Rocks with fine–medium–very fine-grained clasts, such as slate, gneiss, and brecciated schist, were classified as Group 1. In strain–stress curves, it shows that its rock properties of low stiffness, strength, and brittleness have steadily increased, reached a peak of maximum power, and are steadily inclined. Group 1 rocks fractured in two sections and failed in a clean or symmetry failure. In Group 2, the strain–stress curves display a gradual increase to the maximum value of tensile strength, then a sudden fall and a rise in value until the end. Rocks with fine-to-fine grained clasts, such as breccias and brecciated schist, resulted in fractured failure with two to three parts discs. Group 3 characterised fine-to-fine grained rock with clasts such as brecciated schist and schist, as well as rock properties such as low stiffness, strength, and brittleness, as well as strain-stress curves that showed a steady increase and slight fall. The rocks in Group 3 were clean, symmetrical, and failed in two bits. The mechanical properties of mode of failures, stiffness, and brittleness, as well as similarity in texture and grain size where they are grouped, demonstrated that there is no uniformity in the same type of rock, such as metasedimentary rock. To research the primary and secondary cracks as the force propagation guided to the rock, each should be examined by its microstructure.

The strain profiles over the vertical diameter in Fig. 22.1(a) and (b) were used to experiment with the distribution of tensile strain along the sample. The highest strain concentrations are detected at the loading points on both ends of the rock specimens, which are referred to as localised pre-failure. Fig. 22.2(b) illustrates the use of sequential 5-mm diameter circles to monitor the tensile and shear strain histories in these areas using DIC. As can be observed, tensile and shear strains dramatically increase up to 140 s. At 140 s, the tensile and shear strains at the bottom of the disc, at C2, significantly increase, indicating crushing action. Observations of a similar nature have been made in basalt discs. Prior to the peak pressure, the behaviour of sandstone (white and red sandstone) and marble specimens is unknown. Due to the specimens' high fracture velocity, DIC is unable to establish the location of the initial cracking stage. Increased strain concentration at both disc ends results in decreased load-displacement curve responsiveness and tensile strength. As a result, conventional methods for determining the tensile strength of rock disc specimens are ineffective. Additional theoretical research may strengthen this view. Fig. 22.1(a) illustrates the disc's core region's low critical extension strain values (b). Tensile and compressive stresses at the disc centre of specimen WS2-1 are 181 and 387 m/m, respectively. According to Equation 1, the disc's centre has a peak tensile stress of 1.13 MPa, which is less than the specimen's tensile strength at the point of central fracture initiation (4). This contradicts the Brazilian test hypothesis, according to which the disc failed at the bottom or top. P denotes the specimen's failure load (N) (mm). It is thought that rock material properties and load conditions impact indirect tensile strength and rock fracturing. In other words, the requirements outlined in the introduction may result in a Brazilian exam becoming invalid. Indeed, some rock specimens examined during our analysis demonstrated outward crack initiation from the disc centre. As a result, the equation shown here is solely for comparison purposes.

The complete stress–strain curve in tensile compression is the most valuable single definition of mechanical behaviour. The stroke–force curve, which also serves as a stress–strain curve, can be used to demonstrate all of the rock properties for the 16 samples. The curve established and the physic-mechanical properties of the tested rock after tensile force are shown in Table 22.1. The description of strain-stress curve patterns and their associated rock properties is shown in Table 22.2.

The stroke–force curve, like the stress–strain curve, is used to demonstrate the effect of rock microstructure (stroke or stress) and backdrop on mechanical behaviour (force or strain). The horizontal axis indicates strain, which is the relative change in the length of the specimen, and the vertical axis represents stress, which is the load per unit area. Numerous variants on this subject include the presence of distinct microstructures and their effect on the shape of the curve when coupled with the applied loading conditions and rates. The tensile strength rating indicates that the intact rock has properties such as uniformity and anisotropy. The tensile strength value in rock fracturing is the result of generating a geometrical framework of cracks forming rock blocks. Table 22.2 outlines the classification of all rocks into Groups 1, 2, and 3 based on their kind of rock, texture, grain size, and failure mode.

The macroscopic views of the deformed samples up to $t = 18.40$ MPa are shown in Tables 22.1 and 22.2. The distorted samples displayed incohesive fracture with smaller sub-fractures at 7–9 MPa confining strain, with Groups 1 and 2 being the most impacted. The samples failed after splitting into two or three fragmented discs. At 10 MPa confining strain, the sample remains cohesive, and visual inspection confirms that the primary crack accommodated a large percentage of the deformation. Most rocks fall into Group 3 at pressures ranging from 10 to 18.40 MPa, with the rock splitting into two halves, symmetry, and a clean failure.

Group 1 rocks include slate, gneiss, and brecciated schist, which include fine–medium–very fine-grained clasts. Its rock qualities of low stiffness, strength, and brittleness have continuously increased, achieved a peak of maximum power, and are steadily sloped, as seen by strain–stress curves. The rocks in Group 1 broke in two pieces and failed cleanly or symmetrically. The strain–stress curves in Group 2 show a progressive climb to the maximum value of tensile strength, followed by a sharp dip and rise in value till the conclusion. Fine-to-fine-grained clasts in rocks such as breccias and brecciated schist resulting in fractured failure with two to three sections disc. Group 3 consisted of fine to fine-grained rock with clasts such as brecciated schist and schist, as well as rock qualities such as low stiffness, strength, and brittleness, and strain–stress curves that exhibited a continuous climb and little fall. Group 3 rocks were clean, symmetrical, and failed in two chunks. The mechanical qualities of mode of failure, stiffness, and brittleness, as well as texture and grain size similarity when they are clustered, indicated that there is no uniformity in the same type of rock, such as metasedimentary rock. Each primary and secondary fracture should be evaluated by its microstructure in order to research the force propagation guided to the rock.

Fig. 22.1 (a) and (b) illustrates strain profiles along the vertical diameter to quantify the distribution of tensile strain. The maximum strain concentrations are found at the loading points on both ends of specimens, called as pre- failure. In Fig. 22.1(a), the little red dotted dots depict three probable fracture initiation areas in the Brazilian disc, namely C0, C1, and C2. These circles have a diameter of roughly 5 mm and are employed sequentially to monitor tensile and shear strain history in these locations using DIC, as shown in Fig. 22.1(b). As can be observed, the tensile and shear strains both increase somewhat up to 140 s. The tensile and shear strains at the bottom of the disc, where C2 is located, all increase considerably at 140 s, indicating that crushing behaviour occurs there. Similar results have been discovered in the specimens. However, before the maximal load, the crushing behaviour of brittle rocks such as brecciated schist or weathered brecciated schist is not visible. These specimens exhibit significant fracture velocity, which makes it impossible for DIC to determine the position of the first cracking stage. By contrast, the presence of strain concentrations at both ends of the disc nearly always results in an acceleration of the accumulation of damage, which is manifested as a low load-displacement curve response and a low tensile strength.

The critical extension strain values in the disc's core region are comparatively low, as indicated in Table 22.1. The disc's core section exhibits low critical extension strain values. Tensile and compressive strains in the middle of a disc before failure are 181 mm/mm and 387 mm/mm in slate and gneiss specimens, respectively. As shown in Equation, the peak tensile stress in the centre of the disc is 1.13 MPa when linear elasticity is used, which is less than the tensile strength of the specimen with a central fracture start in the disc (4). This means that the failure of the disc began at either the bottom or the top of the disc, which is in direct conflict with the Brazilian test theory.

7. DISCUSSION OF THE FINDINGS

This study's findings reveal that the fracture behaviour of the Brazilian disc is controlled not only by its loading situation, but also by the material properties of the disc. As said at the outset, this could explain why some of the present findings appear to be in conflict with one another. The fact that the rock is anisotropic can have a considerable impact on the failure mechanism of Brazilian discs should also be taken into consideration. The materials used in this investigation were nearly isotropically treated. Consequently, the principal conclusions of the study are not applicable to rock types with anisotropy or transverse isotropy, as a result of this. A further point to mention is that while the ISRM loading form is the most appropriate testing method for the Brazilian test presented in this study, it may result in an invalid failure mode for rock materials with high stiffness and tensile to compressive strength ratios. Another future research topic will be to investigate loading configurations that are appropriate for such rock types. The digitised image analysis results closely match the macroscopic fracture activity of the rock specimens. Crushed sections, such as those observed at the ends of failing discs, show that significant stress has accumulated. It is not, however, advised that the validity of the Brazilian test be judged simply on the basis of the specimen's post-fracture pattern. The following is the definition of the Brazilian Tensile Test:

1. The type of rock, which is largely fine grained with clasts material, has a considerable influence on the failure load and deformation of Brazilian discs, as demonstrated by low tensile strength. The Type 2 test produces the lowest average tensile strength for all rock types, whereas the Type 3 test yields the maximum tensile strength for fine-grained stone.
2. The tensile strength of rocks can be determined using either of the two measures. Because metasedimentary rock has a high stiffness and tensile to compressive strength ratio, this method can be utilised to investigate the failure mechanism of meta sedimentary rock. In this context, alternative testing

procedures and rock types should be investigated in greater depth, which is also the future research direction of the project.
3. When the tensile to compressive strength ratio in rock specimens grows, the highest equivalent stress point (possible crack initiation point) based on Mohr theory tends to occur further away from the disc centre in the Brazilian test using the ISRM standard definition.
4. This is not, however, a set of rules that must be followed at all times. It has been established that the maximum equivalent stress of a disc specimen is affected by the stiffness of the material and the tensile–compression ratio.
5. The validity of the Brazilian test should not be determined solely by the post-fracture pattern of the disc specimens, according to the recommendations in (4). In reality, the digitised picture technique (as depicted in Fig. 22.2) can aid us in better understanding the damage progression process and the modes of specimen failure.

8. CONCLUSION

This study shows the usage of rock mechanics and stress analysis of metasedimentary rock in NATM-1, Karak. The rocks are massive and strong continuous to geological features as faults; joints as can be significant mechanical breaks in the continuum have their own mechanical and geometrical behaviour which often governs by the rock mass properties. Rocks that are simplified in Group 1, Group 2, and Group 3 showed different pattern of stress–strain curves developed due to microcrack propagation because of the tensile force that resulted in certain pattern of mechanical behaviour of their rock properties. Brittleness, stiffness, and strength, which are a combined property, are most important characteristics of rocks. Knowing the degree of these properties of rock would lead to an improved excavation technology.

ACKNOWLEDGEMENTS

This work was supported by the Fundamental Research Grant Scheme (FRGS) awarded by the Ministry of Education of Malaysia entitle 'Enhanced Coalbed Methane Recovery Processes by Coupling Fluid Flow of Mukah-Balingian Coal Deposits' with the referral no. R.J130000.7851.5F371. This work was supported by the Universiti Teknologi Malaysia Encouragement Research Grant (UTMER) awarded by Universiti Teknologi Malaysia entitle 'Diagnosis of Alkali-Aggregate Reaction – Polarizing Microscopy and SEMEDS Analysis' with the referral no. Q.J130000.3851.19J79.

REFERENCES

Akazawa, T. (1943). New test method for evaluating internal stress due to compression of concrete (the splitting tension test) (part 1). *Journal of Japan Society of Civil Engineers*, *29*, 777–787.

Carneiro, F. (1943). A new method to determine the tensile strength of concrete. Paper presented at the 5th meeting of the Brazilian Association for Technical Rules, September 1943 (in Portuguese).

Hajiabdolmajid, V., Kaiser, P. K., & Martin, C. D. (2002). Modelling brittle failure of rock. *International Journal of Rock Mechanics and Mining Sciences*, *39*(8), 731–741.

Howarth, D. F. (1987). The effect of pre-existing microcavities on mechanical rock performance in sedimentary and crystalline rocks. *International Journal of Rock Mechanics and Mining Sciences. Geomechanics Abstracts*, *24*, 223–233.

Kahraman, S. (2001). Correlation of TBM and drilling machine performances with rock brittleness. *Engineering Geology*, *65*, 269–283.

Lim, S. S., & Martin, C. D. (2006). *Estimating in-situ stress magnitudes from core disking; in-situ rock stress – Measurement, interpretation and application* (pp. 159–166). London: Taylor & Francis Group. ISBN 0-415-40163-1.

Mustaffa Kamal Shuib. (2000). The mesozoic tectonics of peninsular Malaysia – An overview. *Warta Geologi*, *26*(3) May–June 2000 P85 Full Paper In: GSM Dynamic Stratigraphy & Tectonics of Peninsular Malaysia: Third Seminar – The Mesozoic of Peninsular Malaysia, University Malaya, Kuala Lumpur, 13 May 2000. Proceedings Volume, pp. 106–126.

Zabidi, H., Rahim, A., & Trisugiwo, M. (2019). L.-N. Moresi (Reviewing Ed.), Structural controls on groundwater inflow analysis of hardrock TBM. *Cogent Geoscience*, *5*, 1. doi:10.1080/23312041.2019.1637556

INDEX

Printed and bound by CPI Group (UK) Ltd, Croydon, CR0 4YY

13/09/2026

14961061-0003